ON *NINETEEN EIGHTY-FOUR*

# ON *NINETEEN EIGHTY-FOUR*

❧

## ORWELL AND OUR FUTURE

*Edited by*
**Abbott Gleason,**
**Jack Goldsmith, and**
**Martha C. Nussbaum**

PRINCETON UNIVERSITY PRESS    PRINCETON AND OXFORD

Copyright © 2005 by Princeton University Press
Published by Princeton University Press, 41 William Street,
Princeton, New Jersey 08540
In the United Kingdom: Princeton University Press,
3 Market Place, Woodstock, Oxfordshire OX20 1SY
All Rights Reserved.

*Library of Congress Cataloging-in-Publication Data*

On nineteen eighty-four : Orwell and our future / edited by Abbott Geason,
Jack Goldsmith, and Martha C. Nussbaum
p.   cm.
Based on papers from a conference held in 1999.
Includes bibliographical references and index.
ISBN 0-691-11360-2 (acid-free paper)—ISBN 0-691-11361-0 (pbk : acid-free paper)
1. Orwell, George, 1903–1950. Nineteen eighty-four. 2. Science fiction,
English—History and criticism. 3. Dystopias in literature. I. Title: 1984.
II. Gleason, Abbott. III. Goldsmith, Jack. IV. Nussbaum, Martha Craven, 1947–.
PR6029.R8N64326 2005
823′.912—dc22      2004059507

British Library Cataloging-in-Publication Data is available.

This book has been composed in Sabon

Printed on acid-free paper. ∞

www.pupress.edu

Printed in the United States of America

1   3   5   7   9   10   8   6   4   2

For Robert Kirschner (1940–2002)

# Contents

As BOB'S WIFE of thirty-seven years, I am delighted that the organizers of the symposium that generated this volume offered to dedicate the book to him. I know that he would have felt honored to have his work in human rights recognized by colleagues whose own contributions to improving society he respected and admired. This passion of Bob's permeated every aspect of his thinking and action; those who knew him personally recognize that he never refrained from expressing his views at appropriate moments. He had such broad intellectual interests and combined them to better the world, while maintaining a modesty and lack of self-promotion that are rare in people who accomplish as much and influence so many.

His independence and drive to speak out against abuse were evident in college in the early 1960s when he wrote an article for his college paper criticizing the House Un-American Activities Committee, which the college administration refused to publish. The force of his convictions in this area was based on his having seen the lives of many of his parents' friends, who were politically liberal or socialist, destroyed by accusations and condemnation. Many lost their jobs as teachers and some took their own lives. From this time on, Bob never refrained from confronting abuse in many areas, although in all cases his energies were directed against man's inhumanity to man.

It was in Argentina, working with Clyde Snow, an anthropologist, that Bob became aware of the power of forensic pathology in documenting human rights abuses. They had recently analyzed remains to identify more than two hundred victims in an airline disaster and recognized that they could use some of the same technologies to identify people who had died in custody of the military junta in Argentina. Bob was forever changed by this experience. He not only examined the remains of the "disappeared" but also delved into the circumstances of their deaths. Talking with the families of those murdered by the regime, especially students, intensified his determination to provide evidence so that those perpetrating such crimes would be held accountable. His intense dedication to this task was validated when several generals were indicted for war crimes.

Through many of the international causes that he undertook, he incurred personal risk, although he made every effort to reduce the likelihood of his not returning from his thirty-six missions. He relied on the advice and assistance of international organizations with which he worked closely, especially Physicians for Human Rights (PHR), Amnesty International, and the American Association for the Advancement of Science (AAAS). He felt that many of the projects for which he was volunteering would have resulted in imprisonment, and probably death, for activists working within their own countries. Incarceration became personal when, while observing the inquest of a political prisoner in Kenya (who was alleged to have committed suicide while in police custody), Bob was unexpectedly removed from the courtroom and jailed. Fortunately, this incident was witnessed and reported immediately to the American embassy by a correspondent from the BBC. Needless to say, this caused much anxiety to our family and to Susannah Sirkin from PHR who was monitoring Bob's activity there. We were greatly relieved later in the day when he was released from jail after pressure from the embassy.

Brutality, as practiced by military and police organizations that were often intertwined, became a focus of his life's work. He meticulously documented the types of wounds inflicted on the victims to document as accurately as possible the type of instruments used, how the injury was caused, and the timing. On occasion this involved individuals (usually political prisoners or social activists) in Czechoslovakia, El Salvador, Guatemala, Israel, Kenya, South Korea, and other areas, but his work was primarily related to large-scale tyrannies (Bosnia, El Salvador, Guatemala, Rwanda, Turkey). He investigated these latter atrocities with many colleagues of whom I will mention only a few: Vince Iacopino, Bill Hagland, Eric Stover, and activists within their countries whom I will not name. Bob felt gratified to have been on the Editorial Committee and a contributing author of *The Istanbul Protocol*, a manual on torture and inhuman punishment that was submitted to the United Nations.

As a father, Bob was particularly disturbed by the mass murder of approximately sixty children under age six in El Mozote, a village in El Salvador. These children, who were shot at close range, were considered future "guerrillas," and the hut in which they died was covered over in a mound of dirt, resembling a hill, to avoid detection. The stigmatization and subjugation of indigenous groups by those in power was a fact of life that Bob found intolerable and against which he fought throughout his life.

Not all the victims of police brutality lived outside of the United States. An example of how Bob used his experience in one situation to understand another is seen in the case against Commander Burge, a member of the Chicago Police Department. Allegations were made of a very specific form of torture endured by prisoners in a district under Burge's command. This was obviously a very politically charged situation with a citizen confronting the city's police department. Bob agreed to look into the charges and concluded that no one who hadn't experienced that form of electrical shock could have had such corroborating wounds and been able to describe the experience in such exact and accurate detail. With forensic knowledge now substantiating the complaint, subsequent cases were investigated and other similar cases of torture within that district were documented. Despite the fact that a judge in the case apparently attempted to undermine Bob's expertise by claiming that there is no field that encompasses special knowledge of torture, Burge retired after the publication of the evidence.

Bob considered the death penalty to be another form of abuse of power. He testified in several death penalty cases, describing the probable suffering that individuals experienced during execution. This was especially so in at least two cases when the instruments of death failed to function properly or were poorly constructed so that the device actually ignited.

Child abuse was an area in which Bob had an enormous impact with individual families but especially as an educator of medical students and house staff, as well as police departments and other practicing pathologists. He wrote numerous chapters in the leading textbooks in the field and lectured locally and nationally on the recognition of abuse. He worked with others on the Academy of Pediatrics Committee on Child Abuse and Neglect to write guidelines for evaluating sexual abuse, unexpected infant and child deaths, and the shaken baby syndrome. He testified on behalf of many children abused or murdered by their caretakers with the goal of making those charged with prosecuting these crimes (lawyers, judges, social workers) aware of the enormity of this problem, and to obtain some justice for the children who suffered. He would often return from these trials angry that adults in empowered positions believed more firmly in the sanctity of a parent's autonomy than in the evidence of abuse.

The formation of the Human Rights Center at the University of Chicago, an endeavor in which Bob collaborated with Jacqueline Bhabha and Rashid Khalidi, was the realization of Bob's great hope—that he could influence students to pursue activities in human rights. He felt great satisfaction in the recognition that the program, now under the leadership of Susan Gzesh, attracted students from diverse backgrounds with a broad range of experiences, talents, and sense of commitment to others.

On a personal note, our family—like so many people around the world—has great admiration and love for Bob. He excelled in everything he participated in. He didn't know what procrastination was—there was hardly a wasted minute. Yet he had a wonderful sense of humor that surfaced all the time, even under the worst circumstances of human misery, and he used it to maintain his spirit and that of others working in the field. He was knowledgeable about classical music and enjoyed it tremendously—especially operas with murderous themes, like *A Masked Ball* and *Peter Grimes*. Even his taste in art, which we shared, was focused on manifestations of the human condition, such as the work of the German

Expressionists and modern Mexican masters including Rivera and Si-
queiros. He incorporated literature, history, and the arts into the annual
program of the American Academy of Forensic Sciences by chairing the
Last Word Society, a session devoted to analyzing forensic aspects of artistic endeavors and historical events.

Bob's death brought great sadness to me, our sons Josh, Dan, and Benjy,
other relatives, and friends, but it is lessened somewhat with the knowledge that his legacy of commitment to human rights will be carried on by
the students he influenced and the activities of his colleagues throughout
the world.

*Barbara S. Kirschner, M.D.*
*Chicago, Illinois*

# Acknowledgments

THIS VOLUME began as a conference at the University of Chicago Law School in 1999, celebrating the fiftieth anniversary of Orwell's novel. The conference was first suggested to us by Law School alumnus and lawyer Marvin J. Rosenblum, whose lifelong passion for Orwell led him to persuade Sonia Orwell to give him the film and television rights to the novel. As a result, he became the executive producer of the admirable film adaptation of the novel directed by Michael Radford and starring John Hurt as Winston and Richard Burton as O'Brien. Rosenblum approached Nussbaum and Goldsmith with the suggestion that a conference celebrating the novel's anniversary and exploring its relevance to our own time ought to take place at his own alma mater. We owe thanks to Marvin for his commitment to Orwell, his vision, and his tireless energy, and to Law School dean Douglas Baird for putting us in contact with Marvin and masterminding the creation of the conference plan. The next dean, Daniel Fischel, generously encouraged our enterprise; we are extremely grateful to him for both institutional and financial support, and to director of external affairs Sylvia Neil for her energy on behalf of the project. Chad Flanders, a Ph.D. student from the Philosophy Department, gave us invaluable assistance as the conference assistant, taking care of correspondence and practical arrangements. For social arrangements we are warmly grateful to Lucienne Goodman, for her well-known efficiency and good taste.

During the subsequent preparation of the volume, we were lucky enough to be able to continue to work with Chad, who did much of the essential work of getting the papers submitted in revised form, and corresponding with authors. In the last stages of the project, Chad's role was taken over by Mark Johnson, who handled scores of details with his usual cheer, graciousness, and efficiency. At this time, too, Abbott Gleason kindly agreed to join the group of editors. Nussbaum and Goldsmith are enormously grateful to him for the painstaking attention he paid to every detail of the final drafts, and for his help in drafting the introduction. Finally, our editor at Princeton University Press, Ian Malcolm, supported us every inch of the way with sage advice and warm encouragement. We are also grateful to two anonymous reviewers for the Press for their helpful suggestions for revision.

There was one major contributor to the conference whose paper we were unable to include, for tragic reasons. Robert Kirschner, professor of medicine at the University of Chicago, internationally renowned expert on the forensic pathology of torture, leader of Physicians for Human Rights, and cofounder of the University of Chicago's Human Rights Program, died of cancer in September 2002, after a long illness. Sometime earlier, he had told us that he was unable to complete his paper. We dedicate this volume to Bob, with deep admiration for his work and life and a sense of the profound loss his death is for our community, and for the cause of social justice. We are most grateful to his widow, Barbara, for supplying the volume's dedicatory foreword.

❧

All quotations from *Nineteen Eighty-Four* are from the same edition, and are cited parenthetically, by page number, within the essays, throughout.

ON *NINETEEN EIGHTY-FOUR*

# Introduction

ABBOTT GLEASON AND MARTHA C. NUSSBAUM

I

GEORGE ORWELL remains at the center of modern political life, just when we might have expected him to depart. In the popular mind, Orwell is the great dramatizer of Cold War values, as seen from an anti-Soviet viewpoint. *Nineteen Eighty-Four*, published in 1949, right at the start of the Cold War, has come to be regarded as one of the great exposés of the horrors of Stalinism. Countless American schoolchildren, required to read the novel in high school, identified with its depiction of the struggle of the lone individual against an omnipresent, omnivigilant state that conducts a systematic and relentless assault against truth, against history, against normal human relationships, and, above all, against the very existence of the individual will. The novel's chilling ending, in which Winston Smith comes to love Big Brother, and thus ceases to be himself, has been seen as a morality tale of the grim future that was possibly in the works for all denizens of the planet, a future involving nothing less than extinction of humanity itself.

But Orwell did not lose his power with the collapse of the Soviet system. Indeed, the new era of ever-vigilant technology seemed to give new relevance to his ideas, just when their specific political occasion had apparently vanished. The conference from which the papers in this volume derive, held in 1999 to celebrate the novel's fiftieth anniversary, set out to ask what it is in the novel that has enabled it to transcend its occasion, what enduring suggestions for our present and future it offers. Starting from the novel's continued ubiquity as a linchpin of popular culture, it set out to probe beyond the Cold War reading of the novel to ask what themes have attached it so securely to the American unconscious, and whether, in fact, it does remain of relevance to our thinking in a changed world situation. *Nineteen Eighty-Four* was published simultaneously in England and the United States in 1949. It has been continuously in print in English from that day to this and has been translated into virtually every European and Asian language. It must be among the most widely read books in the history of the world.

This volume, like the conference, is not an exercise in Orwell criticism. Indeed, we quite deliberately did not include recognized Orwell scholars, and we did not seek standard literary interpretations of the novel. Instead, we asked a wide-ranging group of writers, all with their own agendas in social science, law, and the humanities, to give their own take on the novel, telling a general audience what it does offer us as we try to think about our future. We sought contentious and idiosyncratic papers, leaving open the possibility that they would tell us that Orwell has nothing to offer or is seriously in error in some respect. Almost all our authors, however, feel that the novel merits its central place in our culture. Even when it appears to go wrong in this or that respect, it stimulates our thinking in valuable ways.

Five themes in the novel seemed salient to its continued relevance. First, the novel's role in our culture raises the very general issue of the role of the literary imagination in politics, an issue that was important to Orwell throughout his career. What would lead a social thinker to write fiction, and what, if anything, does fiction offer to an understanding of social events? Second, the novel is preoccupied with the issue of truth and its connection to the possibility of liberal politics. What, if any, is the connection between a belief in the availability of truth (in science, in history) and the ability of liberal democratic societies to sustain themselves? Third, the novel is famously a story of tyranny through technology, and we are living in an era in which possibilities of surveillance and control outstrip even what Orwell could imagine. Have his fears been fulfilled, are they likely to be in the future, or are there features of technology itself that ought to assuage the worries he raises? Fourth, the novel concerns torture and thought control, and we now know a good deal more than we knew in 1949 about how these operate. What do historical experience and psychological research tell us about Orwell's nightmarish idea that humanity itself can be extinguished by psychological techniques? Fifth and finally, there is the theme of sex, which pervades the novel. Orwell's account of the affair of Winston and Julia connects sexual passion with political rebellion, sexual repression with totalitarianism. On what grounds are these connections made, and how successful are they? How helpful is the novel as a starting point for reflection about issues of sexual regulation and the eroticism of politics?

Those were the themes we set out to investigate; as will be no surprise, we got divergent answers, both with respect to the nature of Orwell's contribution and with respect to its value.

Meanwhile, the world continued to change even more radically. From the post–Cold War time of 1999 we have now moved abruptly, post-9/11, into what appears to be a very different era. The remnants of Cold War politics that continued to organize U.S. foreign relations even in the early days of the Bush administration (Russia is still our enemy, freedom is under siege from totalitarianism) have now quite suddenly been replaced by a sharply divergent image of the world, in which the enemy is not an all-powerful state but terrorists, who elude location and identification, and who operate without any easily grasped center or map of connections. We always knew, or at least could vaguely imagine, what the end of the Cold War would look like—one side would win, and that side's economic and political system would be imposed on the other. But it seems impossible even to imagine what the end of this "new war" would look like: would terrorists cease to exist? come to love America? In this changed world, it seems necessary to ask once again, are Orwell's ideas still relevant?

And yet, changed though the world seems to be, we still cannot help finding Orwell in it. Think, for example, of the phrase "America's New War," and of the constant harping on the fact that we are at war. When the president had a colonoscopy (June 2002), it seemed necessary for him to transfer powers to the vice president, despite the fact that he was undergoing mild sedation for a procedure that lasted twenty minutes, even though all presidents sleep during the night and even nap during the day without such a transfer, and even though much more serious medical procedures, during other presidencies, had not led to such a transfer. Why the emergency atmosphere? Because, we were told, we are at war, and it is crucial to let the world see that we have an orderly system for the transfer of power.

In short, the sense of emergency is retained from the Cold War and has simply been reconfigured to fit the new world situation in which the enemy is not single but diffuse. And, in a most Orwellian fashion, the sense of emergency is used to underwrite measures in the area of constitutional law and civil liberty that might otherwise look questionable. Albeit in a changed world, Orwell's ideas survive and help reflection.

Orwell knew that in time of fear and emergency people look for comfort, solidarity, and solace. One striking example of how little our political life has actually departed from the Cold War was given by the recent public and political commotion over the words "under God" in the Pledge of Allegiance. Those words were introduced at the height of the Cold War, with reference to the need to show how we differ from "godless communism." Then as now, their presence raises serious constitutional issues. They lead schoolchildren to connect loyalty to the United States with belief in God, despite the fact that many highly moral people in this nation do not believe in God. (Some of them are atheists, some agnostics, some adherents of nontheistic religions, such as Buddhism and Taoism. The Supreme Court, in deciding what personal creeds count as "religion" for the purpose of military exemptions, has long recognized that "religion" does not require a belief in God.) The subtle coercion and pressure on children, when they are told that they have an "opt-out" and yet the vast majority are reciting the words, has also long been recognized as a salient constitutional issue. So, in the rush to affirm the words "under God" without calm discussion of issues such as the importance of defending minorities, we see an extension of Cold War thinking. Instead of godless communism, godless terrorism. Here again, Orwell's political psychology is a shrewd guide to our present situation.

II

*Part I: Politics and the Literary Imagination*

The volume opens with a section addressing its most general overarching theme, the relationship between politics and the literary imagination. In "A Defense of Poesy," literary scholar and political thinker Elaine Scarry addresses this theme through a surprising extension of the novel's own literary resources. Her essay takes the form of an epistolary treatise from Julia to Winston, arguing that the human ability to think is as dependent on imaginative literature as on history. There is the deepest kind of linkage between the ability to identify "what is the case" and the practice of entering mentally into "what is not the case"; these abilities also link Julia to Winston. In Oceania both the factual and the imaginative counterfactual have been subverted and must be restored together. Great works of art, Julia argues, are independent of the world yet connected to it at its boundaries. Imaginative literature simultaneously provides a density of fact and a liberation from the factual. The counterfactual helps us to penetrate the world more deeply by focusing our attention on selected aspects of it; by revealing to us what is hidden in ordinary life; and by enabling us to think about the most difficult things without risk or penalty.

Homi K. Bhabha's "Doublespeak and the Minority of One" seeks to refute the idea commonly held, with particular relevance to the case of Orwell, that virtuous people should not be "virtuosos." He argues that in fact Orwell is not the plainspoken figure frequently evoked in the vast literature about him, but is in his own way a virtuoso, particularly when he "narrates the vicious." Orwell's language, Bhabha argues, directed against totalitarianism, is itself "suffused with the imagination of totalitarian violence." Orwell turns into a paranoiac in the service of a good cause precisely when he "is at his most inventive and insightful." In order for Orwell to defend Winston Smith's commitment to being at the end of the day "a minority of one" in defense of the truth, there has to be another party that denies the truth. Winston's longed-for relationship with O'Brien is an essential aspect of his struggle for the representation of reality, which can be achieved only by dialogic discourse.

In "Of Beasts and Men: Orwell on Beastliness," novelist and critic Margaret Drabble focuses on a central paradox in Orwell's work: Orwell's belief in the goodness of beasts and the beastliness of human beings. The word "beastly" appears to have been his first word, and it contained fairly direct links, through his mother, to a violent, "farmyard" view of sexuality. A related paradox: Orwell was fond of animals, yet "like a true Englishman" he was fond of killing them. Drabble's essay deals with both *Nineteen Eighty-Four* and *Animal Farm*, whose central narrative device is "the transformation of man into animal" (and vice versa). Drabble concludes that it was above all in Orwell's animal fables that he could express openly and convincingly the essential humanity and decency that he wished to defend and preserve; and even more significantly, perhaps, "write with tenderness." Orwell pitied men, women, and beasts, but he could more easily pity beasts than men, for pity toward men involved pity of himself, and "toward himself he was relentless and unsparing."

Richard A. Epstein, a law professor who has written widely about social issues from a libertarian perspective, closes this section of the book with an essay that is skeptical of the relevance of Orwell's literary work for social theory. Epstein maintains that the normative messages in Orwell's fiction were based too heavily on Orwell's idiosyncratic, and thus unrepresentative, experiences. For this reason, Epstein contends, Orwell's fiction failed to teach us much about the social institutions he criticized. "A literary rendition may well teach someone to be sensitive to the ravages of poverty," Epstein argues, "but it will not indicate whether poverty is in decline or on the increase." Epstein believes that such tasks are best served by the tools of economics and related disciplines. He acknowledges that the literary imagination has "a certain working advantage over a quantitative social science" in explaining deviant behavior, and he deems Orwell to be at his best in identifying and exposing twisted personalities and totalitarian excess. But he insists that Orwell specifically, and writers of fiction in general, are ill-suited to explain complex social systems or to make recommendations for their reform.

## Part II: Truth, Objectivity, and Propaganda

Abbott Gleason has written widely on twentieth-century Soviet history and the history of the Cold War. His essay, "Puritanism and Power Politics during the Cold War: George Orwell and Historical Objectivity," focuses on Orwell's passionate defense of historical objectivity in the approximate decade between the Spanish civil war and the first years of the Cold War, a period when Orwell was concerned above all with the issue of totalitarianism. He argues that Orwell's defense of historical objectivity was less an epistemological position than a defense of a variety of other commitments that played a role in his struggle against totalitarianism: to a historically derived Protestant individualism; to the relevance of history; to sincerity and fair-mindedness in literature; and to opposing theory insufficiently rooted in the materiality of the world. He sees an autobiographical element in Orwell's anguished depiction of O'Brien's total victory over Winston Smith at the end of *Nineteen Eighty-Four*, which suggests Orwell's pessimism about the ability of his most deeply held values to endure in what he regarded as the Age of Totalitarianism.

In "Rorty and Orwell on Truth," philosopher James Conant confronts the relationship between Orwell's views of truth and currently fashionable assaults on truth and objectivity. Taking as his focus philosopher Richard Rorty, who has argued that the norm of solidarity ought to replace a striving for truth in the politics of liberalism, Conant scrutinizes Rorty's attempt to appeal to Orwell as an ally in his assault on truth. He argues that *Nineteen Eighty-Four* shows clearly that Rorty and Orwell are not in alliance, but profoundly at odds. Orwell insists that liberal freedom depends on a strong distinction between truth and mere solidarity. The "really frightening thing about totalitarianism" is not its cruelty but its assault on the concept of objective truth. Insofar as Rorty's position is represented in the novel, it is the position of O'Brien.

Edward S. Herman, an economist and media analyst, looks critically at the relationship between Orwell's Oceania and some aspects of contemporary U.S. politics. In "From *Ingsoc* and *Newspeak* to *Amcap*, *Amerigood*, and *Marketspeak*," he argues that although *Nineteen Eighty-Four* was created to dramatize the threat of the Soviet Union, it contains the germs of a powerful critique of U.S. practice. He argues that propaganda is in fact a more important means of social control in the United States than it is in a closed society like the former Soviet Union. In the United States, the elite does allow controversy, but only within limited bounds. The notion of the United States committing aggression, for instance, is "outside the pale of comprehensible thought." Freedom generally means "freedom of markets" in the American realm of Marketspeak, rather than political freedom. Just as individuals become "unpeople" in Ingsoc, entire populations disappear from the pages of mainstream American media in wartime; unlike American casualties, they have no political cost, and thus large-scale killing of them is permitted. In this and other ways, Amcap is an even more effective means of social control than Ingsoc.

## Part III: Political Coercion

Our third section deals with political control and coercion, one of the novel's most famous and enduring themes. Philip G. Zimbardo, a psychology professor who has done widely recognized research on violence, evil persuasion, and hypnosis (among other things), focuses on the ways that torture can succeed in shaping thought and mind. After reviewing Orwell's conception of human nature and of the techniques of torture, Zimbardo explains the dimensions along which human minds are subject to control and manipulation. He then illustrates how Orwell's mind control techniques have been "embraced, extended, and made more powerful" by modern actors, including the CIA. Zimbardo concludes with a fascinating account of how the Jim Jones–orchestrated mass suicide and murders of 912 U.S. citizens in Guyana in 1978 were modeled directly on the strategies and tactics of mind control outlined in *Nineteen Eighty-Four*.

The essay by Darius Rejali, a political scientist and expert on torture's relation to modernity, focuses on two torture-related themes in *Nineteen Eighty-Four*: the relationship between torture and betrayal, and the various modes of resisting torture. Rejali distinguishes between "great betrayals" (betrayals of great causes and important persons) and "ordinary betrayals" (betrayals at an atomic level in ordinary life). Most accounts of torture focus on great betrayals, and most accounts of *Nineteen Eighty-Four* focus on Winston's great betrayals, especially his betrayal of Julia. Rejali maintains that Orwell was also sensitive to how torture leads to and is shaped by ordinary betrayals. In the course of comparing Orwell's account of betrayal to that of Jean Amery, who was tortured in Auschwitz, Rejali argues that ordinary betrayals are what make surviving torture so difficult and complicated. In the second part of his essay, Rejali classifies various modes of resisting torture and concludes that—in contrast to what *Nineteen Eighty-Four* suggests—present and future torture technologies will never render resistance futile and will never be able to reprogram human beings.

## Part IV: Technology and Privacy

When the adjective "Orwellian" is used, the most common meaning is that of an all-seeing state that has totally effaced personal privacy. Our next group of essays investigates the relevance of Orwell's treatment of that theme, in an age when increasing surveillance of all aspects of people's lives is no mere possibility.

The essay by Richard A. Posner, a founding father of the law and economics movement who has also written widely on the connection between law and literature, compares Orwell's treatment of the relationship between privacy and technology in *Nineteen Eighty-Four* with Aldous Huxley's in *Brave New World*. Posner's essay is wide-ranging and contains many interesting claims growing out of the comparison. He acknowledges that *Nineteen Eighty-Four* successfully recognizes that the human desire for solitude is inimical to totalitarianism, and that the suppression of thought and inquiry are inimical to scientific and technological progress. But beyond these points, Posner thinks that *Nineteen Eighty-Four* and *Brave New World* do not teach us much—or even try to teach us much—about privacy or what it means to live in an age of technological progress. For Posner views the novels as satires rather than as predictions about the future. Posner concludes his essay by arguing, with Epstein, for an aesthetic approach to literature rather than one that tries to mine literature for political or economic significance.

Lawrence Lessig, a law professor and leading Internet authority, demonstrates the Internet's potential threat to privacy by comparing it with Orwell's telescreen. Orwell hated technology and tells us very little in *Nineteen Eighty-Four* about how the telescreen actually worked. But Lessig maintains that it would not have been a particularly useful tool for totalitarianism, for two reasons. First, the telescreen was transparent in the sense that one knew when and where one was being monitored. And second, telescreen monitoring was necessarily imperfect, for it depended (or appeared to depend) on infallible human observers who could misperceive, or forget, what they watched. In these two ways, Lessig argues, the telescreen was more privacy-protecting (or less privacy-invading) than the Internet. For the Internet gathers data beyond our sight and knowledge. And the Internet is a perfect monitor—it stores all data, and it never forgets. Lessig does not believe that these features of the Net are inevitable. To the contrary, he criticizes Orwell for his technological essentialism and closes his essay by suggesting how the Net's architecture could be modified to become, like the telescreen, more transparent and more forgetful.

David Brin's essay suggests a different solution. Brin is a prolific science fiction novelist and the author of the well-received nonfiction book *The Transparent Society: Will Technology Force Us to Choose between Privacy and Freedom?* Unlike Lessig, Brin believes that the erosion of privacy is inevitable; technology is developing, and will continue to develop, in ways that allow "elites" (governments, corporations, criminals, etc.) to monitor every aspect of everyday activity. Brin believes it is futile to put up a wall between the watchers and the watched. He argues that we can best protect privacy by reversing the telescreen and ensuring that those who monitor and observe are subject to monitoring and observation by any citizen. The optimal way to protect privacy in the modern world, Brin argues, is to make observation tools a public resource to ensure that elites do not abuse their powers of observation.

### Part V: Sex and Politics

Orwell's novel is a story of sexual passion at odds with totalitarianism; it contains many suggestions about the likely relationship, in general, between political repression and sexual repression. Three essays ponder this theme of the novel, in very different ways. In "Sexual Freedom and Political Freedom," Cass R. Sunstein, a legal scholar and political theorist, looks critically at the assumptions that lie behind Orwell's account of the Party's control over sexuality. Orwell appears to support the Party's view that sexual energy, repressed, can be transformed into "war fever and leader worship." For Orwell, totalitarianism thrives on the repression of sexual drives; chastity supports political orthodoxy. It is for this reason that the choice to have sex outside the Party's narrow strictures can be connected, as it is in the novel, with political freedom. Sunstein argues that these connections are too neat and easy, and, in particular, that Orwell is insensitive to the domination of women that is frequently linked to movements of sexual liberation. The novel's inadequacy in this area is compounded by Orwell's account of Julia, who is less a full person than an adolescent male fantasy. There is a link worth pondering between totalitarianism and the repression of *women*, but Orwell has nothing to say about it.

In "Sex, Law, Power, and Community," feminist legal theorist Robin West makes a related criticism of the novel's vision of the politics of sexuality. Orwell, she argues, is naive in suggesting that sex is a simple opposite to power, and that state power is the worst threat we face. Thinking about the threats to liberty posed by private power (for example, economic power, power in the family) gives law a different direction from that suggested by Orwell's single-minded focus on the state. She then argues that Orwell expresses a different and richer set of ideas about social control in his biographical and literary essays. There we find Orwell aligning himself with Charles Dickens to espouse a "humanistic" politics that places the expansion of human sympathy at its core. West explores the implications of Orwell's critique of power, when combined with this humanistic vision, for contemporary law.

Philosopher John Haldane, a leading conservative ethical thinker in the Roman Catholic tradition, explores connections between Orwell's ideas about sex and some aspects of Roman Catholic thought, in which Orwell had a serious, albeit overtly hostile, interest. Haldane argues that the novel's relationship to Catholicism is actually very complicated. Although

Orwell expressed the view that Catholicism, like totalitarianism, was a threat to the autonomous individual, the novel itself associates religion not with the totalitarian institutions of Oceania but with the counterculture associated with Goldstein and his dissident following. So too, Haldane argues, the novel's portrayal of sexuality shows surprising sympathy with Catholic ideas of which Orwell was well aware. Winston and Julia's passion is quickly transformed into a quasi-marital domesticity, and the mode of their lovemaking similarly changes, from sadism to tender concern. If we have a sufficiently nuanced understanding of Catholic teaching, moreover, it advocates not body-hating puritanism but the loving and passionate marriage to which Winston and Julia were plainly moving when the Party intervened.

## *Conclusion*

Our conference took place in 1999. During the intervening time, developments in world politics and in the United States's relation to the world have done much to reinforce the novel's continuing timeliness and richness. In a concluding essay, Martha C. Nussbaum contributes a post-9/11 reflection on one little-noticed theme of the novel, the relationship between Oceanian politics and the death of pity. Examining the connection between the emotion of compassion or (tragic) pity and the underpinnings of liberalism, she argues that liberalism requires a public psychology that transcends narcissism, that is, the fantasy of personal invulnerability and omnipotent control. Examining Winston's failure to remain the sort of person who has compassion for others, she argues that his retreat into narcissism does not suggest that all human beings can be so broken: for Winston has some weaknesses that make him far from a "best case" of the human spirit. On the other hand, there are aspects of social life in the contemporary United States that spell danger for the future of compassion, and, hence, for the future of the open and freedom-based society to which we are rightly attached.

# Part I

# POLITICS AND THE LITERARY IMAGINATION

# A Defense of Poesy (The Treatise of Julia)

*Editor's note*: This treatise on poetry was found among the ashes of Oceania. The author is known to us only by the single name Julia. The treatise survives because it was etched in metal, specifically the metal casing of a small lipstick canister. It was found in a mound of soft ash where paper records were routinely incinerated. So microscopic is the writing that it at first appeared to archaeologists only as an ornate wreathing on the case. The fire of the incineration had reacted with the metal in such a way that these tiny marks became burnished and glowing, as though inviting further scrutiny. Once given that scrutiny, the delicate wreathing—which had itself occasioned much excitement since ornamentation was thought to have been nonexistent in Oceania—quickly revealed the secret text contained there. Transcription proved fairly straightforward; the only difficulties came from the fact that no spaces separate the words, and from the fact that once the author finished writing vertically (beginning each line at the bottom of the canister and moving upward), she then turned the canister ninety degrees, continuing her text by now cutting perpendicularly across the already existing lines.

Statements made by Julia inside the treatise suggest what expert analysis of the incision marks confirms: the etching implement was almost certainly a razor blade, a tool regarded as semiprecious in this civilization. Irregularities in the wreathing—whose clarity declines, then resumes, five times—indicate the use of five separate implements. The treatise is addressed throughout to a lover. Occasionally the author refers to "my brother." The scholarly consensus about the identity of the lover and disagreement about the identity of the brother are summarized (along with other lines of scholarly inquiry) in an annotated bibliography now in preparation.

The treatise is widely considered remarkable for its brilliant feat of thinking carried out in a civilization where even modest acts of thinking were discouraged. Occasionally Julia's meaning becomes unclear, and scholars have debated whether the author has lost her way in such passages or whether she has instead made her way onto paths where we have not yet successfully followed. The treatise belongs in a line that includes Sidney's *Apologie for Poetrie* and Shelley's *Defence of Poetry*, though its claims for art go beyond either. Sidney urged that poetry delights and instructs. Shelley said poets were the unacknowledged legislators of the world. The work that Julia's treatise assigns to poetry is anterior to either instruction or legislation, since it claims that *poesis* makes thinking itself possible.

Though the treatise is undated, metallurgical analysis of the inscriptions places its composition in the year A.D. 1984.

THE HUMAN ability to think freely—or, simply, to think—is premised on an ability to carry out two distinguishable mental practices, the practice of accurately identifying what is the case and the practice of entering mentally into what is not the case. The two familiar names for these practices are history and literature.

In Oceania, where the goal is to eliminate thought, each of the two mental practices is systematically damaged by two leading agencies, the Records Department and the Fiction Department. The first dedicates its daily labor to erasing names, dates, and actions that have actually occurred and replacing them with altered substitutes. The second provides machine-generated stories and songs to satiate all longing for the counterfactual before it can arise, thereby preempting the human impulse to generate imaginary objects of its own.

It is easy to see why—in order to think—one must be able to formulate sentences that match physical events in the world. If a woman walks over the footbridge carrying a pink parasol, one must be able to say the sentence "A woman is walking over the footbridge carrying a pink parasol"; and one must also, later in the afternoon, still be able to hold steady the fact "This morning, a woman walked over the footbridge carrying a pink parasol." If the event is memorable enough to be recalled ten months later, the more closely the memory matches the event, the better.

But imagine if the only sentences we could make had to conform to physical events that had actually taken place; our only thoughts would be registrations of already occurring events. We would be prisoners of the actual. We would be like intricate copying machines that could only record factual events happening in close proximity to ourselves (we would not even have any way of choosing among the factual events). But just as primary as the factual reflex of the mind is the counterfactual reflex; and while the factual keeps our thoughts stuck to the world, the counterfactual keeps us unstuck. The factual reflex lets me think *that* a woman walked over the footbridge carrying a pink parasol, while the counterfactual lets me think *about* her.

In all our hours together, it has seemed to me that you keenly appreciate the factual work carried out by the mind but that you consistently underestimate the work of the counterfactual, and it is to open your eyes to the second that I write. You rage at Oceania's assaults on the factual but shrug at its assaults on the counterfactual—as though the imaginary could not be damaged or, upon being damaged, would be no loss.

Yet every day, I also see how strong is your own counterfactual yearning—you, who fell in love with the bright ornament in my name, you who waited to make love until the thrush had sung her song. I have felt your pulse race when you touched the pages of a book. Close this in your hand so your heart will race now.

❧

The counterfactual lets us think *about* events we do not at that moment perceive by sight or touch or one of the other senses. I did not see the woman before she stepped onto the footbridge, but as I watched her gliding across the bridge, this anterior space presented itself to my mind (where did she come from? she must have passed close to me? how did I miss her?), as well as the posterior space (long before she reached the other side, I pictured the small stairway leading from the bridge down to the street level). As for her motion on the bridge itself, I could feel my mind sorting through descriptions, reaching for, then rejecting, adjectives, trying others, starting over.

My thought "*that* the woman is moving over the bridge" enlists the factual reflex of the mind; my thoughts *about* her moving over the bridge enlist the counterfactual. Do I seem to claim too much? What I say is modest compared to what others have argued. Do you remember the night at the Chestnut Tree Café, when young Mary recited passages about imagining from Hume, Kant, and Wittgenstein?[1] She thinks the imagination is at work even in my being able to think "*that* a woman carrying a parasol is moving over the bridge." Her philosophers say it is at work in every perception, no matter how starkly factual.

For example, as the woman moved away from me across the bridge, I only actually saw her at intermittent intervals. It was you I had been waiting for by the bridge. It was your figure, starting across from the other side, that I had searched out, had at last found, and had watched as you began the passage toward me. At first my eyes were steadily on you; then they got tugged away by an anomalous streak on my peripheral vision. I looked to see what it was, and then, struck by the sight of her, I kept moving back and forth, between your two figures—hers and then yours; yours and then hers. The two of you moved toward one another, merged midway on the bridge, then separated again, you moving closer and closer to me, she moving farther and farther away. (You saw me lift my arm,

[1] *Editor's note.* Julia's reference to "young Mary" incited several scholars to speculate that the Chestnut Street Café, identified by Oceania historians as a meeting place of artists, was instead actually an underground church; but no other evidence of religion in Oceania has been found. More recently, "young Mary" has been identified as Mary Warnock, who spent several years in her childhood in Oceania, later lived in Britain, and wrote a book on the place of the imagination in perception that draws on the philosophers Julia names.

and later cautioned me against greeting you so openly in public, but I was not waving to you; my arm lifted because I wanted to arrest her passage.)

Hume says I did not *factually* see the woman carrying the pink parasol over the bridge. I factually saw only intermittent patches of her, now at one station on the bridge, later at another, then another; and another. My confident perception that this discontinuous series of events was a solid and singular person was made possible by the images the imagination supplied for all the missing spaces; just as, more generally, everyday objects in the world—tables and chairs with which we have only very interrupted perceptual experiences—acquire their solidity and integrity and continuity of existence only with the assistance of the counterfactual.

But I, who am more modest, will be content if you will agree to locate the counterfactual only in all that lies "about" or "above" the perception—beginning with the cloud of "not" structures that lie in the field of any perception. In order to perceive what something is, one sees what it is not, and though what it is "not" usually lies inert, it marks out a path for what the thing might have been if it were something other than what it was. This is just the ordinary process of sorting out perceptions—What is that against the sky? an umbrella? no, not an umbrella, a parasol. It is shimmering with light, like sand; no, not sand; like cream, light pink. It has a sheen. Is it metal? But it lets the light through: ah, it is silk. Do you see—the small burst of fireflies of negations that keep shooting out of what is: The woman is carrying a parasol (not an umbrella) that is pink (not tan) and made of silk (not metal).

Ordinarily we have no interest in the cloud of nots, which either go unnoticed or are waved away like gnats, unless there is something about the fact at hand that is aversive. And if it is aversive, then we begin to track out the path of the nots. Let her carry an umbrella, I thought, let it be a drab umbrella, tan or green. (That way she will not call attention to herself on the high footbridge.) Let the pink parasol be made of metal. (That way, she can shield herself once she reaches the other side.) And many more counterfactuals arose in my mind. I surrounded the fact of your own forward motion with a flurry of counterfactual motions. As your path took you near her, I felt dread and accelerated your pace to separate the two of you. (Hurry, hurry past her, out of the path of danger.) But once you were safely past, I wanted you to help her. (Turn around, Winston, look what you are passing, go after her, wrap a coat around her. Pull the silly object from her hand.) But you were all along looking over the railing at me and did not see what was taking place on the bridge: a magnificent woman walking calmly over the river to her death.

What is the point of the counterfactual, on whose behalf she carried out her brief campaign? The counterfactuals my mind so ardently supplied did nothing to alter her fate (though if I were a swift runner, or if you were telepathic, one of us might have reached her in time—you see, the problem was a deficit of counterfactuals, not a surfeit). Even as is, the counterfactual benefits us in two ways. It carries freedom inside itself. It lets us get free of what happened, to picture an alternative world where silk parasols are tolerated—either because no soldier shoots you when you get to the other side, or because, before you get to the other side, a friend has already taken the parasol from your hand. At the same time, it enables us, by lifting a moment away from the facts, to penetrate the facts more deeply. It lets us sense—because she needn't have chosen to do this, she needn't have worn pink, she needn't have held it so high, she needn't have chosen so bright a day when the sunlight would flash around it—the full force of the fact of her courage, the clarity of her defiance.

Not knowing her name, I conferred a name on her as I watched. Will you guess a name such as Odette? Simone? Paulina? All appropriate for her visionary carriage. But no, I called her Polyxena, the young Trojan girl the Greeks decide to slay as a sacrifice to honor Achilles. She consents to die but refuses to be hauled to the altar: "Unhand me, I die willingly." Walking over the footbridge, in her own small corridor of sunlight, the woman with the parasol must have thought what the other earlier thought: "all the light / that now belongs to me is what remains between / this moment and the sword."

In Oceania, where the counterfactual impulse is damaged, it arises not at all or, if at all, only in times of full adversity. But in other empires, where people's lives aren't threatened, and where people wear silk with impunity, the counterfactual comes to be highly prized, easily instigated, prompted at the drop of a hat. In such a world, a color might be not to my liking, and so that alone might prompt me to think of another color, even if no one's life were in danger or even discomfort—except my own exquisitely small discomfort of seeing a hue that is not fully to my liking. Upon seeing a pink dress, I might find its pink not enough inflected with lavender; and this "lavender-deficient state" might count as aversive enough that it would prompt me to mentally revise the color. You complain that empires of aesthetes are decadent, and so they are; but their minds are kept limber, in readiness, and can be pulled toward important work if the need arrives. Because ornament is visibly independent of the structure to which it adheres, it is the material equivalent of the counterfactual. Ornament is there to constantly invite the question, do you like it? do you like it enough? do you wish to change it?

Now do you see why you have *half* fallen in love with the woman washing laundry below our window? (And *fully* fallen in love with the woman who, whenever you turn your back, turns out to be either undressing or dressing up?) In the first years of its rule, Oceania thought it could excise the space of the counterfactual simply by eliminating the paper and canvas on which people write and paint; but soon they saw that people write and paint on themselves in their everyday acts of grooming. This is why Oceania works to control the space of ornament, assigning me a red sash that is obligatory even in the very knot with which it is tied, and removing all tools with which one can voluntarily alter one's own appearance—soap, shirts, linen, and laces, down to the hairpins (on whose heads the angels still dance) and the razor blades (that make the lines of your face and the lines of my thoughts so clear).

❦

Grant me, then, that the counterfactual assists us in every waking moment of our lives. But now comes the key question. What is the relation between the way the counterfactual makes its appearance in everyday consciousness and the way it makes its appearance in great literature? If the counterfactual is omnipresent in waking consciousness, why must we also have poems, stories, pictures, epics in order to be capable of thinking? What further gain to thinking comes from the existence of fictional works? [2]

All the instances of the counterfactual so far given require for their own instigation a feature of the material world; and so, although unstuck from the material world, they are on another level quite stuck to it, taking only brief, fleeting excursions away from it. All the "not" constructions in the perception that the woman is holding a pink (not tan) silk (not steel) parasol (not umbrella or shield) are anchored to, or reined in by, the actual state of affairs. They let us bob away for a split second only. Do you remember when we found in Mr. Charrington's shop the small wooden wheel with the string wound around its central axis? When you tied one end of the string around your finger and let the wooden wheel drop, the string would unspool, then respool so that the wheel would arrive back in your hand a second later. No matter how many times you let it unspool, it would quickly respool, even when you flicked it into unexpected loops and flourishes.

The counterfactual in everyday perception is like this sturdy little toy. But when you open a great piece of literature, the wheel drops from your hand and—rather than respooling and snapping back into place—it instead goes on unspooling and unspooling, maybe not arriving back for two hours, maybe arriving back only at the end of the day. How exactly it keeps unspooling or how far it goes is hard to say, but the string is very long: Homer's *Iliad* is 15,693 lines long; Dante's *Inferno* is 14,320 lines long; and Shakespeare's *Lear* is 3,195 lines long. Time spent in the un-

---

[2] *Editor's note.* Here the author turns the canister and begins to write in lines cutting across all that she has so far written.

spooling motion lets the counterfactual acquire the density and depth of the factual world (so that it is not always being overtoppled and outweighted by the sheer weight of the factual). Once you know the work well, you needn't start at line 1 and proceed forward; you can come in anywhere, through a side window, or up through the floor, then step out again and over into another work. The literary work provides a laboratory for thinking about things that make no claim to being actually the case. And because such a dense array of events is happening inside the fiction, you have to think steadily, fast, and well because, if you don't, why exactly are you there? For relief from the actual? No, sleep is the remedy for that.

So a work of art is a perpetually unspooling counterfactual that exempts you from the actual in order to make you eligible to carry out unrestricted acts of thinking that do not just duplicate the material world as it already exists but constitute a best case. (Not a best case for the world—the world depicted may be dreadful; but a best way of thinking coherently about whatever world has been posed.)

Do you know my brother's historical writings about pre-Oceanic England and India? In one of his essays, he says that a civilization will be capable of producing great works of philosophic thinking only if it is also capable of producing great works of art. About this, I am certain he is right. Now there is a problem with the particular example he came up with, an example by negation. (He claimed that pre-Oceanic England was a country incapable of producing either philosophers or artists. Thanks to Oceania's Empty Shelf policy, he had almost no British books at hand— no philosophy, no art, almost no literature; he based his conclusions only on a surviving archive of picture postcards he gradually assembled from antique shops in Oceania. I have long quarreled with him about this and have enumerated for him the titles of British books shelved at the Fiction Department, awaiting translation.) But never mind the disputed example. His basic insight was right.

Is it imaginable that Plato could ever have thought the thoughts he thought if there were no Homer in his world—Homer, whose work he knew by heart and whom he quotes 150 times in the dialogues? That Aristotle could have thought his thoughts if the world contained no Sophocles or Euripides or Aeschylus? To think what they thought, they had to enter into extended counterfactuals, not taking small fitful veerings away from the actual as we do in everyday perception, but in a kind of strenuous decathlon of the artifactual.

At his trial, Socrates was invited to promise that he would stop teaching and talking: had he agreed, he would have been spared execution. He refused. He said he would never stop talking. He said he would even be pleased to die—would willingly die ten times over—if it meant he could spend all day in conversation with those who had died before him. Do you remember the four he names? Orpheus, Museus, Hesiod, and Homer—poets, all four.

Plato and his friends knew by heart the Athenian calendar of shadows, the places in the city where the best shadows fell in any given week of the year. They went out of their way to meet at such spots. While they were waiting for the full company to arrive and the day's argument to begin, they would narrate the moving shadows, sometimes citing passages from Homer or one of the tragedians, sometimes improvising new stories. In midsummer, a plane tree halfway down a small rounded hill was shadowless at break of day but by early morning sent out a canopied shaft that rapidly rotated a good way around the hillside over the course of a single hour: one of the group would name a fatal event and place a marker on the sunlit ground; then, as the trunk of the plane tree swept swiftly toward the spot, they would together invent circumstances and evolving complications to keep pace with the moving shadow and to account for the concussive moment it crossed onto the marker. (Aristotle was only seven when he first saw this game, and was terrified.) In autumn, when the breezes from the sea picked up, they gathered at a little house belonging to the mother of Timaeus; onto its white wall, a spray of gray and silver shadows from the acacia tree outside produced an unrecognizable garden that seemed to extend into the wall to a depth of forty feet. Those who had arrived took turns, the first positing an event taking place in the first five feet of ground, the second positing occurrences to a depth of fifteen feet, the third inventing an entry originating in the next band of space, and so on until the entire ground, with its changing heights and terraces, was full. Then a die would be rolled and a number, one through five, would appear, and whoever was responsible for that numbered band of space would narrate the next event; until two minutes later, when the die would again be rolled; then two minutes later, again, the story lurching comically from terrace to terrace, the fictional persons in four of the zones always stopping to watch what was occurring in the space under narration. But soon midmorning would arrive, the sun would move on, the shadows and hilarity would fall away, and the slow work of argumentation for which they had gathered would begin.

A work of fiction is—in its full expanse—a counterfactual: it ostentatiously refrains from making any claim that the events it describes actually happened and if pressed will happily acknowledge that they certainly did not happen. But where exactly in the work does the stipulation that it is not factually the case occur? Sometimes people speak as though it comes in every detail, but this would make the play or poem a nightmare of incoherence. Imagine trying to think about my friend Polyxena and the world in which Euripides places her in *Hecabe*. The play is structured around three killings, those of Polyxena (the young daughter of Hecabe taken in sacrifice by the enemies of Troy), Polydorus (Polyxena's younger brother, brutally murdered by Polymestor, a man the Trojans believed was their ally), and Polymestor's two sons (now slain by Hecabe, who also gouges out the eyes of Polymestor). The play conscripts us into deliberating about the legal and ethical differences among the three acts of slaying.

How could we possibly carry out this work of deliberation if each detail in the play were taken as a counterfactual? Here is the way it might sound. Hecabe (not really the case)—the mother of Polyxena and Polydorus (not really the case)—is being held (not really the case) in the camp of the Greek army (not really the case) following the fall of Troy (not really the case). Odysseus (not really the case), a Greek warrior (not really the case) comes to Hecabe (not really the case) to tell her that her daughter (not really the case) . . . and so forth.

Sometimes when one awakens from a terrible nightmare the dream can seem to have, in each of its details, precisely this stark "is and is not" incoherence. One says to whoever will listen—in my dream a man, who was not a man, began to run, but he wasn't really running, toward me, though I don't think I was actually there . . . Such dreams seem to streak right down the center of the rift that separates what the mind takes to be the case and what it recognizes is not the case.

But this has no resemblance to the way events unfold in literature. What are we to make of the sentence "Hecabe (not really the case) is being held (not really the case) in the camp of the Greek army (not really the case)." Are we to understand that there was no woman held by the Greeks, or that there was a woman so held, but a woman other than Hecabe. And when we try to fold in the next phrase, our forward progress becomes even more encumbered: was a woman other than Hecabe held in no enemy camp or held in some enemy camp other than the Greeks', or was it a friendly camp? This is the terrain of dreams.

The fictional work's disavowal of fact takes place on the threshold. The repudiation of the actual is not the content of the work but the precondition for entry and exit. It comes at the moment of passing back and forth between the work and the world, whether these acts take place at the most familiar portals, the first and final lines, or instead through any other window or side door, such as line 531 or line 1626. The membrane of the counterfactual envelope surrounds the entire work. I said it was a precondition for entry, and so it is, but how the precondition works—the consequences that come about if one does not abide by it—becomes clear only at the moment of leaving. If someone reads a fictional work and, upon preparing to exit, declines to agree to regard it as fictional, the person is denied the privilege of exiting; the person stays inside it and never emerges unless or until he changes his mind. This possibility sounds so daunting that you would think we would feel some trepidation at entering into literary works, but for some mysterious reason, we are able—with surprising ease—to comprehend the required repudiation and to carry it out. Yet who has not read a book that so compels belief that one feels a tremor of fear that one will not be able to carry out the eventual repudiation?

The facts of our world are not something we have the option of entering or abstaining from entering, not something we have the option of exiting from; the facts of our world (whether we pay attention to them or not) are part of the world we are abidingly in until we cease to be in the world. Precisely what a fiction is is something that—providing we recognize it as fiction—we can voluntarily enter or exit; and if we don't recognize it as a fiction, the passport dissolves.

Fiction's announcement that it is independent of the actual, and its requirement that we take account of that independence, occurs, then, at the boundaries of the work, at the membrane separating it from the world, and not inside the literary work. A clear statement of this location at the edge rather than the interior was made during the Syme-Searle debates at the Chestnut Tree. They agreed to debate "the logical status of fictional discourse." Now on any topic about language, Syme and Searle usually get into hideous quarrels with one another, but on this particular occasion they startled everyone by agreeing all the way down the line.

Syme began by describing verbs. The same verbs, he argued, are used in ordinary discourse and in fictional discourse, and the same grammatical and semantic rules govern their use. Searle agreed. Then Searle stood up and described nouns. The same nouns are used in ordinary discourse and in fictional discourse, and the same literal meanings are at work. (Here he cast a menacing glance at Syme, but Syme responded by indicating his agreement and urged him to proceed.) If, said Searle, someone tells me something about "a cat," I understand that the person is referring to a furry four-legged creature of a type that often lounges on my doorstep; and so too if I read in a novel or a play about a cat, I understand that what is being referred to is a furry four-legged creature of a type that often lounges on my doorstep. But if the novel says, "This morning a cat lounged on your doorstep," I would know that no claim had just been made about my doorstep or the cats in my neighborhood. The author would have no evidence to bring forward on behalf of the sentence and would be utterly untroubled by that lack of evidence. Were someone to do this in ordinary conversation, I would think the person was either insincere or lying, but the author is guilty of neither insincerity nor lying.

"Bravo Searle! Bravo!" said Syme, as the debate drew to a close. "Will you agree that it is an *odd fact* about human language that it allows for the possibility of fiction at all?" Searle, always the more exuberant of the two, replied, "It is an *odd and amazing fact* about human language that it allows for the possibility of fiction at all." The café (usually full of the hushed whispers of patrons trying to avoid the scrutiny of those passing by) was by now full of laughter and loud applause when Syme, ordinarily the advocate of word reduction, upped the ante on his side of the conjunction by repeating himself shamelessly: "Let us agree, then, that it is an *odd, peculiar, and amazing fact* about human language that it allows the possibility of fiction at all."[3] The two—who were shaking hands—would no doubt have gone on freighting the sentence with mounting expressions of admiration and puzzlement had not the noise of moving chairs ended the evening.

Language—and each of the noun-verb building blocks out of which it is composed—works the same way inside fiction as it does in the realm of fact, with the exception that when one gets to the boundary of the fiction, one is required to break all the referential claims to the world. Now thought—and the building blocks out of which thought is composed—also works inside fiction in the same way it does in the realm of fact. The constant interplay of factual and counterfactual habits of mind that assist us in everyday perception and perceptions about history will again be at work inside the poem or play. The poet presents us with a set of details that, for the duration of the time we are inside the work, we receive as facts (Hecabe is Trojan, Hecabe is in the Greek camp, Hecabe has a daughter, Polyxena), but the counterfactual lets us think *about* these details-presented-as-facts. Here, as in the everyday world, the counterfactual lets us lift away from the facts-as-presented and, by lifting us away, lets us penetrate them more deeply.

During our first encounters with the play, the play itself seems to regulate the amount of time we can exercise the counterfactual: we may say, Let Odysseus not demand Polyxena's death, Let the army not roar its assent to her death, Let Polyxena not agree to die—but the play is moving relentlessly forward, and the very simplicity and clarity of Polyxena's acceptance make our own agitated resistance embarrassing and so abbreviate our own counterfactual protest. Again, when the nurse goes down to

---

[3] *Editor's note.* Searle—who successfully emigrated from Oceania—actually included *all three* of these adjectives when he many years later wrote and published a redaction of the Chestnut Tree debate. (Entitled "The Logical Status of Fictional Discourse," the published version of the argument is close to what Julia reports, though it makes no mention of Syme or the events of the evening.)

Soon after the Chestnut Tree debate, Syme disappeared. There are two schools of thought on the disappearance. Oceania historian George Orwell reports that he was killed by the regime because his acute understanding of verbs was regarded as a threat to the regime. More recently, several historians have speculated that Syme escaped to the United States, changed his name, continued to work on verbs (both regular and irregular), and to this day carries on fierce debates with Searle in intellectual journals.

the ocean for water to bathe Polyxena's newly dead limbs, we may say, Let her not find in the surf the slain body of the other child, Polydorus— but the nurse is narrating what has already occurred, Polydorus is dead, and so again our own resistance is abridged. But now Euripides prepares us for Hecabe's assault on the murderer Polymestor and his two sons, and here—with a set of injuries and deaths about which we feel the least sorrow—we are given ample room (more than we want) to deliberate. Do we try to stay her hand, or do we—like the Chorus—offer to go into the tent of slaughter and assist her? Perhaps we would like to spend much more time countering the deaths of Polyxena and Polydorus, with both of whom we have much sympathy, but Euripides appears to believe that the question at hand is independent of one's sympathies, and so the play conscripts us into deliberating about this third killing.

Yet strange to say, over time—centuries—every detail of the play does in its turn become a site of counterfactual thinking, so that the "is and is not" incoherence of dreams (irrelevant during any single reading) is approximated over the long duration, for do you not agree that countless times in twenty-five centuries people have reflected, "But wait, what if Hecabe had been Greek, what if Polyxena—like Iphigenia—had been Greek? " In the terrain of dreams, every detail at once has this quality; in the work of art, only a small set of details is rolled back at any one time, though eventually they all will be: Hecabe will not have gone down on her knees at the feet of Odysseus; Hecabe will not have saved Odysseus in their earlier lives; Polyxena will not have bared her throat and breast in the breathtaking way that she does; Agamemnon will have conducted Polymestor's trial before, not after, the slayings. Does this begin to answer your question?

For I can picture your face and I see the question you are asking. If the mental acts we carry out inside a literary work resemble so closely the kind of mental acts we carry out in everyday consciousness, why do we so urgently need great literary works in order to be able to carry out strong feats of thinking? What is the difference between the play of factual and counterfactual perceptions applied to the world of fact, and the play of factual and counterfactual perceptions applied to our unspooling counterfactual?

There are five benefits. First, we enter into the literary work for the precise purpose of paying attention to it and thinking about it. In everyday life, we may or may not pay attention to the facts taking place around us, we may or may not think about what we see; we may have to participate in the action in a way that limits the number of perspectives from which we can regard events. Seldom do we draw our chairs up to the arena where facts are unfolding with the purpose of scrutinizing them for an uninterrupted sequence of hours.

Second, inside the literary work, we can think without risk or penalty. Admittedly, this immunity sometimes licenses preposterous statements, but at least it gives the best possible incentive for actually undertaking the work of thinking, and the fact that it also leads to occasional foolishness is a small thing. (I leave aside empires like Oceania where the penalties for entering literary works are grave; other empires have also interfered with the counterfactual reflex by closing theaters, or by prohibiting representation of birds and animals, or by banning particular books, but in such cases the prohibitions are usually narrow, damaging only a thin slice of the full counterfactual sphere, leaving much intact. Only Oceania assaults on every front.)

A third benefit is that the literary work often depicts events that are unusual (or usual, but hidden, in ordinary life). So the work not only occasions deliberation but occasions it on subjects that in waking life we may be explicitly discouraged from talking about, subjects from which we are ordinarily encouraged to avert our eyes. *Oedipus Rex* was for Aristotle always the prototype of the good play, and for the moment it is our prototype as well. But incest is just one among countless subjects that become audible through art. How often is it said about novels that the radical sections occur in the middle? It is only when you are far away from the portals of entry and exit that brush up against our everyday world that the artist's true subject matter emerges.

The fourth and fifth benefits are the greatest, for they concern the ratio of factual and counterfactual as it occurs inside literature, and the ratio of factual and counterfactual as it is found in the historical reality. You suppose I will say that the factual outweighs the counterfactual in historical thinking, whereas the counterfactual outweighs the factual in our skirmishes with great art. There are good grounds for your supposition, since so much historical thinking is dedicated to identifying the facts accurately, whereas in literature we simply take a set of facts as given. But there is one way in which our encounters with literature require of us a heightened reckoning with *both* the factual and the counterfactual.

The fourth benefit, then, is that the details-presented-as-facts in a work of art are often much more dense than the facts in history or everyday life. Yes, of course, the facts in the work of art are just "details-presented-as-though-they-were-facts," or "fact-likenesses"; still, what is at issue is the material the mind is required to seize upon as factual in the act of thinking, leaving aside for the moment the quality or character of the facts themselves. Think of the great historical writings and compare them with the great literary writings (history and literature as they are found in those civilizations whose libraries are intact). The *Iliad*, as Aristotle noticed, is not an account of the thousands of actions that took place in the Trojan War, but an account of a single action whose entire arc can be held within the compass of the mind. Do we have many, or any, equally complete historical accounts of a single action in a given war—say the Napoleonic Wars, or the American Civil War, or any war that occurred in the past twenty-eight centuries?

When we turn from action to character, we again find a much greater density of facts (fact-likenesses) in literature than in history. Have you ever, in reading the biography of an author—even a very great and celebrated biography—been struck by how thin the account is by comparison with what we know about the fictional persons the author invented? How can I ever grasp the mind of Tolstoy in the way I can grasp the mind of Tolstoy's Levin? The biographer tells us that Tolstoy swept his bedroom every morning, but he does not presume to track his perceptions and counterperceptions during the course of a morning's sweeping. How could he without making it up?—he must stay with what is knowable. Yet only if he could do so would I come to know Tolstoy the way I know Levin over the second-by-second, perception-laden twenty minutes Levin wades through a field ready for harvest (or makes his way through the city to visit Kitty, or watches the stars rotating through the sky).

This extraordinary density of factlikeness is outpaced by the fifth and final benefit, the relentless exercise of the counterfactual licensed by the work of art. Right now, all over the world there are people conversing counterfactually about Cordelia (should she have answered her father in a more capacious way?), counterfactually about Hamlet (he should have been more decisive), counterfactually about Ariel (Don't disappear! Chick!). We undo, one at a time and over time, scores of the work's details in a restless way we seldom do with historical persons and events where our regard for what actually happened inhibits any casual rolling back of the facts, unless it is done to get a still more accurate account.

This regard for the factual is precious. Imagine a planet where people contemplated all possibilities equally, and the tiny set of possibilities that happened actually to have come to pass were given no more attention than the far more numerous possibilities that had never come to pass (as though something's having happened were just an accidental and not particularly interesting feature). Our regard for what actually has come to pass—someone's having been born, someone's having spoken, a tree's falling, a house's being built—is the most fundamental way we salute being alive. Sometimes we say of an episode in history, "It has such a coherent design it could be a play," or "The man's speech was so eloquent it could be from an epic." But these qualities of the episode, however notable, have no importance beside what really gives it importance, the fact of its having happened. You will think that I have strayed and have begun to write a defense of history, addressed to one who has no doubt of its value. But calling to mind the value of facts is a way of comprehending the value of art, for by setting aside the claim to actually having happened, a fictional work starts out with a staggering handicap, and what, in compensation, it offers to make itself worthy of attention must be staggering as well.

❦

The factual and the counterfactual do not exist at one another's expense but nourish each other. Conversely, the etiolation of one brings about the etiolation of the other. I bother to say this because someone might think that in Oceania where facts have been damaged, we would be living in the world of the counterfactual: nothing could be further from the truth. Or one might think that Oceania's relentless destruction of the counterfactual at least has the virtue of committing us to the factual: look around for facts in vain. What tempts us to think that the destruction of one marks a strengthening of the other? A blow to either one is a blow to thinking and so necessarily damages both.

Do you remember, Winston, the day you told me you had accidentally held in your hand evidence of the empire's falsification of the Aaronson episode? You mistook my silence for indifference. But I was not indifferent. I was terrified, momentarily struck dumb by the fear that you had lost your clear head, lost your reverence for the very facts you seemed to be defending. The evidence of falsification you recited to me was neither more nor less than the evidence of falsification that every single day passes through your hands in the Records Department, yet so inured had you become to that falsification that its enormity, its gravity, became lost to view until you encountered an unexpected instance. But then, a few seconds later, when you accused me of being "only a rebel from the waist downwards"—like Plato's charioteer, condemned to ride a single horse and the unruly one at that—I felt delight in the fresh reflexes of your mind and knew we had suffered only the briefest of setbacks.

So there you have it, dear Winston. To think even simple thoughts about what is happening, you need the counterfactual, and to think in a sustained way requires that your mind acquire not only an expansive acquaintance with the world as it is, and has in the past been, but, equally, expansive tracts of fiction where you loan your mind to what never was the case.

Soon, I think, we will both be gone. Your guardianship over the factual, and mine over the counterfactual, will end. I do not suppose we will be lucky enough to disappear at the same moment.

If you should disappear before I do, I will hold the factual in place by taking long walks, making maps in my head, then predicting, and fulfilling each step, each turn, each landmark, each plant, each stone. Here is where the red sash fell. Here the bluebell bloomed.

And if I should disappear before you, think that I am only standing behind you—undressing or maybe dressing up—and that soon, any moment now, I will tell you to open your eyes and turn around.

God, and it induces the kind of paranoiac and superstitious be-
children hold, "that the air is full of avenging demons waiting
presumption."[14] Incidentally, Freud's favorite paranoiac, Judge
, presiding judge of the Saxon Supreme Court, shared both the
tion and the paranoia. His description of the "invention" of
nguage (*Grundsprache*) is worth quoting as a precursor to the
in-the-madness of doublethink. This is from Schreber's account
ness written in 1903:

uls to be purified learned during purification the language spoken by
imself, the so-called "basic language" ["Grundsprache"], a somewhat
ated but nevertheless powerful German, characterized particularly by
th of euphemisms (for instance, reward in the reverse sense for punish-
poison for food, juice for venom, unholy for holy, etc.).[15]

Orwell describes as a "deliberate exercise[] in *doublethink*" (178)
recurrent bouts of a kind of "fictional" paranoia as Winston is
ssly pursued for his particular thoughtcrime, his belief in the "mi-
of one." The destruction of Winston's "intellectual apparatus,"
ole body, results in the manipulation of his thoughts or memories.
are passed on from mind to mind; orders come from the "iron
in the wall or through the telescreen. Doublethink destroys the
f memory and the verifiability of history by arresting language
nsciousness in an endless, "frozen" present: a "present" that is
uted through the act of holding two contradictory beliefs in one's
imultaneously. At one moment, the Party intellectuals have to be
ous of the contradiction in order to manipulate reality with strate-
ecision and control the process of "doublethink"; at the very next
nt, the use of the word "doublethink" suggests that reality has been
red with, and one has to subject doublethink to *doublethink*, so
he knowledge of holding contradictory beliefs is erased. The effect,
well describes it, is an infinite process "with the lie always one leap
of the truth. Ultimately it is by means of *doublethink* that the Party
en able . . . to arrest the course of history" (177).
r that horrific scene of electrical torture when Winston feels that
ackbone is about to break, and the torture machine registers 40 on
e of 100, O'Brien begins the process of doublethink. He warns Win-
against the liberal disease of believing in the virtue of the minority
e, or, as he puts it, the belief in "*Your* truth" (203). He charges
ston with having held the treacherous view that the Party had exe-

bid., 8.
aniel Paul Schreber, *Memoirs of My Nervous Illness*, trans. Ida Macalpine and Rich-
. Hunter (London: W. H. Dawson and Sons, 1955), 50.

---

# Doublespeak and the Minority of One

## HOMI K. BHABHA

IT IS ONE of the curious comforts of our lives that we prefer those who
are virtuous not to be virtuosos. It is unclear to me why "strength in
goodness" should somehow seem oddly anomalous with the fluency and
acclaim of genius. In the opinion of many literary critics and political
essayists alike, George Orwell was a virtuous man, somewhat shy of genius. This description of Orwell as a virtuous man is central to Lionel
Trilling's essay in *The Opposing Self*. Virtue makes Orwell no less significant than the great writers of his time; but his *not* being a "genius" is, in
Trilling's opinion, what makes him a "figure."[1] Orwell looks "at things
simply and directly, having in mind only our intention of finding out what
[things] really are, not the prestige of our great intellectual act of looking
at them. . . . [Orwell] tells us that we can understand our political and
social life merely by looking around us," by checking the "tendency to
abstraction and absoluteness."[2] His virtuosity lies in preserving the concrete integrity of language that ensures the authority of the "whole body"
and enables a person to stand courageously in the place of "the minority
of one":

Orwell was using the imagination of a man whose hands and eyes and whole
body were part of his thinking apparatus. . . . He told the truth and told it in
an exemplary way, quietly, simply, with due warning to the reader that it was
only one man's truth.[3]

How do we recognize such virtuousness in language? What strength and
goodness must we exercise to protect ourselves from ideological indoctrination or the utopian indulgence of our imaginations?
    The reform of language, Orwell suggests, is our best hedge against po-
litical hegemony and corruption of public virtue. In his essay "Politics
and the English Language," Orwell insists on the importance of giving
precedence to concrete objects and mental images in our construction of

[1] Lionel Trilling, *The Opposing Self: Nine Essays in Criticism* (New York and London:
Harcourt Brace Jovanovich, 1955), 136.
    [2] Ibid., 139, 143.
    [3] Ibid., 144, 151.

discourse.[4] Words must be held at bay: "it is better to put off using words for as long as possible and get one's meaning as clear as one can through pictures or sensations,"[5] he writes. This process of linguistic clarification keeps consciousness focused and makes it capable of sustaining "one man's truth." Concreteness of thought plays its part by ensuring that the intellectual apparatus—the whole body—is inoculated against ready-made abstractions, prefabricated phrases, and, above all, the epidemic of euphemism. Euphemisms, like "pacification" for the bombing of defense-less villages, or "rectification of frontiers"[6] for the sacking of populations or ethnic cleansing, are "euphonious,"[7] that numbing and dissembling quality of Newspeak that allows doublespeak to prosper. Euphony allows terms and phrases to slip off the tongue, or smoothly slide off the politi-cian's TelePrompTer in a way that allows one to "name things without calling up mental pictures of them."[8]

If we look at the mental pictures projected by Orwell's own writings as he proposes a cure for the language of the body politic, we quickly realize that his underlying metaphors throw up images of some pretty nasty things done to the body of language in the effort to reform it. His own metaphors for the clarification and cure of a language made decadent by ten or fifteen years of European dictatorship are suffused with the imagination of totalitarian violence, even a kind of eugenicist enthusiasm. Let me quote Orwell:

> I said earlier that the decadence of our language is probably curable. . . . Silly words and expressions have often disappeared, not through any evolutionary process but owing to the *conscious action of a minority*. . . . There is a long list of flyblown metaphors which could similarly *be got rid of* if enough peo-ple interested themselves in the job . . . to *reduce* the amount of Greek or Latin in the average sentence, *to drive out* foreign phrases and strayed scien-tific words . . . *scrapping* . . . *every word or idiom which has outworn its usefulness*. (Emphasis added)[9]

"The conscious action of a minority," "[curing] the decadence of our lan-guage," "[driving out] foreign phrases," "the scrapping of every word or idiom which has outworn its usefulness"[10]—all this, proposed as a kind of provisional, if not a "final," solution for the English language, must

have conjured up rather strange sensati[...] when Orwell wrote the essay.

Now before I am accused of "politic[...] ïveté, or the failure to read parodic inte[...] come not to bury Orwell but to praise hi[...] his imagination of violence but to try to u[...] cation with extreme states. In fact, I want[...] he narrates the vicious that the virtuousn[...] of virtuosity. It is when the proselytizer ti[...] service of the good cause that Orwell is[...] sightful. "This invasion of one's mind b[...] *foundations, achieve a radical transforma*[...] make my point), "can only be prevented[...] against them, and every such phrase ana[...] brain."[11] It is this constant vigilance that r[...] by the *action of a minority*, killing *this*, gett[...] "other." The mental image that we form[...] style of writing, and as a *genre* of man—is[...] honest workman of words and things, the[...] passed down to us as the virtuous one amo[...] of our times—Joyce, Stein, Woolf, Lawrence[...]

If *Nineteen Eighty-Four* is about the de[...] tracked in the decadence and deception of do[...] of controlled paranoia among its characters[...] written from a quasi-paranoiac position. I[...] mond Williams does, that Orwell was hims[...] noiac that he evaded the responsibility of dep[...] ductive affiliations between progressive indiv[...] to suggest that the project of reforming the p[...] *peatedly* and *incessantly* demonstrating the[...] structures of doublethink and Newspeak cann[...] of paranoia in the *writer*, not the person, as he c[...] in the narrative. This is supported by an essa[...] "New Words" in which Orwell suggests that "[...] damental thing as language, an attack as it wer[...] our own minds, is blasphemy and therefore da[...] reform of language, he continues, is practically[...]

---

[4] George Orwell, "Politics and the English Language," in *Collected Essays* (London: Secker & Warburg, 1961), 344–45.

[5] Ibid., 350.

[6] Ibid., 347.

[7] Ibid., 345.

[8] Ibid., 347.

[9] Ibid., 349–50.

[10] Ibid., 349, 350.

[11] Ibid., 349.

[12] See Raymond Williams, *George Orwell* (New York: Col[...]

[13] George Orwell, "New Words," in *The Collected Essay[...] George Orwell*, vol. 2, *My Country Right or Left, 1940–19*[...] Angus (New York and London: Harcourt Brace Jovanovich,[...]

cuted three members whose innocence had been established by a New York newspaper photograph. O'Brien produces a copy of the yellowing newsprint and tantalizingly holds it within Winston's angle of vision. Winston writhes, he yells, he forgets the torture dial and cries, triumphantly, "It exists!" (204).

O'Brien, then, burns the incriminating paper in the memory hole, reducing it to ashes, and denies that it ever existed.

> "But it did exist! It does exist! It exists in memory. *I* remember it. *You* remember it.
>
> "I do not remember it," said O'Brien.
>
> Winston's heart sank. *That was doublethink.* . . . If he could have been certain that O'Brien was lying, it would not have seemed to matter. But it was perfectly possible that O'Brien had really forgotten the photograph. And if so, then already he would have forgotten his denial of remembering it, and forgotten the act of forgetting. How could one be sure that it was simply trickery? Perhaps that lunatic dislocation in the mind could really happen: that was the thought that defeated him. (204, emphasis added)

In this brief moment the process of doublethink is no longer a textbook program or a totalitarian theory; it is grasped in the living, writhing form of its performance as a *practice* of mental manipulation and torture. *That was doublethink!* Against all the odds, this horrific exchange allows the victim some faint inkling of "imagined" agency, a futurity that perhaps only fiction allows; or perhaps not. Although Winston is sure that he has just been "doublethinked," he is still able to stand aside and reflect on the procedure which has not succeeded in erasing that movement of memory which allows him to construct an account of what has happened to him—*he has partially escaped the forgetting of the forgetting and is now strangely adjacent to the event.* This account of doublethink, unequal and terrifying though it is, reveals something that pushes Orwell beyond "the minority of one" (179), the figure who stands *by*, and stands *for*, "one man's truth." Winston's concern here is not, primarily, with the vicious circle of deceit that structures *doublethink as the discourse that keeps* "the lie always one leap ahead of the truth." As Winston admits, there is a strong possibility that O'Brien may have really forgotten the photograph so that *he* could not simply be lying. If he had "forgotten the forgetting," then, he may have repressed or disavowed the truth, and who knows, this side of an analyst's couch, what the symptoms of such repression might turn out to be, or where they may be acted out? The issue that concerns Winston is somewhat different from the "content" of lying and truthfulness, although it does *not* neglect that important aspect of the relationship of language to reality. Why does Winston so desperately hope that O'Brien was lying, *and that he was aware of it*? If that were true, it would establish that despite the "deliberate exercises in *doublethink*" (Orwell's phrase) a distinction between truth and falsehood was maintained, however skewed the line between them. If that were so, then there would be some grounds to continue the argument about the existence and significance of the exonerating documents.

There is, however, another intriguing possibility. If O'Brien had genuinely "forgotten the forgetting," then how would Winston—in the minority of one—ever be sure that *he, Winston*, remembered, and would continue remembering? *In this folie à deux, could the minority of one exist without the other?* This opens up an issue about the underlying conditions of social utterance or enunciation, now struggling to be recognized even when they are being hopelessly violated. Any transformation or dislocation of social reality articulated in/*as* social discourse—whether it is manipulative or mutually supportive—requires a dialogic relation or identification between persons. I mean this in the various senses suggested by the work of Bakhtin and Benveniste, and more recently proposed by Charles Taylor. Human existence and expression is crucially marked by its fundamentally dialogical character because, Taylor suggests, "people do not acquire the languages needed for self-definition on their own."[16] He suggests that we are continually in dialogue with, or in struggle against, the things significant others want to see in us—and we in them— and even when they disappear, we continue to be in conversation with them. Now what passes between O'Brien and Winston is hardly a mutual conversation, but it cannot be denied that they are, in Orwell's view, "significant others" to each other.

Breyten Breytenbach, the great South African writer, recognized something about the possibility of a demonic dialogism in conditions of coercion when he addressed his prison poems to his jailer, who was aware of the dire irony and wanted to be "recognized" in them. Language may have its referential realm—factual, concrete, rational—but it also has its dialogic "addressee" who may be an actual person, a virtual presence, an invocatory muse, a superego, a sprite, or a spirit. In each case the significance of the dialogical lies in introducing social discourse to the principle of difference and plurality—to be struggled for or against—in order to "authorize" a perspective or to "take up a position," or yield to someone else's. It is the dialogical process that O'Brien so desperately wants to stamp out; it is the dialogical principle that Winston equally desperately will not relinquish. He might experience himself in the struggle as being in a "minority of one," but there is also a realization that there have to be at least two parties to any struggle over the "truth"; and that within

[16] Charles Taylor, *Multiculturalism and "The Politics of Recognition"* (Princeton: Princeton University Press, 1992), 32.

any one person there are likely to be inner dialogical tensions of the kind that W.E.B. Du Bois called "double consciousness."

One of the strange asymmetries of the human condition is our desire to relate to each other at the level of the unconscious, through projections, fantasies, defensive and compensatory strategies. The dialogical process signifies the quality of *alteritas*, that principle of "otherness" that Hannah Arendt once described as the "paradoxical plurality of unique beings."[17] We *want* access to ourselves and others at levels at which we are least accessible and most vulnerable. Our desire for sociality often arises out of an intimacy that is based on unintelligibility. And our need to affirm the simple human virtue of *affection*—to feel for another—and affiliation—to belong with another—demands that we sharpen our imaginations and instincts to "read" the opacity of others, to get under their signifying skins. Winston holds what he describes as a hope or a "secretly held belief" that O'Brien's political orthodoxy was not perfect: "Something in his face suggested it irresistibly" (13). We are irresistibly led to ask: Is this a belief about himself that Winston projects onto O'Brien? And why is it a secret belief? What is so irresistible in O'Brien's face that can't be described? Is Winston merely hoping against hope, as we are later to discover? Why are there no concrete, mental images to be found that will represent this sensation? When O'Brien tries to break Winston by convincing him that he is mentally deranged, he does so by attacking what Winston had earlier confessed to himself, as his private credo: "Being in a minority, even a minority of one, did not make you mad. There was truth and there was untruth, and if you clung to the truth even against the whole world, you were not mad" (179). Quite apart from our seeking to understand and respond to the intentions and objectives of the speech act, we have to throw ourselves into a form of intersubjective interpretation which works through those figurative, gestural signs of language that have to be interpreted as if there is a kind of "unconsciousness" at work within them. *Is* O'Brien mad *and* bad? Is he a trickster? Is he lying or is he playing a game? Winston has to ask these questions in order to ensure his own survival, but they are not simply matters of textual interpretation or the shrewd calculation of the other person's character and game plan. They are dialogical in a sense that is at once self-questioning and interlocutory: they ask us to confront our own "forgetting of the act of forgetting"; to try to "work through," however imperfectly and tentatively, our own repressions and projections in order to "read" the other person's mind, and the way in which they might hold, or hide, their beliefs *even from themselves.*

---

[17] Hannah Arendt, *The Human Condition* (Chicago and London: University of Chicago Press, 1958), 176.

This is not an invasion of privacy. It is an acceptance of the complex, psychic negotiations that accompany our interactions and utterances. Such "unconscious determinations" may not always sit easily with reasonable or commonsensical explanations, but this does not mean that they cannot be representative of character or personhood in a public sense, or useful for the purposes of democratic dialogue. The very point of subsuming all other selves into the Ideal Ego of Big Brother is to end the struggle over meaning and being that is at the heart of the discourse of the dialogic condition. Orwell makes this very point in "The Principles of Newspeak," an appendix to *Nineteen Eighty-Four*: "Short, clipped words of unmistakable meaning" like Ingsoc, goodthink or prolefeed, were encouraged because they "roused the minimum of *echoes* in the speaker's mind. . . . The intention was to make speech, and especially speech on any subject not ideologically neutral, *as nearly as possible independent of consciousness*" (253, emphasis added). What I have described as Winston's attenuated, though unmistakable, desire for a dialogical relationship should be seen as an attempt to restore an ongoing struggle for "consciousness" to the process of speech. If this were achieved, it would be possible to undo the reductive verbal gagging of "the A vocabulary," which was imposed on ordinary people involved in the business of everyday life:

> All ambiguities and shades of meaning had been purged out. . . . [so] a Newspeak word of this class was simply a staccato sound expressing *one* clearly understood concept. It would have been quite impossible to use the A vocabulary for literary purposes, or for political or philosophical discussion. (247)

The freedom that dialogic discourse envisions is at once fragile and compelling: it is a struggle over the quality and the equality of consciousness; it is evident in the revision and the representation of reality; it is signified in the uses of ambiguity and shades of meaning. A dialogical perspective suggests that there are capacities, capabilities, and qualities of the person—both conscious and unconscious—that should welcome the imaginative, futuristic logic of poetic justice because it puts us in touch with the "paradoxical plurality of unique beings." But what are these paradoxical forms of poetic justice?

Perhaps a story about pigs who are capable of playing the power games that political regimes consider the exclusive preserve of human intelligence—that would certainly turn pigs into unique beings, and human beings into paradoxical animals. Or perhaps poetic justice is to be found in an attempt to write the history of the future, *Nineteen Eighty-Four*, as if it had already happened in 1949, so that what was new was also old, and what we thought we knew was yet to come. In that time warp, History is shadowed by fantasy and Fiction is burdened with fact. They create, in between themselves, a "paradoxical plurality"; a kind of doublespeak that happily condemns fiction and history to a dialogue from which neither one can easily recover the uniqueness of its voice or the singularity of its vision.

# Of Beasts and Men: Orwell on Beastliness

MARGARET DRABBLE

## A SHAKESPEAREAN PROLOGUE

1ST MURDERER:
We are men, my Liege.

MACBETH:
Aye, in the catalogue ye go for men;
As hounds, and greyhounds, mongrels, spaniels, curs,
Shoughs, water-rugs, and demi-wolves, are clept
All by the name of dogs: the valu'd file
Distinguishes the swift, the slow, the subtle . . .
According to the gift which bounteous nature
Hath in him clos'd; whereby he does receive
Particular addition, from the bill
That writes them all alike; and so of men.
Now, if you have a station in the file,
Not i'th'worst rank of manhood, say't . . .;
And I will put that business in your bosoms,
Whose execution takes your enemy off,
Grapples you to the heart and love of us,
Who wear our health but sickly in his life
Which in his death were perfect.

2ND MURDERER:
I am one, my Liege,
Whom the vile blows and buffets of the world
Hath so incens'd, that I am reckless what
I do, to spite the world.

1ST MURDERER:
And I another . . .[1]

---

[1] *Macbeth*, act 3, scene 1.

In the third scene of the act, you may recall, a mysterious third murderer joins the first two nameless murderers in the deed of murdering Banquo. This character has been variously supposed to be Macbeth himself, or Destiny, or some minor character from elsewhere in the play, but is most probably intended to be a suborned spy, introduced as an indication of Macbeth's mistrust of his own henchmen, and, we may now say, as a foreshadowing of the tyrannical or twentieth-century totalitarian all-seeing state.

❦

Macbeth's puzzling catalog of dogs kept coming back into my head when I was thinking of Orwell on the subject of beastliness. According to Orwell's biographer Bernard Crick, "beastly" was George Orwell's first recorded word. On April 11, 1905, his mother wrote in her diary, "Baby much better." (He had been suffering from an ominous bout of bronchitis.) "Calling things beastly."[2] Here, in his early infancy, we note what seems to be an arbitrary association of beastliness and ill health.

"Beastly" is a word that he continued to use a great deal. The word was of course typical English slang of the period and was long to remain popular—it was used by both boys and girls at school, and was still current in my own childhood. It featured a great deal in the schoolboy comics and magazines about which Orwell was to write so well, and which he simultaneously dismissed and celebrated. Orwell must have caught the idea of the beastliness of man directly from his mother, for "beastly" was clearly a word his mother used frequently. She taught him language, and this was his profit from it, for this was one of the curses she taught him. In his last literary notebook there are notes for what may have been intended as a short story or may be an autobiographical reminiscence. The extract reads,

> The conversations he overheard as a small boy, between his mother, his aunt, his elder sister (?) & their feminist friends. The way in which, without ever hearing any direct statement to that effect, & without having more than a very dim idea of the relationship between the sexes, he derived a firm impression that women *did not like* men, that they looked upon them as a sort of large, ugly, smelly & ridiculous animal, who maltreated women in every way, above all by forcing their attentions upon them. It was pressed deep into his consciousness, to remain there till he was abt 20, that sexual intercourse gives pleasure only to the man, & the picture of it in his mind was of a man pursuing a woman, forcing her down & jumping on top of her, as he had often

[2] Bernard Crick, *George Orwell: A Life*, 2nd ed. (London: Secker & Warburg, 1992), 49.

seen a cock do to a hen. All this was derived, not from any remark having a direct sexual reference—or what he recognised as a sexual reference—but from such overheard remarks as "It just shows what beasts men are". . . . Somehow, by the mere tone of these conversations, the hatefulness—above all the physical unattractiveness—of men in women's eyes seemed to be established. It was not until he was abt 30 that it struck him that he had in fact been his mother's favourite child. It had seemed natural to him that, as he was a boy, the two girls should be preferred to him.[3]

The implications of this passage are manifold—that use of the word "feminist," for instance, begs many questions, and Orwell's attitude to women is a subject that deserves examination. But it is the use of the word "beast" and the farmyard analogy to which I draw attention. Orwell used beasts frequently in the current political rhetoric of the day—"Fascist Beasts" popped up everywhere in his journalism, not always in ironical quotation marks. A random sampling of the first pages of *Keep the Aspidistra Flying* throws up remarks about "snooty refined books by those moneyed young beasts" from Eton and Cambridge, and a description of an impoverished old couple as "draggled old beasts," "beetle-like in the long greasy overcoats that hid everything except their feet . . . creeping like unclean beetles to the grave." Both rich and poor are beastly to Gordon Comstock.

The slang use of the word "beastly" was to crop up in Orwell's informal prose right until the end of his life. Here are two examples of many. In his "Hail and Farewell" letter to his early love Jacintha Buddicom (February 15, 1949) he comments lightheartedly on all the "beastly jobs" he had had to take in his early years—and, significantly, the letter toward its end says, "You were such a tender-hearted girl, always full of pity for the creatures we others shot and killed. But you were not so tender-hearted to me when you abandoned me to Burma with all hope denied."[4] A month later he was describing his novel *Nineteen Eighty-Four* in a letter to Ibsen scholar Michael Meyer (March 12, 1949) as "that beastly book."[5]

Yet Orwell was on the whole fond of animals and had far more day-to-day dealings with them throughout his life than many writers have had. His first poem, written when he was four or five, was about a tiger and owed much, he says, to William Blake, that pioneer defender of animal rights. His ill-spelled early letters home from that brutal English institution, the prep school, are dotted with tender inquiries about the Blair family's dogs, cats, and guinea pigs—we find comments such as "Is Togo alright?" and, less pleasantly, "I am very sorry to hear we had those

[3] George Orwell, *The Complete Works*, ed. Peter Davison, with Ian Angus and Sheila Davidson (London: Secker & Warburg, 1998), 20:206.

[4] Ibid., 43–44.

[5] Ibid., 61.

beastly freaks of smelly white mice back. I hope these arnt smelly one. If they arnt I shall like them."[6] A strangely evocative animal reference appears in a letter to Brenda Salkeld (1934?). "The hedgehogs keep coming into the house and last night we found in the bathroom a little tiny hedgehog no bigger than an orange."[7] In his village shop days as a new husband in Wallington he acquired goats, ducks, and hens and a dog called Marx, and the birds that nested between the ceiling and the roof made so much noise that guests often thought they were rats. There were real rats in the homestead in Jura, as well as hens, a pony, many closely observed birds, and snakes.

Orwell was fond of animals, and he was also, like a true Englishman, fond of killing animals. He killed many snakes on Jura, and if witnesses are to be believed, he seemed to kill them with excessive brutality and some pleasure in that brutality. He also shot and fished and hunted. In his first novel, *Burmese Days* (1934), he evokes the beauty of the Burmese landscape:

> Then a single green pigeon fluttered down and perched on a lower branch. It was a tender thing, smaller than a tame dove. With jade-green back as smooth as velvet, and neck and breast of iridescent colours.
>
> . . . So often, like this, in lonely places in the forest, he would come upon something—bird, tree, flower—beautiful beyond all words, if there had been a soul with whom to share it.

But we note that his protagonist Flory is trying to shoot this very pigeon, even as he admires it, and that later in the novel Flory is implicated in the erotic thrill of impressing the newcomer Elizabeth by shooting a leopard—a wild creature that becomes in death "rather pathetic, like a dead kitten." One is reminded, irresistibly, of the sadness of the long-drawn-out and unnecessary death of the elephant in his early essay "Shooting an Elephant." Elizabeth is just as keen on shooting as Flory is, though she does not share his interest in Burmese culture: "He did not realize that this constant striving to interest her in Oriental things struck her only as perverse, ungentlemanly, a deliberate seeking after the squalid and the 'beastly'"[8]—a sentence which reminds one that Orwell saw female human nature as instinctively more racist than was the nature of the male, and that he tended to blame the worst excesses of imperialism on the increasing presence of womenfolk in the colonies: the women in this novel are casually described as hags, pigs, and bitches. He was a prisoner of the brutal sexual politics of his day, and *Nineteen Eighty-Four* was to show

[6] Crick, *George Orwell: A Life*, 64.
[7] Ibid., 248.
[8] Orwell, *The Complete Works*, 2:126.

no sign of liberation from them. There's no space here to discuss Orwell's sexuality, and accusations of sadism and flagellation fantasies that were leveled against him, relevant though these are to any view of anyone's human nature, but I would like to mention in passing Orwell's view of sex in the novel. Sexually explicit descriptions, he complained, were becoming so obligatory and so extreme in the fiction of the 1930s and 1940s that the vogue for them, he said, could not last: he prophesied that one day soon we would find them as absurd as Dickens's indulgence in the death of Little Nell—another of his prophecies not yet fulfilled, and one that reinforces one's sense of his mother's subconscious teachings on the beastliness of sex. Orwell was never happy with the portrayal of sexuality, and I align myself with those who find the description of Julia and Winston's relationship deeply unerotic. He may have intended to portray sexual passion, but if so, he failed.

*Coming Up for Air*, his last novel written before the outbreak of war, is a prophetic lament for the death of pastoral England and a warning against environmental pollution; it uses idyllic descriptions of fish and of fishing to evoke a misogynist, solitary, patriotic love of country. Here is a key passage, which curiously echoes Macbeth's catalog of dogs:

> As soon as you think of fishing you think of things that don't belong to the modern world. The very idea of sitting all day under a willow tree beside a quiet pool . . . belongs to the time before the war, before the radio, before aeroplanes, before Hitler. There's a kind of peacefulness even in the names of English coarse fish. Roach, rudd, dace, bleak, barbel, bream, gudgeon, pike, chub, carp, tench. They're solid kind of names. The people who made them up hadn't heard of machine-guns, they didn't live in terror of the sack or spend their time eating aspirins, going to the pictures, and wondering how to keep out of concentration camp.[9]

(In *Burmese Days*, incidentally, we learn that Buddhists can acquire merit by buying live fish and setting them free in the river.) *Coming Up for Air* also contains, near the end, that prophetic moment leading toward *Animal Farm* when man becomes beast, or rather boy becomes pig: the narrator George Bowling sees rushing down the small-town High Street a herd of pigs, "a sort of huge flood of pig-faces. The next moment, of course, I saw what it was. It wasn't pigs at all, it was only the schoolchildren in their gas masks. . . . At the back of them I could even make out a taller pig that was probably Miss Todgers."[10]

This leads us directly to the transformation of man into animal in *Animal Farm*, an allegory that, despite the bleakness of its message, yet

[9] Ibid., 4:76.
[10] Ibid., 34,

retains a kind of tenderness toward its creation, a tenderness that tempers the savage Swiftian indignation and imagination which learned so much from Swift's treatment of the horses and the Yahoos in *Gulliver's Travels*. (Orwell had been given a copy of *Gulliver's Travels* for his eighth birthday.)

Orwell viewed the Anglo-Irish critic Hugh Kingsmill, his contemporary, as a highly percipient critic, and praised him in particular for his reading of Dickens. He also wrote well on Orwell himself. Commenting on Orwell's "Notes on Nationalism," published in *Polemic*, Kingsmill described Orwell's belief that nationalism implied "the habit of assuming that human beings can be classified like insects and that whole blocks of millions or tens of millions of people can be confidently labelled as 'good' or 'bad.' " Kingsmill goes on to claim that "*Animal Farm*, a fable of the Russian Revolution, revealed the poetry, humour and tenderness in Orwell; but it seems to be only when he thinks of men as animals that he can see them as human beings, and feel at one with them. In his direct relations with them he is always the party man, disgusted with all existing parties."[11]

Here, I think, we have a central point about George Orwell: his attitude toward the goodness of beasts and the beastliness of human nature. The natural goodness of some of the animal characters in *Animal Farm* does not escape the least sophisticated reader, and this universal little work—turned down by several publishers as the kind of animal story that would never sell—remains extremely affecting. *Nineteen Eighty-Four* terrifies and sickens, but it does not touch the heart, whereas in *Animal Farm* the death of Boxer, the betrayed dreams of Clover, the sad dirgelike singing of "Beasts of England" all betray, paradoxically, the essential humanity and decency that Orwell wished to defend and preserve. The last disillusioned singing of the revolutionary anthem "Beasts of England"—sung "very tunefully, but slowly and mournfully, in a way they had never sung it before"[12]—betrays an open emotion that in a human context Orwell found almost impossible to express. When he describes meetings or rallies, even of those with whom he is politically in sympathy, his tone is almost invariably satiric and sardonic, as though he cannot bear the sight of any massed gathering of the human species. Like Dickens, he was sickened by and feared the mob. And unlike Dickens, in his fiction, he could never free character from category. Only in his animal fables could he write with tenderness.

[11] Kingsmill is here quoting from Orwell. See Orwell, "Notes on Nationalism," in *The Complete Works*, 17:141.

[12] Hugh Kingsmill, *The Best of Hugh Kingsmill*, ed. Michael Holroyd (New York: Herder and Herder, 1971), 288.

On the evidence of *Nineteen Eighty-Four* it may easily be argued that Orwell had a low and essentially reductive view of human nature. As we have seen, the novel demonstrates how Orwell believes that we may all, even the bravest of us, be reduced by political manipulation and by violence to the lowest of acts. We become worse than rats. No one resists torture. Altruism does not exist. The gene is selfish, and the individual man is selfish. We are not, ultimately, capable of social or personal altruism. Under pressure, we relinquish our certainties, as the Asch experiment demonstrated in 1952: our desire to conform is greater than our respect for objective facts. We would all steal from a starving sister, as Winston does, or kill our mother to save ourselves. We would all be tricked, as by the notorious Milgram experiment of 1974, into torturing our fellow human beings, if we were persuaded that our acts were part of a legitimate scientific experiment. We wouldn't even have to be paid. We would volunteer. We are all sheep, and we would all march to the goose step, which Orwell describes as "one of the most horrible sights in the world . . . it is simply an affirmation of naked power; contained in it, quite consciously and quite intentionally, is the vision of a boot crashing down on a face."[13]

There has been some discussion of whether Orwell was speaking only of the phenomenon of state power and state control, or did his predictions of mind-manipulation also extend to the power of commercial interests and the mass media? If he was speaking only of the state, it seems we may congratulate ourselves, for triumphant capitalism has moved us—or at least those of us who live in the Western democracies—further from the possibility of totalitarian control. But there are strong indications that he was discussing not merely state power but also the fragility of human nature itself when exposed to various other possible forms of pressure and manipulation. He shows us a world in which an economic elite ruthlessly retains power and suppresses people and freedom in its own interests, but his vision of the collapse of human nature and human dignity under these conditions could equally well apply to a different set of causes. Imagine, for example, severe shortages caused not by political intervention but by natural causes, by so-called acts of God: anthropologists (see Colin Turnbull's worrying study of the Ik people during famine conditions),[14] psychologists, and writers of science fiction do well to warn us that we may quickly revert to barbarity when there is not enough food or water to go round. This seems to me to be one of the central concerns of the novel: who are we, and how can we try to resist our own selfishness?

[13] Orwell, "The Lion and the Unicorn: Socialism and the English Genius," in *The Collected Essays, Journalism and Letters of George Orwell*, ed. Sonia Orwell and Ian Angus (New York: Harcourt, Brace and World, 1968), 2:61–62.

[14] Colin Turnbull, *The Mountain People* (New York: Simon and Schuster, 1982).

Is *Nineteen Eighty-Four* Orwell's final balanced assessment of human nature, or is it an assessment distorted by a near-mortal neck wound, ill-fitting false teeth, and fatally diseased lungs? Did he really dislike and despise the human species? It seems, in view of the suffering and courage of his last years, almost impertinent to ask. While writing this book, he was in considerable pain and knew his life expectancy was minimal: his proposals of marriage to various women, including his proposal to Sonia Brownell, who accepted him, were deathbed proposals. Like Winston Smith, he knew he had a death sentence. Sonia, in effect, married a dead man. When he looked in the mirror, he saw an image that must have closely resembled the tortured face of John Hurt in Marvin Rosenblum's film version of *Nineteen Eighty-Four*. The secondary effects of the new wonder drug streptomycin, flown in from the United States, were so unpleasant, he wrote to a friend, that "it's a bit like sinking the ship to drown the rats" (January 12, 1949, to George Woodcock).[15] (He had what his doctors described as a "fearful allergic reaction"—skin rash, mouth ulcers, hair loss, red eyes, a severe sore throat, nails disintegrating at the roots.) And there is a painful irony in the fact that someone who had always feared himself to be physically unattractive had become literally an untouchable to his own adopted son: he was afraid to have close contact with Richard, for fear of infecting him with tuberculosis.

It is small wonder if his own low health and spirits colored his larger predictions. Many, in 1948 and 1949, would have agreed with him that the younger generation could look forward to nothing but a perpetual future of wars, shortages, and rationing. Many, in less prosperous parts of the world, would still, for themselves, endorse those predictions. Some of us remember well the bleakness and colorlessness of postwar Britain, a world of sensory deprivation only partly exaggerated by Radford and Rosenblum's film: we all dressed in shades of gray and brown, and sweet rationing was so severe that the piece of chocolate stolen by the boy Winston from his sister would have been made to last, carefully eked out, for a family of three children for a week—or so it seems in my bitter childhood memory. That bleakness survived for decades in Eastern Europe, as a permanent indictment of Communism. Yet it might be fair to point out that it would be possible, even today, to find film locations in many prosperous capitalist countries that would look just as convincingly depressing on-screen as those so skillfully filmed by Marvin Rosenblum's cameraman in Britain in 1984. There are such sites in 1999 within a mile or two of where I live in London. There are such sites within a mile or two of the University of Chicago Law School.

[15] Orwell, *The Complete Works*, 20:16.

George Orwell himself was by nature and circumstance deeply sensitized to the suffering of others, to the suffering of both men and beasts, and in his journalism and fiction he tried to conduct us beyond category and catalog, to make us see that others suffer, that they are not debarred from the experience of suffering by belonging to some subhuman or foreign category. We cannot disown or ignore conditions behind the Berlin Wall, beyond the Iron Curtain, or, latterly, in vast faraway areas like Africa, Indonesia, or China. Orwell was an internationalist and an anti-imperialist as well as an English patriot. He wrote an essay for the *Adelphi Magazine*, published in July 1939, called *Not Counting Niggers*, but he himself was always counting niggers, and calling us to account on their behalf. (The word "nigger," incidentally, is, according to my computer spellchecker, an unword. "Unword" is also an unword. But spellchecker, *sic*, is fine.) In the spring of 1939 he went to Marrakech in Morocco, not as a tourist but for the sake of his health, and he wrote of what he described as the people with brown faces: "Are they really the same flesh as yourself? Do they even have names? Or are they merely a kind of undifferentiated brown stuff, about as individual as bees or coral insects?" He feeds bread to a gazelle in the public garden, and an Arab workman says to him in French, "*I could eat some of that bread.*"[16] So Orwell tears off a piece of bread and feeds the man as well as the beast. Like the momentarily brave and generous Prisoner 2713 Bumstead J. (194), he retains the impulse to share. In the same essay, he pities the damnably overloaded Moroccan donkey:

> the most willing creature on earth, it follows its master like a dog and does not need either bridle or halter. After a dozen years of devoted work it suddenly drops dead, whereupon its master tips it into the ditch and the village dogs have torn its guts out before it is cold.
>
> This kind of thing makes one's blood boil, whereas—*on the whole*—the plight of human beings does not. I am not commenting, merely pointing to a fact. . . . Anyone can feel sorry for the donkey with its galled back, but it is generally owing to some kind of accident if one even notices the old woman under her load of sticks.[17]

This passage—indeed this whole essay—is full of passion and paradox and questioning and a kind of angry sick despair. Like *Burmese Days*, it insists on the humanity of those who seem subhuman to the colonial eye. Whatever we may think of its tone, it draws our attention to men, women, and beasts of burden alike. We all live in the land of the prickly pear, where it is "bumpy underfoot, and only a certain regularity in the

[16] Orwell, "Marrakech," in *The Complete Works*, 11:417.
[17] Ibid., 420.

bumps tells you that you are walking over skeletons."[18] Yet Orwell found it easier, less complicated, to show pity for the beast than for the man. For the pity of man involved pity of himself, and toward himself he was relentless and unsparing. He was the unloved child of his mother, and he was a dirty beast.

I would like to come full circle with a Shakespearean epilogue. I began with *Macbeth* and will end with *Lear*. Both plays deal with themes of cruelty and power that the author of *Nineteen Eighty-Four* recognized well. Orwell, in a celebrated essay, defended *King Lear* against Tolstoy's attacks and praised Shakespeare's humanity, his poetry, and his love of "[t]he surface of the earth and the process of life."[19] In Shakespeare, even the three nameless murderers are human. In the catalog, they go for men. And consider the three nameless servants in *King Lear*, who witness one of the most effectively horrible acts of theatrical violence ever staged, the blinding of Gloucester. They react to this shocking scene of violence with ordinary insubordinate human horror. The first servant, when he physically intervenes in an attempt to prevent the blinding, is killed by a stab in the back from Regan, and Servants Two and Three are left to end the scene. To the Third Servant are given the last lines of act 3:

> . . . I'll fetch some flax and whites of eggs
> To apply to his bleeding face. Now, heaven help him![20]

This is a moment of revolt and compassion that could not occur in Orwell's dark totalitarian world. Director Peter Brook, controversially, in 1962 at the Royal Shakespeare Company—in one of the greatest productions of *King Lear* in this half-century—cut those lines, thus removing from the scene its final moment of human kindness and of hope. Many noted but few protested against this ax to the text. History had moved us closer to Orwell's closing 1948/1984 view of the possibilities of human nature, and further from Shakespeare's, and we knew it.

It is fitting that the very last words should be Orwell's own. Part 2, section 2 of *Nineteen Eighty-Four* describes the first secret sexual encounter of Julia and Winston, and before these two doomed lovers come together, they listen for some time to the astonishing and ecstatic song of a solitary thrush. (Orwell, we remember, was a keen observer of birds.) This passionate prelude prompts Winston to wonder, "For whom, for what, was that bird singing? No mate, no rival was watching it. What made it sit at the edge of the lonely wood and pour its music into nothingness?" (103). It is a moment of pointless, impersonal animal delight, which links

---

[18] Ibid., 417.
[19] Orwell, "Lear, Tolstoy, and the Fool," in *The Complete Works*, 19:64.
[20] Act 3, scene 7.

us back to an earlier section when Winston dreams of the Golden Country, a democratic common ground of "rabbit-bitten pasture, with a foot track wandering across it and a molehill here and there" (29). There are elm trees swaying faintly in the breeze, for this was before Dutch elm disease destroyed the elms of England, and those peaceful English dace are swimming in the pools beneath the willow trees. This is a vision of what Orwell's predecessor Cobbett called the countryside of the peasant and the laboring man, land that would never be enclosed by the landlord. Winston's pastoral dream moves into an erotic fantasy, as he summons up the naked body of Julia, who has thrown aside her clothes with a gesture of splendid carelessness. And, writes Orwell, "That too was a gesture belonging to the ancient time. Winston woke up with the word 'Shakespeare' on his lips" (ibid.). Shakespeare here, mysteriously but effectively, stands in as shorthand for all that Winston and Orwell treasure, all that they fear to lose.

# Does Literature Work as Social Science?
# The Case of George Orwell

### RICHARD A. EPSTEIN

## LITERARY AND SOCIAL SCIENCE TRADITIONS

We live in a world that has, to say the least, a certain fascination with public intellectuals. Some public intellectuals are drawn from the academy, but many of the most influential members of this hardy if indefinable breed come from other pursuits. Because they have not undergone the rigors of preparing for a professional or Ph.D degree, they show little respect for the conventional boundaries that separate one field of inquiry from another. They can, and often do, move quickly from the humanities to the social sciences and back again, and are often not aware as to how, or even whether, they have made the journey. Lawyers, especially academic lawyers, are frequently able to fill the niche of public intellectual. Law is a parasitic discipline. It attaches to all human endeavors that involve either disputes or cooperation between two or more people, which is to say that it touches all aspects of human life, either as an unwelcome intruder or as an indispensable aid. Lawyers develop skills to match the breadth of their occupational assignments, so perforce function like public intellectuals who are happy to draw inspiration from whatever source lies close at hand. Often, therefore, they work with materials from both the humanities and the social sciences. The ability to spin a compelling narrative is of course one of the great skills of the trial lawyer. And so is the ability to marshal quantitative data in complex litigation. So our broad portfolio of business contains stock on both sides of the intellectual divide, even if it guarantees mastery of neither.

In dealing with these public issues, we lawyers sometimes work in competition with writers, who often double as journalists. This hardy breed

---

A shorter version of this paper was delivered under the title "Using Literature to Understand Social Institutions: A Critique of the Orwellian Vision" at the John R. Coen/Distinguished White Center Lecture at the Lindsey Memorial Courtroom of the Fleming Law Building at the University of Colorado on November 6, 2001.

specializes in the quick study and may acquire skills in both the arts and the social sciences. These writers also have a penchant for making strong pronouncements about human behavior, so that the question arises as to how their insights and ideas should be incorporated into our evaluation of social phenomena. More specifically, this paper asks the extent to which we, both as lawyers and as citizens, should rely on literature and social science in dealing with the complex forms of human behavior that are subject to legal regulation in all its forms. As already noted, it is dangerous for someone trained in law to move into such heady territory, even when it concerns matters adjacent to legal studies. Nonetheless, the relationship that these two fields have to the law is too important to be left only to persons steeped in either the humanities or the social sciences. Lawyers have to say their piece as well.

My principal target on this occasion is perhaps the most famous public intellectual of the last century, George Orwell, whose work combines literary appeal with powerful critiques of the existing social order. In some sense it is perhaps too strong to call Orwell a social scientist, in that he did not engage in any of the formal or quantitative work. Yet by the same token, he did write serious social commentary on the kinds of large questions that attract the attention of social scientists and political thinkers of all stripes. Perhaps for this reason some people might prefer the term "social critic" or "political philosopher" instead. But I have decided to stick with "social scientist" as reflected in the title. In any event, I do not care about the exact term, for what interests me is the transition from literary work to social theory. On this topic, the connection between literature and politics was exceptionally strong in the turbulent 1930s and 1940s when Orwell wrote. Even within Western democracies there were sharp debates over the desirability, necessity, or futility of central planning. And these were in a sense small beer compared with the challenges that totalitarian forces of the Left and the Right posed to any form of democratic institution.

At one level the interaction between literature and social science might be seen as synergistic. It is commonplace for literary writers to use fiction and narrative to convey their strong dissatisfaction with the present social, economic, or political order. Often their expertise lies in the dissection of character, description, and plot. Sometimes these writers explore the psychological dimensions of the characters they create. Sometimes they examine how normal people respond to dramatic crises. At other times they take the opposite tack to explore how alienated and disturbed people respond to routine events.

As befits his time, however, Orwell wrote with a larger intention. Throughout his life he was both essayist and novelist, and in the case of a "novel" like *Down and Out in Paris and London*, the separation between the autobiographical and the fictional is razor-thin at best.[1] In both settings, Orwell assumed a powerful self-definition as an outsider. Although he grew up within the system, he viewed himself as a man with a mission, as the man who fought against its dominant practices, as the man who could not be tamed or domesticated by it. That sense of having grown up as an outsider, a fighter against orthodox complacency, comes through with great vividness in his posthumous essay "Such, Such Were the Joys . . ." where he recounts the harsh experiences he endured as an impecunious and socially isolated scholarship boy at an English preparatory school.[2] The lesson that shines through is that the fault lies not in Orwell himself but in his stars, that is, in the unthinking and entrenched system into which he was thrown against his will. Orwell often conceived of himself as a minority of one who had to stand firm against the crowd. He projected his determination to fight against the odds, to communicate the sufferings and hardships of life, and to champion the cause of the socially dispossessed. His knack for turning a phrase and for describing a scene both offer obvious clues as to why he was, and is, regarded as one of the great stylists of the twentieth century.

Yet what I find troubling about Orwell's approach is his easy willingness to generalize from his own experiences. To Orwell, private pain was the source of his public knowledge. He never hesitated to treat his life, his pain, or his literary impulses as an accurate description of some larger social reality. It is at this point that the clash between the literary and the social science approaches begins to bite. The point is, of course, not unique to Orwell but applies to many writers who invoke the literary form as a vehicle of social criticism. To go into autobiographical mode for the moment, this point was first brought home to me as a freshman at Columbia College in my course on contemporary civilizations in the fall of 1960. The topic before the class was the condition of the working class in England and France during the middle of the nineteenth century. My teacher on the occasion was an excellent historian who suffered a premature death: Paul Noyes, then a raw assistant professor on his first teaching assignment, back from a Marshall Scholarship, which I believe he held at Oxford. The two excerpts that our class read side by side were a selection from Balzac—I believe that it was from *The Girl with the Golden Eyes*[3]—and an account of the position of the English working

[1] Peter Davison, *George Orwell: A Literary Life* (New York: St. Martin's Press, 1996), 25–26.

[2] See generally George Orwell, "Such, Such Were the Joys . . . ," in *A Collection of Essays* (New York: Doubleday, 1954), 9.

[3] Honoré de Balzac, *The Girl with the Golden Eyes* (1835), cited in *Introduction to Contemporary Civilization in the West*, ed. Contemporary Civilization Staff of Columbia College, 3rd ed. (New York: Columbia University Press, 1961), 263.

class offered by an English industrialist/apologist, Andrew Ure.[4] Balzac used his vast literary powers to capture the desperate plight of the French worker, while Ure, writing in the tradition of Adam Smith, used somber prose and dry statistics to emphasize the steady rate of progress under the system of manufacturers and the vast increases in productivity and longevity that it generated. To the class, Balzac's imagery won the debate in a rout; to Noyes, ever the nonsentimental historian, Ure had the better of the argument by far. And he hammered home the reason why: in the delineation of large-scale social movements the prosaic was more important than the dramatic. We needed to know statistics about life expectancy, literacy rates, caloric intake, and the like. We had to know something about infrastructure, investment, and technical advances. We had to understand the importance of an endless array of small incremental improvements. Noyes was a historian who thought about these matters in the way in which Robert Fogel has thought about nutrition.[5] To Noyes's mind, Balzac's story offers us at best a statistical sample of one, and perhaps not even that.

I cannot speak for everyone in that class, but Noyes won me over. From that time forward, I have been deeply suspicious of the dramatic crossover from literature to social science. The literary author has no obligation to track the truth while writing fiction. But the price that is paid for that liberty—dare one call it a self-indulgence?—is that the fiction cannot be treated as though it is a representative instantiation of some generalized underlying social state of affairs, given the obvious risks of embellishment and fabrication. It is simply too easy for the novelist—or today's docudramatist—to shift weight from one shoulder to another. When the critics are at a distance, and friends are close at hand, literature is projected as an accurate and vivid mirror of the world; when the critics close in, and the friends are absent, oh well, then, some degree of literary license has to be tolerated in the name of creative imagination. The writer is allowed, to use a phrase that the English novelist Margaret Drabble invoked on Gretchen Helfrich's *Odyssey* talk show in evaluating Orwell, the luxury

---

[4] Andrew Ure, *The Philosophy of Manufactures* (1835), cited in *Contemporary Civilization*, 243. The essay was written as response to the Factory Act of 1833. Ibid., 242.

[5] See, e.g., Robert W. Fogel, *Strategic Factors in Nineteenth Century American Economic History: A Volume to Honor Robert W. Fogel*, ed. Hugh Rockoff (Chicago: University of Chicago Press, 1992); Robert W. Fogel, "Exploring the Uses of Data on Height: The Analysis of Long Term Trends on Nutrition, Labor Welfare, and Labor Productivity," *Social Science History* 6 (1982): 401–2; Robert W. Fogel, "New Sources and Techniques for the Study of Secular Trends in Nutritional Status and the Process of Aging," *Historical Methods* 26 (1993): 5.

to speak of "warning not prophecy."[6] To that observation, my response is that this clever equivocation opens the door to literary opportunism. If the world does not turn out as predicted, then the warning has been heeded. If the world does, then warnings can be recast after the fact as the prophecies that they never were at the time.[7] The proposition remains sonorous; but it also becomes nonfalsifiable.

On balance, then, I think the humdrum accounts given by social science are more reliable than the recounting of dramatic incidents that become the stuff of literature. A literary rendition may well teach someone to be sensitive to the ravages of poverty, but it will not indicate whether poverty is in decline or on the increase. It will not give comparative figures across different cities, states, or nations. It will not show its impact on longevity. We are rightly skeptical of social science data that is prepackaged to validate some prior point of view. Adopting the social science method does not require us to accept any and all work just because it falls within the genre. In particular, we should show even greater skepticism of literary works that have the same mission, but that are not subject to the same set of research protocols.

In dealing with grubby data, sometimes we have to look hard for explanations of powerful social trends. Think back to the condition of the working class in Europe in the mid–nineteenth century. One well-documented feature of this period was the expansion of large cities, stoked by migration from the farm.[8] One nagging question asks why people chose to brave the hazards of a long journey in order to work under hellacious factory conditions so vividly described by Balzac and others. Perhaps we can hazard an explanation. One image that dominates popular and social thought conjures up the bucolic pleasures of farm life, and the communion that agricultural workers have with nature. Don't believe it. Even today, farm work ranks among the dirtiest and most dangerous occupa-

[6] Audio recording: Gretchen Helfrich, *Odyssey* talk show on station WBEZ (November 11, 1999), available at http://www.wbez.org/services/ram/od/od-991111.ram (an audio covering Helfrich's interview with Epstein may be downloaded from this Web site).

[7] The same strategy has often been employed by environmental doomsayers, whose predictions of widespread chaos made some thirty years ago have been everywhere falsified by events. For a merciless dissection of that art, see Ronald Bailey, "Earth Day, Then and Now," *Reason*, May 2000, 18, who notes that activists such as Paul Ehrlich and Lester Brown never have to confess error because they know how to "get out ahead of a parade that has already started. When things get better, they claim that it's only because people heeded their warnings, not because of longstanding trends and increased efficiencies." Bailey, "Earth Day," 28. The real risk of course is that someone will believe them even though the firmest protection against environmental risks comes often from new technologies and ideas in what look at first blush to be unrelated areas.

[8] Karl Marx and Friedrich Engels, *The Communist Manifesto*, ed. David McLelland (Oxford: Oxford University Press, 1992).

tions. Accidents and disease are common; exposure to the elements takes its toll upon the farmer.[9] One hour of stoop-labor should convince any objective observer of the false romanticism attached to agricultural work, especially before the advent of the laborsaving (and lifesaving) machines and technologies of the twentieth century.

That observation helps explain why nineteenth-century workers agreed to assume the risk of accident in contracting with their industrial employers. Unfortunately, the usual answer given to that question is one that speaks of the exploitation of the worker by the firm—a leaf from Marx and Engels.[10] The more accurate response does not require any appeal at all to the idea of exploitation. The farmer-worker is often a sole proprietor with no one to sue but himself. The worker who is denied by contract or by law the right to sue his employer has a practical position that is *no worse off* than that of the farmer who labors on his own account—who, after all, has no one else to sue either. Indeed, that person may well be better off if the factory environment he enters turns out to be less dangerous than the farming conditions he left. Now the compensation for injuries on the job comes, as it were, in an *ex ante* form that requires no lawsuit to collect. It is a reduced risk of injury in the first place.

To be sure, workers and employers do not have to stand pat with a no-liability regime just because the current employment is safer for the worker than his next-best job. Competition still drives firms; workers are still willing to accept lower wages in exchange for higher rates of physical security. So once again the more prosaic theories of mutual gain through contracting—theories that would have held scant appeal to Orwell—might help explain the evolution of practices. And to some extent only they can explain what did in fact happen: the early systems of workers' compensation were concentrated in dangerous industries—rails and mines—and they antedated by over thirty years the adoption of the Workmen's Compensation Laws in England in 1897.[11]

Now it may well be that the explanation I have offered is incomplete, for clearly there were many distortions in land markets that could also have pushed workers off the farms and into the cities. The most obvious

[9] Farming (which is lumped together with agriculture, fishing, and forestry) ranks second only to mining in the U.S. rate of job-related deaths. A farm worker is five times more likely than an average American worker to be killed on the job and is more likely to sustain nonfatal work-related injuries as well. U.S. Census Bureau, *Statistical Abstract of the United States* (1999), 450–51, available at http://www.census.gov/prod/00pubs/99statab/sec13.pdf. Agricultural deaths are 20 per 100,000; mining deaths are 24 per 100,000. The general workforce rate is 4 per 100,000.

[10] See generally Marx and Engels, *The Communist Manifesto*.

[11] For a discussion, see Richard A. Epstein, "The Historical Origins and Economic Structure of the Workers' Compensation Law," *Georgia Law Review* 16 (1982): 775.

of these would be the enclosure of lands that stripped many marginal producers of property to which they held only customary title.[12] A strong argument could be made that the legal system should have recognized these claims by some analogy to prescriptive rights. But it would be a mistake to believe that this one shift would have been sufficient to offset the huge pressures that drove England toward industrialization in the nineteenth century. It would be equally misguided to take the position that the proper response to defects in agrarian land policy would have been to alter the rules that governed the employment relationship in industrial settings. What happened in the countryside should, perhaps, have been undone. But for these purposes it hardly matters whether that course of action was just unattainable or also unwise. Either way, it hardly improves matters in the country to adopt an inferior mode of industrial organization in the city. Here, as in general, one cannot counter the adverse effects of one imperfection with the creation of yet another.

## LITERARY OVERGENERALIZATION

The dangers of literature as social science run deeper. Orwell himself was aware of the reporting biases of literary types. In his essay on Charles Dickens, he noted insightfully that "Dickens nowhere describes a railway journey with anything like the enthusiasm he shows in describing journeys by stagecoach."[13] And Orwell further elaborates that Dickens did not have a clue about the businesses and trades of his various merchant characters, who are remembered more for their oddities than for their business acumen. We should never infer national savings rates from the financial habits of *David Copperfield*'s Mr. Wilkins Micawber.[14] We should also take with a grain of salt David's own youthful experiences at Murd-

---

[12] For one such reference, see H. G. Wells, *The Outline Of History* (New York: Macmillan, 1921), 821:

> The bigger men were unchallenged rulers of Great Britain, and they set themselves to enact laws, the Enclosure Acts, that practically confiscated the unenclosed and common lands, mainly for the benefit of the larger landowners. The smaller men sank to the level of wage workers upon the land over which they had once possessed rights of cultivation and pasture.

[13] George Orwell, "Charles Dickens," in *A Collection of Essays* (New York: Harcourt, Brace and Co., 1954), 55, 92.

[14] See generally Charles Dickens, *David Copperfield*, ed. Nina Burgis (Oxford: Clarendon Press, 1981).

stone & Grimby, not to mention the educational oddities of Mr. Grad-grind (even the name is political) in *Hard Times*.[15]

The irony is that Orwell in his own way has fallen into the same trap as Dickens did. Orwell has some great insights about himself, although I must confess that his account of his schoolmates in "Such, Such Were the Joys . . ." was much less credible to me after I raised three children, none of whom is as malleable and impressionable as Orwell supposes his fellow classmates to have been.[16] The last time I read the essay I had uneasy sympathy (perhaps undeserved) for Mr. and Mrs. Wilkes (Bingo), who must have had their hands full with this precocious but problem child whose own hang-ups made it hard for him to adjust to the routines of an English school. At the very least I am convinced that I would not accept Orwell's account of his own youth without first undertaking cross-examination and hearing adverse witnesses, both standard fact-finding precautions. But even if we assume that the adult Orwell had great self-understanding of the youthful Orwell, so that he could see through the foibles of those whom he knew, we still have to challenge his literary method. Quite simply, Orwell cannot win large-scale political debates by generalizing autobiographical information, however compelling.

Let me give an example of what I mean. Recently, I read for the first time Orwell's 1936 novel *A Clergyman's Daughter*.[17] In this book Orwell does little to conceal his overlapping distastes for both religion and capitalism as they operated in England in the 1930s. Orwell himself certainly harbored an immense distaste for totalitarian regimes and an abiding fondness for democratic socialism: "Every line of serious work that I have written since 1936 [the date of the Spanish civil war] has been written, directly or indirectly, *against* totalitarianism and *for* democratic socialism, as I understand it."[18] But even if democratic socialism had the virtues that Orwell attributed to it, the question remains: what could we say about the overall desirability of that system (here understood as the collective ownership of the means of production, or at least extensive government planning and control over industrial policy) in comparison with the decentralized market alternative? Orwell makes that choice easy through

---

[15] See generally Charles Dickens, *Hard Times*, ed. Gwen Jose (Cambridge: Cambridge University Press, 1996).

[16] See generally Orwell, "Such, Such Were the Joys . . ."

[17] George Orwell, *A Clergyman's Daughter* (New York: Harcourt Brace Jovanovich, 1960).

[18] George Orwell, "Why I Write," in *The Collected Essays, Journalism and Letters of George Orwell*, vol. 4, *In Front of Your Nose 1945–1950*, ed. Sonia Orwell and Ian Angus (London: Secker & Warburg, 1968), 313, 318.

his ability to construct a paragon of the old order that embodies the worst of all human traits, no matter what political system one endorses.[19]

The protagonist of the story is a twenty-something woman, Dorothy Hare, whose father is the Reverend Charles Hare, rector of St. Athelstan's, Knype Hill, Suffolk. The worthy Charles has, after a fashion, two claims to fame. The first is his masterful ability to avoid payment of his lawful debts. He is able with astonishing success to berate, bully, feint, insult, parry, postpone, and forestall his gullible creditors (of whom we think the less for their stupidity). His specialty is using his high religious position to insulate himself from his mundane business and moral obligations. His second sin is worse still: he browbeats his daughter Dorothy in a shameless fashion into becoming the unwilling agent of his own self-indulgences: consumption of life's pleasures—the finest cuts of beef, the best wines—off the back of the tradesmen of a lower social class. Religion and capitalism are indissoluble, although perhaps not in quite the way that R. H. Tawney thought.[20] Any social system, Orwell reminds us, that produces or tolerates such base types in high places creates a bastion of privilege that merits our scorn and disapproval.

But what does this denunciation of religion and capitalism tell us about religious parsons and ministers of limited means who are scrupulous in their payment of bills? We should surely not want to generalize that all parsons and ministers are paragons of virtue. Why then take the argument in the opposite direction? Again we see the literary creation of a sample of $n = 1$, without the slightest sense of when literary imagination leaves off and social reality begins.

Once Orwell has dispatched religion, he takes on capitalism. Once again he does not offer a formal demonstration of the inefficiencies of competition in supplying the ultimate level of public goods. Now his literary charge takes the form of a detailed description of the sweaty palms, reddish hue, oily complexion, and revolting secretions of the one businessman, Mr. Warburton, who actively seeks out the attentions and affections of a younger, thoroughly repulsed, Dorothy. And needless to say, Orwell

---

[19] The same is true with documentary re-creations. The Javert-like character of the police officer Vincent Della Pesca in the recent movie *Hurricane* gains its power by making it appear that vengeance is the motive of a single public official who stalks the boxer Ruben Carter from the time that he is a boy. Then we find out that it is all literary creation, to move the plot along, as it were. But this bit of license falsifies the social setting, even if it does not negate the tragedy of what (we still presume) was a false conviction for murders that Carter did not commit. See Amy Westfeldt, " 'The Hurricane' Movie Found to Be Offensive by Victims' Families," *Chicago Tribune*, February 9, 2000, C2.

[20] See generally R. H. Tawney, *Religion and the Rise of Capitalism: A Historical Study* (London: J. Murray, 1926). The central thesis of the book was that the Protestant ethic helped usher in the factory and market systems of modern capitalism.

takes his swipe at education when he plants a desperate Dorothy in the horrid school run by the cheap and loathsome Mrs. Creevy, whose disagreeable name reinforces her low character. Orwell is the master of literary character assassination for political ends. From his writings, it is all too easy to assume that only disfigured individuals engage in commercial transactions.[21]

## HAYEK AND ORWELL

Now this account differs rather dramatically from the way that people who work in commercial trades think about commercial morality. It is worth pausing to comment on the relationship between Hayek and Orwell.[22] The year 1999 was not only the fiftieth anniversary of the 1949 publication of *Nineteen Eighty-Four*, it was also the one hundredth anniversary of the birth of Friedrich Hayek. More to the point, Hayek and Orwell were contemporaries in England from the early 1930s to the late 1940s. Hayek published *The Road to Serfdom* in 1944,[23] to great critical acclaim and equally critical denunciation.[24] Orwell wrote a short, elegant, courteous, ironic, but none-too-perceptive book note about it. Its key passage reads as follows:

> Professor Hayek is also probably right in saying that in this country the intellectuals are more totalitarian-minded than the common people. But he does not see, or will not admit, that a return to "free" competition means for the great mass of people a tyranny probably worse, because more irresponsible, than that of the State. The trouble with competitions is that somebody wins them. Professor Hayek denies that free capitalism necessarily leads to monopoly, but in practice that is where it has led, and since the vast majority of people would far rather have State regimentation than slumps and unem-

---

[21] Nor is Orwell the only author who uses nasty physical descriptions to help in character assassination. Nietzsche, for example, uses the technique in *The Twilight of the Idols*, in which he begins his attack on Socrates by pointing to his ugly appearance, which he treats as "almost a refutation" of his ideas for the Greeks. Friedrich Nietzsche, *Twilight of the Idols*, in *The Portable Nietzsche*, ed. Walter Kaufman (New York: Viking, 1982), 474–75.

[22] For elaboration, see Richard A. Epstein, "Visionaries Revisited," *Chicago Sun-Times*, November 7, 1999, 30A.

[23] The publication history of the book is recounted in Milton Friedman, "Introduction to the Fiftieth Anniversary Edition," of Friedrich A. Hayek, *The Road to Serfdom* (Chicago: University of Chicago Press, 1994), xvii–xx. By 1994 the book had sold more than 250,000 copies in hardcover and paperback.

[24] For instance, see Herman Finer, *Road to Reaction* (Boston: Little, Brown, 1945), singled out by Hayek in his 1956 "Preface to the 1956 Paperback Edition of *The Road to Serfdom*," *The Road to Serfdom*, xxvii, xxx n. 4.

ployment, the drift towards collectivism is bound to continue if popular opinion has any say in the matter.[25]

It takes a fair bit of ingenuity to unpack the sense and nonsense that Orwell jammed into this short passage. On the positive side of the ledger, Orwell joins a long list of authors who have feared and condemned monopoly. But his insistence that competition leads to tyranny reminds me of the contemporary writings of law professors like Friedrich Kessler, who saw in standard form contracts the same dangers of fascism.[26] But of course that entire line of argument misses the point that Hayek stressed so emphatically in *The Road to Serfdom*—free entry into product and labor markets goes a long way to constrain the misbehavior of firms by opening up choices to both workers and consumers.[27] Rather than see this point, Orwell confuses competition in markets with races. Someone wins and loses races, and Orwell's clear import is that races are a zero-sum game. Even that point is wrong as a matter of practice, for participants enter races for the same reasons that they enter any other form of consensual arrangements—because they posit that their expected gain in material and social satisfaction will exceed their anticipated cost. By thinking

---

[25] George Orwell, "Review: *The Road to Serfdom* by F. A. Hayek, *The Mirror of the Past* by K. Zilliacus," in *The Collected Essays, Journalism and Letters of George Orwell*, vol. 3, *As I Please, 1943–1945*, ed. Sonia Orwell and Ian Angus (London: Secker & Warburg, 1968), 118 (a reprinting of Orwell's April 9, 1944, *Observer* book review). The following excerpt summarizes Orwell's argument:

> Taken together, these two books give grounds for dismay. The first of them is an eloquent defense of laissez-faire capitalism, the other is an even more vehement denunciation of it. They cover to some extent the same ground, they frequently quote the same authorities, and they even start out with the same premise, since each of them assumes that western civilisation depends on the sanctity of the individual. Yet each writer is convinced that the other's policy leads directly to slavery, and the alarming thing is that they may both be right. . . .
>
> Between them these two books sum up our present predicament. Capitalism leads to dole queues, the scramble for markets, and war. Collectivism leads to concentration camps, leader worship, and war. There is no way out of this unless a planned economy can be somehow combined with the freedom of the intellect, which can only happen if the concept of right and wrong is restored to politics.
>
> Both of these writers are aware of this, more or less; but since they can show no practicable way of bringing it about the combined effect of their books is a depressing one.
>
> Orwell, "Review," 117–18, 119.

[26] Friedrich Kessler, "Contracts of Adhesion—Some Thoughts about Freedom of Contract," *Columbia Law Review* 43 (1943): 629, 640–42.

[27] "And it is essential that the entry into the different trades should be open to all on equal terms and that the law should not tolerate any attempts by individuals or groups to restrict this entry by open or concealed force." Hayek, *Road to Serfdom*, 42.

of races in static form, Orwell overlooks the *systematic* social gains from competition. Orwell is of course correct to note the peril of monopoly, but wrong to assume that free capitalism "necessarily" leads to monopoly. That conclusion presupposes the absence of new entry and innovation, and, further, that the antitrust law (or competition policy, as it is called in Europe) is helpless to deal with the threats of price-fixing and horizontal mergers. Orwell's somber conclusion that popular opinion would prefer the yoke of government to the bumps and turns of a private economy assumes that separate decisions of firms, as opposed to policies of nations—tariffs, monetary, and fiscal policy—account for the ups and downs in the economy. So while his prediction of popular sentiment was validated in the short run, it did not anticipate either the conservative successes of Margaret Thatcher or, for that matter, the centrist policies of Labour's present prime minister, Tony Blair. It goes without saying that Orwell had no sense of the widely shared gains from innovation in communications, computers, and biotechnology.

Given his lack of sophistication, it is not surprising that Orwell was mistaken in describing Hayek as an eloquent defender of laissez-faire.[28] On this point, he could have usefully referred to the deep intellectual affinities between Hayek and Blair. Alas, Hayek was *not* the thoroughgoing libertarian or utilitarian, even in 1944, that Orwell makes him out to be. Rather, Hayek denied that anyone knows enough to construct any viable social order, so that spontaneous generation of coherent social practices was, for Hayek, the best path to what Hayek later termed (as did Lyndon Johnson, with different intentions) "the Great Society."[29] Recently, I wrote an essay titled "Hayekian Socialism" to comment on, or even lament, how much Hayek was prepared to tolerate government intervention into the market.[30] For starters, Hayek accepted a bloated role for government in the provision of medical services and unemployment benefits.[31] More generally, Hayek's own views reflected something of the social democratic philosophy that permeated his native Austria before he emigrated to England in the 1930s.

But in a sense all this is by the by, for Hayek had a far better sense of the systematic consequences of various economic arrangements; in addition, and perhaps because of this knowledge, he had a much firmer and more accurate read of commercial morality than Orwell ever possessed.

[28] Orwell, "Review," 117.

[29] Friedrich A. Hayek, *Law, Legislation and Liberty: Rules and Order* (Chicago: University of Chicago Press, 1973), 48 n. 11 ("The expression 'the Great Society', which we shall frequently use in the same sense in which we shall use Sir Karl Popper's term 'the Open Society', was, of course, already familiar in the eighteenth century").

[30] Richard A. Epstein, "Hayekian Socialism," *Maryland Law Review.* 58: (1999): 271.

[31] Hayek, *The Road to Serfdom*, 120–21.

Hayek thought that commerce functioned best with unreflective obedience to trade custom by members of any close-knit business group or
community. To Hayek, local knowledge of discrete circumstances cannot
be obtained by anyone who seeks to plan in a top-down way, but can
come only from those who are steeped in the mores and practices of their
own specialized institutions.[32]

That said, Hayek had to ask the question, what kinds of individuals,
with what sort of character traits, are likely to succeed in trade when
entry into and exit from the business are open and when legal enforcement
of the applicable business norms is both costly and spotty? More to the
point, Hayek had to ask not only how a single individual related to the
system, but also how that system continued to maintain some sustainable
equilibrium over time. This is not an easy task, because the theory must
take into account not only the few institutions that flourish over time,
but also those that collapse before starting, and those whose promising
beginnings peter out over time. Working through these calculations requires an appreciation of the many different types of personalities who
interact in the marketplace. The durability of social institutions, like the
durability of firms, cannot be explained through a preoccupation with the
extreme personality types who are least likely to gain the trust needed to
engage in repeat transactions.

Given these constraints, what type of individual is likely to succeed,
and what type is likely to fail? On this view, Hayek's basic position is that
folks who are oily, greasy, unkempt, and generally disreputable turn out,
as the word "disreputable" suggests, to lack the positive reputation that
eases commercial dealings.[33] In reaching that conclusion, I am not speaking of the ineffable even if I am speaking of the intangible. Reputation is
a valuable commercial asset because a good reputation reduces the cost
to others of doing business with you. A good reputation creates trust that
you will keep your word, which in turn confers upon you a real competitive advantage by reducing the costs that others must incur in monitoring
your behavior. In this environment, individuals who are not comfortable
with keeping promises will migrate to some other profession. The assort-
ment of individuals across trades is not random, even on issues of style,
character, and decorum. Certain people fit in better in an office, and others
do better in the field. People generally do better in selling and servicing
products that they like and use as consumers. Commerce thus tends to
self-select individuals who are suited to their particular trade. One cost

[32] For his most famous exposition, see Friedrich A. Hayek, "The Use of Knowledge in
Society," *American Economic Review* 35 (1943): 520.
[33] See Epstein, "Hayekian Socialism," 278–79 (describing Hayek's Darwinian approach
to economic theory).

of the planned economy is that the state tries to match persons with occupations, without having any accurate measure of these subjective predilections.

To be sure, this set of market incentives is not foolproof in the way it "assigns" people to occupations or "polices" their conduct once they get there. But that is something that can be said of any system of legal enforcement as well. In any isolated market transaction, it may pay for someone to breach a deal in order to pocket some large gains. But individuals who have invested heavily in their trade or profession do not have any easy exit options. The gains that they might obtain from breach will therefore be offset by the loss of future transactions that could be worth far more to them than the paltry profits they receive from the immediate transaction. Generally, long experience in the trade is a bonding device that makes it difficult for misfits to prosper in business. When merchants do get old, their horizons shorten—unless they hope to pass their business on to a junior partner, often their son or daughter. The needs of commerce therefore often work at powerful cross-purposes with literary descriptions of outliers, most of whom would wash out early on in their careers. On balance, then, Hayek's account of merchants is both more subtle and more accurate than its Orwellian alternative. Vivid accounts of self-destructive behavior at the brink of ruin—as befalls his protagonist, Gordon Comstock, in the 1936 novel *Keep the Aspidistra Flying*[34]—help "spice up" the plot. But on this point at least Orwell comes off second best to Hayek's more prosaic and workmanlike account of merchant behavior.

## WHEN N DOES EQUAL ONE

Orwell's effort to use literature to illuminate social situations is unpersuasive in seeking to explain patterns of routine behavior. It may well be that no two people have the same desires for milk or music, but none of these perturbations undermines the basic laws of supply and demand. The subjective grounds for valuation may well explain why, with price constant, one individual will purchase goods that another will not. Indeed, we must presuppose variation within human beings in order to explain why all individuals do not desire the same goods with the same intensity. That said, however, we can still infer that any increase in price will result in a reduction in demand, even if we cannot identify which individuals in a large population will stop or reduce their purchases. When we seek to understand this world, the individual variations drop out of the equation. It seems therefore that Orwell's views of market behavior are not insights

---

[34] George Orwell, *Keep the Aspidistra Flying* (London: Secker & Warburg, 1959).

but mistakes. They rely too much on personal introspection and distaste and not enough on empirical generalization. As Orwell said of himself, he was no theorist: "I became pro-Socialist more out of disgust with the way the poorer section of the industrial workers were oppressed and neglected than out of any theoretical admiration for a planned society."[35]

His technique is, however, far more valuable in dealing with the central theme of his great novel *Nineteen Eighty-Four*, that of totalitarian excess. Here the task is no longer to understand the market behavior of large disaggregated groups of consumers. In this context, we do not have a large number of repetitive events—sales, leases, mortgages—of the same type. So it is fair to ask, of what use is general economic theory when it turns out that $n = 1$? Stated otherwise, the key point about totalitarian regimes does not concern the slow movement and migration by the mass of merchants' consumers. Instead, the question before the house is how a single individual—whose actions could be either heroic or demented— shapes the behaviors of political institutions over which he has captured control. In large populations, this one person could be many standard deviations away from the norm. Any judgment as to how that person will respond to ordinary stimuli is likely to be wrong because it rests on the assumption that folks like that are not all that different from ourselves.

The point here does not apply only to these extreme cases, but also to others that are markedly less so. Thus one common feature of economic analysis is to apply the general theories of deterrence to criminals as though they were rational individuals, seeking to maximize their gains when subject to external constraints. Some criminals surely act in this fashion, but most criminals are not drawn from the fat part of the bell curve. The high number of suicides after murders should offer a strong clue that the usual assumptions of deterrence theory do not hold with distraught and distressed individuals, so that it becomes improbable in the extreme to think that changes in legal doctrine or severity of sanctions will have large impacts on the behavior of this subset of the population, even if these same changes will be closely monitored by other individuals for whom criminal behavior is nothing more or less than a way of earning a living.

The same concern applies to some political leaders with extreme personality traits. Now the behavior of individuals trapped in the center of the normal distribution does not offer much guidance as to how any misfit who has bullied his way to the top of the political order will behave. Nor in many cases will it help to think of how other political figures might have acted in particular circumstances. One reason why Hitler was able

---

[35] Orwell, "Author's Preface to the Ukrainian Edition of Animal Farm," in *Collected Essays*, 3:403.

to succeed is not that no one thought he could be quite evil enough to carry out the fiendish plans he outlined in 1925 in *Mein Kampf*.[36] Rather, Hitler's contemporaries compared him to other political leaders who always shrank from their own verbal excesses, and so they all missed the twisted attitudes that warped the man. Since Hitler was outside the domain of common experience, even for depraved politicians, everyone underestimated the extremity of his views because they refused, before it was too late, to treat him as an outlier among outliers. Clearly that mindset had a great deal to do with Neville Chamberlain's ill-fated policy of appeasement in Munich.[37] It is this tactical advantage that truly evil people have over ordinary individuals who from time to time fall from grace.

It is in trying to understand the behavior of extreme deviants that the literary imagination has a certain working advantage over a quantitative social science. The science types deal with the centralizing tendencies of large populations that can be arrayed in normal distributions. The literary author, armed with psychological insights, just might be able to get inside the head of the one isolated person who makes all the difference in the political arena. Indeed, one great weakness of political science generally is that it has no satisfactory theory of how a Hobbesian sovereign is able to aggregate so much personal political power in the first place. Men like Hitler or Stalin are not drawn from the middle of the human distribution, and part of their success lay in the fact that ordinary people were lulled into a false sense of security because they simply could not take these pathological types at their word. Yet the mystery remains, how could these tyrants speak in ways that elicited obedience from millions of independent minds? How is it that such machines of terror and power could sustain themselves for as long as they did?

One reason why Orwell was so effective in his denunciation of totalitarianism is that he was an outlier himself with some understanding of what fueled others who were more troubled, and far more troubled, than he was. I have done no systematic examination of Orwell's life, but from what fragmentary evidence I have been able to assemble, I am taken by what I perceive to be his self-destructive streak—he almost did not survive his self-imposed hand-to-mouth existence, as recorded in *Down and Out in Paris and London*, before he became an established writer in the mid-1930s. I must also confess that whenever I stare at pictures of Orwell, I see a face wracked with tension. The word that comes to mind to describe his appearance is "tortured." That impression is only reinforced by his own account of the arduous conditions to which he voluntarily exposed

---

[36] Adolf Hitler, *Mein Kampf*, trans. Ralph Manheim (New York: Houghton Mifflin, 1943).

[37] John Keegan, *The Second World War* (New York: Viking, 1989), 40.

himself throughout his life. Whether he was in Paris, London, Wigan Pier, or Spain, he always seems to have veered toward the precipice. It is no surprise that he died of tuberculosis and other assorted ailments in January 1950 when he was only forty-six years of age.[38]

All this of course says nothing about personality, but I have been impressed by the remarks of Margaret Drabble, who noted that Orwell had a somewhat unstable personality, with a touch of temper and perhaps even cruelty in his personal relations.[39] Then there is his writing itself. I have already referred to his masterful essay "Such, Such Were the Joys . . ." By his own account, Orwell was a troubled loner who was forced to bear all the indignities of being poor. But other scholarship boys doubtless got on far better than he, so it seems odd to attribute all his travail to the insensitivity of others. Orwell himself was no easy person, and one readily senses his pent-up rage at being close to, but never part of, some elite upper circle.

Orwell's totalitarian impulses are also brought out in passages from his essay "Politics and the English Language," which contains some real fighting words:

> I said earlier that the decadence of our language is probably curable. . . . Silly words and expressions have often disappeared, not through any evolutionary process but owing to the conscious action of a minority. . . . There is a long list of flyblown metaphors which could similarly be got rid of if enough people would interest themselves in the job . . . to reduce the amount of Latin and Greek in the average sentence, to drive out foreign phrases and strayed scientific words . . . with the scrapping of every word or idiom that has outworn its usefulness.[40]

I am not quite sure how to read this passage. As drafted, it does not necessarily require some degree of collective action to cure the English language of some of its internal deficiencies (assuming that one is willing to tar all words of Latin and Greek origins with that designation). It could well be that all Orwell means to suggest is that sound writers will become trendsetters by pruning away the excesses of their own prose. At this point, we could envision a benevolent process of linguistic competition where the better stylists drive out the inferior ones. But for all its imprecision, the passage suggests an intolerant view toward those whose view of language differs from Orwell's. Orwell likes punchy words: "to drive out foreign phrases and strayed scientific words," to "scrap[]. . . every word

---

[38] See Michael Shelden, *Orwell: The Authorized Biography* (New York: HarperCollins, 1991), 442.

[39] See Margaret Drabble's contribution to this volume.

[40] George Orwell, "Politics and the English Language," in *The Collected Essays*, 4:137–38.

or idiom that has outgrown its usefulness," and to "rid" the language of its various imperfections—here are words that invite the image of coercion, not competition, of domination and not exhortation.

Last, I think that we have to look at the situation in *Nineteen Eighty-Four* itself. In one sense the comfortable reading is to assume that Orwell identified himself with Winston Smith, the man who could not quite stand up to the titanic fury of O'Brien. But my reading of Orwell is somewhat different. I think that the author is both repelled by and attracted to O'Brien. It is a bit like the way in which some radical feminists are obsessed by the pornography whose baleful influence they denounce—too frequently. The long description of O'Brien's fiendish intensity; his devious intelligence in cross-examining Winston; and the lavish attention he pays to every detail of the scene—all these elements lead me to think that one reason why Orwell is so effective in his condemnation of totalitarian practices and institutions is that he fought to contain some of those impulses within himself. So he is able to explain some part of the fury associated with the behavior, although to my mind at least, his achievement never quite matches the portrait of totalitarian behavior that is found in Arthur Koestler's 1941 masterpiece, *Darkness at Noon*.[41]

In dealing with the totalitarian impulse, Orwell does a credible job in exposing the twisted personalities of the leaders. But he utterly fails to explain the durability or success of any totalitarian regime. On this point we have Orwell's implicit prophecy that the totalitarian nations will grow stronger over time so that their sheer mass will crush a prostrate world. His reasons for so thinking are outlined in that short review he wrote of *The Road to Serfdom*. He believed that the capitalist system required the prospect of war to keep itself whole. He thought the same thing about most forms of collectivism. So he wrote: to "sum up our present predicament. Capitalism leads to dole queues, the scramble for markets, and war. Collectivism leads to concentration camps, leader worship, and war."[42] There was not much difference between the two systems, at least for one who could not see the distinction between the scramble for markets and war.

Some of what Orwell says is doubtless true. The well-known difficulties in making collective political choices help explain why some nations will pad their defense expenditures for the benefit of the military-industrial complex. But that said, there is far more that Orwell does not understand because of his pervasive ignorance about the operation of both government and markets in a democratic state. In different ways, and for different reasons, both organizations respond to the demands of the median voter who

[41] Arthur Koestler, *Darkness at Noon*, trans. Daphne Hardy (New York: Random House, 1941).

[42] Orwell, "Review," 119.

does not have the same disposition as the outlier.[43] Median voters do not like war. American voters would rather tour Europe than die there. With the increase in wealth that market economies can supply, the military no longer offers *a*, let alone *the*, major path to social advancement. Service in the military no longer carries with it the same cachet that it did in former times. Democracies still fight wars, but the American response to the 1990 Iraqi invasion of Kuwait, to our relentless hunt for Osama bin Laden in Afghanistan, and to a troubled Iraqi occupation should remind us of the extent to which Western governments now go to avoid their own military casualties. The lesson of Vietnam was that when large numbers of soldiers come home in body bags, democratic institutions cannot today support military efforts that do not pertain to national survival. The levels of political protest spread to the middle classes. Lyndon Johnson could not survive politically in 1968 even after a landslide victory in 1964. Far more modest military interventions in Kosovo and Somalia may fail today as public tolerance continues to grow thinner. So what reason was there to think that Stalinism could survive the death of Stalin?

Orwell also misunderstood the direction in which technology would take political discourse. His view, heavily influenced by nineteenth-century developments, was that technological advances always worked in favor of the state. He took what might be termed a "brawny" account of technology. More and bigger tanks, planes, and rockets would carry the day. God would work in favor of the big battalions. The larger populations of the Soviet Union, and perhaps China, would prevail. But he was wrong. Massiveness turns out to be a liability, not an asset. On the economic front, minnows can swim where whales are beached. China and India struggle, while Hong Kong prospers on the strength of trade alone. The image of *Nineteen Eighty-Four* in which the world will devolve into three massive nations—Eurasia, Eastasia, and Oceania—was no more credible in 1949, in the final stages of the breakup of colonial empires, than it is today.

This point was brought home to me when I traveled through Europe in the summer of 1965. I can recall going to East Berlin that July. It did not take a social scientist to figure out that the standard of living was far higher in surrounded West Berlin than in the East German capital. The symbolism of forcing people to purchase East German coinage (which could not be converted back) did not escape us even then: East Germany was an empty amusement park to which you had to pay an admissions fee to tour, so long as you did not open your camera case. The East Ger-

---

[43] For an early discussion of public choice theory, see James M. Buchanan and Gordon Tullock, *The Calculus of Consent: Logical Foundations of Constitutional Democracy* (Ann Arbor: University of Michigan Press, 1962), 3–9.

man money was so light to the touch that it could fly away in a gentle breeze, and East German chocolate was so inedible that it was better to keep worthless East German coins as a souvenir. The local cynicism was often expressed in black humor. I can still recall the shopkeeper who sold me what passed for a chocolate bar—a hollow waferlike structure with a microscopic layer of nasty chocolate on top of it—for my converted East German Marks: "Kapitalismus ist gut wenn man gut unter Kapitalismus isst," which loses only a little of its punning punch in English: "Capitalism is good when one eats well under capitalism."

The measure of progress in the military domain reveals a parallel story. Brawn again takes second place to precision. What is needed is sophisticated weaponry and highly trained personnel. Those advances depend on the ability to develop miniaturized technologies. The chaotic start-up in the United States was more likely than the hierarchical state-run Soviet apparatus to leapfrog some technical obstacle. Monopoly in military organization has the same deadening influence that it has in economic areas. We saw the clear outcome of these divergent paths in the Falkland War in the early 1980s where the British technology swept aside the Argentine advantage in numbers, even in the face of Britain's evident locational and logistical disadvantages in fighting in Argentina's backyard thousands of miles from its home base.[44] The huge tank battles and artillery barrages of the Second World War counted as peak performance in one generation; they were not harbingers of our current tactics that rely heavily on precision electronics, sophisticated air power, and highly trained special forces. In 1950 Hayek believed that socialism would fall of its own weight after two generations, or so my late colleague Walter Blum assured me in conversation. The Berlin Wall came down in 1989 because East Germany's dilapidated economic system could no longer support a military or police state. Orwell had no sense that the monopoly of power at the top would erode because of the inability to feed, house, and clothe people at the bottom.

Orwell was wrong for yet another reason. He argued in *Nineteen Eighty-Four* that a determined state could retain sole control over information and technology. But the transistor radio is a lot smaller than the vacuum tube radio it displaced; the silicon computer chip is smaller still. Long before the rise of the Internet it became clear that improved communications from cheap and miniaturized technology would do more to undermine the power at the center than to prop it up. *Nineteen Eighty-Four* imagines a world of supersurveillance in which determined autocrats bombard a helpless population with constant propaganda. It envisions

---

[44] See generally Max Hastings and Simon Jenkins, *The Battle for the Falklands* (New York: Norton, 1983).

no countervailing forces such as Radio Free Europe, an underground press, or a single Web connection. *Nineteen Eighty-Four* reads as though imaginary wars are enough to keep docile populations in check. It assumes that no one can write letters home from the imaginary front. Now in some circumstances a combination of location, tradition, and language might keep one country isolated from outside influences. That explanation could easily account for the downward spiral in North Korea, from which there may be no easy escape. But the cosmopolitan and open traditions in Europe and the United States work heavily against the worldwide reemergence of any totalitarian regime, with the emphasis on "total." In a word, Orwell proved wrong historically because the last fifty years of the twentieth century in Europe and the United States proved a lot better than the first fifty years of the twentieth century. Yet Orwell could not understand the future path because he could never remove his socialist blinders or overcome his own literary skills.

## PARTING WORDS

Some object lessons should emerge from this analysis. I can think of two. The first is that we should beware of the use of literary imagination as a source of social understanding. The masters of plot and character are best at writing fiction, not at explaining complex social systems and making recommendations for their reform. The second is political, and in a sense more important. It is my prediction that *Nineteen Eighty-Four* will continue to be read but, over time, read more and more as a period piece. People from my own generation—those over fifty, say—will continue to relate to the Soviet threat because, having lived through the time, they understood the risks involved. Yet my children's generation, and—I hope—their children's generation, will not relate to *Nineteen Eighty-Four* as either warning or prophecy, for the best of all reasons. Its gloomy descriptions of life are, and will remain, too far off the mark to raise current fears even if they retain the power to move the abstract imagination. The loss of influence of one work of literature is a small price to pay if it is a reflection of our ability to keep our legal, economic, and political institutions together, and to anchor *Nineteen Eighty-Four* as a relic of Orwell's past, not a part of our future.

# Part II

TRUTH, OBJECTIVITY, AND PROPAGANDA

# Puritanism and Power Politics during the Cold War:
# George Orwell and Historical Objectivity

ABBOTT GLEASON

> In the morning when thou risest unwillingly, let this thought
> be present—I am rising to do the work of a human being
> . . . or have I been made for this, to lie in the bed clothes
> and keep myself warm? . . . Dost thou exist then to take
> thy pleasure and not at all for action or exertion? Dost thou
> not see the little plants, the little birds, the ants, the spiders,
> the bees working together to put in order their several parts
> of the universe? And art thou unwilling to do the work of
> a human being, and dost thou not make haste to do that
> which is according to thy nature?
> —*The Meditations of Marcus Aurelius*[1]

> Prepared ground for beetroot. Cut bean sticks. Some straw-
> berries setting fruits. A good many apple blossoms open.
> Corn in field in front of house well up. Large king-cups in
> marshy places. Primroses out everywhere.
> —George Orwell, *Domestic Diary*, 19/5/47[2]

IT IS ONE OF Peter Novick's significant points in *That Noble Dream* that
broadly speaking both the supporters of and believers in historical objectivity and their opponents invariably had other agendas, that the arguments between them never take place in a vacuum. They come, as he put
it, in "wrapped packages."[3] Orwell's era may be said to have begun with
the outbreak of World War I, took on more coherent shape with the
Russian Revolution and Mussolini's March on Rome, entered a new

---

[1] Quoted in "As I Please," *Tribune*, January 3, 1947, reprinted in *The Complete Works of George Orwell*, vol. 19, *It Is What I Think* (London: Secker & Warburg, 1998), 7–8.

[2] Ibid., 144.

[3] Peter Novick, *That Noble Dream: The "Objectivity Question" and the American Historical Profession* (Cambridge: Cambridge University Press, 1988), 250.

phase with the Spanish civil war, and culminated in the long years of the Cold War. It could be called the "era of totalitarianism," or as the historian Elie Halévy called it, the "era of tyrannies."[4] Underlying many of the political horrors of this period was a growing skepticism about the liberal individualism that had developed in the eighteenth and nineteenth centuries, and that could in important respects be traced back to the Renaissance and Reformation. Orwell's passionate defense of historical objectivity, which took the form of championing that individualism, took shape during his experience fighting in the Spanish civil war, a pivotal moment in this history of our era, and in his later reflections on that experience. Nevertheless, both his defense of certain kinds of objectivity and the bleakness and even defeatism that culminated in *Nineteen Eighty-Four* reflect his own loss of confidence in the values that he most highly prized and had made his signature. Paradoxically, however, the early Cold War years saw a reassertion of the Western belief in liberal individualism in heroic opposition to Communist "totalitarianism," a dynamic in which Orwell's *Nineteen Eighty-Four* played an extremely important role.[5]

"Early in my life," he wrote later of his Spanish experience, "I had noticed that no event is ever correctly reported in a newspaper, but in Spain, for the first time, I saw newspaper reports which did not bear any relation to the facts, not even the relationship which is implied in an ordinary lie. I saw great battles reported where there had been no fighting, and complete silence where hundreds of men had been killed. I saw troops who had fought bravely denounced as cowards and traitors, and others who had never seen a shot fired hailed as the heroes of imaginary victories; and I saw newspapers in London retailing these lies and eager intellectuals building emotional superstructures over events that had never happened."[6] Orwell was obsessed with truth telling and lying, but it was the rise of a new kind of ideologically inspired lying that provided him with the context for his crusade on behalf of objectivity. It was his sense of the power of propaganda to define, to formulate, to *create* reality that horri-

[4] For a general view, see Abbott Gleason, *Totalitarianism: The Inner History of the Cold War* (New York: Oxford University Press, 1995).

[5] See, for example, Anna Krylova, "The Tenacious Liberal Subject in Soviet Studies," *Kritika: Explorations in Russian and Eurasian History* 1, no. 1 (Winter 2000): 119–46, esp. 129–31. A recent student of the subject saw the postwar period as having witnessed a "defiant orientation toward individuation and transcendence, rather than one's embeddedness in a mass society . . . whoso would be a man (or, increasingly, a woman) must be a nonconformist." Wilfred M. McClay, *The Masterless: Self and Society in Modern America* (Chapel Hill: University of North Carolina Press, 1994), 225. McClay's analysis focuses on the United States, but I would hold that in this instance it applies to England as well.

[6] *The Complete Works of George Orwell*, vol. 13, *All Propaganda Is Lies, 1941–1942* (London: Secker & Warburg, 1998), 503.

Orwell's limited disclaimer about his frailty as an observer is far from the radical skepticism prevalent today about the possibility of most sorts of "objectivity."[22] In what might appear to us an excessively straightforward way, Orwell did believe that what a journalist loosely calls "the facts" were more or less discoverable. Indeed, most of his most successful work, fiction and nonfiction, had some quality of the documentary, of an ordinary observer looking for those facts and finding them.[23] But it was really the process of searching for what was going on and the ensuing moral confrontation that was so precious to Orwell. His commitment was to engage with the world, to put himself on the line, as he did in Spain. One can imagine what he would have thought about the way the United States waged war in Kosovo, a military action that truly violated Orwell's deepest convictions about how to engage with the world, as U.S. aircraft rained destruction from the skies, with scarcely a casualty sustained.

Orwell feared that the very biggest lies that we can imagine might seriously be taken for the truth, as did others among his contemporaries. In our age of radical skepticism, when the anxieties of the early Cold War have virtually disappeared, it is hard to recapture the fear that people like Orwell and Hannah Arendt had of what the loss of truth would mean for human life in the future. I think that it was Arendt who reported Clemenceau's remark that whatever the limits on our knowledge, we know for sure that Belgium did not invade Germany at the beginning of the Great War. She and Orwell feared precisely that this kind of certainty was in danger of being lost. Trying to discover the facts was for Orwell a moral obligation, of a very serious kind, and if you worked at it, you could discover quite a lot of them and make some sense out of them. "I believe," he wrote, "that it is possible to be more objective than most of us are, but that it involves a *moral* effort."[24] To make such an effort was important, partly because the people who run the world clearly do not want ordinary people finding out the facts, either under capitalism, or— even more—under the various "fuehrers" that he saw developing everywhere. This commitment to ferreting out what was really going on of

[22] Although we do find O'Brien telling Winston, in an interesting intimation of postmodernism near the end of *Nineteen Eighty-Four* (215), that "no book is produced individually, as you know."

[23] I have been much influenced in what follows by Alan Sandison's perspicacious study *The Last Man in Europe* (New York: Barnes and Noble, 1974). Here, 19.

[24] *Complete Works*, 16:415. Hannah Arendt again provides an interesting parallel. She called for "objectivity in the sense of honesty and impartiality, as 'when Homer decided to sing the deeds of the Trojans no less than those of the Achaeans.' " The ability to do so required " 'a purity of soul, an unmirrored, unreflected innocence of heart' that allows one to narrate a story as it happened." Hannah Arendt, *Eichmann in Jerusalem* (New York: Viking Press, 1964), 229, quoted in David Luban, "Explaining Dark Times," in *Hannah Arendt: Critical Essays*, ed. Lewis P. Hinchman and Sandra K. Hinchman (Albany: SUNY Press, 1994), 80.

fied him, and his understanding of this phenomenon took explicit form in Spain, as he realized the power of the Soviet propaganda apparatus to dominate left-wing opinion in Britain and elsewhere with its lies about what was going on within the Spanish Left. Orwell's preoccupation with ideologically inspired lying (and its political and human consequences, as he saw them) would ultimately result in the creation of "doublethink" in *Nineteen Eighty-Four* (175–77).

Orwell spent the first seven months of 1937 in Spain, returning to England in July. The following year he published *Homage to Catalonia*, in which much of his future focus on "totalitarianism" can be discerned in embryo. It is hard to exaggerate the importance of his Spanish experience for Orwell. After returning, according to Malcolm Muggeridge, Orwell "loved the past, hated the present and dreaded the future."[7] It was not until early in 1939, however, that Orwell began to express his reaction to the wholesale creation of reality directly in print, a time, he thought, of "universal panic and lying." In a review of a new book by Bertrand Russell, he wrote that "it is quite possible that we are descending into an age in which two and two will make five when the leader says so," and he found it "quite easy to imagine a state in which the ruling caste will deceive their followers without deceiving themselves. Dare anyone be sure that something of the kind is not coming into existence already?"[8]

More than a year later, Orwell developed his view into something even more cosmic. In a BBC broadcast on May 21, 1941, he observed that "we live in an age when the autonomous individual is ceasing to exist— or perhaps I ought to say, in which the individual is ceasing to have the illusion of being autonomous." I shall return to that important distinction. "The whole of modern European literature," he continued, "is built on the concept of intellectual honesty. . . ." "To thine own self be true" was an essential maxim for any writer. And again, "the first thing that we ask of a writer is that he shan't tell lies, that he shall say what he really thinks . . . what he really feels."[9] Modern literature, he summed up, "is either the truthful expression of what one man thinks and feels, or it is nothing."

When he wrote these words, Orwell feared that the age of totalitarianism meant that liberty would come to an end "world wide." Totalitarian-

[7] Quoted in Jeffrey Meyers, *Orwell: Wintry Conscience of a Generation* (New York and London: Norton, 2000), 168.

[8] Review of Bertrand Russell's *Power: A New Social Analysis*, in *Adelphi*, January 1939, reprinted in *The Complete Works of George Orwell*, vol. 11, *Facing Unpleasant Facts, 1937–1939* (London: Secker & Warburg, 1998), 312.

[9] "Literary Criticism IV: Literature and Totalitarianism," broadcast May, 21 1941, reprinted in *The Complete Works of George Orwell*, vol. 12, *A Patriot After All, 1940–1941* (London: Secker & Warburg, 1998), 503.

ism not only forbids you "to think certain thoughts," but it dictates what you have to think; it creates an ideology for you. Orwell freely conceded that there had been powerful and coercive orthodoxies in the past, and he cited the European Middle Ages.[10] But for him it was crucial that they did not continually change, as did totalitarian orthodoxies. The very concept of objective truth was now under attack. Literature, he thought, could not survive in such an atmosphere. When people were unable any longer even to perceive the changing orthodoxies, as would sooner or later happen, they would no longer be able to create.

In the spring of 1942, Orwell returned to this theme in his diary, but he now connected the loss of objectivity to a related loss of empathy with others, or ultimately the abandonment of any kind of civility. Even in England, at a time when—we must remember—Orwell was changing his view of England and the war, becoming "a patriot after all,"[11] he felt horror at the wartime atmosphere. "We are all drowning in filth," he wrote. "When I talk to anyone or read the writings of anyone who has an axe to grind, I feel that intellectual honesty and balanced judgement have simply disappeared from the face of the earth. . . . Everyone is dishonest, and everyone is utterly heartless toward people who are outside the immediate range of his own interests. What is most striking of all is the way sympathy can be turned on and off like a tap according to political expediency. . . . All power is in the hands of paranoiacs."[12]

Toward the end of 1942, Orwell wrote in his diary of the Czech town that had sheltered the assassins of Reinhard Heydrich. He began by citing the atrocities visited on the town as a whole by the German army, but his primary point was the way in which these atrocities (like most others) were "believed in or disbelieved in according to political predilection, with utter non-interest in the facts and with complete willingness to alter one's beliefs as soon as the political scene alters."[13]

An early climax of this line of thought came in his important essay "Looking Back on the Spanish War," in which he marveled at the extraordinary political changes of line that the left intelligentsia went through between 1935 and 1942—and in which he might have included something approaching a mea culpa but did not until long afterward.[14] Even with

[10] Ibid., 504. See also Orwell's talk "Culture and Democracy," November 22, 1941, in *Complete Works*, 13:77, where he says essentially the same thing.

[11] That is the subtitle of volume 12 of his recently published complete works.

[12] Ibid., 288–89.

[13] Ibid., 356.

[14] See his mea culpa for all his errors of judgment and prediction in the early days of the war, in *Complete Works*, vol. 16, *I Have Tried to Tell the Truth* (London: Secker & Warburg, 1998), 411–16. The confession was published in the "London Letter' to the *Partisan Review*, Winter 1944–45.

respect to the most dreadful atrocities, he observed, "the truth . . . becomes untruth when your enemy utters it."[15] To sum up, the history of the Spanish civil war was written "not in terms of what happened but of what ought to have happened in terms of various 'party lines.' "[16]

So what ought to be said about Orwell's apparently straightforward belief that a commitment to objectivity and the facts was essential in an age when totalitarian dictators were attempting a massive creation of their own reality? As Orwell remarked in a personal letter toward the end of the war, "If Hitler wins the war, the Jews will be the ones who started it."[17] One thing that seems significant is that Orwell does not seem ever to have said that political or historical reality is actually knowable by any individual, nor that reality can be grasped "wie es eigentlich gewesen ist," to use Ranke's famous phrase. At the end of *Homage to Catalonia* he remarked that he hoped his account of the Spanish war was not "too misleading. I believe," he continued "that on an issue such as this no one is or can be completely truthful. It is difficult to be certain about anything except what you have seen with your own eyes,[18] and consciously or unconsciously everyone writes as a partisan. In case I have not said this somewhere earlier in the book I will say it now: Beware of my partisanship, my mistakes and the distortion inevitably caused by my having seen only one corner of events. And beware of exactly the same things when you read any other book on this period of the Spanish war."[19] In looking back from near the war's end to his opinions of the early 1940s, he was even willing to call them "unconscious falsifications."[20] And indeed, Orwell was often the most passionate of partisans, whose notes reveal that he frequently took even conscious liberties in his finished work with what he had seen. In other words—and I think this is an important point—it was the *concept* or the ideal of objective truth that concerned him, not the possibility or even desirability of objectivity as a practical matter. As he put the matter in a notable essay, his starting point was "always a feeling of partisanship, a sense of injustice. . . . I write . . . because there is some lie that I want to expose, some fact to which I want to draw attention, and my initial concern is to get a hearing."[21]

[15] *Complete Works*, 13:500.

[16] Ibid.

[17] *Complete Works*, 16:191.

[18] An interesting exception to Orwell's broad view of the impossibility of complete objectivity, which presumably would not be allowed by most postmodernists today. But Orwell was committed to the general reliability of the senses.

[19] Orwell, *Homage to Catalonia* (Boston: Beacon Press, 1955), 230–31.

[20] *Complete Works*, 16:441.

[21] Orwell, "Why I Write," in *Complete Works*, vol. 18, *Smothered under Journalism* (London: Secker & Warburg, 1998), 319.

course antedates Orwell's commitment to fight against totalitarianism and goes back to his earliest discernible political attitudes. But the issue was also important because Orwell deeply (if episodically) sensed the limits to his own ability to achieve objectivity and believed that it was vital to undertake the struggle.

Orwell's ideas about "the facts" are obviously connected to that liberal (broadly speaking) individualism which he found so imperiled by totalitarianism. Actually, as we have seen, Orwell seems to recognize that the liberal individual is an "illusion," or, as one might say nowadays, a cultural construction. "The greatest mistake," he wrote in an "As I Please" column for *Tribune* in 1944, "is to believe that the human being is an autonomous individual."[25] And yet everything that Orwell values seems to be connected to that illusion, which, as he saw it, was being dispelled by the age of totalitarianism. The integrity that he valued so highly, then, seems to have had no more solid basis than an act of will, and this fragile, even illusory, quality of the commitment to personal integrity seems to grow throughout the 1940s and to culminate in *Nineteen Eighty-Four*, with Winston Smith's total defeat at the hands of O'Brien.

Alan Sandison pointed out Orwell's love of the earth and its surface, and pointed to the centrality for Orwell of what he called "the direct interplay between man's senses and the world of nature."[26] No one who looks at Orwell's "domestic diary" during his time on the island of Jura, in the final years of his life, can doubt this. Only, according to Sandison, "because nature exists objectively, can our senses affirm themselves as organs of a personal self, which possesses, in consequence, the capacity to reach and sustain individual judgement, and asserts the freedom of the individual conscience."[27] Orwell's view of the facts was connected with his faith in a kind of straightforward, perhaps simplified, version of science, which he often expressed as his belief that no matter what the dictators said, two plus two would go on being four.[28] Scientists would have to be allowed to be scientists, or the rockets wouldn't work. And as a practical matter, the totalitarian rockets did go on working, despite

---

[25] Ibid., 172.

[26] Sandison, *Last Man*, 11. See also Orwell, "Lear, Tolstoy and the Fool," in *The Collected Essays, Journalism and Letters of George Orwell: In Front of Your Nose 1945–1950* (New York: Harcourt, Brace and World, 1968), 300, where Orwell uses the phrase "he loved the surface of the earth" of Shakespeare. He used the same phrase of himself in "Why I Write," in *Collected Works*, 18:319–20.

[27] Sandison, *Last Man*, 23. See also Charles Taylor's words on the "affirmation of ordinary life," which developed at the beginning of the modern era. *Sources of the Self* (Cambridge: Harvard University Press, 1989), 13–14, 27.

[28] See the excellent discussion in William Steinhoff, *George Orwell and the Origins of 1984* (Ann Arbor: University of Michigan Press, 1976), 170–75.

O'Brien's claim that "we make the laws of nature. . . . Nothing exists except through human consciousness" (218).

Most critics who have tried to answer questions about Orwell's identity have seen him as very English, in his empiricism, his practicality, his earthiness (including his love of gardening, bird-watching, fishing), and his obsession with class with a pronounced tory (with a small *t*) streak. Orwell regarded historical memory as a bulwark against loss of contact with actuality, despite its notorious frailty. "Do you realize," he has Winston say to Julia in *Nineteen Eighty-Four*, "that the past, starting from yesterday, has been actually abolished? If it survives anywhere, it's in a few solid objects with no words attached to them. . . . Nothing exists except an endless present in which the Party is always right. I *know*, of course, that the past is falsified, but it would never be possible for me to prove it, even when I did the falsification myself" (128).

Lionel Trilling linked Orwell with the insular English radical William Cobbett (author of *The English Gardener*, with his "working man's countryside") and with the critic William Hazlitt.[29] One can imagine that Orwell would have delighted in Dr. Johnson's "refuting" solipsism by kicking the big stone: "I refute it *thus*, sir."[30] There is something truly Johnsonian about Orwell's fear and dislike of theory and extreme subjectivity.[31] Alan Sandison mentions R. H. Tawney, whose country socialism was very appealing to Orwell.[32] Less obviously, he connects Orwell with John Bunyan, and thus with the puritan and dissenting tradition that played such an important role in English socialism. Sandison's connection of Orwell with the puritan tradition is both accurate and useful in understanding Orwell's individualism. Surely Sandison's quotation from Tawney about the puritan's desire "to crystallize a moral ideal in the daily life of a visible society" illuminates something about Orwell.[33] And an apparent paradox: precisely that part of Orwell's work which most strongly emphasized the documentary at the same time reveals the deepest connection to the spiritual autobiography, the sense of life as a pilgrimage. I am speaking of course of *Down and Out in Paris and London*, *Homage*

[29] Lionel Trilling, introduction to *Homage to Catalonia*, xii–xiii.

[30] Tosco Fyvel likened Orwell's "inner voice" to that of a "latter day Dr. Johnson." T. R. Fyvel, *George Orwell: A Personal Memoir* (New York: Macmillan, 1982), 140–41.

[31] See Michael Zuckert, "Orwell's Hopes and Fears," in *The Orwellian Moment*, ed. Robert L. Savage, James Combs, and Dan Nimmo (Fayetteville: University of Arkansas Press, 1989), 57, and the evocation of Dr. Johnson's poverty and illness, in Meyers, *Orwell*, 325.

[32] R. H. Tawney came and visited Orwell in mid-January 1949 in the Cotswold Sanitorium, where he was being treated for pulmonary tuberculosis. They had apparently never met before. Orwell subsequently wrote that Tawney was "one of the few major figures in the Labour movement whom one can both respect and like personally." *Collected Works*, vol. 20, *Our Job Is to Make Life Worth Living 1949–1950* (London: Secker & Warburg, 1998), 28.

[33] Quoted in Sandison, *Last Man*, 115.

to *Catalonia*, and *The Road to Wigan Pier*. And I think something of Martin Luther can be clearly discerned in Orwell's sometimes despairing sense of the necessity of standing up to tyrants and to churches—especially the Roman and Muscovite ones. Intellectual integrity was certainly for him connected with the idea of rebellion, but his rebellion was a very Lutheran one, supported by the individual conscience. "Throughout the Protestant centuries," Orwell wrote in "The Prevention of Literature" (written in 1945, published early in 1946),

> the idea of rebellion and the idea of intellectual integrity were mixed up. A heretic—political, moral, religious, aesthetic—was one who refused to outrage his own conscience. His outlook was summed up in the words of the Protestant hymn:
>
> > Dare to be a Daniel,
> > Dare to stand alone;
> > Dare to have a purpose firm,
> > Dare to make it known.[34]

The hymn may suggest that there was something a little archaic, as well as embattled, about Orwell's individualism, perhaps with a suggestion of adolescent heroics, for all of Orwell's profound moral seriousness. "Orwell, lonely against the world," as Tosco Fyvel put it, not without affectionate irony.[35] It is significant, too, that most of these comparisons—made by friends and sympathetic students of Orwell—were with figures from the eighteenth or nineteenth century, or even earlier.[36]

Orwell's obsession with endangered objectivity was in abeyance somewhat during 1942 and 1943, when he worked for the BBC, but it returned in full force when he resumed his journalistic career with the socialist weekly *Tribune*. He now insisted on the connection between "the decay of the belief in personal immortality," a theme in which he had earlier been interested, and the increasing indifference to a belief in the importance of truth, thus linking his fears for individualism directly with secularism (which he largely accepted). He was also more and more pessimistic in his fears that ordinary men and women were now becoming infected with the intelligentsia's contempt for "right and wrong."[37] Although he was increas-

---

[34] *Collected Works*, vol. 17, *I Belong to the Left 1945* (London: Secker & Warburg, 1998), 371.

[35] Fyvel, *Orwell*, 184.

[36] George Woodcock, the anarchist, was one of the first writers to attempt a literary portrait of Orwell. He compared him to the final sentences of Orwell's own famous portrait of Dickens, a man "generously angry" and unwilling to endorse any of "the smelly little orthodoxies which are now contending for our souls." Quoted in *Collected Works*, 19:30.

[37] See Orwell's review of Alfred Noyes's *The Edge of the Abyss*, and his "As I Please" essay for *Tribune* (March 3, 1944) in *Collected Works*, 16:103–5, 112, 113, and 150.

ingly ready to say by 1944 and 1945 that the threat of totalitarianism in England in the near future had lessened, he was angered and disheartened by the difficulties he encountered with publishers unwilling to challenge the Russophile sentiments of the English public (and to a degree, government) by publishing *Animal Farm*. In the middle of 1944 he wrote gloomily of how leader worship was on the rise worldwide, and with it "a tendency to disbelieve in the existence of objective truth because all the facts have to fit with the words and prophecies of some invincible fuhrer. Already history has in a sense ceased to exist . . . and the exact sciences are endangered as soon as military necessity ceases to keep people up to the mark."[38]

Orwell seems to have begun what became *Nineteen Eighty-Four* in August 1946, when he was living on the island of Jura in the Hebrides. By the time he was seriously embarked on the project, his mood had been steadily darkening for several years, and it continued to do so. Partly, no doubt, this was due to his long struggle with illness. The awful winter of 1946–47 contributed to his contraction (or recontraction) of tuberculosis, and during the summer and fall of 1947 his health deteriorated drastically. But it was above all the unexpected death of his wife, Eileen, on the operating table at the end of March 1945, a blow from which he never fully recovered, that dramatically increased his loneliness and isolation. And it made matters worse that during his seven-month bout with TB in 1947 and 1948 he was physically separated from his adopted son, Richard, for fear that the boy might contract the disease, and then again after his condition worsened at the end of his life.[39]

During this miserable period, Orwell was much preoccupied with how the war had caused English men and women to deteriorate, to enter, as he saw it, a stage of pretotalitarianism. The refusal of a fair hearing to opponents, the falsification of history, libelous attacks on enemies, the willingness of people to yield to propaganda without checking the evidence, and Orwell's long-distance repulsion at the violence done to Nazi collaborators in France—these were predominant themes of his journalism throughout 1945 and 1946.[40] He may well have had an exaggerated view of this alleged deterioration—and it seems not to have been a view that he consistently held—but that was how he was often prepared to see the matter.[41]

The development of the Cold War exacerbated his sensibility in two ways. He became, if possible, more anti-Soviet, and in reaction to atti-

[38] Ibid., 191.

[39] "I am afraid of his [Richard's] growing away from me, or getting to think of me as just a person who is always lying down and can't play," Orwell wrote sadly to Richard Rees on March 3, 1949. *Collected Works*, 20:53.

[40] See *Collected Works*, vol. 17, passim.

[41] For indications of Orwell's mood, see "Towards European Unity," *Partisan Review*, July–August 1947, reprinted in *Collected Works*, 19:163–67; and in particular "Writers and Leviathan," *Politics and Letters*, Summer 1948, in ibid., 288–94.

tudes he detected among British left intellectuals, he became rather pro-American. "I particularly hate," he wrote, "that trick of sucking up to left cliques while relying on America to feed & protect us."[42] He became eager to choose the United States over the Soviet Union publicly, in the teeth of British anti-Americanism. He and Richard Rees often played an unpleasant little game together, trying to decide which of the "cryptos" and fellow travelers they knew would become quislings in the event of a Soviet takeover of Britain. Orwell also left a lengthy list of such people, with brief descriptions appended, in his papers.[43]

The writing and typing of *Nineteen Eighty-Four* in the ultimately inhospitable Scottish Hebrides virtually guaranteed that Orwell would not survive, and indeed it is hard not to see in the undertaking some kind of death wish. By the summer of 1946, he had become a semi-invalid and was about to be separated from Richard for some seven months and confined to a sanatorium. He was also inclined to believe in the inevitability of nuclear war, even before the Russians detonated an atomic weapon.[44] The book represented, among other things, a kind of integrated anthology of his fears of the Party elite's ability to shape reality.[45]

In the course of writing the novel, which was finished in December of 1948, he had concluded that the Party elite rejected not only "the validity of experience, but the very existence of external reality. . . . The heresy of heresies was common sense. . . . The Party told you to reject the evidence of your eyes and ears. It was their final, most essential command" (69). And increasingly, Orwell had come to believe that they who "control all records, and . . . control all memories" might be able to pull off their seemingly fantastic enterprise of creating a self-generated, impenetrable social reality over large portions of the world (205). Orwell's deepening despair, however, seems also to have had to do with something more personal: not only with gloom about the potential totalitarianization of the world, but also with an increasingly vivid realization that the autonomous individual with a morally based personal agency was an unsustainable fiction. This conclusion, emphasized by Alan Sandison, seems evident in Winston's total submission to O'Brien at the end of *Nineteen Eighty-Four*. And no doubt Orwell's own wretched physical condition played a role in his vivid description of both the poor health and the physical deterioration of Winston Smith over the course of the novel—his varicose ulcer,

---

[42] Letter to Julian Symons, January 2, 1948, in ibid., 250.

[43] *Collected Works*, 20:87–90, 104–6, 247–59.

[44] See his letter to Julian Symons of October 29, 1948, in *Collected Works*, 19:462.

[45] The fact that the Spanish Communists had come after him in Barcelona, presumably to shoot him, increased his fear and hatred in a personal way. They considered him "a rabid Trotskyite." See Meyers, *Orwell*, 164–67, 233–34.

his coughing fits, his bad teeth—and of course his virtual annihilation at the hands of O'Brien at the end of the book.[46]

It seems very likely that Orwell's constant and occasionally extravagant anger and scorn at power-worshiping intellectuals was connected to some kind of fear—perhaps partly conscious—that he could under certain circumstances be capable of succumbing to hero worship, or some mixture of persuasion and coercion, or of subsuming his puritan individual identity in some kind of larger entity. In other words, Orwell's detestation of power-worshiping Stalinists was probably not posited on a secure sense of his difference from them but connected to a secret fear that he might ultimately turn out to be like them. One may clearly presume some considerable identification between Orwell and Winston Smith, an identification that would extend to Winston's vulnerability and failure at the end of *Nineteen Eighty-Four*. The refrain "Under the spreading chestnut tree / I sold you and you sold me" then becomes not merely a totalitarian rewriting of a (not very inspired) piece of verse but, it may be, a form of confession, or an exercise containing elements of fear and self-contempt (241). One may even guess that Orwell's self-contempt might have had some relationship to his willingness, over the course of several years, to be unfaithful to Eileen.

The conflict in Orwell between the solitary outsider that he essentially was and the person who longed to be part of the group was lifelong, and it was one reason why he was sometimes able to write about childhood and adolescence with such extraordinary power and sympathy. Even a cursory look at Orwell's earlier work suggests the degree to which—despite his social reticence, his occasional cynicism, his upper-class presence, his determined liberal individualism, and his self-conscious integrity—he longed to be swallowed up in collectivities and experiences that transcended his workaday, puritan self. His whole commitment to socialism at least suggested this, but it may be most evident in the description of liberated Barcelona at the beginning of *Homage to Catalonia*. It is also evident, I would argue, in the past-tense meditations on nature: the reveries about the "Golden Country" in *Nineteen Eighty-Four* and George Bowling's memories of Lower Binfield in *Coming Up for Air*. But the nature reveries all contain a strong sense of a world that is past recovering and indeed may never have truly existed outside the observer's head. And Orwell's early hopes for a real revolution, kindled again in his Barcelona experiences, were mutilated by his understanding of Stalinist betrayal. Big

---

[46] Orwell told Tosco Fyvel in the spring of 1949 that because of his illness, *Nineteen Eighty-Four* "might have turned out duller and more pessimistic than intended." *Collected Works*, 20:21.

Brother was a very powerful enemy, against whom, he came gradually to conclude in his weakened state, it might be impossible to stand.

Thus I would argue that the end of *Nineteen Eighty-Four* has a deeper autobiographical dimension than is often realized, that the atmosphere of defeat and despair was quite personal, that it reflects Orwell's belief that the chosen underpinnings of his worldview would be unable to sustain the proactive individual self in the new era into which the world was moving. Orwell, despite his apparently secular self, had a strong sense of guilt (which Sandison identifies with the puritan's "negative conscience") and seems to have felt, at some level, a good deal of the painful futility he ascribed to Winston Smith.[47] Not only is freedom slavery, as O'Brien tells Winston, but the reverse is also true. "Alone—free—the human being is always defeated. It must be so, because every human being is doomed to die, which is the greatest of all failures. But if he can make complete, utter submission, if he can escape from his identity, if he can merge himself in the Party, so that he *is* the Party, then he is all-powerful and immortal" (218).

In sum, Orwell's commitment to the principle of "objectivity" was not really an epistemological position at all. It was a commitment to the reality of ordinary things, to the surface of the earth, to the observable regularity of nature, to the pleasure of tools. It was a political commitment to the ordinary people with whom Orwell longed to be at one. It was the belief in a way of life involving the necessity of discovering how things really were, and in making an effort to put wrong things right.

The half-century of the Cold War did a great deal to undermine belief in the importance of peer acceptability and conformity with unanalyzed community values, and to inspire fears of the mass society—in David Riesman's terms, to make inner-directedness attractive again, and the prevailing other-directedness seem repugnant.[48] No individual life could have more graphically suggested inner-directedness than that of George Orwell; no biography could have seemed more inspiring to the liberals of the Cold War period; no one contended more valiantly with those "smelly little orthodoxies."[49] Even though Orwell's own struggle ended in something close to despair, his posthumous legacy to the generations that followed was very different.

[47] Sandison, *Last Man*, 55.

[48] My thinking was much stimulated by James Conant's "Freedom, Cruelty and Truth: Rorty versus Orwell," in *Rorty and His Critics*, ed. Robert B. Brandom (Malden, Mass.: Blackwell Publishers, 2000).

[49] "Charles Dickens," in George Orwell, *A Collection of Essays* (New York: Harcourt, Brace, Jovanovich, 1953), 104.

# Rorty and Orwell on Truth

## JAMES CONANT

I AM GOING TO discuss the political upshot of Richard Rorty's epistemological doctrines. I shall do this by comparing Rorty's and George Orwell's respective conceptions of what it means to be a liberal—that is, their respective conceptions of the relation among preservation of freedom, prevention of cruelty, and regard for truth. In a chapter of his book *Contingency, Irony and Solidarity*, Rorty reads Orwell as espousing the variety of liberalism that Rorty himself seeks to champion.[1] The aim of this paper is to suggest, not only that what is offered in that chapter is a misreading of Orwell, but that it is an instructive misreading—one that illuminates the shortcomings of some of Rorty's central doctrines.

If you look at Rorty's replies to his critics, you'll notice that they tend to be quite similar in content. What they end up saying could often be most economically expressed simply through a shrug of the shoulders. The common subtext of these extended verbal shrugs of the shoulders might be put as follows: "Yeah, yeah, you want to accuse me of having made a *philosophical* mistake, or of slighting the importance of a *metaphysical* insight, or of violating *common sense*, or of being out of touch with *reality*; but don't you see that that sort of criticism is effective only against someone who *cares* about philosophical correctness, metaphysical insight, common sense, being in touch with reality, and so on; and don't you see that my whole goal is to try to get you to stop caring about the problems to which these ways of talking give rise and to start caring about problems that are worth caring about. My whole point is that we don't *need* to care about the sorts of problems that philosophers say we have to care about— we only think we have to; and my aim is to demonstrate the utter dispensability of caring about such problems by offering a practical demonstration of just how well one can get on without caring about them."

This paper is a slightly revised excerpt from a much longer paper titled "Freedom, Cruelty and Truth: Rorty versus Orwell" [henceforth FCT], in *Richard Rorty and His Critics*, ed. Robert Brandom (Oxford: Blackwell, 2000). For Rorty's reply to the criticisms advanced in this paper, see his "Response to Conant" in the same volume.

[1] *Contingency, Irony and Solidarity* (Cambridge: Cambridge University Press, 1989) [henceforth CIS], chap. 8, passim.

Thus Rorty and those who sympathize with his doctrines tend to experience criticisms to the effect that their views are philosophically unsound as point-missing. So what sort of criticism might strike home? What sort of criticism has a hope of eliciting something other than the verbal equivalent of a shrug of the shoulders? Rorty himself likes to recommend his epistemological doctrines on *political* grounds—that is, on the ground that his doctrines cohere more comfortably with the sort of politics that we (i.e., citizens of our sort of liberal democracy) cannot help wanting. One sort of criticism therefore which has a hope of striking home is one that could demonstrate that the political upshot of Rortian doctrines is not only not what those who enthusiastically embrace such doctrines presume it to be, but roughly the opposite of what they presume it to be. So what I shall try to show is that Rorty's epistemological doctrines not only fail to cohere comfortably with his liberal politics, but that they cohere far more comfortably with a radically illiberal politics.

I am concerned here, above all, with two Rortian doctrines:

**1.** *The doctrine that solidarity should replace objectivity*—which I will summarize as the doctrine that justification is a purely sociological matter, a matter of seeing whether something is acceptable to my peers.[2]

**2.** *The doctrine of Rortian liberalism*—which I will summarize as the doctrine that *cruelty is the worst thing we can do* and that "morality" should not be taken to denote anything other than our abilities to notice, identify with, and alleviate pain and humiliation.[3]

Rorty takes Orwell's novel *Nineteen Eighty-Four* to be concerned, above all, with championing these two doctrines. Rorty is aware that certain admirers of Orwell's novel have advanced what he calls a "Realist reading" of the novel—one that attributes to Orwell an attachment to the very conception of objectivity that Rorty wishes to credit Orwell with having put behind him. Rorty concedes that there are passages which, when taken out of context, appear to support this reading—especially, he thinks, the following passage:

The Party told you to reject the evidence of your eyes and ears. It was their final, most essential, command. [Winston's] heart sank as he thought of the enormous power arrayed against him, the ease with which any Party intellectual would overthrow him in debate. . . . And yet he [Winston] was in the right! . . . The obvious, the silly, and the true had got to be defended. Truisms are true, hold on to that! The solid world exists, its laws do not change. Stones are hard, water is wet, objects unsupported fall toward the earth's

---

[2] For a more detailed statement of the Rortian thesis in question here, see FCT.
[3] For a more detailed statement of the Rortian thesis in question here, see FCT.

center. With the feeling that he was . . . setting forth an important axiom, [Winston] wrote:

> Freedom is the freedom to say that two plus two make four. If that is granted, all else follows. (69)[4]

Rorty takes this passage to be the main support of the Realist reading of *Nineteen Eighty-Four*. Since this passage occupies a central place in the quarrel Rorty takes himself to have with other readers of Orwell, and since we will have occasion to recur to it, I refer to it as "the focal passage."

Rorty offers the following gloss on where Orwell's concerns as an author lie: Orwell's main concern is to "sensitize an audience to cases of cruelty and humiliation which they had not noticed." According to Rorty, Orwell is to be read, above all, as a good "liberal ironist": someone whose aim is to "to give us an alternative perspective, from which we liberals . . . could describe the political history of our century."[5] Rorty explains:

> [T]he kind of thing Orwell . . . did—sensitizing an audience to cases of cruelty and humiliation which they had not noticed—is not usefully thought of as a matter of stripping away appearance and revealing reality. It is better thought of as a redescription of what may happen or has been happening—to be compared, not with reality, but with alternative descriptions. . . .[6]
>
> In his better moments, Orwell himself . . . recognized that he was doing the same *kind* of thing as his opponents, the apologists for Stalin, were doing.[7]

Orwell, according to Rorty, has no use for the idea of truth—for the idea that some descriptions are superior to others in virtue of the relation in which they stand to the subject matter that they describe. According to Rorty's Orwell, some descriptions just happen to be more *useful* than others.

Rorty insists that what is supposed to be really *scary* about the prospect with which the novel presents us is that it forces on us the thought that "as a matter of sheer contingent fact" the future could, at least in principle, resemble the future depicted in the novel.[8] That thought is, no doubt, scary. But, in insisting upon this, what Rorty is most concerned to deny is an alternative view of what might be scary about the possible future that the novel depicts. Rorty knows that some of Orwell's other admirers manage to be frightened by the idea of living in a society in which our leaders have the power to deprive us of (something they call) "our hold on the concept of objective truth." But only a raving metaphysical Realist,

[4] Quoted in CIS, 172.
[5] CIS, 173.
[6] CIS, 173.
[7] CIS, 173–74.
[8] See CIS, 183.

Rorty thinks, could find *that* prospect frightening. What such readers of Orwell fear losing, Rorty regards as well lost. According to Rorty, loss of contact with truth or the world or reality can be frightening only to someone who has failed to realize that the idea of answerability to the world is a secular surrogate for the idea of answerability to an infallible Deity. The only way Rorty can see of giving content to talk of "answerability to something non-human" is through an appeal to dubious metaphysical theses (such as the thesis that the world has a preferred description of itself). Hence he concludes: once we abandon such theses, there is no longer any reason to think it would be hubris on our part to abandon the traditional language of "respect for fact" and "objectivity."[9] He identifies a continued attachment to such ways of speaking as a sure sign that the speaker has failed to take the final and crucial step in the post-Enlightenment project of attaining to full intellectual maturity. The speaker still longs for something outside our contingent historically situated practices. He longs for something transhuman that would underwrite practices of which he approves and condemn practices of which he disapproves. Rorty cannot see how such a person could, in speaking in these sorts of ways, possibly be speaking for Orwell.

Rorty takes Orwell to be sympathetic to his own preferred strategy for bringing fruitless forms of philosophical controversy to an end. The strategy is to adopt a mode of discourse from within which one no longer has any occasion to call upon the vocabulary requisite for the formulation of metaphysical theses about "matters of fact," "truth," or "objective reality."[10] The underlying injunction concerning how to dissolve philosophical problems might be summed up as follows: "Free yourself from the problems by *jettisoning the vocabulary* in which the problems are couched!" But this strategy for dissolving philosophical problems is a wise one only if the sole function within our linguistic community of the vocabulary in question is to enable dubious theses to be formulated. If there are other discursive possibilities—apart from the formulation of such theses—whose availability depends upon the availability of that vocabulary,[11] then a pragmatist (of all people) has no business enjoining us to jettison that vocabulary unless he can first demonstrate that the loss of

---

[9] The last six sentences are largely a paraphrase of CIS, 21.

[10] Though he no longer *requires* such vocabulary, a Rortian may continue to employ it in either of two ways: (a) he may continue to employ it as a means of warding off the enemy (e.g., by saying things like "We should replace objectivity with solidarity"); (b) he may interpolate a revisionist account of its meaning that enables him to continue to speak with the vulgar (by declaring things like "For the pragmatist, 'knowledge' and 'truth' are simply compliments paid to beliefs we think well justified").

[11] Or more precisely: whose availability depends upon the availability of concepts traditionally expressed by means of that vocabulary.

those other discursive possibilities is vastly outweighed by the gain of rendering ourselves immune to the temptations of (putatively) bad philosophy.[12] The ultimate aim of this paper is to suggest that one effect of the adoption of Rorty's favorite method of dissolving philosophical problems—namely, the elimination of vocabulary such as "objective reality" and so on—would be to render Orwell's *Nineteen Eighty-Four* as unreadable to us as, I believe, it presently is to Rorty.

The real point of the novel, according to Rorty, lies in its defense of the idea that cruelty is the worst thing we do. Now Rorty is certainly right that cruelty figures prominently in one of the climactic scenes of *Nineteen Eighty-Four*. Through the infliction of much pain and humiliation, O'Brien eventually succeeds in getting Winston Smith to believe that he is speaking the truth when he says, "2 + 2 = 5" (206–15, 228). Rorty insists that on a proper understanding of this scene, it does not matter that "two plus two is four" happens to be true or that the answer "O'Brien is holding up four fingers" happens at the time to be true. All that matters for the scene, according to Rorty, is that Winston believes what he says (when, e.g., he says "two plus two is four"). The horror of the scene lies entirely in the fact that he is not permitted to say what he believes without getting hurt. What Orwell cares about, according to Rorty, is your ability to talk to other people about what seems to you to be true; it doesn't matter in the least for Orwell's purposes whether what is believed is in fact true.

Rorty offers two options for how to think about what matters in this scene: either (a) what matters is *truth* (i.e., that what you say is answerable to something beyond what your community holds to be true), or (b) what matters is *freedom* (i.e., the freedom to say 2 + 2 = 4 if, that is what you believe, or to say 2 + 2 = 5, if that is what you believe). Rorty represents the alternatives for reading Orwell as requiring a forced choice here between these options and concludes that Orwell's view is that what matters is freedom and not the answerability of what we say to something outside of what we say. What, Rorty in effect asks, do we lose if we conclude that what destroys Winston is not the loss of the concept of objective truth but rather the loss of his freedom? We lose nothing, Rorty suggests, and we save Orwell from the charge of being needlessly preoccupied with fruitless metaphysical issues. Winston's real loss in the novel is his loss of freedom. I lose my freedom to say and think what I believe, according to Rorty's Orwell, not when I fail to be answerable to something outside of a human community, but when the failure of my beliefs to cohere with each other results in the loss of my ability to justify myself to myself:

---

[12] Of course, if there are less drastic and yet equally effective ways of disarming Realism, then there are *no* good reasons to jettison the vocabulary. This is in fact my view. But since my aim in this paper is not to disarm Realism, I shall not argue the point here.

The *only* point in making Winston believe that two and two equals five is to break him. Getting somebody to deny a belief for no reason is a first step toward making her incapable of having a self because she becomes incapable of weaving a coherent web of belief and desire. It makes her irrational, in a quite precise sense: She is unable to give a reason for her belief that fits together with her other beliefs. She becomes irrational not in the sense that she has lost contact with reality but in the sense that she can no longer rationalize—no longer justify herself to herself.[13]

According to Rorty, at the beginning of their conversation, O'Brien and Winston have equally coherent but distinct sets of beliefs; and, by the end of their conversation, only one of them—namely, O'Brien—continues to have a coherent set of beliefs. Now Rorty is certainly right that O'Brien does not *experience* any lack of coherence in his web of beliefs. He is in this sense able to justify himself to himself. Does that mean his beliefs are justified? Since Rorty assumes that only someone mired in an unprofitable metaphysics could be of the view that O'Brien's beliefs remain open to some further criticism (e.g., that his beliefs are out of touch with reality), he concludes that Orwell neither wants nor should want to be able to rebut O'Brien's claim to be able to justify himself to himself.

So much by way of a brief summary of Rorty's reading of *Nineteen Eighty-Four*. Now I am going to say a few things about Orwell's own understanding of what he was trying to do in the novel.

In an essay about the novel, Orwell sums up what he "really meant to do" in *Nineteen Eighty-Four* by saying that his aim was to display "the *intellectual* implications of *totalitarianism*."[14] As Orwell defines the term, "totalitarianism" refers to the abolition of the freedom of thought in a positive as well as a negative respect. Orwell writes:

> [Totalitarianism's] control of thought is not only negative, but positive. It not only forbids you to express—even to think—certain thoughts, but it dictates what you *shall* think. . . . And as far as possible it isolates you from the outside world, it shuts you up in an artificial universe in which you have no standards of comparison.[15]

Totalitarianism seeks to isolate you from the outside world. The aim of totalitarian tactics, according to Orwell, is to bring it about that the sole standards of comparison available to you are precisely those which Rorty urges are the only ones you should ever want: the standards supplied by

[13] CIS, 178.

[14] *The Collected Essays, Journalism and Letters of George Orwell*, ed. Sonia Orwell and Ian Angus (New York: Harcourt Brace Jovanovich, 1968) [henceforth CEJL], 4:460. My emphases.

[15] CEJL, 3:88.

the aspiration to remain in agreement with a community of "comrades" with whom you presently express your solidarity. Concentration camps and secret police forces are peripheral to the set of cultural, social, and political phenomena that Orwell wants to identify as totalitarian. What is integral is a kind of "organized lying" that, if the logical consequences of its inherent tendencies were fully drawn out, could be seen (as Orwell puts it) "to demand a disbelief in the very existence of objective truth."[16]

Orwell thinks that one of the consequences of totalitarianism is that it undermines the possibility of your leading a life in which you are free to think your own thoughts. Another of its consequences, he thinks, is that it leads to the proliferation of great cruelty. But neither of these is what he calls "the really frightening thing about totalitarianism"—they are rather, in his view, merely consequences of it. "The really frightening thing about totalitarianism," Orwell says, "is not that it commits 'atrocities' but that it attacks the concept of objective truth."[17]

In order to see what Orwell takes "the really frightening thing about totalitarianism" to be, it helps to notice how the central themes of his novel emerge directly out of his writings about his experiences as a soldier in the Spanish civil war:

> Early in life I had noticed that no event is ever correctly reported in a newspaper, but in Spain, for the first time, I saw newspaper reports which did not bear any relation to the facts, not even the relationship which is implied in an ordinary lie.[18] I saw great battles reported where there had been no fighting, and complete silence where hundreds of men had been killed. I saw troops who had fought bravely denounced as cowards and traitors, and others who had never seen a shot fired hailed as the heroes of imaginary victories; and I saw newspapers in London retailing these lies and eager intellectuals building emotional superstructures over events that had never happened. . . . This kind of thing is frightening to me, because it gives me the feeling that the very concept of objective truth is fading out of the world.[19]

The really frightening case, for Orwell, is one in which you continue to form perfectly determinate beliefs about happenings in the world, yet the

---

[16] See CEJL, 4:64, see also CEJL, 3:149.

[17] CEJL, 3:88.

[18] Compare: "[A]ctually, [Winston] thought as he readjusted the Ministry of Plenty's figures, it was not even forgery. . . . Most of the material that you were dealing with had no connection with anything in the real world, not even the kind of connection that is contained in a direct lie" (37).

[19] CEJL, 2:256–58. Caleb Thompson, in his article "Philosophy and Corruption of Language" (*Philosophy*, January 1992), adduces this passage in the context of an illuminating discussion of the importance to Orwell of the contrast between telling lies and those uses of language which impede or erode our attaining the sort of relation to truth implicit even in a direct lie.

mechanisms by means of which those beliefs are formed are no longer guided by the happenings that form the subjects of those beliefs. During the Spanish civil war, intellectuals in Britain held certain beliefs about what was happening in Spain and attached great importance to the happenings that formed the subjects of those beliefs. Many acted on those beliefs; some died acting on them. The totalitarian dimension of the situation, according to Orwell, was a function, on the one hand, of the loyal determination of these intellectuals to believe only accounts accredited by their respective political parties and, on the other hand, of the unwavering determination of the political parties to admit only politically expedient accounts of what was happening in Spain. The following situation was therefore in place: the beliefs of these intellectuals were answerable solely to the standards by means of which a prevailing consensus was reached within their party, but the means by which that consensus was reached was not answerable to *what was happening in Spain*. So the beliefs of British intellectuals concerning what was happening in Spain bore no relation to what was happening in Spain, not even the relationship that is implied in an ordinary lie.

The situation Orwell has in mind when he says "the very concept of objective truth is fading out of the world" is a situation in which belief-formation is subject to the following three conditions: (a) the resulting beliefs are answerable solely to the mechanisms through which consensus is achieved within a certain community, (b) those standards yield beliefs about the facts that do not bear any relation to the facts, not even the relationship implied in an ordinary lie, and (c) systematic means are employed by the community to render access to any other standard impossible. I will henceforth refer to such a state of affairs—in which the formation of someone's beliefs with respect to some subject matter is subject to these three conditions—as "a totalitarian scenario."[20] *Nineteen Eighty-Four* is an attempt to depict a scenario that is totalitarian with respect to an extraordinarily wide class of beliefs—a world in which the formation of as many of a person's beliefs are subject to the above three conditions

---

[20] As I use the term, a "totalitarian scenario" is always relative to a set of beliefs and the subject matter of those beliefs. The British intellectuals discussed by Orwell inhabit a totalitarian scenario with regard to the formation of their beliefs about the Spanish civil war (and no doubt certain other matters); but there is no reason to suppose that the formation of their beliefs about what is happening at any given time in their vegetable garden is unable to be appropriately sensitive to the subject matter of those beliefs. Thus by a "totalitarian scenario" I always mean only to refer to a *locally* totalitarian scenario. (I don't think any sense is to be made of a *maximally global* totalitarian scenario—though *Nineteen Eighty-Four* offers what I take to be a depiction of the most global version of a totalitarian scenario of which one can form an at least minimally coherent conception.) When I use the term "nontotalitarian scenario," I mean to refer to a scenario that is not even locally totalitarian.

as can possibly be the case.[21] The novel is about the possibility of a state of affairs in which the concept of objective truth has faded as far out of the world as it conceivably can.[22] The attempt to depict such a state of affairs is one of the central ways in which Orwell's novel seeks "to draw out the logical consequences" inherent in certain modes of thought—modes of thought that Orwell found were suddenly beginning to become prevalent among certain British intellectuals during the 1930s.

In *Nineteen Eighty-Four*, the Party aims to ensure that the concept of objective truth ceases to apply, for example, to the way history is recorded or remembered:

> The Party said that Oceania had never been in alliance with Eurasia. He, Winston Smith, knew that Oceania had been in alliance with Eurasia as short a time as four years ago. But where did that knowledge exist? Only in his own consciousness, which in any case must soon be annihilated. And if all others accepted the lie which the Party imposed—if all records told the same tale—then the lie passed into history and became truth. "Who controls the past," ran the Party slogan, "controls the future: who controls the present controls the past." And yet the past, though of its nature alterable, never had been altered. Whatever was true now was true from everlasting to everlasting. It was quite simple. All that was needed was an unending series of victories over your own memory. "Reality control," they called it. (32)

Numerous passages in the novel characterize the purpose of "reality control" as "the denial of objective reality"; and some equate such a denial with the denial of "objective truth" (e.g., 68–69, 129, 205, 219). Winston speaks for Orwell when he reflects, "If the Party could thrust its hand into the past and say of this or that event, *it never happened*—that, surely,

---

[21] "The process of continuous alteration was applied not only to newspapers, but to books, periodicals, pamphlets, posters, leaflets, films, sound tracks, cartoons, photographs—to every kind of literature or documentation which might conceivably hold any political or ideological significance.... [E]very prediction made by the Party could be shown by documentary evidence to have been correct; nor was any item of news, or any expression of opinion, which conflicted with the needs of the moment, ever allowed to remain on record. All history was a palimpsest, scraped clean and reinscribed exactly as often as was necessary. In no case would it have been possible, once the deed was done, to prove that any falsification had taken place.... It might very well be that literally every word in the history books, even the things that one accepted without question, was pure fantasy.... [T]he claim of the Party . . . had got to be accepted, because there did not exist, and never again could exist, any standard against which it could be tested. . . . [Members of the Party] could be made to accept the most flagrant violations of reality" (36–37, 64, 79, 129).

[22] For reasons that we will come to, this is not to say that the concept of objective truth has altogether faded out of the world of a Party member. When I say here it "has faded as far out of someone's world as it conceivably can," that means as far out of someone's world as it conceivably can without that person's losing her mindedness—her ability to direct her thought at reality—altogether.

was more terrifying than mere torture and death" (32). Glimpses into the possibility of just such a nightmare scenario figure prominently in Orwell's writings about the Spanish civil war:

> If you look up the history of the last war [i.e., World War I] in, for instance, the *Encyclopaedia Britannica*, you will find that a respectable amount of the material is drawn from German sources. A British and a German historian would disagree deeply on many things, even on fundamentals, but there would still be that body of, as it were, neutral fact on which neither would seriously challenge the other. It is just this common basis of agreement . . . that totalitarianism destroys. . . . The implied objective of this line of thought is a nightmare world in which the Leader, or some ruling clique, controls not only the future but *the past*. If the Leader says of such and such an event, "It never happened"—well, it never happened. If he says that two and two are five—well, two and two are five. This prospect frightens me much more than bombs—and after our experiences of the last few years that is not a frivolous statement.[23]

This last sentence is a reference to the fact that these lines were written in London in 1942 just after Orwell had witnessed the cruelty inflicted through the bombing of a defenseless urban civilian population. It was the most devastating example of cruelty that Orwell, in his not uneventful life, had witnessed firsthand. The example is chosen to make it clear that the author means to be taking the full measure of the horror of cruelty in concluding that cruelty is not the worst thing we do.

This passage concludes with the claim that "the implied objective" of a totalitarian line of thought is "a nightmare world": a world in which if the Leader says of such and such an event, "It never happened"—well, it never happened; and if he says that two and two are five—well, two and two are five. This passage clearly anticipates the topic (and, to some extent, the exact wording) of the focal passage. The author of these passages does not intend the truth of "2 + 2 = 4" to drop out as irrelevant to an understanding of the point of the passage. Two paragraphs before the focal passage in the novel we find this:

> In the end the Party would announce that two and two made five, and you would have to believe it. It was inevitable that they should make that claim sooner or later: the logic of their position demanded it. Not merely the validity of experience, but the very existence of external reality was tacitly denied by their philosophy. . . . And what was terrifying was not that they would kill you for thinking otherwise, but that. . . . the mind itself is controllable. (69)

[23] CEJL, 2:258–59.

What does it mean to say "not merely the validity of experience, but the very existence of external reality was tacitly denied by [the Party's] philosophy"? It means that one is asked to form one's beliefs about how things are in a manner that is no longer beholden to how things are. There are two sorts of examples of truth-claims that figure centrally in this passage (and in the focal passage and, indeed, throughout the novel): perceptual judgments (claims based on "the evidence of your senses") and elementary arithmetical judgments (such as two and two make four). Why do these two sorts of examples recur throughout the novel? Once a member of our linguistic community has become competent in the application of the relevant (perceptual or arithmetic) concepts, these are the sorts of judgments the truth or falsity of which can easily be assessed by an individual *on her own*. Her ability to assess the truth of such judgments does not wait upon the development of a consensus within her community. (It is this ability on the part of the individual—to arrive at a view of the facts that does not depend on a knowledge of the Party's preferred version of the facts—that the focal passage announces must be undone: "The Party told you to reject the evidence of your eyes and ears. It was their final, most essential, command.") Indeed, when the judgment concerns, say, something you saw and no one else saw, you have excellent prima facie reasons to trust your own view of what happened over, say, a conflicting version that, say, appears in the newspaper.[24] It is this capacity of individuals to assess the truth of claims on their own that threatens the hegemony of the Party over their minds. (If the freedom to exercise *this* capacity is granted, then—as the focal passage says—all else follows.) The "mind itself" is fully "controllable" only when the Party's version of the facts is taken as true even in the face of contradictory testimony from one's own senses and against the grain of the norms built into the concepts employed in the formulation of the Party's version of the facts.

Recall now Rorty's reading of the focal passage: O'Brien's object, Rorty says, is merely to deprive Winston of the freedom to believe what he wants to believe—the truth of what Winston believes drops out as irrelevant: O'Brien forces Winston to believe "two and two make five" because Winston *happens* to believe that "two and two make four" and because Winston *happens* to have attached great importance to this belief.[25] But what

---

[24] Winston reflects: "[The photograph] was concrete evidence; it was a fragment of the abolished past. . . . [T]he fact of having held [the photograph] in his fingers seemed to him to make a difference even now, when the photograph itself, as well as the event it recorded, was only memory" (67–68).

[25] Rorty's reading of the novel leaves it generally mysterious why words such as "truth" and "objective reality" should figure in the manner in which they do throughout the discussions between O'Brien and Winston, but especially so with respect to that moment of the novel for which one would have expected Rorty to be most concerned to have a textually

the novel says (just prior to the focal passage) is: "In the end" the moment would come when "the Party would announce that two and two made five" because "the logic of their position demanded it." Claims such as "two and two make four" and "O'Brien is now holding up four fingers" figure as central examples of claims the truth of which in the end must be denied by the Party because of the kind of claims they are: ones that are true and moreover easily seen to be true by anyone competent in our practices of claim making. The novel is here working out one of the "intellectual implications of totalitarianism." The Party's practice of wholesale "organized lying" is sustainable only if, in the end, it deprives its members of their ability to autonomously assess the credentials of a claim—any claim: even a straightforward perceptual or arithmetic claim. The reason claims such as "two and two make four" and "I see a photograph before me" figure prominently as examples in the novel is this: it makes no sense

---

plausible reading: namely, the moment in the pivotal torture scene in which O'Brien refers back to the convictions to which Winston gives voice in the focal passage and begins to undertake to strip him of those convictions:

> "You believe that reality is something objective, external, existing in its own right. . . . But I tell you, Winston, reality is not external. Reality exists in the human mind, and nowhere else. Not in the individual mind, which can make mistakes, and in any case soon perishes; only in the mind of the Party, which is collective and immortal. Whatever the Party holds to be the truth *is* the truth. It is impossible to see reality except by looking through the eyes of the Party. That is the fact that you have got to relearn, Winston. It needs an act of self-destruction, an effort of the will. You must humble yourself before you can become sane."
>
> [O'Brien] paused for a few moments, as though to allow what he had been saying to sink in.
>
> "Do you remember," he went on, "writing in your diary, 'Freedom is the freedom to say that two plus two make four'?"
>
> "Yes," said Winston.
>
> O'Brien held up his left hand, its back toward Winston, with the thumb hidden and the four fingers extended.
>
> "How many fingers am I holding up, Winston?"
>
> "Four."
>
> "And if the Party says that it is not four but five—then how many?" (205–6)

Notice: O'Brien undertakes to destroy Winston's conviction that "$2 + 2 = 4$" only (and immediately) after charging him with clinging to the belief that "reality is something objective, external, existing in its own right" and failing to acquiesce in the belief that "whatever the Party holds to be the truth *is* the truth." Before going on to remind Winston of what he wrote in his diary and undertaking to make him believe otherwise, O'Brien pauses for a few moments to allow what he here says to sink in (so that Winston will keep in view why he is being tortured while he is being tortured). Rorty does not pause; he skips over O'Brien's remarks to what Winston wrote and latches onto the word "freedom," thus ignoring the entire context of the novel's discussion of the question of what is involved in the "freedom

to suppose that the criteria for determining the truth-value of such claims could require that prior to arriving at a judgment on such matters one first had to consult the latest bulletin from the Party. They are the sorts of claims that can be known to be true by someone like Winston without reference to higher authority and, once known to be true, will sometimes inevitably fail to cohere with the rest of the Party's version of the facts.[26]

Rorty thinks that Orwell's novel describes a set of practices of claim making which happen to differ radically from our own, and that its point in doing so is to urge that, apart from our culturally and historically provincial predilections, there is nothing that entitles us to prefer our practices to these possible future practices. Is *that* Orwell's view of the Party's practices?

When O'Brien asks Winston how many fingers he is holding up, he doesn't merely want Winston to overrule the testimony of his senses in favor of what the Party tells him. Nor does O'Brien want Winston, in concluding that there are five fingers in front of him, to be adopting a revision in our concepts (of "see," "five," "fingers," etc.). He doesn't merely want Winston to believe something that can be expressed in Newspeak by the statement "I see five fingers," but that has a completely different meaning from its homophonic English counterpart; he wants Winston to believe *that there are five fingers* in front of him. O'Brien wants Winston to look at him holding up four fingers and, if the Party wants him to believe that there are five fingers, to *see* five fingers in front of him, and to have the ground of his belief that there are five fingers in front of him be (not that the Party wants him to believe that, but) that he sees five fingers. The Party's ambition is therefore neither—as Rorty suggests—so modest as merely to want to change the ground rules for how to use certain philosophically freighted portions of our vocabulary (e.g., "truth," "reality") nor so ambitious as to want to effect a wholesale revision in the norms for applying our entire present battery of concepts, completely jettisoning our familiar norms for making claims. The ways in which the Party wants its members to think and judge cannot be captured in terms of a coherent set of ground rules for the application of concepts: Party members are supposed to abide by our ordinary norms for making claims and not to abide by these norms.

---

to say that two plus two make four."

[26] This may seem less obvious with respect to arithmetical claims. It is for just this reason that Orwell goes out of his way to include scenes such as the scene in which Winston is asked to alter the figures of the Ministry of Plenty, the scene in which the quantity of the chocolate ration is altered, etc. These scenes require a certain plasticity in a Party member's conviction of the need for arithmetical results to tally: in all of these scenes alterations of quantitative fact are made by the Party, but Party members are required to believe both that no alteration of quantity has taken place and that the figures tally.

The Party wants its members to be able to think and judge—which requires that they retain their mastery of our familiar norms for the application of concepts—but never to think or judge in a manner that conflicts with what the Party wants them to think or judge; yet, all along, while thinking and judging in accordance with the Party's decrees, to believe that they are never arriving at a judgment about how things are that conflicts with a judgment at which someone who had no knowledge of the Party's decrees, but who simply abided by the norms built into our concepts, might have occasion to arrive. The Party therefore places an incoherent set of demands upon its members, the incoherence of which must itself be rendered *invisible* if those demands are to serve the Party's purposes.[27] How is this invisibility to be achieved? The rules for the formation of beliefs that Party members are in fact required to follow and the rules that they are asked to *believe* that they are following cannot be the same.[28] How is it possible for Party members successfully to follow a set of rules that they never believe they are following? By engaging in the practices of "reality control" and "doublethink." Party members are expected to "adjust" their beliefs about reality in accordance with the Party's decrees but then are asked to believe that the justification for their beliefs lies (not merely in their accord with the Party's decrees, but) in their accord with the facts. Party members are asked, for example, not only to believe that such-and-such happened in the past (if the Party presently decrees that this is what happened), but to adjust their memories of the past so that they now remember such-and-such as having happened in the past and to believe that the ground of their present belief that such-and-such happened in the past is (not the Party's present decree to that effect, but rather) their present memory of its having happened in the past.[29] This is why the novel insists that reality control can be successfully practiced only by someone who has also become adept in the practice of doublethink. In order to be a Party member, Orwell says, one needs "to deny the existence of objective reality and all the while to take account of the reality which one denies. . . . [O]ne must be able to dislocate the sense of reality" (177). One must not only adjust one's beliefs about reality, but one must

[27] "A Party member is required to have not only the right opinions, but the right instincts. Many of the beliefs and attitudes demanded of him are never plainly stated, and could not be stated without laying bare the contradictions inherent in Ingsoc" (174).

[28] "[T]he essential act of the Party is to use conscious deception while retaining the firmness of purpose that goes with complete honesty. To tell deliberate lies while genuinely believing in them" (176–77).

[29] "To make sure that all written records agree with the orthodoxy of the moment is a merely mechanical act. But it is also necessary to *remember* that events happened in the desired manner. And if it is necessary to rearrange one's memories or to tamper with written records, then it is necessary to *forget* that one has done so" (176).

also be proficient in the art of forgetting that one continuously so adjusts them.[30] "The denial of external reality" demanded by the logic of the Party's position can be approximated only to the extent that members of a community learn to cultivate a tremendously thoroughgoing form of self-deception—so thoroughgoing that they succeed in hiding from themselves that (as Orwell puts it) "the truth goes on existing, as it were, behind [their] back[s]."[31]

Rorty talks as if our practices and the "practices" of the future totalitarian society depicted in Orwell's novel represented a pair of equally viable alternatives (with the interesting difference that, as it happens, talk of "objective reality" is frowned upon in the future "practices" and all that is thereby lost, according to Rorty, is a proclivity to engage in fruitless metaphysical controversies).[32] But this isn't right. There are overwhelming grounds from *within* their "practices" for preferring our practices to theirs. What Orwell calls "the denial of objective reality" is a denial that can be at most partially sustained and then only within a set of "practices" regulated by what Orwell calls a "schizophrenic system of thought"[33]—a system that simultaneously respects and disregards our present norms for making claims.[34]

Passages such as the following recur throughout *Nineteen Eighty-Four*:

> Being in a minority, even a minority of one, did not make you mad. There was truth and untruth, and if you clung to the truth even against the whole world, you were not mad. . . . [Winston] fell asleep murmuring "Sanity is not statistical," with the feeling that this remark contained in it a profound wisdom. (179)

---

[30] "[T]he labyrinthine world of doublethink. To know and not to know, to be conscious of complete truthfulness while telling carefully constructed lies, to hold simultaneously two opinions which cancelled out, knowing them to be contradictory and believing in both of them, to use logic against logic, . . . to forget, whatever it was necessary to forget, then to draw it back into memory again at the moment it was needed, and then promptly to forget it again, and above all, to apply the same process to the process itself—that was the ultimate subtlety: consciously to induce unconsciousness, and then, once again, to become unconscious of the act of hypnosis you had just performed. Even to understand the word 'doublethink' involved the use of doublethink" (32–33).

[31] CEJL, 2:259.

[32] I place "practices" here (and in the next two sentences) in scare quotes to signal that—in contrast to the expression when it occurs here (and in the next two sentences) without scare quotes—it does not refer to a coherent set of norms for making claims.

[33] "A totalitarian society which succeeded in perpetuating itself would set up a schizophrenic system of thought" (CEJL, 4:64).

[34] "The empirical method of thought, on which all the scientific achievements of the past were founded, is opposed to the most fundamental principles of Ingsoc. . . . But in matters of vital importance . . . the empirical approach is still encouraged, or at least tolerated. . . . [B]ut once that minimum is achieved, [members of the Party] can twist reality into whatever shape they choose" (159, 164).

Rorty's doctrines presuppose that sanity *is* a statistical matter: a matter of the congruence of one's beliefs with those of one's peers. Admittedly, in a nontotalitarian scenario, such congruence is generally a reliable measure of sanity. But Orwell is concerned to depict a world in which it is not a reliable measure:

> [Winston] was a lonely ghost uttering a truth that nobody would ever hear. But so long as he uttered it, in some obscure way the continuity was not broken. It was not by making yourself heard but by staying sane that you carried on the human heritage. (26)

What Orwell's depiction of a totalitarian scenario brings out is that a statistical gloss on sanity cannot serve as a definition of sanity.

In the world of the novel, there is a fact of the matter as to whether Winston's statement that he saw a photograph of Rutherford is warranted. (It is warranted and remains so even after all the corroborating evidence has been destroyed by the Party.) Moreover, it is important to the narrative of the novel that whether Winston's statement is warranted or not is independent of whether the majority of his cultural peers in the Party would *say* it is warranted. Even though Winston constitutes a minority of one, his statement remains warranted. Rorty not only fails to see that such a state of affairs is envisioned in the novel, he fails to see that it can so much as represent a perfectly coherent possibility:

> There being a fact of the matter about warranted assertibility must, for [philosophers like] Putnam, be something *more* than our ability to figure out whether S is in a good position, given the interests and values of herself and her peers, to assert *p*. But what more . . . can it be? Presumably it is whatever makes it possible for a statement not to be warranted even though a majority of one's peers say it is. *Is* that possible? . . . Well, maybe a *majority* can be wrong. But suppose everybody in the community, except for one or two dubious characters notorious for making assertions even stranger than *p*, thinks S must be a bit crazy. They think this even after patiently sitting through S's defense of *p*, and after sustained attempts to talk her out of it. Might S still be *warranted* in asserting *p*? Only if there is some way of determining warrant *sub specie aeternitatis*, some natural order of reasons which determines, quite apart from S's ability to justify *p* to those around her, whether she is *really* justified in holding *p*.[35]

Rorty does not see how to allow for a scenario in which both of the following are true: (a) S's willingness to assert *p* furnishes practically everybody in S's community (except perhaps for one or two dubious charac-

---

[35] "Putnam and the Relativist Menace" [henceforth PRM], *Journal of Philosophy* 90, no. 9 (September 1993): 450.

ters) with a ground for thinking that S is crazy, and (b) S is, nonetheless, fully warranted in asserting *p*. *But—in Orwell's novel—Winston finds himself in just such a situation.* Orwell, in depicting the conversation between Winston and O'Brien, aims to furnish an example of just the sort of case that Rorty (in the passage quoted above) does not allow for: Winston's claims are warranted because they are in accord—not with what his peers in fact say, but—with what his peers *should* say. Winston's statement that he saw a photograph of Rutherford is warranted (not because he possesses some way of determining warrant *sub specie aeternitatis*, but rather) because he faithfully adheres to the only *coherent* norms members of his community have for applying concepts (such as the concept *photograph*) and for making claims (such as the claim "I saw such-and-such").[36] Such a situation can come about whenever what one's peers *ought* to believe (given the norms inherent in the community's practices for making claims) fails to coincide with what they, as a matter of brute sociological fact, happen to believe. If one inhabits a nontotalitarian scenario, then one is not likely to find oneself in such a situation—a situation in which one's community as a whole goes wrong, leaving one in a minority of one. What *Nineteen Eighty-Four* makes vivid, however, is that, if one has the misfortune to be an inhabitant of a totalitarian scenario, then, unless one is adept in practicing the arts of reality control and doublethink, it is not only possible but *probable* that one will find oneself in such a situation a great deal of the time and with respect to a great many of one's beliefs.[37] (The more totalitarian the scenario one inhabits, the greater the number of beliefs one will have that are likely to be both warranted and unacceptable to one's peers.)

Rorty writes:

> [T]he terms 'warranted', 'rational acceptability', etc., will always invite the question 'to whom'? This question will always lead us back, it seems to me, to the answer '*Us*, at our best'. So all 'a fact of the matter about whether *p* is a warranted assertion' can mean is "a fact of the matter about our ability to feel solidarity with a community that views *p* as warranted."[38]

[36] The norms that Winston follows in making his claims are internal to a worldview, just as Putnam urges norms must be. If we plug "Winston" in for S, it should be easy to see that there is no tension—as Rorty claims—between Putnam's rejection of Realism and his claim that S can be completely out of step with the beliefs of other members of his community and yet be warranted in asserting *p*.

[37] I do not mean to suggest that Orwell thinks that one finds oneself in the situation in which Winston here finds himself—i.e., in which, e.g., one believes a statement to be unwarranted even though the majority of one's cultural peers believe it to be true—only if one inhabits a totalitarian scenario. Orwell is perfectly happy to say about this or that belief of his contemporaries: "I am not saying that it is a true belief, merely that it is a belief which all modern men do actually hold" (CEJL, 2:185).

[38] PRM, 453.

The only sense Rorty can make of notions such as warrant or rational acceptability is in terms of the idea of passing muster with our peers. In the world of the novel, Winston knows that the Party did not invent the airplane (33). He has clear and vivid memories of airplanes from his childhood, way back before the days of the Party. But his belief will never pass muster with any of his peers. All of the history books and all other forms of documentary evidence have been altered to reflect the Party's version of the facts. Every member of the Party now dutifully believes the official version of the facts (putatively) documented in the history books. Winston's belief to the contrary is an act of thoughtcrime punishable by death.[39] His peers have no interest in entertaining beliefs that might lead to their being vaporized, so they have all internalized the mental habit of crimestop.[40] Under these circumstances, is Winston's belief (that the Party did not invent the airplane) warranted? If the question "Is Winston's belief warranted?" is simply equated with the question "Is it acceptable to his peers?" then the answer clearly is: "No, his belief is not warranted." For Winston, under the totalitarian conditions in which he finds himself, is in no position to bring anyone round to his belief. The only existing "community that views $p$ as warranted" is in this case a community of one. There is no larger community with whom Winston can seek solidarity, if to seek solidarity means—as Rorty thinks it does—to seek de facto agreement with a presently available community of peers.[41] What this shows is that there is something missing in Rorty's theory of justification. Implicit in the practices of Winston's community are norms that, if properly abided by, underwrite Winston's belief. Assuming (as the author of the novel clearly intends us to) that Winston's memory does not deceive him (i.e., that there were airplanes when he was a child) and given the norms that govern the application of the concept *invention* (e.g., that it is impossible for X to invent Y if there were Ys before X existed), then Winston's belief (that the Party did not invent the airplane) *is* warranted; and it remains warranted even if it also remains the case that none of his peers are willing to (engage in an act of thoughtcrime in which they) credit the possibility that his belief is warranted.

[39] "[Winston] had committed—would still have committed, even if he never set pen to paper—the essential crime that contained all others in itself. Thoughtcrime, they called it. Thoughtcrime was not a thing that could be concealed forever. You might dodge successfully for a while, even for years, but sooner or later they were bound to get you" (19).

[40] "*Crimestop* means the faculty of stopping short, as though by instinct, at the threshold of any dangerous thought. It includes the power of not grasping analogies, of failing to perceive logical errors, of misunderstanding the simplest arguments if they are inimical to Ingsoc, and of being bored and repelled by any train of thought which is capable of leading in a heretical direction" (174–75).

[41] "For whom, it suddenly occurred to [Winston] to wonder, was he writing his diary? For the future, for the unborn" (10).

In nontotalitarian scenarios, the following two tasks generally coincide: the task of seeking to justify a claim to the satisfaction of other people and the task of seeking to establish that a claim is justified in the light of the facts. In totalitarian scenarios, these two tasks diverge radically. It is manifest to Winston that the question whether it is true that the Party did not invent the airplane and the question whether or not someone will be allowed to get away with saying "The Party did not invent the airplane" are different questions. In our world, as long as the question "Who invented the airplane?" does not become too ideologically fraught, the tasks of seeking an answer to that question and of seeking an answer to the question "What will my peers let me get away with saying about who invented the airplane?" ought to more or less coincide. In Winston's world they do not coincide. If our world were like Winston's world in the respect in which Rorty suggests that it already is—if our only aim in inquiry were to remain in step with our peers— then there would be no reason to suppose that our claims had any more bearing on the world than the claims that appear in the newspapers in *Nineteen Eighty-Four* have on the events which those newspapers report. Yet even the inhabitants of Winston's world are (at least in principle) able to distinguish the questions "Who invented the airplane?" and "Who does practically everyone *say* invented the airplane?" *Not even the Party goes quite as far as Rorty!* It does not aim to deprive its members of the capacity to distinguish between these questions. What members of the Party believe is that the answers to these two clearly distinct questions happily coincide. The Party wants its members to believe that their ground for believing what the Party says is that it accords with the facts. Not even the Party aims to do away altogether in theory with (what Orwell calls) "the very concept of objective truth"—i.e., the very idea of the answerability of claims concerning how things are to how things are. Nevertheless, Orwell's depiction of the world in which Winston lives— a world in which, as Orwell puts it, this concept is on the verge of "fading out"—is perhaps as close as we can come to contemplating in imagination the implications of the adoption of a resolutely Rortian conception of objectivity (i.e., a conception in which the concept of objectivity is exhausted by that of solidarity).[42]

---

[42] I say this is "*as close as we can come* to contemplating in imagination the implications of the adoption of a resolutely Rortian conception of objectivity" because I do not think that Rorty's conception is sufficiently coherent actually to permit of such contemplation. Even the inhabitants of a totalitarian scenario are still able to make claims. Rorty's conception, I would argue, deprives us of the resources for being able to understand those who engage in the practices Rorty describes as even so much as making claims. Since such an argument is out of place in this section of the paper—which is concerned with how Rorty would look to Orwell—I leave it for another occasion.

Rorty writes:

[T]here seems to be no obvious reason why the progress of the language-game we are playing should have anything in particular to do with the way the rest of the world is.[43]

It is precisely in scenarios which approximate the conditions of a totalitarian scenario that the progress of our language-games for making claims are sure to have nothing to do "with the way the rest of the world is"—as, for example, the progress of the highly ideological language-game for making claims about what was happening in Spain played by British intellectuals during the Spanish civil war failed to have anything to do with what was happening in Spain. In the scenario depicted in *Nineteen Eighty-Four*, abiding by (some of what pass in that world for) norms of inquiry—such as taking newspaper accounts of events as true—does not improve a person's chances of having beliefs about the world that are right about the world. Following those "norms" leaves a person with a set of beliefs about the world that (can quite properly be said to) have nothing "in particular to do with the way the rest of the world is." That is the problem with those (putative) norms of inquiry. In a nontotalitarian scenario—i.e., the sort of scenario we generally take ourselves to inhabit—part of the point of abiding by (what Rorty calls) "the rules of language-games" for making claims is that, in abiding by them, we strengthen the probability that the claims we come out with will have something to do with the way the world is. If abiding by these rules did not have this consequence, this would reveal that there was something wrong with these rules. We do occasionally discover that our rules for conducting inquiry do not improve our chances of being right about the world; and when we discover this, we modify our rules. In the world of *Nineteen Eighty-Four*, the emergence of a felt need for some modification of the prevailing norms of inquiry is forestalled only through a tremendous expenditure of effort—through a systematic falsification of the evidence (which constantly threatens to accumulate) showing that some of what pass in that world for norms of inquiry do not improve one's chances of being right about the world.

Perhaps the single most perverse feature of Rorty's reading of *Nineteen Eighty-Four* is that, in attributing Rortian doctrines to Orwell, Rorty comes extraordinarily close to attributing to Orwell the very views that Orwell chose to put into O'Brien's mouth.[44] O'Brien, in the following

---

[43] *Objectivity, Relativism and Truth* (Cambridge: Cambridge University Press, 1991), 129.

[44] Rorty himself takes some time over the question whether O'Brien should be counted as an ironist, and expresses only one reservation about declaring O'Brien to be one: O'Brien has mastered doublethink and therefore is not troubled by doubts about himself or the

portion of his dialogue with Winston, opens with an argumentative gambit strikingly reminiscent of some of Rorty's own tactics:

> O'Brien smiled faintly. "You are no metaphysician, Winston," he said. "Until this moment you had never considered what is meant by existence. I will put it more precisely. Does the past exist concretely, in space? Is there somewhere or other a place, a world of solid objects, where the past is still happening?"
> "No."
> "Then where does the past exist, if at all?"
> "In records. It is written down."
> "In records. And—?"
> "In the mind. In human memories."
> "In memory. Very well, then. We, the Party, control all records, and we control all memories. Then we control the past, do we not?" (205)

O'Brien moves here from an affirmation of the hopelessness of a hyper-Realist, hyper-metaphysical construal of the reality of the past (as "a place, a world of solid objects, where the past is still happening") to an unqualified denial of the idea that (what Orwell calls) "the concept of objective truth" has application to the past. According to O'Brien, the Party controls the past because it controls all mechanisms for achieving an informed consensus about the past. It does not take much of a stretch to formulate O'Brien's view in Rortian vocabulary. O'Brien would, I think, find the following reformulation of his view perfectly congenial:

> There is no past, as it were, "out there" against which to assess the veridicality of memories and records. There is nothing independent of the community's present practices of making claims about the past against which to assess the truth-values of such claims. The "truth" about the past is simply a matter of how the community's memories and records as a whole *cohere* and has nothing to do with how well those memories and records "represent the facts." To seek an answer to the question "What happened at such-and-such a point in the past?" is to seek a *consensus* with one's peers. If a Winston Smith comes along and challenges the coherence or integrity of the community's beliefs, the truth is to be arrived at through a process of *conversation* between Winston and his peers. The "true" story will be the one that *prevails* as the outcome of that conversation.

---

Party. Rorty concludes, "[O'Brien] still has the *gifts* which, in a time when doublethink had not yet been invented, would have made him an ironist. . . . In this qualified sense, we can think of O'Brien as the last ironist in Europe" (CIS, 187). What Rorty misses is that, on Orwell's view, O'Brien's ironist "denial of objective reality" can be put into practice only by someone who has perfected the art of doublethink.

The convergence between O'Brien's and Rorty's views is striking.[45] Hence the perversity of Rorty's reading of Orwell. For O'Brien's answers to his own questions in his dialogue with Winston represent Orwell's most resolute attempt "to draw the logical consequences of totalitarianism" out to their ultimate conclusion.

At the beginning of his forbidden diary, Winston inscribes the following greetings to his potential readers:

> To the future or to the past, to a time when thought is free, when men are different from one another and do not live alone—to a time when truth exists and what is done cannot be undone:
> From the age of uniformity, from the age of solitude, from the age of Big Brother, from the age of doublethink—greetings! (26–27)

Three central concepts of the novel are linked here: freedom, community, and truth. Orwell, as I read him, seeks to show that you have freedom of thought only when you are free to arrive at your own verdict concerning the facts; and that such freedom can be exercised only where there is genuine community.[46] Such community can be sustained only where the norms that regulate inquiry are guided not only by a demand to remain in step with one's peers but by a demand to make one's claims concerning how things are answerable to how things are. The point of Winston's complex description of his potential readership is that the possibility of freedom, the possibility of community, and the possibility of truth are seen by him to stand or fall together. This contrasts starkly with how Rorty sees the relationship among these three concepts. Rorty takes freedom to be the central theme of Orwell's novel; he takes community to be something anyone can get for free (as long as one lives with other people and does things a sociologist might want to study); and, truth, Rorty declares, is a red herring. Rorty is certainly right that the novel seeks to "sensitize" its readers to some of the ways in which "cruelty is a bad thing"; but most of the point of the novel is missed if one misses the

---

[45] See also *Nineteen Eighty-Four*, 219: " 'I told you Winston,' [O'Brien] said, 'that metaphysics is not your strong point. The word you are trying to think of is solipsism. But you are mistaken. This is not solipsism. Collective solipsism, if you like. But that is a different thing; in fact, the opposite thing.'" And 229: "What knowledge have we of anything, save through our own minds? . . . Whatever happens in all minds, truly happens."

[46] This is not quite right, insofar as it appears to assert that if I were to become stranded on an uninhabited island, I would suddenly cease to be able to arrive at a free verdict concerning what transpires in my environment. To put the point more carefully: (a) initiation into a genuine community is a condition of the acquisition of the capacity to arrive at such verdicts, and (b) insofar as one continues to live in the society of one's fellow human beings, one can fully exercise freedom of judgment in their company only to the extent that they are not devoted to undermining one's capacity to do so (i.e., only to the extent that the "community" one forms with them is not a totalitarian one).

internal relation between its concern with cruelty and its concern with the interrelated concepts of freedom, genuine community, and truth. The novel seeks to exhibit how cruelty becomes commonplace in a world in which these three concepts no longer have secure foothold.[47]

In failing to grasp the connection among these three concepts, Rorty misunderstands what freedom, community, and truth are for Orwell. In the latter half of the above passage, Winston employs three other concepts, equally central to the novel, to specify what prevails in the absence of freedom, community, and truth: uniformity, solitude, and doublethink. Freedom of thought is not—as Rorty suggests—merely the freedom to say or think whatever you happen to feel like saying or thinking at a given moment; it is the freedom fully to exercise one's intellectual resources, to make the most of one's capacity for thought. The fundamental deprivation of freedom suffered by a Party member lies not in the prohibitions on what he is allowed to say, but in the undermining of the conditions that would enable him to develop his capacity to arrive at something worth saying. Once such conditions are undermined, you can say whatever you like, but it will hardly differ from what anyone else says.[48] The

[47] A central theme of all of Orwell's writing—especially his writings on the relative strengths and shortcomings of English versus other kinds of imperialism—is that once all forms of answerability are effaced except accountability to the demands of those who happen to have power, then the lives of those who are not in power are flooded with cruelty. Rorty, of course, might be perfectly willing to concede that the fact that the Party possesses virtually limitless power (a power "more absolute than had previously been imagined possible") over its members and the fact that the most apt image of the life of a Party member is an image of "a boot stamping on a human face" (220) are not, for Orwell, externally related facts about the world of *Nineteen Eighty-Four*. But the fact that the Party has such complete power over the minds of its members is, as we have seen, a function of the inability of its members to arrive at an independent verdict concerning how things are (of "the dislocation of their sense of reality"). Thus there obtains, for Orwell, an internal relation between the fact that the life of a Party member is "a boot stamping on a human face" and the fact that the world in which a Party member lives is one in which "the very concept of objective truth is on the verge of fading out."

[48] Thus Orwell's notion of freedom is considerably weightier than Rorty's. Officially, there are no prohibitions on what a Party member is allowed to say, for there are no laws that prohibit anything in the world of *Nineteen Eighty-Four*. A Party member is simply expected to act, speak, and think in the appropriate fashion. The average "well-adjusted" Party member—unlike Winston—is not conscious of any deprivation of freedom. According to Rorty's purely negative concept of freedom, he is free (he can say anything he likes and no one will hurt him); and Winston is comparatively lacking in freedom (there is much that he wants to say but cannot). But, on the positive concept of freedom central to the novel, the average Party member is, in comparison to Winston, utterly lacking in freedom. The following point is central to Orwell's concept of freedom: the more completely captive a mind is, the less conscious it is of its lack of freedom. If one identifies freedom with the freedom from juridical constraint accorded to the well-adjusted Party member, then there is a reading of the Party's slogan about freedom on which, in the world of the novel, it (like all of the Party's slogans) is true: Freedom *is* slavery.

aim of the Party is to bring about a state of affairs in which all people are free to say what they like and yet perfect consensus reigns.[49] Hence uniformity. A community of genuinely free people is not simply one in which a high level of de facto consensus has been achieved and can be sustained, but one in which vigorous disagreement is welcomed as a spur to refining a shared set of norms for adjudicating and resolving present and future disagreements. In the absence of *such* practices for resolving disagreement, regardless of how much one talks to others, one will always find oneself sealed off by one's heterodox convictions. Hence solitude. Truth, for Orwell, is not simply a compliment we pay to those of our assertions that, as it happens, our peers will let us get away with. Regardless of what our peers say, "The Party invented the airplane" is true if and only if the Party invented the airplane. If you know that the Party did not invent the airplane, but in order to survive (in a world controlled by the Party) you have to believe otherwise, then you must believe to be true what you know to be false.[50] Hence doublethink.

I want to conclude by returning to the topic of Rorty's favorite method of dissolving philosophical problems—that of "vocabulary replacement."

[49] For reasons given in the previous note, it would be more precise to say: the aim of the Party is to bring about a state of affairs in which everyone is juridically free to say what they like. Hence O'Brien explains to Winston:

"We are not content with negative obedience, nor even with the most abject submission. When finally you surrender to us, it must be of your own free will. We do not destroy the heretic because he resists us: so long as he resists us we never destroy him. We convert him, we capture his inner mind, we reshape him. We burn all evil and illusion out of him; we bring him over to our side, not in appearance, but genuinely, heart and soul." (210)

The above remarks constitute O'Brien's answer to Winston's question (if "nothing will remain of" him, not even "a name in a register" or "a memory in a living brain") "why bother to torture me?" (210). Rorty's answer to this question (O'Brien tortures people solely for the pleasure it affords him) obliges him to overlook O'Brien's own answer to the question.

[50] Orwell takes one of the things Rorty claims really matter to Orwell—namely, a preservation of the sense of the coherence of one's own identity—to depend on the thing Rorty views as a red herring. The novel makes vivid how the answerability of your beliefs concerning how things are to how things are is a condition of maintaining your sense of self. Without such answerability—in the absence of any "external records that you [can] refer to"— even the narrative "outline of your own life [loses] its sharpness." You no longer fully have an identity—your identity is on the verge of "crumbling"—if, when you try to remember who you are and what you have done, "[y]ou remember[] huge events which [you have good reason to think] had quite probably never happened" and most of your memory of the past is simply filled with "long blank periods to which you [can] assign nothing" (30). Under such conditions, only someone who is a master of self-deception can retain the impression that she is able to "justify herself to herself."

Among the many ironies in Rorty's attempt to find an apologia for his own doctrines in *Nineteen Eighty-Four*, perhaps the most wonderful lies in the fact that the novel—in its discussion of Newspeak—contains one of the most searching meditations ever written on the potential intellectual implications of replacing one vocabulary with another. One purpose of Newspeak in the novel is, of course, the production of vocabulary for new concepts—concepts such as *doublethink*, *thoughtcrime*, and *crimestop*—vocabulary whose daily employment is essential to maintaining the practices and beliefs of members of the Party. But the most important purpose of Newspeak is the destruction of concepts.

What appeals to Rorty about vocabulary replacement as a method of dissolving philosophical problems is that it holds open the promise of making it *impossible* to formulate old putatively useless problems. The underlying premise is that a problem which can no longer be formulated is a problem that no longer exists.[51] Now such a method, no doubt, can sometimes be liberating. A change of vocabulary usually entails a change in the sorts of things we can talk about. If there are no such things as phlogiston or witches, and the only purpose formerly served by the vocabulary of "phlogiston" and "witches" was to make talk about such things possible, then nothing is lost and something is gained by junking the vocabulary. Moreover, in changing vocabularies, we can also sometimes effect a change in the sorts of things we want. We may discover more interesting things to care about and divert our attention away from less rewarding inquiries. All of these features of vocabulary replacement appeal to Rorty. But the point of the discussion of Newspeak in *Nineteen Eighty-Four* is that all of these features of vocabulary replacement cut both ways. A change in vocabulary can also deprive us of the ability to talk about some things we might still want to talk about, if only we still could. A sufficiently radical change in the discursive resources available to us might also change *us* so radically that we become no longer able even to *want* to talk about those things which formerly most occupied our thoughts; and it can deprive us of the discursive resources necessary to explore—and thus reopen—the question whether we are now better off in our present condition, in which we are unable to imagine our previous wants and ineluctably stuck wanting what we now want. Thus the feature of vocabulary replacement that most appeals to Rorty is just the one that most appeals to the Party: it renders certain "modes of thought impossible" (246). Winston's colleague in the Ministry of Truth, who is busy at work on the eleventh and definitive edition of the Newspeak dictionary, explains the chief objective of Newspeak to Winston as follows:

---

[51] I think that with respect to most philosophical problems the premise is false, but I shall not argue the point here.

[O]ur chief job is . . . destroying words. . . . [T]he whole aim of Newspeak is to narrow the range of thought[.] In the end we shall make thoughtcrime literally impossible, because there will be no words in which to express it. . . . The Revolution will be complete when the language is perfect. . . . Even the literature of the Party will change. Even the slogans will change. . . . The whole climate of thought will be different. In fact there will *be* no thought, as we understand it now. Orthodoxy means not thinking—not needing to think. (45, 46–47)

Some of the concepts that Newspeak aims to abolish—such as the concept of freedom—are ones for which Rorty himself expresses considerable fondness. But a good many of the forms of words that Newspeak aims to "destroy" are ones that Rorty's own proposals for vocabulary replacement earmark for destruction, forms of words such as "objective truth" and "objective reality." In the novel, one of the intended consequences of the implementation of Newspeak is to render most of the literature of the past utterly incomprehensible. An unintended consequence of Rorty's own proposals for vocabulary replacement, were they to be embraced, would be to render a work such as Orwell's *Nineteen Eighty-Four* equally incomprehensible.[52]

---

[52] This paper is indebted to conversations about Rorty over the past decade with Stanley Cavell, John Haugeland, and Hilary Putnam and to comments on earlier drafts of this paper by David Finkelstein and Lisa Van Alstyne. Its two largest debts are to Cora Diamond and John McDowell: to Diamond's article "Truth: Defenders, Debunkers, Despisers" (in *Commitment in Reflection*, ed. Leona Toker [New York: Garland, 1994]), to McDowell's paper "Towards Rehabilitating Objectivity" (in *Richard Rorty and His Critics*, ed. Robert Brandom [Oxford: Blackwell, 2000]), and to conversations with each of them about Rorty.

# From *Ingsoc* and *Newspeak* to *Amcap*, *Amerigood*, and *Marketspeak*

EDWARD S. HERMAN

ALTHOUGH *Nineteen Eighty-Four* was a Cold War document that drama-tized the threat of the Soviet enemy, and has always been used mainly to serve Cold War political ends, it also contained the germs of a powerful critique of U.S. and Western practice. Orwell himself suggested such ap-plications in his essay "Politics and the English Language" and even more explicitly in a neglected preface to *Animal Farm*.[1] But doublespeak and thought control are far more important in the West than Orwell indicated, often in subtle forms but sometimes as crudely as in *Nineteen Eighty-Four*, and virtually every *Nineteen Eighty-Four* illustration of Ingsoc, Newspeak, and doublethink has numerous counterparts in what we may call Amcap, Amerigood, and Marketspeak. The doublethink formulas "War Is Peace" and "Ministry of Peace" were highlights of Newspeak. But even before Orwell published *Nineteen Eighty-Four*, the U.S. "De-partment of War" had been renamed the "Department of Defense," re-flecting the Amcap-Amerigood view that our military actions and war preparations are always defensive, reasonable responses to somebody else's provocations, and ultimately in the interest of peace.

Furthermore, Americans have been much more effective dispensers of propaganda, doublespeak, and disinformation than were the managers of Ingsoc, in either *Nineteen Eighty-Four* or the real-world Soviet Union. The power of information control in this country was displayed during World War I in the work of the Creel Commission, and in its aftermath the United States pioneered in the development of public relations and advertising. Both of these industries have long been mobilized in the ser-vice of politics. During the 1994 election campaign in the United States, the Republican "Contract with America" was formed with the aid of a consultant who first polled the public to find out which words resonated with them, and then incorporated those words into the contract without

---

[1] The "Fiftieth Anniversary Edition" of *Animal Farm* (New York: Harcourt, Brace and Company, 1995) includes this preface as appendix 1.

regard to the contract's substance. This yielded, for example, a "Job Creation and Wage Enhancement" title for proposed actions that would reduce the capital gains tax.

Consider also the fact that in this country, as the role of rehabilitation in the treatment of imprisoned criminals has diminished, the name of their places of incarceration has been changed from "jails" and "prisons" to "corrections facilities." Or that civilians killed by U.S. missiles or bombs in Yugoslavia, Afghanistan, Iraq, or earlier in Indochina are always unintended "collateral damage," and the deaths are therefore morally acceptable, although there is always an official lack of interest in such numbers, and sometimes even an effort made to keep this toll under wraps. Or that the 2002 war in Afghanistan was briefly called "Infinite Justice," altered to "Enduring Freedom" in the wake of complaints that only God offers infinite justice. Amcap represents a significant advance over Ingsoc.

## THE ROLE AND MECHANISMS OF THOUGHT CONTROL

In fact, a good case can be made that propaganda is a more important means of social control in open societies like the United States than in closed societies like the late Soviet Union. In the former, the protection of inequalities of wealth and power, which frequently exceed those in totalitarian societies, cannot rest on the use of force, and as political scientist Harold Lasswell explained back in 1933, this compels the dominant elite to manage the ignorant multitude "largely through propaganda."[2] Similarly, in his 1922 classic, *Public Opinion*, Walter Lippmann argued that "the common interests [sometimes called the "national interest"] very largely elude public opinion entirely, and can be managed only by a specialized class whose personal interests reach beyond the locality," "responsible" men who must "manufacture consent" among the thoughtless masses.[3] The claim that such collective action is impossible in a free society, and that it implies some form of conspiracy, is mistaken. This claim is refuted both by the record of collective action, discussed and illustrated briefly below, and by an examination of how Amcap is implemented. Amcap works in part because it is the responsible men (and women) who own and run newspapers, TV stations and networks, and the other power centers in society. They manage national affairs, and "cri-

[2] Harold Lasswell, "Propaganda," in *Encyclopedia of the Social Sciences* (New York: Macmillan, 1933).
[3] Walter Lippman, *Public Opinion* (New York: Harcourt, Brace and Company, 1922), 31–32, 248, 310.

ses in democracy" are identified by the fact that, as in the infamous 1960s, important sectors of the usually apathetic general population organize and press hard for recognition of their needs. The power of this responsible elite is also reflected in society's ideological assumptions and ways of thinking about issues, as this elite manages the flow of advertising and the work of public relations firms and think tanks, as well as controlling access to the mass media. It takes only a small extension of Beckerian analysis—which insists on economic motives explaining virtually anything—to understand how a powerful demand for particular lines of economic and political thought might well elicit an appropriate supply response, which will be a "responsible" economics and politics that serves the "national interest."

This system of thought control is not centrally managed, although sometimes the government orchestrates a particular propaganda campaign. It operates mainly by individual and market choices, with the frequent collective service to the national interest arising from common interests and internalized beliefs. The responsible men (and women) often disagree on tactics, but not on premises, ends, and the core ideology of a free market system. What gives this system of thought control its power and advantage over Ingsoc is that its members truly believe in Amcap, and their passion in its exposition and defense is sincere. In their patriotic ardor they put forth, accept, and internalize untruths and doublethink as impressive as anything portrayed in *Nineteen Eighty-Four.* But at the same time they allow controversy to rage freely, although within bounds, so that debate appears to be fully open when it is in fact sharply constrained. And if the responsibles agree that the "national interest" calls for a military budget of $400 billion, this is not even subject to any debate whatever, even though studies of public opinion have regularly shown that the "proles" would like that budget sharply cut.[4]

Occasionally the powerful do use the police and armed forces, and sometimes covert programs of disinformation and disruption—as in the CIA's Operation Chaos and the FBI's Cointelpro programs—to keep oppositional movements under control.[5] More frequent are propaganda campaigns to sell policy to the general population. In 1983—only one year before the time imagined in *Nineteen Eighty-Four*—the Reagan administration organized a so-called Office of Public Diplomacy to sell its

[4] See Steven Kull, "Americans on Defense Spending: A Study of Public Attitudes," Report on Findings, Program on International Policy Attitudes, School of Public Affairs (University of Maryland, June 19, 1996).

[5] Nelson Blackstock, *Cointelpro: The FBI's Secret War on Political Freedom* (New York: Vintage, 1975); Frank Donner, *The Age of Surveillance* (New York: Vintage, 1981).

war against Nicaragua to the media and general public. Run by a CIA specialist in psychological warfare, it was explicitly designed to demonize the left-wing Sandinista government of Nicaragua by tactics that included the spread of disinformation. An office to engage in covert "public diplomacy" with the American people, its specific program titled "Operation Truth," sounds like something straight out of *Nineteen Eighty-Four*. But it was successful, as the media rarely if ever mentioned or criticized the OPD or Operation Truth.[6]

One manifestation of this accommodation provides us with an almost perfect illustration of doublethink in action. The Reagan administration wanted to build public support for the government of El Salvador, so it sponsored elections there in 1982 and 1984, in which it highlighted the high voter turnout and long lines of smiling voters, and played down the legal requirement to vote, the destruction of the two independent newspapers, the ongoing state terror, and the inability of the Left to enter candidates. In the very same time frame, the Sandinista government of Nicaragua held an election, but here the Reagan administration wished to deny the government legitimacy, so it used a different set of criteria to judge that election. Here it ignored the high turnout and smiling voters (and the absence of a legal requirement to vote) and focused on the harassment of *La Prensa* and the voluntary refusal to participate by one oppositional candidate (who was on the CIA payroll). In a miracle of doublethink, forgetting a set of electoral criteria "and then, when it becomes necessary again, [drawing] it back from oblivion" (177), the *New York Times* and its confreres followed the Reagan agenda and called the Nicaraguan election a "sham" on the basis of criteria they had completely ignored in finding the Salvadoran elections heartwarming moves toward democracy.[7]

## AMCAP AND AMERIGOOD AND THEIR CHALLENGES

There are two dominant strands of thought in Amcap. One is that America is a global paterfamilias that does good and pursues benevolent and democratic ends. This has a Newspeak corollary that we may call Amerigood.

The second strand of Amcap thought and ideology is the belief in the "miracle of the market" and the view that the market can do it all. In this

---

[6] For an account of OPD and Operation Truth, see Peter Kornbluh, *Nicaragua: The Price of Intervention* (Washington, D.C.: Institute for Policy Studies, 1987), chap. 4.

[7] For details, Edward S. Herman and Noam Chomsky, *Manufacturing Consent: The Political Economy of the Mass Media* (New York: Pantheon Books, 1988 and 2002), chap. 3.

system of thought, and in its Newspeak counterpart, Marketspeak, the market is virtually a sacred totem, "reform" means a move toward a freer market irrespective of conditions or effects, and accolades to and proofs of the market's efficiency crowd the intellectual marketplace. This system corresponds closely to Orwell's "goodthink," a body of orthodox thought immune to evidence, and it approximates Orwell's view of the outlook of "the ancient Hebrew who knew, without knowing much else, that all nations other than his worshipped 'false gods' " (251).

There has been a major conflict between Amerigood and Marketspeak, however, in that market openings and a prized "favorable climate of investment" have often been expedited by military leaders willing to destroy trade unions, kill social democrats and radicals, and ruthlessly terminate democracy itself. The United States has very frequently supported those serving the market at the expense of human rights and democracy.[8] But Amerigood and Marketspeak have met this challenge brilliantly, with much greater efficiency than Ingsoc and Newspeak ever met the needs of the Soviet Union.

### *Resolution by Definition*

One mode of handling the problem in Amerigood is by an internalized belief system in which words with negative connotations simply cannot be applied to us. Thus this country is never an aggressor, terrorist, or sponsor of terrorism, by definition, whatever the correspondence of facts to standard definitions. Back in May 1983, for five successive days the Soviet radio broadcaster Vladimir Danchev castigated the Soviet assault on Afghanistan, calling it an "invasion" and urging the Afghans to resist. He was lauded as a hero in the U.S. media, and his temporary removal from the air was bitterly criticized. But in many years of study of the U.S. media performance during the Vietnam War, I have never found a single mainstream journalistic reference to a U.S. "invasion" of Vietnam or U.S. "aggression" there, although the United States was invited in, like the Soviets in Afghanistan, by its own puppet government lacking minimal legitimacy. There was no Danchev in the U.S. media. Here, as in Ingsoc, where "Big Brother is ungood" was "a self-evident absurdity" (254), the notion of the United States committing "aggression" was outside the pale of comprehensible thought.

---

[8] For details, Edward S. Herman, *The Real Terror Network* (Boston: South End Press, 1982), esp. chap. 3; Herman, "The United States versus Human Rights in the Third World," *Harvard Human Rights Journal*, Spring 1991; William Blum, *Rogue State* (Monroe, Me.: Common Courage Press, 2000).

### Resolution by Forgetting and Remembering according to Need

The intellectual mechanism of forgetting and remembering according to momentary need is also urgently important, because in Amerigood this country favors and actively promotes democracy abroad, whereas in real-world practice it supports democracy only very selectively. The pro-democracy stance can be emphasized when the United States attacks Cuba and passes a "Cuban Democracy Act," but the media do not discuss and reflect on the absence of a "Saudi Democracy Act" (and the presence of U.S. troops in Saudi Arabia to protect that authoritarian regime) in the same or nearby articles. In the case of the steadfast thirty-two-year U.S. support of Suharto's military regime, or its support of Marcos's dictatorship in the Philippines, it was necessary to forget that the United States was devoted to democracy, as long as these tyrants delivered a "favorable climate of investment." But once they ceased to be viable rulers, suddenly the U.S. concern for democracy moved front and center, and this occurred without the mainstream media's dwelling on the long positive support of autocracy, or looking closely at any compromising elements in the shift (such as continued support for the Indonesian army). In both cases, also, the media suddenly discovered that Suharto and Marcos had looted their countries (and U.S. aid) on a large scale, a point that had somehow escaped their attention while the looters were still serving the U.S. "national interest." This is a virtual media law and displays their dependable service in forgetting and remembering.

### Resolution by a Resort to the "Long Run"

Some "realists" and Marketspeak philosophers who believe that "what's good for America is good for the world" have a different way of reconciling U.S. support of dictators and state terrorists with the U.S. devotion to democracy. They argue that the support for a Castillo Branco in Brazil or Pinochet in Chile is pro-democracy because the freer markets they introduce will serve democracy in the long run. In Marketspeak there is in fact a strong tendency to make "freedom" synonymous with freedom of markets rather than political (or any other kind of) freedom. This tendency, plus the complaisance and even enthusiasm at the termination of democracy in the short run, suggests that elite interest in a "favorable climate of investment" may be stronger than any devotion to democracy. The realists' case also suffers from its use of an argument long projected onto Big Brother: namely, that ugly means are justified by a supposedly benign end and do not themselves contaminate and even contradict that end.

## Resolution by "Disappearing" People

In the world of Ingsoc, individuals become "unpeople" and simply disappear. In Amcap we have a comparable phenomenon whereby entire populations become expendable for political reasons, effectively "disappear" from the mainstream media, and can be massacred or starved without political cost. When the United States fights abroad, U.S. deaths are politically costly and must be avoided. From the Vietnam War era onward this has resulted in the increased use of capital-intensive warfare that reduces U.S. casualties but increases those of enemy soldiers and their civilian populations. But those casualties have no domestic political cost, and official and media reporting of such losses is exceedingly sparse, if not absent altogether. This permits large-scale killing of target forces and civilians who have been rendered "unpeople."

It also permits entire populations to be held hostage and starved to achieve some political objective. Back in 1996 former secretary of state Madeleine Albright replied to a question on the costs and benefits of the estimated death of half a million Iraqi children as a result of sanctions. When she said that this result of U.S. policy "was worth it,"[9] her calculus rested in part on the fact that with the help of the mainstream media the Iraqi children were "unpeople" whose deaths involved no political costs to U.S. leaders.

This process of dehumanization is also evident in the treatment of client state terror and mass killings. When Pol Pot killed large numbers in Cambodia between 1975 and 1978, official and media attention and indignation were great. When in the same years Indonesia invaded East Timor, killing an even larger fraction of the population than did Pol Pot, media attention was minimal and fell to zero in the *New York Times* as Indonesian terror reached its peak in 1977 and 1978. Indonesia was a U.S. client state providing a favorable climate of investment, and the mainstream media treatment of the East Timorese as an unpeople was closely coordinated with U.S. policy.[10]

Even more dramatic, when the priest Jerzy Popieluszko was murdered by the police of Communist Poland in 1984, U.S. official and media attention and indignation were intense. In fact, media coverage of the Popieluszko murder was greater than its coverage of the murder of one

---

[9] Albright's statement was made in answer to a question by Leslie Stahl on the CBS program *60 Minutes*, May 12, 1996.

[10] For details, Noam Chomsky and Edward S. Herman, *The Washington Connection and Third World Fascism* (Boston: South End Press, 1979), chap. 3; Edward S. Herman and David Peterson, "How the *New York Times* Protects Indonesian Terror in East Timor," *Z Magazine*, July/August, 1999.

hundred religious victims in Latin America in the 1970s and 1980s taken together, even though eight of these victims were U.S. citizens.[11] Popieluszko was a "worthy" victim, as he was killed by an enemy state and propaganda points could be scored against the enemy; the one hundred religious in Latin America were killed in U.S. client states, and attention to their victimization would have been inconvenient to U.S. policy ends. This channeling of benevolence toward Polish victims (and victims of Pol Pot) and away from victims in our own backyard (and in East Timor) made it possible for the leaders of the National Security States (and Indonesia) to kill large numbers with quiet support from the United States, and without disturbing the ideology of Amerigood.

## No Agreements with Demons Possible

As one other illustration of an Ingsoc analogue in Amcap, in Ingsoc, "any past or future agreement with him [the demonized enemy] was impossible. . . . The Party said that Oceania had never been in alliance with Eurasia. He, Winston Smith, knew that Oceania had been in alliance with Eurasia so short a time as four years ago" (32). In Amcap things are done more subtly. We simply pretend that our high moral stance in fighting the demon represents continuous policy, and the mainstream media cooperate by not discussing the subject.

After Pol Pot was overthrown by the Vietnamese in December 1978, the United States quietly supported him for more than a decade, giving him aid directly and indirectly, approving his retention of Cambodia's seat in the UN, and even bargaining to include him in the election process of the 1990s. The U.S. media kept this support for the demon under the rug. The United States invaded Panama and captured Noriega in 1989, allegedly because of his involvement in the drug trade, but actually because he failed to meet U.S. demands for support in the war against Nicaragua. Noriega had been involved in the drug trade for more than a decade previously without causing any withdrawal of U.S. support. The mainstream media did not discuss the earlier agreement with the demon.

Saddam Hussein became "another Hitler" on August 2, 1990, when he invaded Kuwait. All through the prior decade he had been given steady U.S. support in his war against Iran and thereafter. He had received billions in loans, access to weapons, and intelligence information on Iranian military deployments, and his use of chemical weapons against Iran and his own Kurds did not result in his being ostracized. Following August 2, 1990, when he became an enemy, it would be difficult to find in the

---

[11] For a full account, Herman and Chomsky, *Manufacturing Consent*, chap. 2.

mainstream media any reference to the fact that this demon "had been in alliance with the U.S. as short a time ago as" August 1, 1990.

The Taliban government in Afghanistan moved beyond the pale in 1998, following the bombing of two U.S. embassies in Africa by cadres affiliated with Osama bin Laden, who made his headquarters in Afghanistan. Then, following the deadly World Trade Center and Pentagon bombings on September 11, 2001, by terrorists allegedly linked to bin Laden, the Bush administration issued an ultimatum to the Taliban to deliver bin Laden and his al Qaeda cadres to this country or suffer the consequences. The Taliban not complying, U.S. forces attacked Afghanistan, deposed the Taliban, and installed a replacement government. Following 9/11, the Taliban government was declared to be monstrous and intolerable, even apart from its sheltering bin Laden, and this was the general view in the mainstream media. But here again, it would be hard to find mainstream news reports or commentary recounting these facts: that the Taliban and al Qaeda had been organized and supported by the United States and its allies Saudi Arabia and Pakistan in the 1980s to fight Soviet forces in Afghanistan, and that the United States had backed the Taliban's assumption of power in 1996 because that faction brought "stability" and might make possible the construction of an oil pipeline through Afghanistan.[12]

## MARKETSPEAK

As in the case of Ingsoc, Marketspeak serves to consolidate the power of the dominant elite. In Ingsoc, the claim that Big Brother could do it all served Party domination and Party economic advantage, and it helped contain the incomes of the proles. Marketspeak does the same for the dominant elite in America. Ingsoc helped assure "that economic inequality has been made permanent" (170), and Marketspeak has done the same here, even facilitating its substantial increase in recent decades.

In fact, in an interesting turnabout, the supposedly permanent condition of the victims of Ingsoc has proven to be impermanent (i.e., the Soviet Union was dissolved and its component parts have been struggling since 1989 to enter the world of Amcap and Marketspeak), whereas the victims of Amcap and Marketspeak in both the former Soviet Union and the West have been placed in the condition where, as Mrs. Thatcher so happily pronounced, "there is no alternative." The power of capital and finance to dominate elections, to limit policy options by the threat of their enhanced

---

[12] Ahmed Rashid, *Taliban: Militant Islam, Oil and Fundamentalism in Central Asia* (New Haven: Yale University Press, 2000); Michael T. Klare, "Bush's Master Oil Plan," *Alternet.-Org*, April 23, 2002.

mobility, and their domination of the means of communication has seem-ingly ended challenges to the policy dictates of capital. Under the regime of Ingsoc "there is no way in which discontent can become articulate" (171). Under the regime of Amcap and Marketspeak as well there is no way discontent can materialize in meaningful political choices or pro-grams; rather, it will be channeled into bursts of anger and scapegoating of "government" and other convenient targets.

Under the regime of Ingsoc, the proles were kept down by "heavy physi-cal work, the care of home and children, petty quarrels with neighbors, films, football, beer, and above all gambling" (61–62). Orwell mentioned television as a valuable diversionary instrument for keeping the proles in line. The transformation of U.S. commercial broadcasting into essentially an entertainment vehicle—with its heavy emphasis on films, football, and other sports and its virtual annihilation of any public service and public sphere role—is Amcap's and Marketspeak's clear improvement over the primitive workings of Ingsoc. The growth of lotteries and casinos, partly driven by capital's pressure on governments to seek funding outside of taxes, also improves on Ingsoc's methods of providing prole diversion and depoliticization.

Under the regime of Amcap and Marketspeak, the proles are kept down not only by physical work and diversions, but also by insecurity. In 1997, Fed chairman Allan Greenspan explained to Congress that the inflation threat was minimal because of a generalized worker insecurity, which he presented as a bonanza—although such insecurity would seem to be in itself a serious welfare detriment, on the assumption that the condition of the proles was an important policy consideration. His instrumental view of the proles can also be seen in economic theory, where the "natural rate of unemployment" ties inflation (the bad) very closely to excessive wage demands on the part of the proles.

This view of prole wage increases as a threat to the national interest is a throwback to mercantilist attitudes and doctrine, where high wages were deemed bad "because they would reduce England's competing power by raising production costs," in the words of the historian of mer-cantilism Edgar S. Furniss.[13] He notes that in this class-biased view of the national interest "the dominant class . . . attempt[ed] to bind the burdens upon the shoulders of those groups whose political power is too slight to defend them from exploitation and will find justification for its policies in the plea of national necessity." In this mercantilist and Marketspeak view of the proles, as a cost and instrument rather than a group whose

[13] Edgar S. Furniss, *The Position of the Laborer in a System of Nationalism* (Boston: Houghton Mifflin Co., 1920), 201, 203.

well-being is the policy objective, the proles, like citizens of an enemy state, become "unpersons."

The accommodations of economic science to the demands of Amcap and Marketspeak have been extensive, and in many of these cases the intellectual abuses and somersaults carried out to salvage Marketspeak are similar to those used to defend Ingsoc. As one example, during each merger wave from 1897–1903 onward, Marketspeak economists have found the movement to be based on efficiency considerations and have downgraded the importance of other bases of merger activity and any negative effects on competition. They have struggled valiantly to prove that the market works well in providing net public benefits here as elsewhere.

In recent years Marketspeak economists have done this by measuring the efficiency of mergers on the basis of stock price movements before and at the time of the merger, not postmerger results, although stock price measures suffer from problems of timing and contamination by influences other than efficiency, and they are at best indirect. In one classic of this genre, Michael Jensen and Richard Ruback, as an afterthought, did look at postmerger financial results, which turned out to show "systematic reductions in the stock price of bidding firms following the event."[14] They concluded that such results "are unsettling because they are inconsistent with market efficiency and suggest that changes in stock prices during takeovers overestimate the future efficiency gains from mergers." But as Marketspeak says that free market behavior enhances efficiency, the authors did not allow those "systematic" findings to alter their conclusions.

### CONCLUSION: A PROMISING AMCAP FUTURE

Ingsoc has given way to a potent replacement in Amcap, and Amcap has actually taken on more vitality with the death of Ingsoc. The ideologists of Amcap have proclaimed an "end of history": freedom and liberal democracy triumphant and doublethink and thought control presumably ended with the close of the system of tyranny. But such claims have little basis in reality. History has not "ended," and since the death of the Soviet Union, wars, political and economic instability, ethnic cleansing, the global polarization of incomes, and environmental distress and threats seem to have increased in frequency and/or intensity. Freedom and liberal democracy are increasingly constrained by national and global power structures that sharply limit any actions helpful to the proles.

[14] Michael Jensen and Richard Ruback, "The Market for Corporate Control: The Scientific Evidence," *Journal of Financial Economics* 5 (1983): 30.

In the increasingly inegalitarian system that prevails, Amcap, Amerigood, and Marketspeak are flourishing and have a more important role to play than ever. They have been doing their job—"largely the defense of the indefensible," as Orwell put it—with a sophistication and effectiveness that Ingsoc could never command. Their innovations in language are continuous, filling all emerging propaganda gaps. At home, a law encroaching on civil liberties is called a "Patriot Act"; laws that free the weak and poor from their "entitlements" by pushing them into the labor market are referred to as "reform" and "empowerment," and they are said to reflect "tough love" of the suffering proles. In military and foreign policy, a government agency openly designed to disseminate disinformation is called the "Office of Strategic Influence";[15] missiles are "Peacekeepers," and military alliances are "Partnerships for Peace." The appeasement of amenable state terrorists (Mobutu, Suharto, the governments of apartheid South Africa) is called "constructive engagement"; civilian deaths from the "humanitarian bombing" of "rogue states" are "collateral damage."

The progress and prospects of Amcap are impressive. This immensely powerful system of thought control should get the credit and recognition that it deserves.

---

[15] This organization was quickly closed down after receiving considerable negative publicity. However, the contract for services to be carried out on behalf of the Office of Strategic Influence was not canceled.

# Part III

POLITICAL COERCION

# Mind Control in Orwell's *Nineteen Eighty-Four*: Fictional Concepts Become Operational Realities in Jim Jones's Jungle Experiment

### PHILIP G. ZIMBARDO

IMAGINE THAT your Enemy's mission is to control your every thought, feeling, and action so that they become alienated from the core of your being. The State assumes their ownership as part of its master plan for the total domination of you and the wills of all your kin. Consider further how you feel when you discover that the goals of this omnipotent Enemy are boldly proclaimed thus: "to extinguish once and for all the possibility of independent thought" (159); to eliminate the conditions that enable even one "erroneous thought [to] exist anywhere in the world" (210); to crush the core of humaneness so that no person is "capable of ordinary human feeling" (211); and for good final measure, to enforce such total obedience to its authority that every citizen is "prepared to commit suicide, if and when we order you to do so" (142).

Now imagine further that this terrifying Enemy is not some external force emanating from a foreign nation, but it is your own Government; it is The Party of your Government. How do you resist becoming a brainwashed, gut-cleansed slave of such a system? How do you instigate a rebellion, organizing the might of the minority who do not want to be controlled and dehumanized by their own government?

Before you can start to develop a plan of resistance, you must understand the strategy and tactics of mind control being put into operation by your Enemy. In this battle of the Forces of Inhuman Totalitarian Control against the Spirit of Every Man and Every Woman, the system loses if even one person is able to maintain autonomy, preserve free will, and sustain a sense of compassion for fellow human beings. The absolute power of this oppressive system is threatened by the presence of even a single dissident, someone who can laugh at its pretentiousness, energized by remembering when life was different and better, and by imagining future realities, future possible selves, with meaningful options and viable choices. But the System views such dissidents as "a stain that must be wiped out" (210). And the Party uses all its might to cleanse such stains from the fabric of its domination.

George Orwell gives us a model of resistance, the reluctant hero Winston Smith, who stands against the omnipotence of the *Nineteen Eighty-Four* version of the System. What can we learn from his trials and tribulations that may help us cope more effectively with the contemporary version of the System that has been operating since Orwell shared his insights with us some fifty years ago? What is the reality of his fictional portrayal of mega-governments at war for the control of the human mind? Are there significant lessons to be learned about dealing with current and future threats to our freedom and liberty? My answers come packaged in six parts.

First outlined are Orwell's views of what is essential in human nature, since they form a "reversed blueprint" that reveals the justifications for his use of so many different devices of mind control, each of which is designed to undermine a particular aspect of humanity.

Next reviewed are the key features of those exotic mind control devices—the psychological technologies for modifying behavior and altering the functions of the mind—that Orwell "gifts" to the System.

The issue of the malleability of man, and of course, woman, when pitted against powerful situational forces, is then analyzed. I show how Winston, like most of us, increases his vulnerability to social influence, while paradoxically believing he is becoming more resistant, by making what is known as "the Fundamental Attribution Error." Social-psychological research on situational power illustrates this dual tendency to overestimate individual strength and character while underestimating the force of subtle aspects of the social situation when we try to understand what causes us to act as we do.

A contrast is presented showing what it takes to become a "True Believer" instead of merely a Party Conformist, and demonstrating that the System errs in seeking only group conformity and individual compliance; the vital process of seeding its ideology for future growth without constant external control must rely, rather, upon the internalization of its persuasive message.

Briefly illustrated is how Orwell's fictional mind control conceptions have been embraced, extended, and made more powerful by modern influence peddlers in our real world. We see this among those who would cure, care for, convert, and educate us. Most notably featured is the CIA in its MK-ULTRA program, used against many unwitting Americans from the 1950s to the 1970s, and probably well beyond that time.

Finally, I advance the hypothesis that the processes that led to the mass suicide/mass murders of 912 U.S. citizens in the jungles of Guyana in 1978—orchestrated by their reverend Jim Jones, pastor of the Peoples

Temple—were borrowed wholesale from Orwell. Jones's dominating mind control approaches were modeled directly on many of the strategies and tactics of mind and body control that he learned as a student of Orwell's System in *Nineteen Eighty-Four*. It became the Devil's bible that replaced Jones's Christian Bible.

## WHAT IS THE ORWELLIAN VIEW OF HUMAN NATURE AS REVEALED IN HIS MIND CONTROL TECHNOLOGIES?

Each of *Nineteen Eighty-Four*'s technologies of mind control is aimed at either undermining or overwhelming some personal attribute central to the human spirit.

- For freedom of action there is Obedience Training.
- For freedom of association and interpersonal trust there is Social Isolation, Enforced Solitude, and the Spy Network.
- For independence of one's thought there is Newspeak, Thought Control, and the Thought Police.
- For reality-based perceptions and decisions there is Sense Impression Denial, Doublethink, and Reality Control.
- For human pride there are pernicious Interrogation Tactics and the humiliating terrors of one's most terrible fears realized in the living nightmare of Room 101.
- For sharing tender sentiments with friends and loved ones, there is Aversive Emotional Conditioning, elimination of sexual impulses, and the implementation of pro-war, hateful emotions.
- The use of language to convey and focus cognitive functions is devastated by Crimestop and Newspeak.
- Personal privacy and solitude wither under the glare of Big Brother's Telescreen Surveillance.
- Individuality, eccentricity, and diversity also yield to the forces of Crimestop.
- A sense of Self that is based on personally experienced events stored in episodic memory is no match for the Ministry of Truth's falsification tactics of selective amnesia.

Orwell confronts us with some of the most profound questions about human existence. What is reality? What is truth? What are the central, most vital qualities of the human psyche? What happens when intelligence is allowed free rein without constraint by compassionate feelings or social conscience? And can an individual survive in an inhospitable environment without the tangible support of a social group, family and friends, or the spiritual support of a religious-mythical ideology?

## *What Is Unique and to Be Valued in the Human Condition?*

By illustrating what can happen when our basic assumptions and beliefs are negated or reversed, Orwell forces us to see anew what there is to value, and thus preserve against all odds, in sustaining the beauty and meaning of the Human Condition. The uniqueness of our species and of each individual emanates from the combination of intelligence, consciousness, motivation, and affect.

> *Intelligence* gives us the capacity to learn, to remember, to imagine alternatives, to transform current existence.
>
> *Consciousness* gives us the awareness of the self as a uniquely time-bound entity able to distinguish inner from external realities, wishes from what is, and to construct a worldview of potentialities that transforms our vision beyond the constraints of current actualities.
>
> *Motivation* energizes human resolve, moves us from intention to action, enables us to persevere toward goals despite adversity.
>
> *Affect* colors the quality of experience in infinitely complex hues that enrich it and transport us beyond a life limited to the experiencing of animal pleasures and pains.

### *Time Perspective*

However, vital to each of these fundamental functions is the development of a balanced temporal perspective that optimally blends conceptions of past, present, and future. The human mind is designed to partition the flow of experience into these temporal categories and thereby to enrich our experiences by becoming totally enmeshed in what was, is, and will be at any given moment. A focus on the past connects us to our roots, to our sense of self over time, and is critical for the development of a sense of personality. A focus on the hedonistic present nourishes daily existence with the joys of playfulness and sensuality. A focus on the future gives people wings to soar to new heights of achievement. People need this temporal trilogy harmoniously operating in a balanced perspective to realize fully their human potential. This uniquely human temporal perspective, in recognizing its own frailty and mortal limits, serves to establish principles of justice and a transcendent vision of spiritual life. Anything that limits use of a part of this temporal trilogy, such as eliminating the past, constraining the future, or restricting the present, creates a cognitive bias that distorts the fullest use of our mental faculties.

## Social Support

But the social psychologist in me asserts that beyond all these human attributes, in order to thrive people need to be part of a society that reasonably and equitably trades off self-interests, rights, and privileges with social obligations that foster the common good. People need other people to create a system of supportive interdependence, a bonded unit that helps each to resist assaults from destructive influences in the physical, social, and political environments. One of the most important lessons from modern social sciences, psychiatry, and epidemiology is that social isolation is the cause and consequence of a host of pathologies of both body and mind. And its corollary is that being part of a social support network is the most effective prophylaxis against mental and physical illnesses. Anything that isolates us from our kin kills the human spirit; anything that makes us feel anonymous perverts the human spirit into not caring for others—and makes vandalism and violence more probable. Orwell recognizes this essence of human nature and encourages us to reflect on its vitality and tenuousness by acknowledging how easily it can be corrupted, transformed, destroyed—as much by a totalitarian enemy force as by a brain disease or a paralyzing stroke.

## A MIND CONTROLLER'S CATALOG

Let us briefly review some of the main strategies for transferring Self-Control to Party Control.

## Obedience Training

Obedience training enforces unquestioned submission to the will of authority. The individual develops a behavioral intention to act on command by repeatedly agreeing "to cheat, to forge, to blackmail, to corrupt the minds of children, to distribute habit-forming drugs ... " (142). Author C. P. Snow reminds us that more crimes against human nature have been committed in the name of obedience than in the name of rebellion. The blind obedience to authority that characterized Eichmann's defense and that of other Nazi criminals was not fashioned by Hitler or Himmler; it was originally nurtured by elementary school teachers issuing coercive rules to stay seated until given permission to move, and a host of other forms of authoritarian and sometimes mindless rules of discipline. The problem is that our teachers and parents never taught us how to discriminate between just and unjust authority when they both demand our obedience and the resistance and opposition we owe the latter must be as strong as the respect and amenability we grant the former.

## Newspeak

Newspeak diminishes the range of thought by cutting the choice of words to a minimum (247). "Every year fewer and fewer words, and the range of consciousness always a little smaller" (46). By canceling a lexicon of purged words, such as honor, justice, morality, and democracy, Newspeak abolished the underlying concepts that they expressed. Then, through the substitution of new words for old concepts, all conceptual analysis came to be meaningless and therefore stopped; liberty and justice became *crimethink*, objectivity and rationalism became *oldthink*, and sexual relations not state prescribed became *sexcrime*.

## Crimestop

Crimestop goes beyond destroying and simplifying language to distort basic cognitive functions. "It includes the power of not grasping analogies, of failing to perceive logical errors, of misunderstanding the simplest arguments if they are inimical to Ingsoc. . . . *Crimestop*, in short, means protective stupidity. . . . a control over one's own mental processes as complete as that of a contortionist over his body" (174–75).

## Doublethink

Doublethink "is a vast system of mental cheating" (177) in which doubt and certainty coexist about the same event that one can honestly say never happened, knowing that it is deceptive to so state. By involving the person as his own agent of conscious self-deception, Doublethink frees Party members to engage in more strenuous forms of interrogation (199–200) and torture (202 ff.).

Doublethink is similar to "trance logic" among hypnotized subjects when they try to create a rational explanation for an irrational perception of a hallucinatory experience suggested by the hypnotist. At one level of consciousness, they know the hallucination they are experiencing is not an empirically valid perception, while at the same time, at another level of consciousness, they do not grasp that fact and believe the suggested hallucination is real. Thus they vigorously try to rationalize this anomaly to themselves and to others in order to make sense of the nonsensical experience. Doublethink similarly induces doubt and the need for the person to convince him- or herself that what is not really should be so.

## Reality Control

Reality Control is Oldspeak for what in Newspeak would be a primary function of Doublethink, "to reject the evidence of your eyes and ears" (69). The process of abolishing reliance on external reality as the validation check for internal perceptions, beliefs, and desires wipes away the fundamental dualisms of internal-external, subjective-objective, and covert, private mental activities as separate entities from their overt, public statement. Without these dualities, can there be any absolutes in truth and reality or freedom of choice? Schizophrenic patients reverse the ordinary validity checks of internal beliefs assessed against criteria anchored in external reality. Instead, they validate external reality by its fit with their subjective, idiosyncratic reality. In *Nineteen Eighty-Four*, Reality Control forces individual subjective reality to be determined by Party consensus; reality is the Collective Subjective.

## Big Brother Is Watching You

Telescreen surveillance permanently intrudes an external presence into the once private life of every individual, thereby making privacy a criminal luxury. "Always the eyes watching you. . . . working or eating, indoors or out of doors, in the bath or in bed—no escape. Nothing was your own except the few cubic centimeters inside your skull" (26), and each day that private vault was being robbed of some of its contents. Surveillance has a psychological "chilling effect" in suppressing individual actions through intimidation and feelings of powerlessness, above and beyond the objective facts of the surveillance itself.

Beyond this omnipresent Telescreen intrusion of Big Brother is an even more sinister mind control tactic used in *Nineteen Eighty-Four* by the Party. Institutionalized spying by friends, family, and neighbors eliminates interpersonal trust—the basis for a social support network—and in its place distrust, suspicion, and conspiracy theories abound. When social bonds are broken, social isolation becomes common, and individuals exist in "locked loneliness" that diminishes the human spirit. In prisons, the worst crime a prisoner can commit in violation of the prisoner's code of conduct is to become a snitch, an informer for the guards. Whenever there is a prison riot, the first people to be brutally murdered by prisoners are usually these informers. Hitler also institutionalized rewards for children spying on and informing against parents, as did Jim Jones for all members of his church, providing them with powerful incentive to inform against anyone expressing the least dissidence.

### Emotional Control

Emotional control in *Nineteen Eighty-Four* meant "there will be no emotions except fear, rage, triumph, and self-abasement. Everything else we shall destroy—everything" (220). Orwell utilizes a variant of what was in his time a new conditioning paradigm in clinical psychology, aversive emotional conditioning. Practitioners change emotions by visually exposing people to various emotional stimuli and then gradually fading out responses to originally strong stimuli, while fading in a new stimulus to-be-hated. This is achieved through the generalization of the negative emotion elicited by the first stimulus to any new person, object, or symbolic concept now associated with that feeling of hate or fear. (Some psychotherapists in the 1950s and 1960s used such aversive conditioning to try to induce homosexuals to loathe the sight of pictures of naked men they had previously desired, and to transfer that sexual desire so that they would be aroused by pictures of female bodies.)

But Orwell adds a nice Nietzschean twist to this emotional conditioning by showing us how the Dionysian side of human nature revels in destruction and is intoxicated with the unlimited, mindless passion for power. It is that irrational, chaotic, libertine aspect of every human being that bursts free from the control of our Apollonian rationally guiding vision by joining in the revels of the mob mentality. The Two Minutes Hate exercise lured even the reluctant into its "hideous ecstasy of fear and vindictiveness, a desire to kill, to torture, to smash faces in with a sledge hammer" (16).

When exclusive Party loyalty was threatened by passions and the spontaneous seeking of intimate pleasure, the Party punished such *sexcrime*. It is more difficult to dehumanize those who are in touch with primitive instincts, who are intimately connected with another person as a vital physical unit that might resist more vigorously than either partner in an isolated test-tube existence. "The sex impulse was dangerous to the Party, and the Party had turned it to its account" (111). Emotions are what separate men from robots, giving us both our animal and our human nature, and when the State wants people to act as its robots, then emotions must go.

## *Time Manipulation*

Perhaps the Party's most potent technology for mind control was its insidious manipulation of time. The Ministry of Truth fabricated the past by deleting all records that were not acceptable to its belief system, while rewriting others to fit current ideology. "Day by day and almost minute by minute the past was brought up to date" (36). "The Party could thrust its hand into the past and say of this or that event, *it never happened. . . .* 'Who controls the past,' ran the Party slogan, 'controls the future: who controls the present controls the past.' And yet the past, though of its nature alterable, never had been altered. . . . All that was needed was an unending series of victories over your own memory" (32).

What follows then is the bleakest question of the successful mind controller and his or her horrified subject: "If both the past and the external world exist only in the mind, and the mind itself is controllable [by the confluence of these mind control technologies]—what then?" (69). Curiously, and foreshadowing my concluding remarks, Jim Jones had erected above his throne in the jungles of Guyana a simple painted sign with the powerful message "Those who do not remember the past, are condemned to repeat it." These foreboding words of American philosopher George Santayana are also inscribed on a Holocaust memorial outside Munich, near the Dachau concentration camp, with "relive it" in place of Jones's "repeat it."

## THE MALLEABILITY OF HUMAN NATURE

Thus we see that the Party's ambitious experimental objective was destroying every independent mind in all human creatures. Dr. Frankenstein's fictional achievement in discovering the secret for infusing the spark of life in dead creatures pales in comparison to the Party's fictional achievement: "We make the laws of nature," and O'Brien might add, "we can undo them" (218). The Party represents a master analytical intelligence striving toward an ideal of omniscience and omnipotence—but unconstrained by moral values, ethical principles, and love, it becomes a monster-maker run amok, worse than the feared Frankenstein solitary monster.

O'Brien, the Party's spokesperson, says, "You are imagining that there is something called human nature which will be outraged by what we do and will turn against us. But we create human nature. Men are infinitely malleable" (222). Is that doctrine of the total malleability of man and woman another Orwellian fiction? Listen to the rhetoric of some of the most influential realists from our world of fact:

"Give us the child for eight years, and it will be a Bolshevist forever," wrote
Lenin, in 1923;

"Give me a dozen healthy infants," wrote J. B. Watson, the pioneer of American behaviorism, in 1926, "well-formed, and my own specified world to
bring them up in and I'll guarantee to take any one at random and train
him to become any type of specialist I might select, doctor, lawyer, artist, merchant-chief, and yes, even into beggar-man and thief, regardless
of his talents, penchants, tendencies, abilities, vocations, and race of his
ancestors";

"An agitator who is capable of communicating an idea to the masses has to
be a psychologist, even though he be but a demagogue. He will always be
better as a leader than the retiring theorist who knows nothing about men.
For leadership means ability to move masses of men," Hitler told the world
in *Mein Kampf* in 1933.[1]

These master mind controllers all work on the Orwellian principle that
situational forces can overwhelm the defenses and resilience of the individual. We would all prefer to think it was otherwise. Indeed, coming
from a society whose dominant values are individualistic, where people
get the credit for their success and the blame for failure, we are led down
a narrow cognitive pathway to accepting a pair of false assumptions about
the causes of human actions. Unfortunately, doing so increases our vulnerability to mind control attempts and our malleability to influence professionals—exactly the opposite of our intention when we assert our sense
of individual strength over the forces of external situations.

We commonly believe that we have more strength to resist behavior-
modifying attempts than we really have. We rely on the abstractions of
"force of character," "spirit of self-determination," "ego strength" to
steel us against assaults on our personal values and beliefs. That is the
belief in the power of dispositional determinants of behavior, good and
evil residing within individual psyches. But at the same time, we entertain
a second misperception by underestimating the true power of social pressures to make people conform, comply, and obey. This dual tendency is
called the Fundamental Attribution Error, overestimating person power
and underestimating situational power, when we try to understand the

---

[1] Behaviorist John B. Watson made this bold assertion in 1926 in a provocative essay,
"What the Nursery Has to Say about Instincts," in *Psychologies of 1925*, ed. C. Murchison
(Worcester, Mass.: Clark University Press), 1–34. Bolshevist revolutionary Vladimir Lenin's
belief in the persuasive power of his ideological beliefs prompted this proclamation in a
speech to the Commissars of Education, 1923. Fascist dictator Adolph Hitler forewarned
the world in 1933 about his intentions of conquest in *Mein Kampf* or *My Battle*, trans.
E.T.S. Dugdale (Boston: Houghton Mifflin Co., 1933), 250.

reasons for any behavior, or try to predict behavioral outcomes.[2] Paradoxically, we, like Winston Smith, become more vulnerable to mind control attempts to the extent that we deceive ourselves into believing we are personally invulnerable and can will ourselves to resist, so we do not realistically appraise the ubiquitous influences that operate in social norms, rules, roles, uniforms, contracts, peer pressure, authority models, authoritative signs, and more such features of our behavioral setting.

## The Lessons of Contemporary Social Psychology

Orwell's fictional depiction of the concept of the "power of the situation" has had many counterparts in our nation's social psychology laboratories. The first lesson of social psychology is that social situations can exert powerful influences over human behavior. The situation matters more in controlling the behavior of individuals and groups than we suspect or possibly believe it could. Behavior always takes place in a context, and that context shapes and defines what behavior is appropriate, gets rewarded or punished, gets emulated by others or is ignored. The second lesson underscores the importance of the personal meaning of the situation to the actor. Functional reality is created in the mind of the person in a behavioral setting by that actor's cognitive construals, personal values, and biases, as well as by the consensual validation of group members—the mind matters. The third lesson is that individuals behave differently when they are faced with group pressure and have a group identity than when alone—groups matter.

In the most notable demonstration of situational power, my colleague Stanley Milgram[3] demonstrated how easy it was to get the majority of research participants, from among a thousand people of diverse backgrounds, to believe they were electrocuting a stranger on the orders of an authority figure, and to carry out his command to deliver the maximum of 450 volts of shock to a mild-mannered, pleasant man, the victim. They did so not from malice or evil motives; rather, they did so from distorted pro-social motives, wanting to help science, to help education, to help this researcher. Their blind obedience to authority came not from the charismatic appeals of a Hitler or a Saddam Hussein, but from accepting a role as teacher, agreeing to a behavioral contract, and following the

---

[2] L. Ross, "The Intuitive Psychologist and His Shortcomings: Distortion in the Attribution Process," in *Advances in Experimental Social Psychology*, ed. L. Berkowitz, vol. 10 (New York: Academic Press, 1977), 173–220.

[3] S. Milgram, *Obedience to Authority* (New York: Harper and Row, 1974).

white-coated experimenter's injunction, "Teacher, you must continue to shock, the rules state that . . . "

Curiously, while two-thirds of the subjects were totally obedient in this paradigm, when Milgram's protocol was described in detail to forty mental health experts, they underestimated the extent of compliance, concluding that fewer than 1 percent would go all the way to deliver the ultimate shock level, and then only the sadists, they said. How could these expert judges of human behavior have been so wrong? The answer: the Fundamental Attribution Error at work, since these professionals are trained to see pathology in the minds of individuals and not in situational forces. Across a series of nineteen separate experiments, Milgram was able to reduce this obedience to 10 percent or escalate it up to 90 percent by changing one variable in the situation in each study. The effect vanishes when the victim demands to be shocked, and it is highest when the subject first witnesses a peer modeling the blind obedience to authority.[4]

My own research on the psychology of deindividuation also underscores the truth in some of Orwell's analyses. College students made to feel part of an anonymous group were much more likely to hurt innocent victims than were comparison research subjects who felt individuated in that setting. Women participants administered twice as much shock to other women when they felt anonymous—wearing hoods, in the dark, in a group, names replaced by numbers—than did those who were in the same situation but not anonymous.[5] Anthropological research supports and extends this general conclusion about the destructive power of anonymity. It was shown that the majority of societies that prepare young men for war by first changing their appearance through painted faces or masks tend to kill, mutilate, and torture their captives significantly more than do warriors in other comparable cultures that do not undergo this anonymity-inducing ritual.[6] Cultural wisdom acknowledges that for young men to kill other young men in wars, usually fashioned by old men, the most effective preparation is to arrange for them to make an external transformation of identity so they can do normally evil deeds with impunity.

Similarly, anonymity conferred not by masks or costumes but by living in an anonymity-conferring environment increases the probability of destructive vandalism, as I showed in a field study in which cars were abandoned in the Bronx, New York, and Palo Alto, California, all near a local

---

[4] See T. Blass, ed., *Obedience to Authority: Current Perspectives on the Milgram Paradigm* (Mahwah, N.J.: Erlbaum, 2000).

[5] G. Zimbardo, "The Human Choice: Individuation, Reason, and Order versus Deindividuation, Impulse, and Chaos," in *1969 Nebraska Symposium on Motivation*, ed. W. J. Arnold and D. Levine, vol. 27 (Lincoln: University of Nebraska Press, 1970), 237–307.

[6] R. J. Watson, "Investigation into Deindividuation Using a Cross-Cultural Survey Technique," *Journal of Personality and Social Psychology* 25 (1973): 342–45.

college. Only in the anonymity of life in the urban New York setting was vandalism unleashed immediately and furiously, within minutes of the car's being left on the street with its hood lifted and license plate removed. In the course of two days there were twenty-three separate daytime destructive contacts with that car, all but one by adults, many well dressed or driving by in their own cars. In the Palo Alto community, no one touched the similarly abandoned car left on the streets for a full week, and when I removed the car, three neighbors alerted the police that an abandoned car was being stolen.[7] That is one definition of a social community, where neighbors care about the person and property of others within the realm of their territory, with the assumption of reciprocal caring. Contrariwise, a sense of personal anonymity engages such thoughts as "nobody knows or cares who I am, so my behavior is not under public scrutiny or personal accountability." Community then becomes a jungle of self-interest and exploitation.

Another demonstration of the power of situations to induce pathological behavior in normal individuals, even without the intense pressures of an ever present authority figure commanding them, is the Stanford Prison Experiment.[8] College students enacted randomly assigned roles of prisoners and guards within the setting of a simulated prison, in an experiment planned to run for two weeks. But I had to terminate the study prematurely after only six days because it had gotten out of control. Young men we had premeasured on a battery of psychological tests, and had selected because of their normality across many dimensions, were suffering emotional breakdowns and irrational thinking if they were the powerless mock prisoners. Those enacting the mock guard role became abusive and hostile, and some even qualified as sadistic torturers—despite being avowed pacifists and normal on all prior personality measures. The inhumanity of the evil prison situation had come to totally dominate the humanity of most of the good people who were trapped in that total situation. I had to end this experiment because the sight of the malleability of human character was too much for me to witness among some of the best and the brightest of our nation's youth.[9]

Can we demonstrate that our mental construction of social situations influences significant behavioral outcomes in positive directions as well as negative? Yes, indeed, as seen in research that modified health and

[7] G. Zimbardo, "A Field Experiment in Auto Shaping," in *Vandalism*, ed. C. Ward (London: Architectural Press, 1973), 85–99.

[8] G. Zimbardo, C. Haney, W. C. Banks, and D. Jaffe, "The Mind Is a Formidable Jailer: A Pirandellian Prison," *New York Times Magazine*, April 8, 1973, 3 ff.

[9] G. Zimbardo, C. Maslach, and C. Haney, "Reflections on the Stanford Prison Experiment: Genesis, Transformations, Consequences," in Blass, *Obedience to Authority*, 193–237.

mortality outcomes in elderly patients living in a home for the aged.[10] Some patients were asked to make active choices about minor aspects of their dinner menu or movie schedule and given the responsibility of caring for a gift plant, while comparable other patients were randomly assigned to a no-choice, no-responsibility condition. These comparison patients functioned under standard care procedures of the institution, remaining passively tended by the staff. Three weeks later these two groups diverged, with the choice/responsibility patients reporting feeling happier, more alert, and more active than the controls. A year and a half later this seemingly minor variation in their sense of personal choice and personal responsibility translated into nurses' ratings of greater vigor and sociability, and doctors' assessment that these patients' health was better than that of the control subjects. Finally, the researchers discovered that those with this rather minimal new meaning in their generally bleak existence lived significantly longer than those peers without such a sense of choice and responsibility. The mind matters and situations matter, even in issues of life and death.

The classic demonstration of social psychology's lesson of the power of groups comes from the "Asch effect."[11] College student participants found themselves in a perception study of judgments of the relative sizes of lines. When subjects were alone, their judgments were very accurate, but when they were in a group, their judgments were very distorted. The group was composed of experimental confederates who, after several honest trials, gave consensus false judgments that diverged from the obvious perceptual reality. Long lines were judged to be the same size as much shorter standards or vice versa on various trials. The group norm exerted a powerful influence over the individual judgments even in this highly structured, unambiguous perceptual judging situation—on 70 percent of the critical trials there was at least one conforming error, and fully a third of all participants conformed on the majority of critical trials. Seeing is not believing when your group says big is small, black is bad, war is good, or terrorism is virtue.

Concluding this brief detour into some social psychology laboratories to illustrate the validity of some of Orwell's stated and implied assumptions about situational power, mind manipulation, and the power of the group, we return to the main themes of our story.

---

[10] E. J. Langer and J. Rodin, "The Effects of Choice and Enhanced Personal Responsibility for the Aged: A Field Experiment in an Institutional Setting," *Journal of Personality and Social Psychology* 34 (1976): 191–98; J. Rodin and E. J. Langer, "Long Term Effects of a Control-Relevant Intervention with Institutionalized Aged," *Journal of Personality and Social Psychology* 35 (1977): 897–902.

[11] S. E. Asch, "Studies of Independence and Conformity: A Minority of One against a Unanimous Majority," *Psychological Monographs* 70, no. 416 (1951).

## CREATING TRUE BELIEVERS

The major weakness in the mind control armament with which Orwell endowed the Party is the *visibility or transparency of its coercive power.* Winston and his countrymen knew they were being controlled, both the How and the Who, since the Party wanted full credit for its victories over their psyches. O'Brien declares: "Always, at every moment, there will be the thrill of victory, the sensation of trampling on an enemy who is help-less. If you want a picture of the future, imagine a boot stamping on a human face—forever" (220).

Coercive controls create compliant conformists while the boot is in your butt or on your face. We know from psychological research on atti-tude change that people who perceive their discrepant acts as justified by the magnitude of the pressures on them comply publicly but do not accept privately.[12] They surrender, they yield, but they do not internalize the new ideology. To become a True Believer requires attitude and value change under conditions where there is at least an illusion of personal choice and insufficient extrinsic justification for changing. The cognitive dissonance created by the belief that one's alien action was intrinsically motivated comes to transform the person into an agent of self-persuasion, and that leads to the most enduring form of attitude/value/behavior change: it leads to becoming a True Believer.[13]

This point has been amply demonstrated in the overthrow of Eastern European Communist regimes that had ruled for decades with an iron boot on the backs of citizens. The people conformed to the dominating rules of the Party but did not internalize the ideology. At the first sign of weakness in the might of Communist Party control, they rebelled. Throughout time, governments have tried to enslave people, but people have resisted and in some cases successfully revolted to gain their freedom and liberty.

A related point of contention is the Party's error in relying on technol-ogy to do the work of mind control. It is not so much exotic tactics, like hypnosis and drugs, and high-tech devices that influence attitudes and values in directed paths as it is the most mundane aspects of human expe-rience. Effective mind control is best platformed on people's basic needs to be loved, respected, recognized, and wanted. It comes from the power of desired social groups that can reject deviants and embrace believers.

[12] G. Zimbardo and M. Leippe, *The Psychology of Attitude Change and Social Influence* (New York: McGraw-Hill, 1991).

[13] L. Festinger, *A Theory of Cognitive Dissonance* (Stanford: Stanford University Press, 1957); G. Zimbardo, *The Cognitive Control of Motivation* (Glenview, Ill.: Scott, Foresman, 1969).

Let us, then, in our analysis of human action, recast the definition of the Fundamental Attribution Error as a mental bias underestimating the true power of these mundane social-situational determinants of human action, while overcrediting external physical forces and nebulous dispositional qualities of the actors.

## CONTEMPORARY MIND CONTROL IN OUR LIVES

In a sense, Orwell's most telling prediction about human control is not to be found in the heavy-handed practices of the Ministry of Justice, but in the treatment protocols of the Ministry of Love. "Shall I tell you why we have brought you here? To cure you! To make you sane! Will you understand, Winston, that no one whom we bring to this place ever leaves our hands uncured? . . . The Party is not interested in the overt act: the thought is all we care about. We do not merely destroy our enemies; we change them" (209).

### Control by Cure, Education, and Cults

Twenty-five years after his involuntary commitment to a Russian mental hospital for political crimes, a Soviet dissident, Viktor Feinberg, was told by the psychiatrist: "Your release depends on your behavior. And your behavior, to us, means your political views. In all other respects your behavior is perfectly normal. Your illness consists of dissenting opinions. As soon as you renounce them and adopt a correct point of view, we will let you go."[14]

The current, real-world practitioners of the Ministry of Love come from the ranks of the mental health establishment, social welfare, education, and even business. As the fabric of the national social life becomes frayed in our time, ever more Americans are being turned over to institutional care providers from preschool to senior citizen homes. Orwell deserves credit for seeing the potential power of society-sanctioned professionals who intervene in our lives "for our own good." It is hard to rebel against something that is being done "for you" and not "to you." Instead of the "tricks of the tyrant trade"—punishment, torture, exile—we are seeing the "tricks of the treatment trade": therapy, education, reform, retraining, rehabilitation, designed to make people fit the norm, achieve the social ideal.[15]

[14] Federation of American Scientists, *Public Interest Report* 26 (October 1973): 6.
[15] See M. Galanter, *Cults: Faith, Healing, and Coercion*, 2nd ed. (New York: Oxford University Press, 1999).

Orwell, like the Totalitarian Soviet State, had no use for religion in *Nineteen Eighty-Four*. But in our time of ontological insecurity, religion plays a major role as a social influence institution. Not only the old-time religions, but the plethora of more than three thousand nontraditional religious groups and cults in America, and untold numbers of them throughout the world. Many of these New Time cults are big business, with billion-dollar revenues, tax exempt, of course.[16]

The Christian Broadcasting Network is the largest nonprofit broadcasting company in the country, with hundreds of stations and millions of faithful subscribers, with its own news staff and foreign bureaus and a research department that "tells the harsh truth," according to Pat Robertson, its director-minister. In his words, "[W]e determined that people weren't interested in religion or the church, they were interested in God's power." With that power in his pocket, the minister boldly proclaimed, "I seldom fight, but when I do, I seldom lose. God himself will fight for me against you and he will win."[17] During a visit to his TV studio for a book promotion tour, I discovered that his church educates and informs his followers on which side of that fight is the right side, through the auspices of the only two academic departments in his university in Norfolk, Virginia—the Departments of Education and Communication. I think Orwell would have chuckled over that narrow view of the essentials in a university curriculum.

### The CIA's MK-ULTRA Mind Control Program

But Orwell might have been pleased to have foreseen the role of the scientist-researcher distorted when employed by the state for its nefarious purposes, as happened for several decades from the 1950s on in CIA-sponsored experiments on extreme forms of mind control and behavior modification using exotic technologies. MK-ULTRA was the code name of their most notorious program designed to develop and make operational technologies for disrupting and then reprogramming individual habitual patterns of perception, thought, and action. Orwell presciently describes some of the operatives in this ambitious program used by our government against its citizens in the following passage: "The scientist of today is either a mixture of psychologist and inquisitor, studying with extraordinary minuteness the meaning of facial expressions, gestures, and tones of voice, and testing the truth-producing effects of drugs, shock therapy, hypnosis, and physical torture; or he is a chemist, physicist, or biologist concerned

---

[16] See S. Hassan, *Combatting Cult Mind Control* (Rochester, Vt.: Park St. Press, 1988).
[17] *San Francisco Chronicle*, 1983.

only with such branches of his special subject as are relevant to the taking of life" (159–60). And indeed, this CIA program employed a host of psychologists, psychiatrists, chemists, biologists, physicians, hypnotists, nurses, and other professionals in mental hospitals and universities. They tested LSD and other psychoactive drugs on both consenting and naive subjects; they explored new forms of electroshock treatment, hypnosis, cognitive reprogramming, and sensory deprivation used on unwitting mental patients whose minor mental disorder diagnoses did not warrant such extreme treatments. Some victims died, others were permanently impaired, and many brains were scrambled by these horrendous tactics. Nevertheless, these exotic technologies could not direct a single target person's action in a predetermined way. The MK-ULTRA program failed to meet any of its strategic objectives of developing deployable agents who would carry out assigned missions with efficiency and without regard for consequences. But it did have two clear effects: it underwrote the start of wide-scale experimentation with mind-altering drugs by middle-class citizens in the 1960s, and it demonstrated that a host of respectable professionals recruited to their staff could be mind-controlled into violating their values and beliefs by low-tech persuasive devices and concepts: flattery, prestige, camaraderie, ideological fear of the Communist menace at America's doorstep, and the last refuge of scoundrels, patriotism.[18]

## JIM JONES AS ORWELL'S SECRET AGENT MAN

Finally, I would like to highlight briefly parallels between the mind control tactics and strategies employed by Peoples Temple leader Jim Jones and those found throughout *Nineteen Eighty-Four*. In an earlier analysis, I argued that there were curious similarities between Orwell's depictions and the procedures that Jones put into effect to dominate his followers both in San Francisco and in the jungle compound in Guyana.[19] Now the strong form of my argument is that Jones learned those techniques directly from reading Orwell's *Nineteen Eighty-Four*. He field-tested the operational utility of these imaginative, fictional techniques with him as Party Head and his System in control of the minds and lives of more than a thousand real people, U.S. citizens, whom he had transformed into True Believers.

My personal connections with the Peoples Temple (PT) run wide and deep. I have studied much written evidence, theories, stories, and letters

[18] See A. W. Scheflin and E. M. Opton, Jr., *The Mind Manipulators: A Non-fiction Account* (New York: Paddington Press, 1978), for a detailed legal and psychological analysis of the work of these mind manipulators; see also P. Schrag, *Mind Control* (New York: Pantheon, 1978).

[19] G. Zimbardo, "Mind Control: Political Fiction and Psychological Reality," in *On Nineteen Eighty-Four*, ed. P. Stansky (Stanford, Calif.: The Portable Stanford, 1983), 197–224.

about Jones and Peoples Temple activities.[20] I counseled and extensively interviewed several Temple members shortly after they returned from Jones's jungle experiment and for a few years subsequently. They were escape survivors of the mass suicide/murders, Diane Louie and Richard Clark.[21] I arranged for Jeanne Mills, an early defector, to speak to my Stanford University class on the psychology of mind control about her personal experiences and had long conversations with her shortly before she was murdered in her home, in a still unsolved mystery. I also organized a Peoples Temple cult night program at Stanford University with cult experts, former members, and relatives of deceased members. I was an expert witness in the defense of Larry Layton, charged with conspiracy to murder Congressman Leo Ryan (on the jungle airstrip as he was leading a party of twenty defectors, relatives, and media to safety), and in that capacity was privy to much information and tape recordings by and about Jones and about PT. I also engaged in a number of long interviews with Layton both in jail and in my home. I was one of the expert panel members in a national call-in on National Public Radio in 1978 following the airing of the audiotapes *Father Cares: The Last of Jonestown.*

In recent times, I have had extensive discussions of various aspects of the functioning of PT and about Jones with Debby Layton, one of Jones's inner circle, who defected and led the exposé of the evils being perpetrated at Jonestown.[22] She introduced me to Mike Cartmell, who had been adopted

[20] M. Kilduff and R. Javers, *The Suicide Cult: The Temple Sect and the Massacre in Guyana* (New York: Bantam Books, 1978); M. Kilduff and P. Tracy, "Inside Peoples Temple," *New West* 30 (August 1977): 30–38; C. A. Krause, *Guyana Massacre: The Eyewitness Account* (New York: Berkeley Publishers, 1978); M. Lane, *The Strongest Poison* (New York: Hawthorne Books, 1980); D. Layton, *Seductive Poison: A Jonestown Survivor's Story of Life and Death in the Peoples Temple* (New York: Anchor Books, 1988); M. Meiers, "Was Jonestown a CIA Medical Experiment? A Review of the Evidence," *Studies in American Religion*, vol. 35 (New York: Lewiston Press, 1989); J. Mills, *My Six Years with God: Life inside Reverend Jim Jones's Peoples Temple* (New York: A and W Press, 1979); R. Moore, *A Sympathetic History of Jonestown: The Moore Family Involvement in Peoples Temple* (Lewiston, N.Y.: Edwin Mellen Press, 1985); W. S. Naipaul, *Journey to Nowhere: A New World Tragedy* (New York: Penguin, 1982); J. Nugent, *White Night: The Untold Story of What Happened before and beyond Jonestown* (New York: Rawson, Wade Publishers, 1979); N. Osherow, "Making Sense of the Nonsensical," in *Readings about the Social Animal*, ed. E. Aronson (New York: Freeman), 1980; T. Reiterman and J. Jacobs, *Raven: The Untold Story of Rev. Jim Jones and His People* (New York: Dutton, 1982); J. Reston, Jr., *Our Father Who Art in Hell* (New York: Times Books, 1981); U.S. Congress, *The Assassination of Representative Leo J. Ryan and the Jonestown, Guyana Tragedy* (Washington, D.C.: U.S. Government Printing Office, 1979); J. M. Weighten, *Making Sense of Jonestown Suicides: A Sociological History of Peoples Temple* (New York: Edwin Mellen Press, 1983); and M. S. Yee and T. N. Layton, *In My Father's House: The Story of the Layton Family and the Reverend Jim Jones* (New York: Holt, Rinehart, and Winston, 1982).

[21] D. Sullivan and G. Zimbardo, "Jonestown Survivors Tell Their Story," *Los Angeles Times*, March 9, 1979, View section, pt. 4, 1, 10–12.

[22] See Layton, *Seductive Poison.*

by Jones and was his heir apparent, and also to Stephan Jones, Jim Jones's biological son, who was in Georgetown playing basketball on the day of the massacre. The three of them gave me new insights and information that formed the basis of my strong argument that Jim Jones modeled his mind control tactics directly on those he learned from George Orwell's handbook for would-be mind controllers, *Nineteen Eighty-Four.*

Did Jim Jones read *Nineteen Eighty-Four*? The affirmative answer is revealed in this excerpt from an electronic message sent to me by his son, Stephan Jones (reproduced with his permission, March 10, 2000). "Dad did read *Nineteen Eighty-Four*, talked about it plenty to frighten us. I think he may have even attached some kind of prophetic significance to the date, nuclear holocaust or fascist takeover or something. Yup, there was a song [*"Nineteen Eighty-Four"*] written and performed by Diane Wilkerson, our lead performer from the time she joined 'til she died in Jonestown."

Debby Layton was the first to inform me of Jones's fascination with *Nineteen Eighty-Four*: "Jim talked about *Nineteen Eighty-Four* all the time. There is a film with Diane singing '*Nineteen Eighty-Four*' in Jonestown and Jim is singing along with her, saying, 'that's right, that's right.' Diane wrote it in California and Jim loved it, probably edited it. He would sing, 'Got to watch out. They are coming to get us. They are going to kill us,' and similar phrases that I can't exactly remember now."[23] During that same conversation in my home, Mike Cartmell also recalled Jones's interest in *Nineteen Eighty-Four*, as well as his close reading of the reports of the Nuremberg trials and Goering's defense of Hitler in his writing on the "leadership principle." Jones would say of the creation of a totalitarian state, of an all-powerful dominant leader, "That's exactly the point!" according to Cartmell. He recalled that Jones also read Louis Fischer's biography of Lenin and a lot of other books about cults. In 1967, Jones told him that he had had a revelation that in an earlier life he was Lenin, so that Cartmell would be his Trotsky, and the youth group he was going to head would be named "The Red Army."

### Direct Parallels of Orwellian and Jonesian Mind Control Tactics

BLACK/WHITE DISTORTION OF LANGUAGE AND NEWSPEAK DISTORTION
OF REALITY REFLECTED IN JONES'S "BIG LIES"

Jones went further than to distort the reality of the past. Amazingly, he was able to distort reality as it existed in followers' perceptions of the present. These hungry, fearful, exhausted, overworked, abused people

---

[23] Personal communication, San Francisco, December 6, 2000.

were forced to say their "gratitudes" regularly as they meditated upon "Dad," a.k.a. Jim Jones. Gratitudes were a litany of praise for Dad's providing them with good food, a good home, and good work because he loved them so—despite the contrary evidence provided by their senses. People held captive in this jungle concentration camp policed by armed guards also had to give thanks daily to Dad for their freedom and liberty. In addition, members told themselves a series of big lies, such as the assertions that the food was good and abundant, when it was horrible and scarce; the weather was lovely, when it was brutally hot; there were no insects, when mosquitoes attacked ferociously; they were happy, when many were depressed and frightened. They also had to write these lies to their relatives. He went a bit too far by asserting that in Jonestown there was no sickness, and there would be no death! Not even he could control those forces, and he had to deal with that discontinuity when members of his flock, including his mother, got ill and died. Jones even played films of Nazi concentration camps, such as *Night and Fog*, to remind his followers that their condition could get worse if they did not obey him totally and blindly.

During the tape of the last hour in Jonestown, one can hear his lies escalating as he says, "I have never lied to you," entreating the people to take their "medicine"—the cyanide poison—"it will not hurt, there is nothing to fear." The tape exposes the reality of children crying, screaming, as they were convulsing and dying.

While the Ministry of Truth rewrote history in *Nineteen Eighty-Four*, Jones was able to get his god-fearing, religious followers to tear up and discard their beloved Bibles after he exposed the lies and errors he claimed to have found in Scripture. And then he got them all to profess to reject the Bible as a source of lies. In passing, I am struck by Jones's mimicking of Orwell's imaginative titles for the various departments in The Party, such as the Ministry of Truth in charge of distorting truth. Jones created a "Department of Diversion," headed by Terri Buford, whose purpose was to carry out sensitive work in the government involving gathering data on selected politicians that could be used to persuade them to cooperate with the goals and needs of PT.

BIG BROTHER IS WATCHING YOU: BIG DADDY IS INFILTRATING
YOUR EVERY THOUGHT

The formulation "24/7" appears to denote a new concept initiated in Silicon Valley to describe the around-the-clock daily work and services of high-tech firms, but it accurately describes Jim Jones's day and night broadcasts of sermons, speeches, and fiery attacks on the government, defectors, and other enemies. In place of the Telescreen surveillance in

*Nineteen Eighty-Four,* Jones reached into the minds of his followers by blasting them with these endless messages that blared from loudspeakers in the central pavilion and could be heard for great distances, sometimes live, sometimes taped; but always his presence filled the airways and thus the "mind ways" while members worked, ate, and slept.

### SPY NETWORK: JONES'S INFORMER SYSTEM

Jones rewarded those who informed on other members who complained about the hard work, awful rations, and enforced separation of spouses, and he severely punished the dissidents publicly. He even announced that he would send around comrades who would pretend to be dissenters to lure others into agreeing to complain or to defect, and then mete out the punishment due to these traitors. He initiated his spy system much earlier in the United States by having members of his security force find out as much as possible about various members by breaking into their homes, checking their garbage, tapping their phones, or having family members inform on each other.

### BOTH THE PARTY AND JONES ENFORCED FOOD DEPRIVATION

This tactic was a means to weaken the ability to resist or rebel. The diet in Jonestown was almost protein free, consisted of small portions, and tasted bad; it was heavy on ricelike gruel, with few fruits or vegetables. Jones chided those who might complain that it was better to be lean than fat, and that they were rejecting capitalistic values in making such sacrifices. What is both amazing and quite sad is that people in Jonestown were often near starvation while Jones was regularly sending millions of dollars to secret bank accounts in Switzerland, Panama, and elsewhere with his couriers, Debby Layton[24] and other trusted aides. A small part of these funds could easily have fed the congregation well, but sustenance was intentionally denied to them. Image this deprivation against the background of working ten-hour days, often in the blazing jungle sun.

### SEXCRIMES

Jones separated married couples into different barracks, and they could be intimate only with his permission, at prescribed times. He openly accused men of homosexual improprieties with him and had them publicly ridiculed and punished. Similarly, he accused woman of forcing him to sexually favor them, when, of course, he was the coercive agent. Sex was

[24] Layton, *Seductive Poison.*

a powerful motive for Jones, who often seemed obsessed with sexual desires: part of his image among his followers was as a man of extraordinary sexual appetites and performances. But he also realized the powerful bonds that human sexuality could create among his followers, and so such Sexcrimes by anyone else had to be controlled, limited, and dominated by his authority.

### SELF-INCRIMINATION, WRITING ONESELF UP, CATHARSIS, AND PUNISHMENT

These tactics were a central part of Orwell's and Jones's control systems. All members had to engage in self-analysis and prepare statements of their errors, weaknesses, fears, and wrongdoing, allegedly so that they could purge themselves of these negative thoughts and thereby achieve a catharsis. Instead, these reports became part of each member's permanent file and were used against them in public meetings, when errant individuals were "called on the carpet" to be ridiculed, humiliated, tormented, and physically tortured.

### ORWELL'S ANALYSIS OF THE PARTY MENTALITY AND THE PSYCHOLOGY OF WAR APPLIES DIRECTLY TO JONESTOWN IN ITS FINAL DAYS AND LAST HOUR

Orwell writes: "The social atmosphere is that of a besieged city. . . . It does not matter whether war is actually happening. . . . All that is needed is that a state of war should exist" (158), and when capture was inevitable, "[t]he proper thing was to kill yourself before they got you" (86). Jones had his group practice middle-of-the-night suicide drills called "White Nights." They were full group exercises that were realistic preludes to the final performance that Jones orchestrated, just as Orwell had depicted, with Jones's lie of the threat of the U.S. military on its way to take away and harm PT's children and elders. "Revolutionary suicide," he said, was preferable to being massacred at the hands of this ruthless American enemy; he compared the resistance of PT members with that of the besieged Jews at the battle of Masada. It is not clear how many of the 912 dead willingly committed suicide by drinking cyanide, how many were murdered with poison injections or shot for refusing to die for the cause, but the important thing to remember is that those compound guards who did kill PT members were themselves the friends and family members of those who were killed. Here Jim Jones imitates Heinrich Himmler's SS oath to Hitler, "I swear to thee, Adolf Hitler, loyalty and bravery. I vow to thee and to the superiors whom thou shall appoint, obedience until death." So total blind obedience to unjust authority ruled that fateful day in November 1978, as it had for so many years earlier in Nazi Germany, and later in the experimental demonstrations of Stanley Milgram, described earlier.

### TORTURE ROOM 101 MIRRORED IN JONES'S BLUE-EYED MONSTER, BIGFOOT, AND THE BOX

Having confessed earlier to a rat phobia, Winston Smith finally breaks down when in Room 101 he is faced with his worst fear of having rats run at his face. Jones did exactly that, had members write out their fears, and when they disobeyed, were late for a meeting, fell asleep during his endless harangues, or engaged in some rule violation like giving an orange to a child without his permission, they were forced to face their worst fears.

Consider the case of an Oregon youngster, Garry Scott, who followed his father into Peoples Temple but somehow was found to be disobedient. Listen to his brief statement as he called the national call-in following the broadcast of the NPR show *Father Cares: The Last of Jonestown*, by James Reston, Jr. Listen to the tape of the nature of his punishment for a minor infraction as his worst phobia is made manifest in Jones's Room 101. But more important, listen to his articulation of his lasting reaction to this torment. Does he hate Jones? Not one bit. He has become a True Believer; even though his father died in Jonestown, and he was tortured and humiliated, Garry still admires and loves Dad. Not even Orwell's omnipotent Party could honestly claim such a victory.

SCOTT:
Like a lot of other young people, I had my sort of rebellion against some of the doctrinal methods that were taking place in the church, and I rebelled, and for that I was punished to become a better Christian. I was physically abused. Beaten with a two-by-four. I was whipped. One of the big problems I have in life is I have a phobia against snakes and for one punishment I was tied up and a snake [a boa] was put on top of me and that was psychological torment that I had to go through for a while. And I was sexually abused as well.

Moderator Bill Moyers then asked, "What did you see in Jim Jones when you were in the Temple that caused you to be faithful despite your treatment?"

SCOTT:
I think the guilt. I felt that I was responsible for everything that was taking place around me. If there was any bad attitudes or any bad feelings emitting from persons in the Temple, I felt that they were my actions. . . . I followed

Jim Jones because he was a very caring person. And even today, you know, despite the fact that a lot of my friends, which I considered my brothers and sisters, died, and a lot of them were forced to their death, there is a very personal part of Reverend Jim Jones that still lives today. And even though I'm very frustrated and very disappointed by what happened to my father, there's still a peace [piece?] here that I see in Reverend Jones.[25]

Like Winston Smith, Garry Scott seems "to have won a victory over himself": in the end, they love Big Brother and Father Jones, alike.

Before discussion of Jones's other torture chambers, it is well to point up one way in which Jones was able to create such True Believers, when Orwell's *Nineteen Eighty-Four* system, or Soviet Communism in Eastern Europe, could not. Jones had the ability to make a uniquely personal connection with each member of his church. Many PT members told me that when listening to his sermons, each one felt as if Jones were talking to him or her personally. "Jones had personal touch down," Mike Cartmell told me. "He was like a priest, a personal counselor, coming to see each person who was important to him in some way, and spoke to them personally about what is troubling them, what are they afraid of. Jones could make everyone feel as if he or she was the guest of the day, he made each one feel special in some way. *He gave you your five minutes, and in return, you gave him your life.*" And so, despite the public punishment they often received, members, like Garry Scott, retained the sense that down deep, in his private heart, "Dad Loves Me, and I am responsible for being a bad person who needs to change his evil ways to deserve Dad's love."

Jeanne Mills presents her young daughter's account of torment when faced with the "Blue-Eyed Monster," where she and other children were punished. "They took me into this dark room and the monsters were all over the room. They said, 'I am the Blue-Eyed Monster and I'm going to get you.' Then the monster grabbed my shirt and tore it open."[26] Mills surmised that the children were being given electric shocks, because she had heard that "Jim was using the Blue-Eyed Monster as 'behavior modification' for the small children."[27] Mills describes other torture chambers in PT. "Debbie [Layton] told us about 'Bigfoot,' a punishment that had replaced the 'Blue-Eyed Monster.' It's a deep well about forty-five minutes' walk away from the camp," she said sadly. "Counselors have to sit in there, and when the child is disciplined they throw the child down the well. The kids would cry hysterically as soon as Jim would tell them

[25] *Father Cares: The Last of Jonestown*, National Public Radio, 2-vol. set of audiotapes (1978).
[26] Mills, *My Six Years with God*, 55.
[27] Ibid., 56.

they'd have to go visit Bigfoot. We'd hear them scream all the way there, and all the time they had to be down in the well, and by the time they got back they were begging for mercy. It was really awful. Some young people were forced to eat hot peppers or even have hot peppers put up their rectums as disciplines."[28]

"The Box" was a simple feared torture chamber. Troublemakers were sentenced by Jones to spend time in a sealed metal box placed in the ground, where temperatures would soar and Temple members would fear dying of suffocation. Interestingly, in the classic prison movie *Cool Hand Luke*, Karl, the yard-boss, describes the consequences of breaking any of the many prison rules, as "then you spend a night in the box."

Obedience training, Newspeak, Crimestop, Doublethink, Reality Control, Emotional Control, sexual control, surveillance, hard work on starvation diets—the staples of the Orwellian Mind Controller's repertoire—were adapted and put into effective strategic operation by Jim Jones in his attempt to demonstrate total behavior modification beyond anything that MK-ULTRA had ever achieved. Jones succeeded in his perverted mind control "experiment" by creating a mass mentality "Manchurian Candidate" that killed the Enemy on demand, only the Enemy was one's children, one's parents, one's mate, one's friends, and finally oneself.

I believe that Orwell would not have been pleased to see his warning about the dangers of a totalitarian state actually acted out by a latter-day disciple in the jungles of Guyana. I am sure that Orwell wanted his ideas to serve as a precautionary tale and not as a mind control operations manual. All the sadder when similar destructive scenarios were recently reenacted by cult leaders in many other countries around the world— Japan, Canada, Switzerland, the United States, and Uganda—all extracting the ultimate sacrifice for the cause of domination of free will, of suppression of individuality, of distortion of critical thought, and the destruction of the spirit of independence.

We have seen evil in Orwell and evil in Jones, and that evil is us. We will go down as they did, if we do not learn from the lessons of the past to oppose tyranny at its first signs, to be vigilant in cutting through political rhetoric and semantic distortions by all those with any power to control communications media and educational systems. Despots and dictators, whether demonic or benevolent, demean human nature and defile the human connection. In defying Big Brother, we assert our community with all those who value freedom over security, who would die for liberty rather than live a life of mindless obedience to unjust authority.

[28] Ibid., 60.

## ORWELL AND OUR FUTURE

Orwell's future vision of governmental massive deception and endless wars is on our current radar screen; that cynical vision is visiting the United States now and is likely to worsen in the foreseeable future. We learned recently that the Pentagon was in the process of creating a new office of "Strategic Influence." "The Pentagon is developing plans to provide news items, possibly even false ones, to foreign media organizations as part of a new effort to influence public sentiment and policy makers in both friendly and unfriendly countries, military officials said."[29] This attempt at furthering efforts in America's war on terrorism through systematic deception was disbanded in response to pressures from the public, the media, and other governmental agencies. That may simply mean that the Pentagon's "black" operation of spreading disinformation goes underground and attracts less publicity in doing its dubious deeds. It has also become evident that the Bush administration plans to make this war on terrorism a long war, extending into an ill-defined future space and time. The original enemy, al Qaeda forces, was expanded to include Afghanistan's Taliban; then the net widened to all governments that supported terrorism in any way, then to countries that qualify as belonging to the "axis of evil" because they make weapons, have not been friendly to the United States, and may be supporting terrorists.

The Bush administration has learned a basic Orwellian lesson from the terrorists responsible for the attacks of September 11, 2001, namely, how to "weaponize human fear" of random, unexpected attacks against this nation. They raised the banner of "Homeland Security" as the most important national value and "Terrorists" as our most hated enemy. They put a face on this faceless terrorism, Saddam Hussein, as conspiring with a known villain, Osama bin Laden, and they put a place on the ambiguous origins of global terrorism, the nation of Iraq. Then they upped the fear ante from just violent attacks to threats of potential nuclear destruction and worse by asserting that Saddam and sons possessed something termed "Weapons of Mass Destruction!" They made the threat appear so great that only immediate preemptive war against Iraq (our former ally against our earlier enemy, Iran) could prevent imminent disaster for our helpless nation. In the process, the administration parlayed this escalating national fear into creating a new self-image of America as "Victimized," and recrafted the image of the formerly bumbling president into that of the "Decisive-Commander-in-Chief" who led the armed forces to military victory and restored America's pride in its might.

[29] *San Francisco Chronicle*, January 24, 2002, D3.

They took another leaf from Orwell in stifling any dissent as an unpatriotic challenge to national security—now punishable as a federal offense within the labyrinth of rules and laws of the newly created so-called Patriot Act. When all the justifications for the Iraq war later vanished upon subsequent analysis of the false and flimsy intelligence evidence used for the rush to the "Shock and Awe" military campaign against Iraq, the president and his staff declared that it did not matter since the ends justified the means. Even if Saddam did not have any WMD or contacts with Osama, he was a bad guy and the world is better off with that "regime change." This is so even when weighed against the extensive destruction wrought against Iraq, the deaths of tens of thousands of Iraqis, and more than a thousand American and "Willing Coalition" forces, not to mention thousands seriously wounded, perhaps a trillion-dollar ultimate tab for the costs of war and its endless aftermath, the loss of respect of many of America's allies, and the loss of any sense of moral superiority from the scandal of rampant abuses in the Abu Ghraib Prison.

Dear Mr. Orwell, did you really have to get so much right on that is proven so wrong for America?

# Whom Do You Trust? What Do You Count On?

DARIUS REJALI

> "I *know* that you will fail. There is something in the uni-
> verse—I don't know, some spirit, some principle—that
> you will never overcome."
> "Do you believe in God, Winston?"
> "No."
> "Then what is it, this principle that will defeat us?"
> "I don't know. The spirit of Man."
> "And do you consider yourself a man?"
> "Yes."
> "If you are a man, Winston, you are the last man. Your kind
> is extinct; we are the inheritors. Do you understand that
> you are *alone*? You are outside history, you are non-exis-
> tent." (222)

WINSTON SMITH fails to resist torture. This failure is utter and complete. Fear grips the reader as he hopes, against all odds, that Winston Smith will be able to resist. But there is no redemption for either the reader or Winston Smith. He is, Orwell tells us in a peculiar Nietzschean langu-age, the "last man." Like the pink coral paperweight shattered at the time of his arrest, the pink flesh of a human being seems to be deeply vulnerable no matter how well encased it is in ideas. There is no protec-tion in ideas. Ideas, like glass, are hard to see and, it seems, can be de-stroyed by violence.

Upon consideration, however, a different reading is possible. We are apt to forget how fiercely and how successfully Winston Smith resisted Oceania. We forget this because in the end Smith betrayed everything. But considering how few opportunities he had to develop his character, how methodically state and society had been structured against him, it is amazing that Smith fought as fiercely as he did. This should remind us how little opportunity a man may need to resist and how many years he may survive even in a society that is a virtual prison. Yet this reading poses a further question: what are the characteristic sources of value by which one may resist? What are these principles? On this point Orwell is less than clear.

In fact, Orwell gives a better account of betrayal than he does of resistance. Orwell is right in identifying how torture is shaped by what might be called "ordinary betrayals," betrayals at an atomic level of ordinary life. It is these kinds of betrayals, not so much the great betrayals ("betraying Julia"), that make being a survivor of torture so difficult and complicated. Once these atoms of trust are shattered, they are not only hard to reassemble; they are hard to fill with something else. Torture in the end produces only shattered bodies, and that is all it does.

Unfortunately, Orwell obscures his accurate insight into the nature of ordinary betrayals with what I might call "great betrayals," that is, trials in which one betrays a true cause. *Nineteen Eighty-Four* is a great novel of the Cold War, and often Orwell conflates the historical reality of his times—torture as he saw it in Stalin's show trials, for example—with an account of the essence of torture as such. In this respect, the novel is misleading: while ordinary betrayals are inevitable, indeed terrifyingly so, great betrayals are not. Many prisoners never betray their great causes, though they too suffer from ordinary betrayals. Modern torture centers provide us with an exemplary range of models of how individuals shape and change themselves in the face of their extreme misfortune and helplessness, models that are read and imitated widely today by political prisoners everywhere. Indeed, if anything, the range of possible forms of resistance to torture is far greater than anything Orwell imagined.

Orwell does endow Winston Smith with some standard techniques used today. If these techniques fail for Winston Smith, this has less to do with torture technology and more to do with the fact that Smith lives in a particular kind of state which progressively undermines characteristic sources of value outside the torture chamber. Here again, Orwell conflates the historical reality of his times, torture as he saw it in Stalinist Russia or Nazi Germany, with an account of the reality of torture as such. He reads back into the past his present, and out of that he constructs an unchanging vision of what torture "really" is. Orwell here suffers from a narrowness of vision, and this narrowness bears the marks of the Cold War period in which the novel was written.

In what follows, I consider first the nature of betrayal. I compare the strengths and weaknesses of Orwell's account to that of Jean Amery, who was tortured by the SS. Amery offers us a rather special narrative, a narrative of torture that is not one of resistance, but one that recognizes the complexity of betrayal. I then classify modes of resistance to torture, identifying the strengths and weaknesses of each. Here I will draw on many different accounts: Don Foster's interviews with South African political prisoners; Cuevas's accounts of Republican women incarcerated during the Spanish civil war; various accounts of Iranian guerrillas in prison; a manual for dissidents in the former Soviet Union; Milovan Djilas's account of his torture in 1933; Henri Alleg's torture by French paratroopers in 1959; Jacobo Timmerman's torture at the hands of the Argentine junta in the 1970s, Palden Gyatso's torture in Tibetan prisons in the 1990s, and last, but not least, Niccolò Machiavelli's prison poetry from his tortures in 1511. Having clarified what kinds of resistance are possible, I return to Winston Smith's resistance in the novel. I ask how well these forms of resistance would have fared in Oceania. Here I consider critically Orwell's account of modern torture, identifying its strengths, as well as its limitations.

## MODES OF BETRAYAL

Winston Smith betrayed others. This was also the case of Jean Amery. As with Winston Smith, Amery's betrayal was utter and complete. And as with Smith, Amery asks not "how did I resist?" but "How did I betray? What inside me failed to resist?" His narrative is one well worth exploring because it shows the pitfalls of Orwell's narrative of betrayal.

Betrayal is not a mode of resistance; it is sheer and utter surrender. Suspended on a hook, Amery writes, "I had to give up rather quickly. And now there was a crackling and splintering in my shoulders that my body has not forgotten until this hour."[1] In torture, he writes, "the transformation of the person into flesh becomes complete. Frail in the face of violence, yelling out in pain, awaiting no help, capable of no resistance, the tortured person is only a body, and nothing else besides that."[2] When asked, Amery replied truthfully. He was lucky he did not know very much himself, but this, he recognizes, was not due to his virtuousness:

To come right out with it: I had nothing but luck, because especially in regard to the extorting of information, our group was rather well organized. What they wanted to hear from me in Breendonk, I simply did not know myself. If instead of aliases I had been able to name the real names, perhaps, or probably, a calamity would have occurred, and I would be standing here now as the weakling I most likely am, and as the traitor I potentially already was. Yet it was not at all that I opposed them with the heroically maintained silence that befits a real man in such a situation and about which one may read (almost always, incidentally, in reports by people who were not there themselves). I talked. I accused myself of invented absurd political crimes and even

[1] Jean Amery, *At the Mind's Limits: Contemplations by a Survivor on Auschwitz and Its Realities* (Bloomington: Indiana University Press, 1980), 32.
[2] Ibid., 33.

now I don't know at all how they could have occurred to me, dangling bundle that I was. Apparently, I had the hope that, after such incriminating disclosures, a well-aimed blow to the head would put an end to my misery and quickly bring on my death, or at least unconsciousness.[3]

Winston Smith could not have said it better.

Amery has no secrets to give regarding resistance. He has seen too many variations, cases where the pain was hardly enough to justify the confession and cases of heroic martyrdom. "Where does the strength, where does the weakness come from? I don't know. ONE does not know. No one has yet been able to draw distinct borders between the 'moral' power of resistance to physical pain and the 'bodily' resistance (which likewise must be placed in quotation marks)."[4] Choosing between moral and physical factors seems to yield unpalatable choices. If we reduce it to the purely physical capacity of an organism, then every form of cowardice and whiny reaction is pardoned. If we emphasize the moral factors, exhorting others to endure more pain, then we hold physically weak people to the same standards as the biologically superior. "Thus, we had better let the question rest, just as at that time I myself did not further analyze my power to resist, when, battered and with my hands still shackled, I lay in the cell and ruminated."[5]

What obsesses Amery are not the great betrayals; even if he had known the names of his colleagues, even if he had given them up, this is not the aspect of torture he fastens himself to. Rather, it is what I want to call the ordinary betrayals, and on this score, I think Amery is onto something important, something that Orwell conflates with great betrayals. Ordinary betrayals are not like the great betrayals (the religion I followed, the cause I fought for, the person I loved: let us call these the "Julian events"). Ordinary betrayals are not often remarked upon. Yet they can cut deeper than we think.

Ordinary life has a rhythm that is embodied in the way our bodies reach or hear sounds, things that are second nature to us. This embodied agency confers intelligibility on the experiences we have. Ordinarily we don't notice this embodied universe in which we live; we *do* notice it when the structures and rhythms are interrupted, that is, in the course of ordinary betrayals. When ordinary betrayals occur, when habits that are second nature cease to make sense of our world, we experience our finitude. I do not mean that we discover that our body is causally finite. It is true enough that I cannot walk through the wall before me, but that is not very interesting. It is rather that I cannot act or reach as I used to without wondering simultaneously who I am, what I am doing, where I am, because each

---

[3] Ibid., 36.
[4] Ibid., 37.
[5] Ibid., 38.

time I do so, my hand falls on thin air. We live in a world of concerned relatedness to objects around us, and their first and primary relationship to us is not as neutral objects but as things that are part of our projects and goals, what we might call our form of life. When these involvements are gone and when the things no longer lie at hand, we experience our finiteness in a far more profound sense than a simple causal one. The world becomes simply less intelligible.[6]

What does this have to do with torture? Often when we reflect upon torture, analysis focuses on the great betrayals. Did he confess the names of his conspirators? Did she commit treason against the state? But Amery focuses on ordinary betrayals that happen in the course of violence, when one reaches for something and finds that it is not at hand or that it has changed. For some people, this experience—where ordinary people behave in ways they never did, where ordinary places become nightmares, where ordinary things are used to do horrible things—is, one is inclined to say, a kind of madness. But that would signal only the fact that we have given up trying to make sense of our experiences. And in general, in the study of violence, we get no closer to understanding violence by saying how horrible it is. Rather, we get closer by comparing it to the ordinary, showing its similarities and differences. And that is, indeed, the power of the final section of *Nineteen Eighty-Four*, the way it is both ordinary and extraordinary.

Let me list some of the ordinary betrayals that happen in the course of torture, all of which Winston Smith also experiences. First, in many cases, you are being tortured by your friends and neighbors, people with whom you have interacted daily for many years. Second, you are betrayed by ordinary professionals, by the doctor, for example, who attends the torture session and takes your pulse, or the nurse who hooks up the IV after the session is over. Third, there is the role played by ordinary objects, not just dental drills and hypodermic needles, but the field telephone used to shock you or the music played while you are tortured. Fourth, there is the questioning itself, the bureaucratic solicitations for information, which are delivered in a calm reassuring voice. Fifth, there are the bureaucratic professionals who attend the session, the secretary outside the colonel's office or the stenographer who writes out your profession of guilt. Sixth, there are the exercises that you are compelled to perform or the machines to which you are strapped. Seventh, there are the forms of self-expression that are involved, such as writing out your confession. And finally, there is the betrayal of the body itself, as you lose control over

---

[6] The following analysis draws on the works of Martin Heidegger, Ludwig Wittgenstein, Charles Taylor, and Judith Shklar. See Martin Heidegger, *Being and Time* (New York: Harper and Row, 1962); Ludwig Wittgenstein, *Philosophical Investigations* (London: Basil Blackwell, 1976); Charles Taylor, *Philosophical Arguments* (Cambridge: Harvard University Press, 1995); and Judith Shklar, *Ordinary Vices* (Cambridge: Harvard University Press, 1984).

your bodily processes. " 'You are rotting away,' he said; 'you are falling to pieces. What are you? A bag of filth. Now turn around and look into that mirror again. Do you see that thing facing you? That is the last man. If you are human, that is humanity' " (224).

Torture, then, gathers to itself accomplices, and these accomplices are not just other human beings but ordinary things for which bodies reach and are familiar. They are the large kitchen rice paddles used to beat detainees in Sri Lanka,[7] the kindergarten chairs to which Palestinians are tied for the Shabeh torture in Israel.[8] They also include the things forensic pathologists working at gravesites refer to as the "Associated Objects," the clothing, crosses, toys, and shoes that somehow found their way into the grave. Again, it is often said that torture destroys communities, families, and identities, but less frequently that torture also destroys many other forms of relatedness, things like cooking, dancing, writing, or simply moving. These too constitute ordinary betrayals that follow from modern torture. For this reason, Amery concludes:

> Whoever has succumbed to torture can no longer feel at home in the world. The shame of destruction cannot be erased. Trust in the world, which already collapsed in part at the first blow, but in the end, under torture, fully, will not be regained. That one's fellow man was experienced as the antiman remains in the tortured person as accumulated horror. It blocks the view into a world in which the principle of hope rules.[9]

It is important to recognize Amery's belief that ordinary betrayals characterize not only the life of those who committed great betrayals, but even that of those who, for whatever reasons, did not betray their colleagues and friends and, therefore, resisted successfully. Amery himself committed suicide in 1978.

## MODES OF BEING

Amery's account is not very typical of modern torture narratives. While there are many modern narratives, they are often stories of resistance.

---

[7] Patricia Lawrence, "Survivors' Tasks: Narratives from Sri Lankan Detention Camps" (paper presented at the Conference on Investigating and Combating Torture, University of Chicago, March 1999), 6.

[8] Yuval Ginbar, *Routine Torture: Interrogation Methods of the General Security Service* (Jerusalem: B'Tselem, Israeli Information Center for Human Rights in the Occupied Territories, 1998), 16; Lori A. Allen, "Why Position Abuse? How Israeli Torture of Palestinians Makes Sense" (paper presented at the Conference on Investigating and Combating Torture, University of Chicago, March 1999), 5–6.

[9] Amery, *At the Mind's Limits*, 40.

One must use such stories cautiously. Writers present their sources of resistance in passing and with surprising indifference. They mix and match strategies; what works one day for you may not work the next. The stories they recount cannot tell us whether the strategies worked. There is simply no easy way to determine this. Even survival may, in fact, be as much due to accident as it is to deliberate planning on the part of the victim or the torturer. Still, what makes these stories valuable is that they tell us about ways of being in prison, and they are philosophically interesting because they show some of the characteristic problems, as well as characteristic sources of value for people.

There are five particular modes of being in prison: modes of alertness, modes of governance, modes of compassion, modes of forgetfulness, and modes of laughter. I shall consider these, in turn, contrasting them with each other and teasing out what is being invoked as a source of value for the self in its confrontation with misfortune. In the section that follows this analysis, I shall consider which modes are invoked in *Nineteen Eighty-Four.*

### Modes of Alertness

When we think of torture, we think of the classic Orwellian confrontation of the victim and the torturer. Ordinary people think of this misfortune in terms of strategy: the question is how to hold out against or outwit the torturer or how to avoid betraying one's comrades. In countries where torture settled into a particular kind of routine, political dissidents did not merely criticize the government: they also produced self-help literature for the incarcerated. A good example of this sort is *A Manual of Psychiatry for Dissidents* produced for dissidents handed over by the KGB for psychiatric terror.[10] Manuals like this set out to describe the entire organizational process of torture. They identify the process of arrest and preliminary interrogation. They offer typologies of the kinds of people, including torturers, one is likely to meet. They identify the terminology, concepts, and jargon that characterize the torture system. They describe the actual tortures themselves and how to manage the pain. They recommend tactics for how to answer questions and thus minimize one's torture or frustrate the torturer. These kinds of strategies are to be studied, memorized, and implemented by the individual when he or she is tortured. In short, manuals set out to prepare victims for the worst, to dispel the fear of the un-

---

[10] Harvey Fireside, *Soviet Psychoprisons* (New York: W. W. Norton, 1979), 92–117. See also Ervand Abrahamian, *Tortured Confessions: Prisons and Public Recantations in Modern Iran* (Berkeley and Los Angeles: University of California Press, 1999), 106–7.

known through enhancing their awareness of the system, and thereby to empower them.

In modes of awareness, a lost and anxious imagination, not pain or torture, is the greatest enemy of the incarcerated. Awareness of what is to come, a calm and deliberate mind: these are what the manuals seek to cultivate. Above all, the victim can remain alive only by overcoming the greatest fear of all, the fear of death. This is why Milovan Djilas's torture memoir remains the most articulate expression of this mode of resistance. Djilas spells it out rather clearly. If one lives in the service of an idea, says Djilas, then one "need not fear, and has no reason to fear, prison, torture, or even death. He will survive. He will live on in the lives of his comrades, in the life of the idea. Nevertheless, he will also be more confident and able to bear torture all the more easily if he is familiar with certain 'weak points' innate to the act itself and those who practice it."[11] Djilas advances several reasons why one should not fear death: If one does not fear death, one cannot fear torture, if only for the simple reason that torture fails if it produces death. At any rate, there is no point to the fear: because death is not in one's control, because they'll kill you if they want to, so you can't change that; and because the body creates a limit to too much pain anyway, so you'll faint long before it matters.

For Djilas, it is the people who cling too fast to life who are at serious risk, for their love of life betrays them to the torturer. They calculate "when" they will betray, not "if." As he puts it, "Almost always, one does not become a traitor *under* torture, but *before* torture . . . most people prepare themselves to give in under torture before arrest, while they are still free."[12] It may appear that torture breaks individuals; in fact, individuals who crack have rehearsed their betrayal long in advance precisely because of their attachment to life. The traitor tries to "avoid any presentiment of pain, to keep from thinking of the horrible torture that faces him." He deliberately avoids precisely the kind of awareness and alertness the resistance manuals try to cultivate. In this, he is just like the agent provocateur who is revealed by his indifference to theory or his feigned interest in it. Both the provocateur and the potential traitor "share a boundless frantic love of life and all its pleasure; both are alike in their need for security and warmth."[13]

If these prudential reasons do not suffice, Djilas offers two other techniques designed "to stifle the imagination from the start, to trick it, and to master it." The first is preoccupation with activities that keep one alert, but focused. He urges playing chess, chatting with one's comrades, occu-

---

[11] Milovan Djilas, *Of Prisons and Ideas* (New York: Harcourt Brace Jovanovich, 1986), 7.
[12] Ibid., 4–5.
[13] Ibid., 6.

pying oneself mentally in one's cell. Even when one is shackled, one should concentrate on insignificant concrete things—spots on the ceiling, for example—with a constant steady stare until one's surroundings and all other details utterly vanish. "That's hard and painful to make happen, but it brings calm and strength and may be resorted to again and again." One is reminded here of many other such examples: the Soviet spy who played chess on the plaid blanket of his cell bed using small pieces of lint, or the Soviet dissident who invented an entire field of mathematics while in prison.

The other technique Djilas urges is to transform one's living attachments in one's imagination. "Whoever wishes to do battle, to sacrifice himself for an idea, to become an idea so as to become the master of his life, must beware of life. He dare not waver between life and the idea—except when that hesitation serves to promote the idea. For life is itself a mistake and a betrayal."[14] Attachments to one's beloved, for example, offer powerful reasons to choose life over one's ideas. How, then, to transform such attachments? In April 1933, Djilas was whipped on the bastinado and tossed into a cell "like a sack of junk." With pain burning through his entire body, his thoughts turn to his beloved. Notice, then, how Djilas transforms his imaginings in a different direction.

> This scene in the Police Department took place on the top floor. Below us and around us Belgrade slept peacefully, and in it, somewhere, lay a beloved girl. Yet somehow the city did not seem to exist, as though it had evaporated into amorphous space. And the girl—she was transformed into a compassionate presence before whose gaze I was able to stand proud, having offered her one more reason, the very highest, insuperable reason—for deserving her love. I had become the master of the outer world of reality if only because, insofar as it existed at all, it was for me no longer a thing unto itself, a thing alienable.[15]

Djilas's consolation, then, lies in the fact that he will be remembered and cherished by his beloved for having sacrificed himself for the idea. Djilas will be loved all the more by his beloved for having died in the service of an idea.

## Modes of Governance

Despite the urge to reduce torture to the confrontation of victim and torturer, torture does not happen in a vacuum. It is one incident in a long

[14] Ibid.
[15] Ibid., 4.

journey through many rooms involving many people. This is why even strategic accounts of resistance are embedded in broader republican narratives of self-governance. Governance here means the careful regulation of one's body movements and mind in the service of social solidarity. Self-government turns out to furnish its own foundation for resistance. The Republican women of Franco's prisons tell their resistance stories by telling of all the things they did together. Their lives are characterized by hunger strikes, reading groups, plays, communal singing, caring for the sick, and slowing down the forced labor lines. Generations of Iranian prisoners tell similar stories, stories of hunger strikes, lectures for self-improvement, gossip, reading groups, caring for the sick, and remembering lost comrades through memorials. Above all, there is the government of the cell, which can be a source of tremendous preoccupation and solidarity. Such self-government includes everything from the menial tasks of daily survival (e.g., cleaning) to electing cell officials.

Once again, the point of such activities is to reduce inappropriate memories of home or wild imaginings of things to come. Of course, not every prisoner can be so fortunate as to belong to a cell community. The South African prisoners certainly were not. Many spent a very long time in solitary confinement.[16] But even in the absence of ordinary human contact, we should not underestimate the role played by other things that become part of one's community or the ingenious ways in which human beings reach out to other beings. In the absence of humans, prisoners expand their universe to include all biological beings. People in solitary tell of the endless amusements provided by ants and mice as fraternal friends and constant companions. Nor should we underestimate the crafty ways prisoners manipulate their oppressors into providing contact. They make mistakes and generate complaints in order to get guards to argue with them and touch them, thereby receiving the human element they hungered for. Finally, there is civic memory, the community of the honored dead who stand beside the prisoner. Henri Alleg opens his own account of torture by pointing to the civic sources of his self:

> On reading this account, one must think of all those who have "disappeared" and of those who, sure of their cause, await death without fear; of those who have known tortures and who have not feared them; of those who, faced with hatred and torture, reaffirm their belief in future peace and friendship between the French and Algerian peoples. This could be an account of any one of them.[17]

---

[16] Don Foster, Dennis Davis, and Diane Sandler, *Detention and Torture in South Africa: Psychological, Legal and Historical Studies* (New York: St. Martin's Press, 1987).

[17] Henri Alleg, *The Question* (New York: George Braziller, 1958), 43.

Civic memory, then, stands for civic community. Whether one thinks of the past, as Alleg does, or toward a future community, memory furnishes social solidarity when reality does not. In this respect, modes of governance and modes of awareness are deeply interlinked; if one finds one of them in a narrative, one eventually finds the other.

## Modes of Compassion

It may seem that those who depend on modes of governance, who are empowered by participating in such communal processes, are making themselves ever more vulnerable. I now want to turn to a third mode of being in prison that is perhaps even more vulnerable, namely, modes of compassion. If the mode of awareness draws a bright, closed circle around the self, shutting it off from the world, the mode of compassion expands that circle to include the entire world, not just one's friends but also one's enemies. It is best illustrated by the work of the Tibetan monk Palden Gyatso, who was tortured in various Chinese prisons for some forty years. When he was asked what he feared most in all the years he was tortured, he replied that what he feared most was that he would lose compassion for his torturers. I want to return to this, but first I would like to highlight how this modality of being in prison is similar to the previous two.

Modes of compassion emphasize alertness and awareness. Gyatso is well aware of the "tricks" of interrogators, and he has mastered many different strategies, including omission, deception, and silence. He is skilled at hiding things.[18] He is fully focused on the Dalai Lama,[19] and he has, like Djilas, no fear of death.[20] But as a monk, he venerates life. Indeed, Gyatso is remarkable in his willingness to think compassionately of all living creatures and reach out to them. He affirms all these fragile relationships. He takes on pupils whom he teaches to read, only to see them tortured. He makes friends only to witness their suicides or their public denunciations of him. He reveals to his captors who his family is and where they can be found. He speaks with prisoners and enjoys their company, only to see them executed.

All this makes Gyatso profoundly vulnerable. He experiences anger, the delicious feeling of revenge, and the agonies of his friends as though they were his own. He mourns the loss of freedom. Though he was forced to walk in shackles for years, there was no such thing as happiness on the

---

[18] Palden Gyatso with Tsering Shkya, *The Autobiography of a Tibetan Monk* (New York: Grove Press, 1997), 76, 116, 119, 144, 180, and 182.

[19] Ibid., 231.

[20] Ibid., 135.

rack for him. "The loss of freedom," he writes, "is so tangible." And it leads to great unhappiness:

> Many prisoners committed suicide. Some thought they were cowards, others that it was an act of courage. I dare not pass judgment. No one can understand the extreme despair that drives someone to take their own life. As a Buddhist monk, I was brought up to regard human life as the most precious thing in the world, and I found strength in the desire to show my tormentors they had not beaten me, that I still had the courage to live.[21]

He himself becomes suicidal more than once.[22] Above all, he suffers through the many denunciations of his friends. "The fear of being criticized was a constant source of mental torment."[23] Yet his compassion extends even under such conditions. "I never got used to the pain that the denunciations of a friend could cause. But we had to learn how to forget the endless forced betrayals."[24]

Gyatso's compassion extends to his torturers. He describes the arrival of the Red Guard during the Cultural Revolution and the destruction of the prison administrators.

> At first I thought that these officials were getting a taste of their own medicine. This feeling of revenge ran contrary to my religious upbringing, but it is a powerful human impulse. Although prison officers and guards were at the very bottom of a long chain of command, it was their brute force that caused us pain. It was only natural for them to be the prime object of our anger. The Red Guards were spitting on them, accusing them of obstructing the Revolution by refusing to expose the enemies of the Party.[25]

But Gyatso's strategy is different. He expands himself to include the torturers as part of humanity. In the modes of alertness and governance, the torturer stands apart as an enemy. When humanity is invoked, it is invoked as part of the strategy of the torturer or of the victim to gain a hold on the other. That is not the case here with Gyatso. The center of Gyatso's approach is that even in the absence of hope, one opens oneself up fully to the world, and it is this openness that allows one to remain whole in the end. Although in a place of death, Gyatso dreams of escape not through death but by affirming life.

One may well wonder whether anyone other than a monk could live a mode of compassion so fully. But we would do well to recognize that

---

[21] Ibid., 117.
[22] Ibid., 135–37.
[23] Ibid., 135.
[24] Ibid., 152.
[25] Ibid., 126.

Gyatso was not a well-trained monk. He was a very young man when he was arrested, and he admits that he did not understand his faith very well, though he had taken the vows. For most of his life he neither lived in monasteries nor was allowed to practice his faith. He lived, after all, during the Cultural Revolution, when so mundane an activity as washing one's face could be interpreted as a ritual ablution and could lead to denunciation and possible death. The mode of compassion was, in other words, something he achieved in prison, not something he brought to it.

## Modes of Forgetfulness

Now there is an entirely different way to approach torture, one that rejects all reflection. To understand it, we might begin by considering the limits of modes of awareness, modes of governance, and modes of compassion. Modes of awareness seem to prompt higher kinds of thought. Yet the more one thinks, the more one can worry and remember. South African prisoners in solitary tell of how repetitive thoughts tormented them, how they entered into intense dialogues with themselves and made vows about what they would or would not do in life again. And, of course, the more one depends on other humans as a source of comfort, the more one values life. One becomes vulnerable to its loss, and one can become obsessed with it.

Modes of forgetfulness remind us that a great deal of emotional energy is spent, and to no purpose. The alternative is to champion not memory but forgetfulness. Contrary to what one might think, it is forgetfulness rather than memory that is essential to all life. For if we did not forget, we could be tormented by our past. Nietzsche puts it this way:

> To close the doors and windows of consciousness for a time; to remain undisturbed by the noise and struggle of our underworld of utility organs working with and against one another; a little quietness, a little *tabula rasa* of the consciousness, to make room for new things, above all for the nobler functions and functionaries, for regulation, foresight, premeditation (for our organism is an oligarchy)—that is the purpose of active forgetfulness, which is like a doorkeeper, a preserve of psychic order, repose and etiquette: so that it will be immediately obvious how there could be no happiness, no cheerfulness, no hope, no pride, no *present* without forgetfulness. The man in whom this apparatus of repression is damaged and ceases to function properly may be compared (and more than merely compared) with a dyspeptic—he cannot "have done" with anything.[26]

[26] Friedrich Nietzsche, *On the Genealogy of Morals; Ecce Homo* (New York: Vintage Books, 1969), 57–58.

How, then, to induce active forgetfulness is the main concern of this kind of resistance, and Jacobo Timmerman's work is its most exemplary expression.

"Memory," writes Timmerman, "is the chief enemy of the solitary tortured man."[27] The tortured man needs no manuals; he does not need to remember the great civic martyrs; he does not need to manage his self democratically; he does not even need to remain alert. "Once it's been determined that a human being is to be tortured, nothing can prevent that torture from taking place. And it's best to allow yourself to be led meekly toward pain and through pain, rather than to struggle resolutely as if you were a normal human being. The vegetable attitude can save life." The same applies to solitary confinement: no chess or friendship with mice. As Timmerman says of his time in isolation, "More than once I was brusquely awakened by someone shouting: 'Think. Don't sleep, think.' But I refused to think." Why is thought so dangerous? To think meant becoming "conscious of what was happening to me, imagining what might be happening to my wife and children; to think meant trying to work out how to relieve this situation, how to wedge an opening in my relationship with jailers. In that solitary universe of the tortured, any attempt to relate to reality was an immense painful effort leading to nothing."[28] Thought leads to memory, and with memory comes hope, and with that, anxiety and anguish and the need for compassion and tenderness. Hope fulfilled is a great benefit, but then Pandora did not find hope in a box of evils by chance. Hope unfulfilled is surely a great evil, perhaps the greatest evil of all. Is that why hope follows all other evils into the world? As with all Greek gifts, hope is a double-edged offering.

And one that Timmerman will not accept. If the stoic and the republican can embrace hope and rise above life, Timmerman sinks into the muck of organic existence and finds safety there. His goal is to preserve biological energy:

> In the year and a half I spent under house arrest, I devoted much thought to my attitude during torture sessions and during the period of solitary confinement. I realized that, instinctively, I developed an attitude of absolute passivity. Some fought against being carried to the torture tables; others begged not to be tortured; others insulted their torturers. I represented sheer passivity. Because my eyes were blindfolded, I was led by the hand. And I went. The silence was part of the terror. Yet I did not utter a word. I was told to undress. And I did so, passively. I was told when I sat on a bed, to lie down. And, passively, I did so. This passivity, I believe, preserved a great deal

[27] Jacobo Timmerman, *Prisoner without a Name, Cell without a Number* (New York: Vintage Books, 1982), 36.
[28] Ibid., 35.

of energy and left me with all my strength to withstand the torture. I felt I was becoming a vegetable, casting aside all logical emotions and sensations—fear, hatred, vengeance—for any emotion or sensation meant wasting useless energy.[29]

Timmerman's basic advice, then, is something like this: Let the body dominate everything, even the mind, and you will survive. For torture is an attack on the body, and the body needs all the energy it can muster to heal itself. Thought will not heal it, and neither will emotion or memory. As with all advice of this sort, passivity does not come easily to the prisoner. On the contrary, active forgetfulness is a technique that has to be mastered. "I managed to develop certain passivity-inducing devices for withstanding torture and anti-memory devices for those long hours in the solitary cell."[30] During interrogation, he barely speaks. He stands apart during his torture. "What does a man feel? The only thing that comes to mind is that they are ripping apart my flesh. . . . And what else? Nothing that I can think of. No other sensation? Not at that moment. But did they beat you? Yes, but it didn't hurt."[31] Timmerman approaches all conversation with weariness, resignation, or perhaps a presentiment of imminent death—in any case, like a plant, he bends with the blows and says nothing. These are not techniques unknown to other survivors. An Iranian manual advises that one should eat less, so one faints sooner.[32] Even Djilas tells us that "our bodies have limits of endurance. When the infliction of pain reaches the latter limits, the body and spirit protect themselves by lapsing into unconsciousness. In those moments of unconsciousness even torments become sweet, turning to the most subtle, the most spiritual joys imaginable. This is the beginning of the victory over torturers and tortures alike."[33]

For the one in solitary confinement, the most basic technique involves repetitive physical activity: exercises, folding and refolding the bedding, marking time by cracks of light, removing dust from one's hair, cleaning the room, shining the floor. "I behaved," writes Timmerman, "as if my mind were occupied with infinite diverse tasks. Concrete, specific tasks, chores."[34] The basic mental techniques also involve repetition and very little novelty or ingenuity: following the movement of a fly around the room. A somewhat more challenging mental technique was to engage in "professional activity, disconnected from the events around me or that I

---

[29] Ibid., 34–35.
[30] Ibid., 36.
[31] Ibid., 33.
[32] Abrahamian, *Tortured Confessions*, 107.
[33] Djilas, *Of Prisons and Ideas*, 9.
[34] Timmerman, *Prisoner without a Name*, 35.

imagined going on around me. Deliberately, I evaded conjecture on my own destiny, that of my family and the nation. I devoted myself simply to being consciously a solitary man entrusted with a specific task."[35] The kinds of professional development Timmerman chose were very formal. For example, in his mind, Timmerman devises a bookstore, determining which books to put where, what to carry, in short, envisioning the infinite, pointless movement of books.

Timmerman concedes, though, that techniques of forgetfulness are not foolproof. They can be undermined by "some lingering physical pain following an interrogation, hunger, the need for a human voice, for contact, for a memory." What he was not able to avoid were two powerful emotions: the desire for suicide and the feeling of madness. But suicide turns out to be manageable, even usable, when one realizes what a definitively hopeless gesture it is. One can plan one's suicide with "unforeseen originality," since the "possibility of suicide no longer exists."[36] Then there is the temptation of madness, which cannot be dealt with so rationally, so here passivity is the way forward. "You must await madness, and think that perhaps it will come. You must try to yield to it, and possibly it will engulf you. Await it and yield to it—that is the grim part. For if it fails to arrive, your impotence is conclusive, and your humiliation greater than a kick on the behind from some voiceless, faceless stranger who leads you blindfolded from your cell." You await madness, but under no circumstances do you expect it, for that would be vanity and a false belief in one's omnipotence. All you can do is grow like a plant. "You keep on going, and here I am."[37]

### Modes of Laughter

I cannot overlook a further strain of resistance: namely, ways of acting that constantly introduce comic relief into the condition of incarceration. It is perhaps true, as Foucault says, that revolutionaries do not have to be grim and so serious, but it is rare to meet laughing revolutionaries in prison. Yet laughter does happen there, as the movie *Life Is Beautiful* reminds us—as do the tales of the Republican prisoners from Spain. Consider this moving tale of the trial of Generalissimo Franco. One needs to imagine a room in which women, in hushed voices, have to quell their laughter as they think of awful wicked ways to make Franco suffer.

---

[35] Ibid., 37.
[36] Ibid., 89.
[37] Ibid., 92.

In spite of the horrible conditions—and naturally the food and hygiene were terrible—we young women didn't lose our good humor. We were always happy, always singing and planning some joke to distract the older women, and sometimes the younger ones too, from thinking about their homes, their children, their husbands. We would do all sorts of pranks to divert the women who spent so many days under the death penalty. I remember vividly one such prank. Almost every night, we staged a mock trial where we judged Franco. We cast lots for the part of Franco because naturally no one wanted to play the role. The unlucky woman would sit on a sleeping mat that served as the defendant's chair and the popular tribunal was formed around her. The entire room had the right to speak and render opinions. It was like an army of devils rising up. No one can begin to imagine what tortures the prisoners dreamed up to make Franco die little by little to make . . . well, what can I say? It was horrifying.[38]

There are other such examples. "One thing that made me laugh, yes laugh, was that one of the officials kicking us lost his shoe and a prisoner grabbed it and passed it to another who, in turn, threw it down to the patio. He got really mad. I laughed so hard I almost fell in his hands."[39] Abrahamian describes similar scenes in Iranian prisons, where prison routine is thrown into chaos by a comic and serene personality. The main occasions were the forced public confessions, often televised.

These tense shows could easily be subverted into carnivals—at least, by those willing to risk death. E.A. recounts that a teenage boy was invited to the podium by Ladjevardi to explain why he was in prison. He explained that he had first joined the Tudeh but had left it once he discovered that the party supported the Islamic Republic. He had looked around for a party to his liking, but finding none, had formed his own organization with a total membership of one—himself. At that point, much of the audience was smirking, for it was clear that he was in Evin simply because he did not like the regime.[40]

This was Winston Smith's dilemma, but, unlike the boy, he found no humor in it.

To understand the role of the comic in torture, we need to remember that in this context, the comic is a kind of magic. The comic, like magic, "brings about a sudden and rationally inexplicable shift in the sense of reality."[41] It is by this shift between worlds, sudden juxtapositions, that—

---

[38] Tomasa Cuevas, *Prison of Women: Testimonies of War and Resistance in Spain, 1939–1975*, ed. Mary E. Giles (Albany: State University of New York Press, 1998), 53–54.

[39] Ibid., 54.

[40] Abrahamian, *Tortured Confessions*, 145–46.

[41] Peter L. Berger, *Redeeming Laughter: The Comic Dimension of Human Experience* (New York: Walter de Gruyter Press, 1997), 117.

even if it does not offer catharsis—it serves to console. Machiavelli is certainly the greatest expositor of this modality in prison.

Machiavelli wrote two prison sonnets, and they represent the irrepressible humor with which Machiavelli accepted his misfortunes, even torture.[42] This did not mean that he did not suffer. That he composed poems at all, of course, is astounding, since the torture he underwent on the strappado involves being hoisted, with one's arms tied behind one's back, and dropped from a great height. As the prisoner is hoisted, the shoulders must bear his entire weight, an excruciating torture that eventually pulls the bones from their sockets.

Machiavelli's first poem tells of his night in the cell after he was tortured. It is a humorous rejection of the consolations of religion. He lies in the cell with chains on his feet. He is aching from six falls on the strappado. Next door they are torturing into the night; the victim complains that they have raised the strappado too high in violation of the law, but to no avail. The place smells. It is infested. It is, as all prisons are, very noisy. As Timmerman says, "the police need to shout; shouting helps them."[43] Machiavelli's prison is a scene of confusion, chaos, and corruption, and he tries hard to piece it together into a dainty hospice. But, he says, at dawn he hears the priests chanting, "We are praying for you." This, he complains, is truly unbearable, the most torment a man can bear, so he addresses the Medici, Have pity on me, free me from these bonds so I don't suffer such horrible torture.

Machiavelli's second poem attacks the stoic view, this time, through a wicked adaptation of Boethius's *Consolation of Philosophy*. Like the imprisoned Boethius, Machiavelli calls out to the Muses to console him and intercede for him with the Medici. A nameless Muse appears, flustered and angry. She decides to torture him, slaps him across the face, and silences him. Even worse, she does not recognize him at all, saying, "Who are you?" and decides that he must be the madman Dazzo, not Citizen Niccolò. Machiavelli wants to argue with the Muse, but the Muse, clearly Philosophy, will not listen. Reversing his plea that the Muse intercede with the Medici, Machiavelli now begs the Medici to intercede with her and tell her that this is Niccolò Machiavelli. In the end it is civic identity, not philosophical identity, that is the most precious item of all to Machiavelli.

There is a serious philosophical point to these poems. Machiavelli's poems are a humorous attack on people who resist using modes of awareness. People like Djilas think that one can be happy on the rack. Yet amid

[42] Niccolò Machiavelli, *Chief Works and Others* (Durham, N.C.: Duke University Press, 1965), 2:1013.
[43] Timmerman, *Prisoner without a Name*, 83.

the chaos and noise of prison, only madmen would think of their prisons as dainty hospices, as Don Quixote did. What is more, incarceration and torture lead to a distressing loss of self. To contemplate the great idea, one needs to have some assurance of who one is, but this is precisely what prison and torture interrupt. It is silly to think that one can lead a complex inner life under torture. Indeed, someone who is truly committed to the proposition that happiness is simply a good state of mind is talking about falling into something like a coma or a sleep or a trance. He should probably imitate the life of Jacobo Timmerman in prison: live the life of the madman Dazzo, not the life of Djilas. But if one really wants to affirm life in prison, one should laugh and laugh and laugh and live the life of Machiavelli.

Both modes of forgetfulness and modes of laughter flirt with madness, and this is, of course, their weakness. Laughter can become hysteria, and forgetfulness can become delusion and fantasy. In the film *Brazil*, as the torture victim escapes into fantasy, the torturers say regretfully, "We have lost him." What Timmerman says, though, then serves as a caution. Hysteria and delusion are indeed dangers, but they may not come, and besides there's no point in worrying about it. One just proceeds.

## THE ORDINARY FUTURE PAST

One may object to all this that I have analyzed resistance outside of the context of Oceania. In Oceania, the Party seems to undercut the possibility of resistance to torture by shaping a particular kind of state and society, and by developing excruciatingly painful torture technology. One brings to torture the totality of one's life experiences, and Smith had so few opportunities to develop his character that he was handicapped. Perhaps, but this credits Smith with too little. Smith does practice modes of alertness (by outwitting the Party for so long), governance (by joining the "resistance"), and compassion. But in the end the Party had anticipated these. In Oceania's prisons, modes of alertness, governance, laughter, and compassion are not available—though, interestingly, modes of forgetfulness do persist, for it is possible that the cells of Oceania are full of Smiths who escape into forgetfulness and fantasy, as does the hero in the movie *Brazil*.

Nevertheless, the question remains: is Oceania the future? Will there be torture technologies against which resistance is futile, technologies that reprogram individuals? "Orwell is purposely vague about the machine which first tortures Smith. Nothing like it existed in 1948, but for Orwell it was a solid and predictable piece of the future; since pain could achieve the conversion of recalcitrant individuals, the dismantling and recreation of personalities, then a device for producing adequate volumes of pain for this purpose would have to be invented."[44]

There are two facets to this observation, technological and political. Let me deal first with the technological objection. How inventive are torturers? Will they invent the perfect torture machine? The answer to that is no. Orwell is right to say that contemporary torture is scientific and modern, but it is important not to conflate this with the attribution of technological genius to torturers. Sociological studies of torture technology show that torturers are not innovators but adapters of previously existing technology invented for other purposes.[45] They simply have better things to do than to tinker. Djilas is absolutely on target when he states:

> Torturers are seldom possessed of a particularly inventive imagination in devising their terrors. Most frequently, they find it easiest to follow long trodden paths and make use of those tried and true methods handed down from the past. They rely on ready-made instruments: whips, truncheons, sandbags, needles, castor oil, electric currents, and the like. It is common, of course, especially where torture is not standard procedure, for the police to use, particularly in anger and haste, whatever instruments may be at hand—pencils (for jabbing between fingers), drawers (for crushing hands), chairs (for jamming bodies against the walls), and most frequently, to be sure, the most direct, handiest instrument of all, their fists.[46]

And the results are often the same. As the Soviet dissidents write:

> But do not despair! Scores of your comrades have been undergoing compulsory treatment for long years without any serious injury to their health. Despite the whole arsenal of psycho-pharmacological methods and shock therapy, contemporary science has—fortunately—not yet reached the point where it can work irreversible changes in the human individual or destroy a man's personality.[47]

Orwell is also a great adapter of torture techniques, and his torture techniques are, in fact, adaptations of previously existing technologies as well.

---

[44] Edward Peters, *Torture*, 2nd ed. (Philadelphia: University of Pennsylvania Press, 1996), 162.

[45] Darius Rejali, *Torture and Modernity: Self, Society and State in Modern Iran* (Boulder, Colo.: Westview, 1994), 135–36; Rejali, "Electric Torture: A Global History of a Torture Technology" (paper presented at the Conference on Investigating and Combating Torture, University of Chicago, March 1999); Steve Wright, "The New Trade in Technologies," in *A Glimpse of Hell*, ed. Duncan Forrest (London: Amnesty International, 1996).

[46] Djilas, *Of Prisons and Ideas*, 7.

[47] Fireside, *Soviet Psychoprisons*, 116.

The torture with rats had already been used by the Cheka in the 1920s.[48] As for the electric table, contrary to Edward Peters's assertion,[49] machines that modulated electricity for torture had already been in use for at least thirty years prior to the appearance of Orwell's novel. Electric torture had been used in Argentina, civil war Spain, Royalist Iran, and Vichy France. Specialized machines were in use in Argentina and Italy. In this respect, Oceania is not the future. It is the past.

Orwell's torture scenes are gripping not so much for their technology as for the psychological techniques that O'Brien employs. These techniques are what Foucault might call examples of "pastoral power." The torturer presents himself as mediating between the prisoner and the benefits of the world.[50] He claims that he wields this power in the interests of the subject, and the pain will stop when the subject cures himself.[51] He employs psychological techniques designed to elicit the confession that he wants to hear. As Philip Zimbardo argues, these techniques are very insidious and very effective. For example, in Japan, where confession to crime is valued even more highly than it is here, 86 percent of all criminal cases end with a full confession by the accused.[52] While these techniques are effective, they work best *without torture*. "Thus, psychology has generally replaced the physical abuses of the third degree, not only because the courts have made invalid physically coerced confessions, but largely because the third degree is not as effective."[53] As an FBI agent stated: "When you break a man by torture, he will always hate you. If you break him by your intelligence, he will always fear and respect you."[54] Peters, after reviewing the state of torture technology, concurs: "Rather more psychological sophistication is evident than medical or technological, except in the use of pharmacological methods of torture. The mysterious machines of *Nineteen Eighty-Four* seem, for the most part, not yet to be in use."[55]

So much, then, for the technological objection. Let me turn now to the political question. Orwell presents a particular model of the kind of state, the kind of society, that tortures. Let me sum it up. Torture is sanguinary

[48] Peters, *Torture*, 162.

[49] Ibid., 162–63.

[50] Timmerman, *Prisoner without a Name*, 39–41.

[51] Rejali, *Torture and Modernity*, 75–77.

[52] G. McCormick, "Crime, Confession and Control in Contemporary Japan," in *Democracy in Contemporary Japan*, ed. G. McCormick and Y. Sugimoto (Armonk, N.Y.: M. E. Sharpe, 1986), 187.

[53] Philip Zimbardo, "Coercion and Compliance: The Psychology of Police Confessions," in *Triple Revolution Emerging: Social Problems in Depth*, ed. Robert Perrucci and Marc Pilisuk (Boston: Little Brown, 1971), 499.

[54] In ibid.

[55] Peters, *Torture*, 172.

violence conducted by party officials on behalf of state interests. It leaves scars and marks all over the body from broken bones to chewed-up faces. It is done as part of a proactive police strategy to reduce the internal enemy: political crime and terrorism. The goal is not that the victim should confess to a crime, for that is already taken for granted, but to come up with a complete file on a person's political contacts and to gather to the state an ever widening net of dependent and insular individuals. Torture, then, happens mainly to political criminals, not to ordinary criminals who actually live it up in prison (187).

Most important, torture is scientific and modern. It is characterized by the modes of rationality that characterize other professions (medicine, engineering, administration, and psychology) that arise in our modern universe. It comes from within our societies, not from without. It is a form of routinized and ordinary cruelty. Torture is a cancer: it is not a virus that comes from without but something that arises owing to some pathology within the democratic body politic. If one were to ask why torture is characterized by ordinary betrayals, the answer is simple: it should be no surprise that a practice that draws on so many activities constitutive of modern life should also have so many disruptive effects on the substrata of the lives on which it is inflicted.

There is much to recommend this model of torture. Orwell clearly was right in rejecting older views of torture as an atavistic survival. He correctly identified the fact that, in the twentieth century, torture once again assumed its traditional place within the state apparatus, and we witnessed the second great revival of torture since the end of the Roman Empire (the first being the creation of inquisitional torture in the twelfth century, which lasted until its abolition in the eighteenth). He correctly identified the ways in which modern forms of rationality could become complicit in the practice of torture. This is why modern torture is characterized by ordinary, as well as great, betrayals.

As a historical description of what torture has been like in the latter twentieth century, there is much to recommend this model. But it is a model of torture that has become increasingly antiquated even as we gain a purchase on it. There are four trends that ensure the irrelevance of this model. Oceania, once again, is the past.

First, the state is changing. In a world that emphasizes the movements of peoples and goods, otherwise known as globalization, states are changing the ways they exercise their monopoly on violence. Rather than emphasizing enclosed military bureaucratic administration of space, states are turning increasingly to policing—that is, a form of coercion that allows one to discriminate between different kinds of people (legal and illegal immigrants) and goods (commodities and contraband) while they are in motion. This kind of policing state governs not through enclosed societies but through the reinvention of policing.[56]

And this is my second point: policing itself is changing. For a variety of reasons, policing is becoming privatized.[57] In South Africa, for example, the ratio of private to public police is now 5:1, but trends like this are evident in all sorts of societies to greater or lesser degrees. This rapid decentralization of policing is pushed, in part, by the commodification of policing—that is, the sale of security products and services for multinational conglomerates and the creation of a "Robocop" universe. In the words of Michael Kaye, president of burgeoning Westec, a subsidiary of Japan's Secon Ltd.: "We're not a security guard company. We sell a *concept of security.*"[58] But commodification is not the only factor that pushes this change, as Martha Huggins has shown in the case of Brazil: privatization can also follow from bureaucratic politics and professionalization of police.[59]

Increasingly, what is emerging is a specialization of functions; the Los Angeles police may be a shape of things to come. The Los Angeles police focus on the movements of illegal goods and people, the kinds of issues that are central to the new crimefare state. Private, decentralized policing focuses on the control of local space: the restricted use of public space, the creation of unwelcome street environments, the panoptic malls, and gated residential communities, all of which have their private police.[60] Public/private partnerships—which go by many names, including community policing—are now the rage[61] and prey on a democratic public's fears of urban crime and on their personal insecurity. Proactive international policing works in tandem with reactive private policing of neighborhoods.

---

[56] Peter Andreas, "Political Economy of Narco-Corruption in Mexico," *Current History*, April 1998; Andreas, "The Rise of the American Crimefare State," *World Policy Journal*, Fall 1997; Peter Andreas and Andreas Friman, eds., *The Illicit Global Economy and State Power* (Lanham, Md.: Rowman and Littlefield, 1999).

[57] Clifford Shearing, "The Relation between Public and Private Policing," in *Modern Policing*, ed. Michael Tonry and Norval Morris (Chicago: University of Chicago Press, 1992); Shearing, "Reinventing Policing: Policing as Governance," in *Policing Change, Changing Police: International Perspectives*, ed. Otwin Marenin (New York: Garland Publishing, 1996).

[58] Mike Davis, *City of Quartz: Excavating the Future in Los Angeles* (New York: Vintage Books, 1992), 250.

[59] Martha K. Huggins, *Political Policing: The United States and Latin America* (Durham, N.C.: Duke University Press, 1998), 161–87; see also Paul Chevigny, "Changing Control of Police Violence in Rio de Janeiro and São Paulo, Brazil," in Marenin, *Policing Change, Changing Police.*

[60] Davis, *City of Quartz*, 221–65.

[61] Shearing, "Reinventing Policing."

In this context, torture is changing. Torture used to be the lot of the political criminal but is now increasingly the lot of the ordinary criminal, the vagrant, the illegal immigrant, or the drug runner.[62] In retrospect, in some countries such as Iran,[63] the Cold War was actually a golden age for ordinary criminals, since even the most authoritarian states liked to operate the civilian prison system in exemplary ways and keep the focus off the prisoners in the political prison system. This technique was used to satisfy local and international critics of the regime. But with the end of the Cold War, there is no particular need for such pretenses, and torture has once again become commonplace for ordinary as well as political criminals.

Finally, torture technology itself is changing. One of the increasingly disturbing trends in modern torture is that police forces are becoming interested in forms of torture that leave no marks and hence no story to tell. Such tortures are especially common in semidemocratic states, where a press, left-wing politicians, and intellectuals are apt to denounce torture, and increasingly in authoritarian states that are closely scrutinized by international human rights organizations.[64] One might describe this as a police captain's way of saying, "This person claims to have been tortured, but, in fact, you see, there are no marks, you see them exactly as they always were." How far this process can go, no one knows, but one hopes the Israeli Supreme Court set a standard when it condemned such invisible torture techniques in September 1999. In the absence of such explicit judicial condemnation, torture of this sort may not only be more tolerable, it may be increasingly regarded as legal by police, media, and the public.

At its grandest level, Orwell's vision of state and society presupposed military bureaucratic states locked in alternating "Cold" and "Hot" wars. This background informs his vision of torture. His account draws on certain characteristic features of torture in Franco's Spain, Nazi Germany, and Stalinist Russia to complete the picture. This model of torture had many imitators during the Cold War and in countries where a version of a "Cold War" still exists. Orwell would not have been the least surprised by torture in the Islamic Republic of Iran, with its show trials, public forced confessions, and constant "War with the American Great Satan."[65] In many ways, that nation provides the best current exemplar of what Orwell thought torture would be like.

---

[62] See, for example, Geoffrey York, "Study Finds Russian Police Use Torture Routinely," *Globe and Mail*, November 10, 1999.

[63] This was not the case everywhere, though. See Chevigny, "Changing Control," on Brazil.

[64] James Ron, "Varying Methods of State Violence," *International Organization* 51, no. 2 (1997): 296–97; Rejali, "Electric Torture."

[65] Abrahamian, *Tortured Confessions*. See also International Solidarity Front for the Defense of the Iranian People's Democratic Rights, *The Crimes of Khomeini's Regime* (N.p.:

But even in places like Iran, this model is now becoming history, and Iran itself is a curious backwater as far as concerns security concepts for the modern state. With the end of the Cold War and the dawning of globalization, everything is changing: states, police forces, prisons, community security, and torture. We have every reason to fear a world of torture in the twenty-first century, but not for the reasons Orwell has suggested. We may be entering an age of "Cold Peace," and torture as I have described it will have a place in that world. And that world will be populated by people who betray others or resist in the ways I've described. And resist they will. Nothing that is human, even something so seemingly inhuman as torture, is alien to man, and whatever one man makes, another can understand and undo. That is the rule of the human world.

---

ISF-Iran, 1982); Reza Baraheni, *The Crowned Cannibals: Writings on Repression in Iran* (New York: Vintage Press, 1977); Amnesty International, *Iran: Violations of Human Rights* (London: Amnesty International, 1987).

# Part IV

## TECHNOLOGY AND PRIVACY

# Orwell versus Huxley: Economics, Technology, Privacy, and Satire

RICHARD A. POSNER

THE EDITORS asked me to discuss what *Nineteen Eighty-Four* may have bequeathed to us in the way of useful thinking about technology and privacy; for many people believe that the relentless advance of science and technology in recent decades has endangered privacy and brought us to the very brink of the Orwellian nightmare. With the editors' permission, however, I enlarged my canvas to take in another famous English satiric novel from the era that produced *Nineteen Eighty-Four*. Aldous Huxley's *Brave New World*, published in 1932, has many parallels to Orwell's novel, published in 1949—and Orwell borrowed extensively from the earlier work (as both works did from Yevgeny Zamyatin's novel *We* [1924])—yet it is far more technology-intensive and in ways that bring out the limitations of Orwell's social vision. Indeed, the contrast between these two celebrated dystopian novels, notably in their ideas about the relation between sex and privacy, is striking. But relating the two works to technology, and more broadly to what I am calling "technocratic modernism," the kind of outlook that fosters and is fostered by technological progress, is no easy matter, and I need two mediating approaches: that of economics, in relation to technology, and that of literary criticism, in relation to satire, which is the genre of both novels, although I shall argue that Orwell's novel is not only a satire.

To telegraph my punch, I don't think either novel has much to teach us about what it means to live in an age of technology, though both are fine novels. They don't have much to say about privacy (a particular concern of those who fear technology), although what they do say about it is important—in particular, that a taste for solitude is inimical to totalizing schemes of governance and social organization, whether the utilitarianism

This is the amplified text of a talk given at a University of Chicago Law School conference, "*Nineteen Eighty-Four*: Orwell and Our Future," on November 12, 1999. I thank Paul Choi for his helpful research assistance and Wayne Booth, Larry Downes, Joseph Epstein, Lawrence Lessig, Joan Mellen, Charlene Posner, Eric Posner, Eric Rasmusen, Richard Rorty, and Richard Stern for their helpful comments on a previous draft. A longer version of the paper appears under the same title in *Philosophy and Literature* 24, no. 1 (April 2000).

184 ORWELL VERSUS HUXLEY

of *Brave New World* or the totalitarianism of *Nineteen Eighty-Four*, because when people are alone they are more apt to have wayward thoughts about their community than when they are immersed in it.[1] This is not a new idea; it lies behind Jeremy Bentham's proposal for the "Panopticon," a domed prison the cells of which would have no ceilings so that the prisoners could be kept under continuous observation by warders stationed at the top of the dome. Privacy and technology are related in Orwell's novel through the "telescreen," a means of universal surveillance. They are largely separate in Huxley's novel, except insofar as reproductive technology is related to privacy.

I do not mean to rest with making negative points. I shall try to explain what in my view these novels are most importantly about and where they succeed and where they fail. And I shall suggest[2] that it is a mistake to try to mine works of literature for political or economic significance—even when it is political literature.

## SOME ECONOMICS OF TECHNOLOGY

I imagine that anyone who thinks that these two novels—both in their different ways distinctly dystopian, if not downright dyspeptic—are commentaries on technology thinks they are critical commentaries. Economics can provide focus, structure, and critique to the widespread fear that technology is a danger to humankind as well as a boon—indeed, a master as well as a servant, so that technological "progress" may be, at the same time and perhaps more fundamentally, retrogressive from the standpoint of civilization. There are five ways in which the economist can help us to see the downside of technological change.[3] I shall call them externality,

---

[1] "[T]o do anything that suggested a taste for solitude, even to go for a walk by yourself, was always slightly dangerous. There was a word for it in Newspeak: *ownlife*, it was called, meaning individualism and eccentricity" (70).

[2] As I have done elsewhere: see my essays "Against Ethical Criticism," *Philosophy and Literature* 20 (1997); and "Against Ethical Criticism: Part Two," *Philosophy and Literature* 22 (1998).

[3] This is not the usual focus of economic analysis of technology. The usual focus is on the relation between science and technology (the former being a major input into the latter), the different incentive structures of the two activities, the social benefits of technological progress, and the means (such as patent rights) for encouraging private individuals and firms to produce these benefits. See, for an excellent discussion, Partha Dasgupta and Paul A. David, "Information Disclosure and the Economics of Technology," in *Arrow and the Ascent of Modern Economic Theory*, ed. George R. Feiwel (New York: New York University Press, 1987), 519.

marginality, rent seeking, interaction effects, and economies of scale and scope, and shall explain them very briefly.[4]

*Externality.* The seller may not take the full costs of a new technology into account, in which event technology may be introduced even though its net social benefits are negative. As economists say, some of the costs may be *external* to his decision-making process. A transcontinental supersonic airline service would reduce travel times, but it would also generate sonic booms, which would annoy people and break windows beneath the flight path. These harms would be a cost of supersonic travel, but not a cost borne by the airline unless the law made the airline liable for it. External effects can be positive as well as negative, however, and on balance the external effects of modern technology have been positive. The positive effects stem largely from the fact that most technological innovations are imitable, and patent laws provide only very limited protection against imitation. The benefits to consumers of most technologically advanced products, ranging from pharmaceuticals to color television, greatly exceed the profits of the manufacturers.

*Marginality.* The level of output in a competitive market is determined by the intersection of price and marginal cost (the cost of increasing output by one unit). This implies that the marginal purchaser—the purchaser willing to pay a price no higher than marginal cost—drives the market to a considerable extent. It follows that a technological innovation that is attractive to the marginal consumer may be introduced even though it lowers consumer welfare overall because it reduces the welfare of the inframarginal consumers more than it increases the welfare of the marginal ones; this is a kind of negative externality.

*Rent Seeking.* This term refers to the fact that economic activity is generally guided by the prospects for private gain rather than the prospects for social gain. As a result, costs may be incurred that do not increase society's overall wealth but merely alter its distribution among persons. For example, a more lethal gun has value both to criminals and to the police, but after both sides in the war against crime are equipped with it, the only effect of the innovation may be to increase the costs of crime and crime control. Likewise, but on a much larger scale, with military weapons. The "arms race" is indeed the classic example of wasteful competition. Both crime and conquest are close to being purely rent-seeking activities. The costs incurred in trying to obtain a competitive advantage by adopting a new technology are entirely wasted from the standpoint of overall social welfare except to the extent that the technology can be bene-

---

[4] For a fuller discussion, see the longer version of this article published in *Philosophy and Literature.*

ficially adapted to civilian use—a spillover analogous to the informational or entertainment quality of advertising designed purely to wrest business from a competitor.

A form of arms race that is particularly relevant to the two novels under discussion is the struggle on the one hand to invade and on the other hand to protect privacy. For example, advances in electronics have both increased the efficacy of surveillance and, through such devices as electronic encryption and computer "burn" programs, made certain communications more private.

*Interaction Effects.* Technological innovations can interact with each other or with the social structure to produce unforeseeable long-run consequences that may be good or bad, a possibility dramatized by World War I, which revealed the unexpected destructiveness of warfare under conditions of technological progress. The problem of technology's unanticipated consequences, the subject of a vast literature in history, sociology, and cultural studies,[5] is merely the problem of externalities writ large. For I am speaking now of external effects that cannot be predicted; often they cannot be evaluated even after they have come to pass. Consider such innovations of the last half-century as improved contraceptive and labor-saving devices, fast food, and the automation of many tasks formerly requiring substantial upper-body strength. Their interaction probably is largely responsible for women's emancipation from their formerly constrained role in society, an emancipation that has brought in its train a high divorce rate, a low marriage rate and high age of first marriage, a high rate of abortions and of births out of wedlock, a low birthrate, an increase in fertility problems that has contributed in turn to an increased rate of innovation in reproductive technology, and a profound change in sexual morality, including increased tolerance of homosexuality. None of these consequences was foreseen, and the net impact on social welfare is unclear, or at least unmeasurable, though I am inclined to think it positive.[6]

The four reasons that I have discussed thus far for uncertainty about whether technological innovation will increase or reduce social welfare can help us understand the sense that many people have that scientific and technological progress is "out of control" and leading us into a future that may not be a net improvement on the present. Those of us who have lived most of our lives in the second half of the twentieth century are

---

[5] See *The Intellectual Appropriation of Technology: Discourses on Modernity, 1900–1939*, ed. Mikael Hård and Andrew Jamison (Cambridge: MIT Press, 1998), and references cited there.

[6] For a historical example, see the fascinating story of the effect of the invention of the stirrup on medieval society in Lynn White, Jr., *Medieval Technology and Social Change* (Oxford: Clarendon Press, 1962), chap. 1.

likely to be optimistic rather than pessimistic about where technology is leading, though perhaps only because technology has been on the whole very good to us. But the economics of technological innovation that I have been sketching suggests the need for caution about projecting the beneficent trends of the recent past into the future.

*Economies of Scale and Scope.* None of the specific concerns so far discussed figures in either Orwell's or Huxley's novel. What worried the authors was that technology, and "technocratic" methods and attitudes more generally, might destroy both economic competition (the market) and political competition (democracy). Our authors believed, like many of their contemporaries, that engineering methods, applied both to production and to people ("social engineering"), epitomized rationality, entailed central planning and centralized control, were much more efficient than the market, and implied political as well as economic rule by experts. In economic lingo, the concern was that technology was bringing about radically increased economies of scale and scope—was making the efficient size and scope of enterprises so large that eventually all activity would be conducted on a monopoly basis.

The relation between monopoly and technology is complicated. When technological innovation is risky, too little of it may be undertaken if competitors can appropriate the benefits of the innovation. This is the rationale of patent protection, which is a form of monopoly. So technology may invite monopoly and at the same time may lower its costs, perhaps by reducing the cost of control. Computers were once expected to facilitate central planning of an economy; recently they have been effective in reducing middle management, thereby reducing the costs of internal control of enterprises and so presumably increasing the span of effective control and thus the optimum size of enterprises. But equally technology can foster decentralization, for example by reducing transaction costs among independent firms.[7] Another possibility is that new (hence small) firms may be better at technological innovation,[8] in which event technological progress will favor small firms over large, competition over monopoly. It is an empirical rather than a theoretical question whether technological progress on balance favors monopoly or competition. As of now it appears, contrary to widespread fears in the 1930s and 1940s, not only that competition generally is a more efficient method of organizing production than central planning but also that the more technologically advanced the economy, the greater the advantage of competition.

---

[7] This effect is emphasized in Larry Downes and Chunka Mui, *Unleashing the Killer App: Digital Strategies for Market Dominance* (Boston: Harvard Business School Press, 1998).

[8] As argued in Clayton M. Christensen, *The Innovator's Dilemma: When New Technologies Cause Great Firms to Fail* (Boston: Harvard Business School Press, 1997).

Nor has technological progress imperiled democracy; rather the opposite. Technological progress has increased average incomes in most nations, and income not only is strongly positively correlated with political freedom but also appears to play a causal role in that freedom.[9] We should consider, however, the possibility that technology may threaten freedom through its effect on privacy. Consider the two principal aspects of privacy when it is distinguished from autonomy, for which "privacy" has become a common synonym in constitutional law, where rights of sexual and reproductive freedom are described as aspects of the "right of privacy." The two nonautonomy aspects of privacy are solitude and secrecy, and to a totalitarian regime the social costs of both are great. Solitude (not complete isolation, but enough private space to enable a person to think for himself) fosters individualistic attitudes; conversely, the constant presence of other people, or the sense of being under constant surveillance, enforces decorum and conformity. Secrecy, in the sense of concealment of what one is thinking, or writing, or saying to friends or other intimates, enables subversive thinking and planning to be hidden from the authorities. Indeed, planning implies communication, and serious independent thinking is hardly possible without having someone to "bounce ideas" off, but the communication of "dangerous" thoughts is itself dangerous if there is no privacy of communication. So solitude creates the elementary conditions for independent thought, and concealment creates the essential conditions for the refinement and propagation of that thought. In both *Brave New World* and *Nineteen Eighty-Four*, the high social costs of privacy to the regime, conjoined with technological advances that make it costly to maintain privacy, result in dramatically less privacy compared to that of our society.

Each of these aspects of privacy can be regarded as an economic good, and its demand and supply conditions investigated. Notice first that the cost of invading privacy has fallen with the "information revolution"— now the "cyberspace revolution."[10] (We shall see this when we see how labor-intensive the means of surveillance employed in *Nineteen Eighty-Four* are.) But it is unlikely that the net amount of privacy has declined, since it is what economists call a superior good (that is, more of it is demanded as people's incomes rise), and since, as I mentioned earlier, technological progress fosters protection as well as invasion of privacy. What is certain is that people today are better informed, more individual-

---

[9] Richard A. Posner, "Equality, Wealth, and Political Stability," *Journal of Law, Economics, and Organization* 13 (1997): 344.

[10] See, for example, Lawrence Lessig, *Code—and Other Laws of Cyberspace* (New York: Basic Books, 1999), 142–56.

istic, and more self-assertive than they were in Huxley's and Orwell's time—which is what we would expect if privacy had, on balance, grown.

An even more important point is that privacy as secrecy is not an unalloyed good. Charismatic political leadership—the most dangerous kind—depends on the leader's ability to control public information about him. If he loses that ability—if he loses his "privacy"—his mystique, and with it his power, erodes. The same technological advances that have made it costly for private persons to protect their privacy have, by making government more transparent, made it more costly for public officials to conceal bad acts—including snooping into the private affairs of the citizenry. Secrecy, in short, is a bad as well as a good, and so the net effect on social welfare of making secrecy more costly to maintain is difficult to assess.

I anticipate the argument that in examining issues of technology and privacy from the standpoint of economics, I am instantiating the problem rather than analyzing it. Modern economics is itself a form of "technocratic" thought closely allied to such clearly technocratic fields as statistics, engineering, computer science, and operations research. Max Weber would have thought that modern economic thinking, especially when it is applied to noneconomic behavior—as I have done in many of my writings—is a prime example of the triumph of the trend, which he thought defined modernity, toward bringing more and more areas of human life and thought under the reign of rational methods. This theory, which as we'll see influenced both Huxley and (under the rubric of "managerialism") Orwell, is indeed worth considering in a discussion of the relation of *Brave New World* and *Nineteen Eighty-Four* to issues of technology, and I shall do so. Specifically, I shall argue that the disenchantment of the world which Weber predicted as a by-product of the triumph of rational methods appears in Orwell's novel as a nostalgia for Romantic values. We might think of this as a spiritual consequence of technology and technocracy that is separate from the economic and political consequences that I have been discussing and that are often, though I think erroneously, considered the heart of the novels' critique of modernity.

### SATIRE

We need to think about the genre, satire,[11] to which both novels belong, though *Brave New World* more obviously. Satire is a genre of fiction that invites the reader's attention to the flaws in his society, or in society (or humanity) more generally. Often, as in such classics of the genre as *Gulli-*

---

[11] Superbly discussed in Alvin Kernan, *The Cankered Muse: Satire of the English Renaissance* (New Haven: Yale University Press, 1959), chap. 1.

*ver's Travels*, it is set in a fantastic world, seemingly remote in time, place, or culture from the satirist's (and reader's) world. This point is directly applicable to both *Brave New World* and *Nineteen Eighty-Four*. The fact that they are set in the future (six hundred years and thirty-five years, respectively) need not imply that they are efforts at prophecy, rather than critiques of, or warnings against, tendencies visible in the writer's own society. In both novels, as we shall see, futuristic technology is a straight-forward extrapolation from well-known technologies of the author's day.

Extrapolation is the key. The satirist criticizes repulsive tendencies in his society by providing an imaginative picture of the logical outcome of those tendencies. He shows (not argues) the inner logic of whatever contemporary tendency troubles him.

It is also characteristic of satire that there is a satirist *character* in the work—a denouncer of the flaws to which the author wishes to invite the reader's attention, but not necessarily identical to the author. Often he is a gloomier, shriller figure than the author, and sometimes he embodies many of the flaws that he denounces. *Brave New World* has two main satirist characters—the Savage, who like Gulliver is an outsider to the "world" that is being satirized, and Bernard Marx, the insider, a classic satiric misfit.[12] In *Nineteen Eighty-Four* the satiric character is also an insider, Winston Smith, who, being like Bernard something of a misfit[13] and also like Bernard (and relatedly) having the taste for solitude that both authors deem the precondition for independent thinking, is able to see through the lies that undergird his society and is thus able to denounce it. The satiric figures in both novels come to a bad end—death, "unper-sonhood," or, in the case of Bernard Marx, exile to Iceland—which is also typical of the genre. Likewise the fact that both provide an anchor to the real world of the present by dwelling on certain familiar objects, such as the Savage's copy of Shakespeare's complete works, or, in Orwell's novel, the paperweight, thrush, statue of Oliver Cromwell, real coffee, silver-foil-wrapped chocolate, and other objects left over from before the Revo-lution. Characters in satires tend to be cardboard figures, "humors" rather than three-dimensional human beings. Winston and Julia, in *Nine-teen Eighty-Four*, are the only richly human characters in either novel,

---

[12] Marx is bitter, marginal, excessively intelligent, insecure, timid, boastful, and socially inept—all apparently stemming from his being short. " 'They say somebody made a mistake when he was still in the bottle—thought he was a Gamma and put alcohol into his blood-surrogate. That's why he's so stunted.' " Aldous Huxley, *Brave New World* (New York: Perennial Classics, 1932), 46. He is probably meant to remind the reader of a Jew, though there are no Jews in the society depicted in the novel. Winston Smith is physically challenged as well, as we shall see.

[13] Though, in keeping with the quite different tone of Orwell's novel, he is not ridiculous, as Bernard becomes.

and some doubt that even they are that. Satire tends, finally, to be topical. This makes it perilous to try to understand a satire without some knowledge of social conditions in the time and place in which it was written. Satire is akin to parody, and to understand a parody you have to understand the conditions being parodied, which are usually those of the satirist-parodist's own society. To understand Swift's *A Modest Proposal*, you have to understand eighteenth-century English attitudes toward both cannibalism and the Irish.

Simply identifying the genre of the two novels that I am examining is helpful in dispelling common misunderstandings about them: that the authors were trying to predict the future, that they were pessimists (as they would have to be regarded if they thought they *were* predicting the future), and that Huxley identifies with the Savage (or, less plausibly, Bernard) and Orwell with Winston Smith. To write in a particular genre is to adopt the conventions of that genre, and this need not reveal anything of the character, emotions, or even beliefs of the author. Of course, from all we know about Orwell it is obvious that *Nineteen Eighty-Four* is a warning about communism, specifically its Stalinist variant.[14] But that is not necessarily the most important thing that it is; among other things he was warning us about tendencies that he believed latent in capitalism.

## BRAVE NEW WORLD

Huxley's novel is much more high-tech than Orwell's. This is not surprising; Huxley came from a distinguished scientific family and studied to be a doctor, whereas Orwell had no familial or educational background in science. Futuristic technology is a pervasive feature of the society depicted in *Brave New World* and is meticulously described and explained. It is of three types. The first is reproductive technology. Contraception has been made foolproof yet does not interfere with sexual pleasure. So sex has been separated reliably from procreation at last, and, at the same time, procreation has been separated from sex. Ova extracted from ovaries are mixed in the laboratory with sperm, and the fertilized ova are brought to term in incubators. The procedure has enabled the perfection of eugenic breeding, yielding five genetically differentiated castes, ranging from high-

---

[14] Though it can be argued, from the meeting in O'Brien's apartment at which the tactics of the "Brotherhood" (led by Emmanuel Goldstein, the Trotsky figure) are laid out and Winston pledges his willingness to throw sulfuric acid in a child's face if that will advance the Brotherhood's cause, that Orwell believed that a Trotskyite version of communism would have been no better than the Stalinist. It is merely arguable, because it is uncertain whether the Brotherhood or Goldstein actually exists. Goldstein is probably no more a real person than Big Brother is.

IQ Alphas to moronic Epsilons, to enable a perfect matching of genetic endowment with society's task needs.[15]

Second is mind- and body-altering technology, including hypnopaedia (hypnosis during sleep), Pavlovian conditioning, elaborate cosmetic surgery, and happiness pills (*soma*, similar to our Prozac, but nonprescription and taken continually by everyone). For the elderly, there are "gonadal hormones" and "transfusion of young blood."[16] Third is happiness-inducing entertainment technology, including television, synthetic music, movies that gratify the five senses (the "Feelies"), and, for the Alphas, personal helicopters for vacations.

These technological advances are represented as having profound effects. They induce mindless contentment, including guiltless promiscuous sex. They induce complete intellectual and cultural vacuity, and complete political passivity. Marriage, the family, and parenthood—all conceived of as sources of misery, tension, and painful strong emotions—have gone by the board. But none of these consequences is presented as an *unintended* consequence of technological innovation; it is unintended consequence that we fear in technology, and the economics of technology suggests some rational basis for that fear. Technology in *Brave New World* is the slave of a utilitarian ideology. Above everything else, Huxley's novel is a send-up of utilitarianism. "The higher castes . . . [must not] lose their faith in happiness as the Sovereign Good and take to believing, instead, that the goal was somewhere beyond, somewhere outside the present human sphere; that the purpose of life was not the maintenance of well-being, but some intensification and refining of consciousness, some enlargement of knowledge."[17] Technology has enabled the creation of the utilitarian paradise, in which happiness is maximized, albeit at the cost of everything that makes human beings interesting.[18] The Savage is unhappy but vital; the "civilized" people are fatuous, empty. The role of technology is to create the conditions in which a tiny elite can combine complete control over social, political, and economic life with the achievement of material abundance. This is an echo of the 1930s belief in the efficacy of central planning.

The topicality of satire, well illustrated in Huxley's novel by the caste system that is obviously a satiric commentary on the English class system and by the exhibiting of the Savage and his mother to the shocked Londoners as exotic specimens of New World savagery (though the two of

[15] "We decant our babies as socialized human beings, as Alphas or Epsilons, as sewage workers or future . . . Directors of Hatcheries." Huxley, *Brave New World*, 13.

[16] Ibid., 54.

[17] Ibid., 177.

[18] " 'Yes, everybody's happy now,' echoed Lenina. They had heard the words repeated a hundred and fifty times every night for twelve years" (when they were children). Ibid.

them are in fact English), invites us to consider conditions in England when *Brave New World* was written. It was in the depths of a world depression that Keynes was teaching had resulted from insufficient consumer demand and could be cured only by aggressive government intervention. Capitalism was believed to have failed for lack of sufficient coordination or rationalization, resulting in excessive, destructive competition. Capitalism (competition, the "free market") was not merely unjust; it was inefficient. There was also great anxiety about falling birthrates and the quality of the genetic pool.

All these concerns are mirrored in *Brave New World*. One of the salient features of the society depicted in it is consumerism, which encompasses planned obsolescence and a "throwaway" mentality ("ending is better than mending").[19] People are brainwashed to want ever more, ever newer consumer goods, lest consumer demand flag. Everything is planned and directed, down to the smallest detail of culture, technology, and consumption, from the center. And eugenic breeding solves the population and gene-pool problems. The society of *Brave New World* is the "logical" outcome of reform measures advocated by advanced thinkers in England and other countries during the depression. Developing the logic of an existing social system to an absurd or repulsive extreme (Huxley appears to have thought it the latter, not doubting its feasibility) is a typical technique of satire; we shall see it at work in *Nineteen Eighty-Four* as well.

Without technology, the "solution" that Huxley limns to 1930s-type problems would not be workable. But the technology plays a supporting rather than initiating role. It is the tool of a philosophical and economic vision. There is no sense that technology has merely evolved, unplanned, to a level that makes the regimented, trivial society depicted in the novel likely, let alone inevitable. There is no law of unintended consequences operating. Technology enables but does not dictate.

What makes *Brave New World* still a good read today is mainly the fact that so many of its predictions of futuristic technology and morality have come or are rapidly coming to pass. Sex has been made largely safe for pleasure by the invention of methods of contraception that at once are reliable and do not interfere with the pleasure of sex, while, as I noted earlier, a variety of other technological advances—ranging from better care of pregnant women and of infants to household labor-saving devices and advances in the medical treatment of infertility and the automation of the workplace—have (along with the contraceptive advances, and safe abortion on demand) liberated women from the traditional restrictions

---

[19] Ibid., 49.

on their sexual freedom.[20] The result is a climate of sexual freedom, and of public obsession with sex and sexual pleasure, much like that depicted in Huxley's novel, though "mother" is not yet a dirty word, as it literally is in the novel, and marriage has not yet been abolished, though the marriage rate has fallen considerably.

The society of happy thoughtless philistines depicted by Huxley will thus strike some readers as an exaggeration rather than a distortion of today's America. We, too, are awash in happiness pills, of both the legal and the illegal variety, augmented by increasingly ambitious cosmetic surgery to make us happier about our appearance. We are enveloped by entertainment technology to a degree that even Huxley could not imagine; in our society, too, "cleanliness is next to fordliness."[21] We have a horror of physical aging and even cultivate infantilism—adults dressing and talking like children. "Alphas are so conditioned that they do not *have* to be infantile in their emotional behaviour. But that is all the more reason for their making a special effort to conform. It is their duty to be infantile, even against their inclination."[22] We live in the present; our slogan, too, might be, "Never put off till to-morrow the fun you can have today."[23] Popular culture has everywhere triumphed over high culture; the past has been largely forgotten. We consider it our duty as well as our right to pursue happiness to the very edge of the grave. In the "Park Lane Hospital for the Dying . . . we try to create a thoroughly pleasant atmosphere . . . , something between a first-class hotel and a feely-palace."[24] Our culture is saturated with sex. Shopping is the national pastime. Although Americans are not entirely passive politically, we are largely content with the status quo, we are largely free from envy and resentment, the major political parties are copies of each other, and a 1930s-style depression seems unimaginable to most of us. Depression in both its senses is becoming unimaginable.

We may even be moving, albeit slowly, toward a greater genetic differentiation of classes, although not by the mechanism depicted in *Brave New World*—yet that mechanism will soon be feasible. With the decline of arranged marriage and the breaking down of taboos against interracial, interethnic, and religiously mixed marriage, prospective marriage part-

---

[20] "In some areas, despite its being a dystopia, *Brave New World* offers women a better deal than the contemporary British society of the 1930s. There is no housework, no wifely subjugation, no need to balance children and a career." June Deery, "Technology and Gender in Aldous Huxley's Alternative (?) Worlds," in *Critical Essays on Aldous Huxley*, ed. Jerome Meckier (New York: G. K. Hall, 1996), 103, 105.

[21] Huxley, *Brave New World*, 110.

[22] Ibid., 98.

[23] Ibid., 93.

[24] Ibid., 198–99.

ners can be expected to be sorted more by "real" similarities, including intelligence.[25] IQ has a significant heritable component, so the implication of more perfect assortative mating is that the IQ distribution will widen in future generations.

But all this has come (or is coming) about without foresight or direction, contrary to the implication of Huxley's novel. It turns out that a society can attain "Fordism"[26]—the rationalization, the systematization, of production that was originally symbolized by the assembly line—without centralization. Huxley was mistaken to equate efficiency with collectivization.[27] Our society has no utilitarian master plan and no utilitarian master planner. Nothing corresponds to *Brave New World*'s "Controllers," the successors to Dostoyevsky's Grand Inquisitor: "Happiness is a hard master—particularly other people's happiness."[28] And despite its resemblance to Huxley's dystopia, what we have seems to most people, even the thinking people, rather closer to Utopia.

## NINETEEN EIGHTY-FOUR

By 1948, the year in which Orwell completed *Nineteen Eighty-Four* (he had begun writing it two years earlier), the depression of the 1930s was over and concern with rationalizing production and stimulating consumption had diminished. The thought of politically conscious people was dominated instead by vivid recent memories of World War II and the menace of the Soviet Union, and these gloomy, foreboding thoughts are everywhere reflected in the novel. The dinginess of London in 1984 is recognizably the dinginess of that city during and immediately after the war, a time of shortages, rationing, and a prevailing grayness of life; and rocket bombs are falling on London in 1984 just as they did in the last year of World War II. The novel dwells obsessively on these features of life in Orwell's imagined dystopia, making a stark contrast with the consumer's heaven of *Brave New World*. Orwell depicted the future London as he did less, I suspect, because he was prescient about the incapacity of the Soviet economy, or of socialist central planning in general, to bring about abundance—a loyal member of the Labour Party to the end of his

---

[25] On the tendency to "assortative" mating—likes mating with likes—see Gary S. Becker, *A Treatise on the Family*, enl. ed. (Cambridge: Harvard University Press, 1991), chap. 4.

[26] Henry Ford is the Karl Marx of the society depicted in *Brave New World*. Instead of making the sign of the cross, the denizens of the world make a T, which stands, of course, for Ford's Model T.

[27] His equation of them is well discussed in James Sexton, "Brave New World and the Rationalization of Industry," in Meckier, *Critical Essays on Aldous Huxley*, 88.

[28] Huxley, *Brave New World*, 227.

life, he never relinquished his belief in democratic socialism—than because he was extremely sensitive to squalor, and to the sights and sounds and texture of lower-class life in London. Orwell's ambivalence about the lower class (the "proles," in *Nineteen Eighty-Four*), which he seems to have found at once repellent and appealing, is strongly marked.

The novel's take on technology is a curious one. On the one hand, the world of 1984 is presented[29] as technologically retrogressive, and this is explained by the fact that it is an oligopoly of three perfected totalitarian "superstates," Oceania, Eurasia, and Eastasia, which have tacitly agreed to impose rigid thought control on their populations, thus stifling the scientific and inventive spirit. On the other hand, this development is inevitable because of technology, which in the form of machine production enables an almost effortless creation of wealth. (Shades of Huxley.) When wealth is abundant, people cease believing in the necessity of a hierarchical society with marked inequalities. To stave off equality, the ruling classes channel the "overproduction" enabled by technology into warfare, which has the further advantage that in times of war people are readier to submit to collective control. So technology leads to totalitarianism, though by a more indirect route than its simply fostering centralization at all levels because of the greater efficiency of technocratic methods (which Orwell also believed, however, as we are about to see).

*Nineteen Eighty-Four* is correct that the conditions of a totalitarian society, in particular its suppression of freedom of thought, inquiry, and communication, are inimical to scientific and technological progress. This (another reason, by the way, to doubt that technology conduces to the elimination of political freedom) is one of the lessons of the fall of communism—we now know that much of the technological success of the Soviet Union in the domain of weaponry, the only domain in which it had such successes, was due to espionage. The other half of the novel's technology thesis, however, is clearly wrong; the great increase in material wealth in the developed countries of the world since Orwell wrote has produced both greater economic inequality *and* greater political stability.

The silliness of supposing that economic development leads to the Orwellian nightmare is brought out in Erich Fromm's afterword to the 1961 edition of *Nineteen Eighty-Four*. Fromm attributes to Orwell the view (with which Fromm makes clear that he agrees) that the danger of the Orwellian nightmare is "inherent in the modern mode of production and organization, and relatively independent of the various ideologies [that

---

[29] In *The Theory and Practice of Oligarchical Collectivism*—the treatise ostensibly written by Emmanual Goldstein (the Trotsky figure in the novel), but actually forged by the Inner Party—from which Winston reads a long selection aloud to Julia shortly before they are arrested.

is, capitalist and communist]" (267). But the attribution of this view to Orwell, or more precisely to the implied author of *Nineteen Eighty-Four*, as it is perilous to read off an author's personal views from his imaginative writings, seems approximately correct. (One clue is that the currency of Oceania is the dollar, not the pound.) Among the unmistakable sources of Orwell's novel is the concept much touted in his day of "managerialism," which predicted incorrectly that capitalism would evolve into a *dirigiste*, bureaucratized, centralized economic system indistinguishable from Soviet communism.[30] The superior efficiency of competitive markets for coordinating production was not widely understood.

The only technological innovation that figures largely in *Nineteen Eighty-Four* is two-way television (the telescreen) by which the securities services keep watch over the members of the Party, though there is also reference to music and verse synthesizers. (The technology is that of modern "videoconferencing.") The telescreen is a powerful metaphor for the loss of privacy in a totalitarian state. But it is inessential to the political theme of the novel, which is the feasibility of thought control through propaganda, education, psychology (including behavioral modification), informers (including children), censorship, lobotomizing, stirring up war fever, terror, and, above all, the manipulation of historical records and of language. The most interesting single feature of the novel is Newspeak, a parody of Basic English, as well as of Nazi and Soviet rhetoric, designed to make dangerous thoughts unthinkable by eliminating the words for them.[31] None of the instruments of thought control described in the novel, except the telescreen and possibly the lobotomizing-like machine that eliminates portions of Winston's memory, involves any technological advance over Orwell's time (as he emphasizes—it is, remember, part of his take on technology). Indeed, all but the telescreen and the lobotomy machine were in use in the Soviet Union of the 1930s and 1940s, though in a less thoroughgoing form than in Orwell's imagined world. *Nineteen Eighty-Four* would be less vivid and suspenseful, but not different in essentials, without any telescreens.

Because there is so little futurism in Orwell's novel, he had no reason to set it in the *remote* future; he was extrapolating only modestly from contemporary conditions; one can imagine Soviet leaders reading *Nine-*

---

[30] See, for example, James Burnham, *The Managerial Revolution: What Is Happening in the World* (Bloomington: Indiana University Press, 1941). Burnham's prediction that World War II (then in progress) would result in a division of the world into three indistinguishable superstates (see, for example, 264–65) is another of Orwell's conspicuous borrowings in the novel.

[31] For a comprehensive discussion, see John Wesley Young, *Totalitarian Language: Orwell's Newspeak and Its Nazi and Communist Antecedents* (Charlottesville: University Press of Virginia, 1991).

*teen Eighty-Four* for ideas.[32] Yet, oddly enough, Huxley's far-futuristic extravaganza comes closer to describing our world. The reason is not that Huxley could foresee the future (no one can) but that science is the story of our time, and Huxley was genuinely interested in science and his interest is reflected in his novel.[33] Although Soviet-style brainwashing undoubtedly had considerable effect on the minds of the people of the communist countries,[34] the rapidity and completeness with which communism collapsed (today only Cuba and North Korea are genuinely communist countries) demonstrated its ultimate ineffectuality. The combination of techniques described in *Nineteen Eighty-Four* seems frighteningly plausible, but this is a tribute to Orwell's artistic imagination. The system he describes is not realistic.[35] To see this, one need only ask who is to man all the telescreens. There are several in every apartment and office occupied by members of the Party—of whom there are a total of about 45 million, for we are told that 15 percent of the population belongs to the Party and that Oceania's total population is 300 million—and it is implied that all the telescreens are manned. Suppose there are 100 million telescreens; that would probably require 10 million watchers.[36] This is a clue to the element of fantasy in the novel, which is important to an understanding of it as literature.

Without the (infeasible) telescreen surveillance, the system of thought control depicted by Orwell is essentially the Soviet system under Stalin, which began eroding shortly after Stalin died,[37] four years after *Nineteen*

[32] A defector from the Polish Communist Party claimed that members of the "Inner Party," who alone could easily obtain copies of *Nineteen Eighty-Four*, were fascinated by Orwell's "insight into details they knew well." Czeslaw Milosz, *The Captive Mind* (New York: Vintage International, 1990), 40.

[33] A subordinate explanation of Huxley's prescience is that until recently there was a long lead time between scientific discovery and widespread practical application. Helicopters, television, mind-altering drugs, eugenic breeding, and large-screen color movies with wraparound sound and (if desired) tactile and olfactory sensations were all known in the 1930s to be technologically feasible, but it was decades before any of them became an important part of our culture. For example, it wasn't until the 1950s that television, which had been developed in the 1930s, became a major factor in American culture, and it was not till the 1960s that it became a major factor in political campaigns. The longer the lead time between invention and application, the easier it is to foresee the future technological condition of society.

[34] See Timur Kuran, *Private Truths, Public Lies: The Social Consequences of Preference Falsification* (Cambridge: Harvard University Press, 1995), chap. 13.

[35] Not a new point; see, for example, George Anastaplo, *The American Moralist: On Law, Ethics, and Government* (Athens: Ohio University Press, 1992), chap. 13.

[36] I am assuming two shifts, so that each watcher would be responsible for monitoring twenty telescreens.

[37] See, for example, Abbott Gleason, " 'Totalitarianism' in 1984," *Russian Review* 43 (1984): 145.

*Eighty-Four* was published; even in the Stalin era, the Party's control of public opinion was spotty.[38] Orwell may have had an inkling of the fragility of thought control. Eighty-five percent of the population of Oceania consists of the proles, who are much like Huxley's lower castes except that the proles' stupidity is not genetic—and, potentially, is redemptive. Having no "brains," the proles are immune to being brainwashed, as is Julia, who is not "clever."[39] Most brainwashing is directed at Party members, and it is only imperfectly successful; Winston and Julia, we discover late in the novel, are not the only imperfectly socialized Party members.[40] Hence the large number of "vaporizings" (liquidations), though, just as in Stalin's Soviet Union, many of those liquidated are in fact loyal Party members, notably the lexicographer Syme.

Most important, the Inner Party—the directing mechanism, 2 percent of the population—necessarily comprises people who see through the lies they are trying to foist on the rest of the society. Like the rulers of the Soviet Union, the members of the Inner Party have their own shops, which stock otherwise unobtainable luxury goods of traditional bourgeois character. The novel denies, however, that the fanaticism of the members of the Inner Party has been undermined by comfort or hypocrisy, arguing that through the mental technique of "doublethink" the members both know and don't know that their ideology is false. This was indeed a characteristic of thought under communism,[41] but the novel exaggerates its effectiveness and tenacity.

Orwell seems to have realized that a system of thought control will be unstable if major nations remain outside the totalitarian sphere and knowledge of the conditions in them cannot be wholly masked from the subject population. The novel emphasizes that there are no such nations in 1984. But this is not a plausible equilibrium—another point of which Orwell may have had an inkling: he notes that the three totalitarian superstates have tacitly agreed to refrain from competing in military research. Without such an agreement the totalitarian oligopoly would be unstable because each superstate would have a compelling incentive to seek a mili-

[38] "The normal posture of a Soviet citizen was passive conformity and outward obedience. This did not mean, however, that Soviet citizens necessarily had a high respect for authority. On the contrary, a degree of skepticism, even a refusal to take the regime's most serious pronouncements fully seriously, was the norm." Sheila Fitzpatrick, *Everyday Stalinism. Ordinary Life in Extraordinary Times: Soviet Russia in the 1930s* (New York: Oxford University Press, 1999), 222.

[39] Though Julia, like Winston, is broken by torture, the ultimate method of control.

[40] Consider the egregious Parsons, a Party zealot turned in by his seven-year-old daughter who overhears him saying in his sleep, "Down with Big Brother!" (193). Maybe, though, his real sin is being proud of his daughter for turning him in; it shows that he continues, contrary to Party doctrine, to attach great importance to family.

[41] Kuran, *Private Truths, Public Lies*, 218.

tary advantage by relaxing its thought control sufficiently to foster scientific and technological innovation. We now know that liberal nations, like the United States, are politically and militarily more formidable than authoritarian or totalitarian ones because they create far better preconditions to rapid social and economic development, more than offsetting the loss of centralized control and direction. A particular weakness of totalitarian states is the tendency to "subjectivism,"[42] the view much emphasized in *Nineteen Eighty-Four* that truth is what the Party or Leader says is true. Subjectivism led to such disastrous totalitarian misadventures as the Nazi rejection of "Jewish physics," the Soviet embrace of Lysenko's crackpot genetic theories, and Maoist China's "Great Leap Forward."

The Orwellian nightmare is unstable in a second sense as well. Neither Stalin nor Mao, the greatest practitioners of the kind of thought control depicted in Orwell's novel, was able to *institutionalize* the system of thought control, which disintegrated rapidly after their deaths. Their tyrannies were personal, while that depicted in *Nineteen Eighty-Four* is collective. Big Brother is not a living person but a symbolic fabrication. The collective leaderships that succeeded Stalin and Mao in their respective nations were authoritarian, but they were unable to maintain the degree of control that Stalin and Mao had achieved and that *Nineteen Eighty-Four* parodies. Orwell does not explain how the Party, and its counterpart in the other totalitarian superstates, have managed this trick.

The political significance of *Nineteen Eighty-Four*, as of Orwell's earlier political satire, *Animal Farm*, is to depict with riveting clarity the *logic* of totalitarianism—not its practice or its prospects, but the carrying of its inner logic to extremes that are sometimes almost comic, though darkly so. An example is the sudden, *retroactive* substitution of Eastasia for Eurasia as Oceania's eternal enemy (an allusion, obviously, to the Nazi-Soviet pact of 1939) on the sixth day of Hate Week. An orator of the Inner Party is handed a slip of paper in the middle of his speech, and without missing a beat he completes the speech with "Eastasia" replacing "Eurasia" wherever the latter name appears in his prepared text.

It is natural for intellectuals, even one like Orwell who was contemptuous of intellectuals ("the more intelligent, the less sane"[177]),[43] to exaggerate the efficacy of attempts at brainwashing, since, loosely speaking, intellectuals are in the business of brainwashing as well as being principal

[42] For an excellent discussion, see George Watson, "Orwell's Nazi Renegade," *Sewanee Review* 94 (1986): 486.

[43] "One has to belong to the intelligentsia to believe things like that: no ordinary man could be such a fool." George Orwell, "Notes on Nationalism," in *Collected Essays, Journalism and Letters of George Orwell*, ed. Sonia Orwell and Ian Angus (New York: Harcourt, Brace and World, 1968), 3:361, 379. The "that" was that American troops had come to England during World War II not to fight the Germans but to crush an English revolution.

targets of it.[44] It is noteworthy that Orwell got the political significance of television backward. He thought it a medium of surveillance (the telescreen) and indoctrination (the "Two Minutes Hate"). It has proved to be a medium of subversion, vastly increasing people's access to information about society and politics. It played a role not only in the fall of communism but also, long before that, in the thwarting of Lyndon Johnson's attempt to conduct a war in Vietnam without the informed consent of the American people.

Michael Shelden, Orwell's most recent biographer, takes the "message" of *Nineteen Eighty-Four* to be that

> there must be a place in the modern world for things that have no power associated with them, things that are not meant to advance someone's cause, or to make someone's fortune, or to assert someone's will over someone else. There must be room, in other words, for paperweights and fishing rods and penny sweets and leather hammers used as children's toys. And there must be time for wandering among old churchyards and making the perfect cup of tea and balancing caterpillars on a stick and falling in love. All these things are derided as sentimental and trivial by intellectuals who have no time for them, but they are the things that form the real texture of a life. . . . Readers see Winston fail, but they also see how a whole society failed years before "1984" when the people of that society allowed the state to strip them systematically of their right to be sentimental and trivial, taking away their rich language and replacing it with an ugly, utilitarian one and denying them the ordinary pleasures of a private life.[45]

I find this largely unconvincing. For one thing, there is no basis in the novel for foisting blame on "the people of that society [who] allowed the state to strip them systematically of their right to be sentimental and trivial." The origin of the totalitarian dictatorship of Oceania is not described, and so there is no more reason to blame the people for it than to blame the Russian people for the communist dictatorship; Lenin seized power in a coup, and Stalin achieved absolute control through terror. For another thing, Newspeak is a project; it has not yet replaced standard English, even within the Party.[46] Nor is there anything to suggest that

<hr/>

[44] The same exaggeration is visible in another notable novel about Stalinism, Arthur Koestler's *Darkness at Noon*. See Richard A. Posner, *Law and Literature*, rev. and enl. ed. (Cambridge: Harvard University Press, 1998), 138. It is notable that Winston, Julia, and the other targets of thought control and intimidation in *Nineteen Eighty-Four* are themselves all engaged in "political work"; it is such people who pose the largest political threat to a totalitarian regime and who therefore must be watched most closely.

[45] Michael Shelden, *Orwell: The Authorized Biography* (New York: HarperCollins, 1991), 436–37.

[46] I have made the same mistake as Shelden. See Posner, *Law and Literature*, 297.

trivia and sentimentality are the keys to freedom—Huxley thought they were the keys to a kind of slavery.

But there *is* something to Shelden's belief that Orwell is trying to tell us that if political freedom is to be preserved, "there must be time for . . . falling in love." For if you ask yourself what other "party" of "thought controllers" disfavors sex among party members (and the Party in Orwell's novel is emphatic in teaching that the sole legitimate function of sex is procreation, and in discouraging sexual pleasure),[47] the answer is the Roman Catholic priesthood. It is a fair guess that one model for the Party is the Roman Catholic Church, though a more important one is, of course, the Communist Party of the Soviet Union, which, however, no doubt borrowed some of its techniques from the Church.[48] Orwell explicitly compares the "adoptive" (as distinct from a hereditary) oligarchy of the Church with that of the Party. The Church preaches love, but in its heyday tortured and burned people. The junction is symbolized by Orwell's "Ministry of Love," which is the torture and liquidation bureau. Love the sinner, hate the sin.

One of the distinctive elements of Christianity—it is dramatized in the Catholic practice of confession to a priest—is its concern with people's thoughts (the confessional is a mode of surveillance, though also of absolution—and there are elements of that, too, in Winston's ordeal), and its placing of thought on a moral par with action, so that adultery in the mind is a mortal sin just like adultery in the flesh. Another name for this concern is thought control—priests correspond to the Thought Police of Orwell's novel—and it is linked to hostility to sex through the fact that sexual pleasure involves thoughts that are in the control very largely of our animal nature rather than of a priestly caste that tells us what we ought to be thinking about. "Not merely the love of one person, but the animal instinct, the simple undifferentiated desire: that was the force that would tear the Party to pieces" (105). In this respect, *Nineteen Eighty-Four* is the opposite of *Brave New World*, where promiscuous sex is mandatory for good citizens. "Orgy-porgy, Ford and fun, / Kiss the girls and make them One. / Boys at one with girls at peace; / Orgy-porgy gives release."[49]

---

[47] Though only among the members of the Party, that is, the 15 percent of the population that corresponds to the middle and upper class of a normal society. The leaders of the Party have no interest in the morals of the proles.

[48] Orwell personally was hostile to Catholicism and at times compared it to communism—John Rodden, "George Orwell and British Catholicism," *Renascence* 41 (1989): 143, 144; John P. Rossi, "Orwell and Catholicism," *Commonweal* 103 (1976): 404—but I am reluctant to use a writer's personal opinions to interpret his imaginative writings.

[49] Huxley, *Brave New World*, 84.

The contrast between the two authors' views of the political consequences of a society's sexual mores suggests that there may not be a unique totalitarian "position" on sexual freedom.[50] Perhaps, however, any kind of intimacy is a potential threat to a totalitarian society, which seeks to mobilize the population for selfless communal projects; and the issue is then what policy toward sex discourages intimacy. The societies depicted in both novels are hostile to the family. In *Brave New World* it has been abolished, while in *Nineteen Eighty-Four* its abolition is one of the Party's long-term goals, to be achieved in part by perfecting the system under which children are encouraged to report thoughtcrime by their parents. The problem, so far as assigning a political valence to sexual freedom is concerned, is that promiscuity can undermine the family, but so can a degree of puritanism that weakens the sexual bonding of married people. Maybe that's why some communes encourage free love and others celibacy, or why the Soviet Union veered from sexual liberalism in the 1920s to puritanism in the 1930s. Notice that if Huxley is right, the U.S. Supreme Court is wrong to think that contraception and abortion protect privacy viewed as a precondition of intimate relationships, while if Orwell is right, those things do protect privacy in that sense. But, as I say, either extreme may be inimical to intimacy.

I doubt the underlying premise, however—that totalitarianism is inherently hostile to the family. Some radical Islamic nations are quasi-totalitarian, but they are strongly pro-family. They are hostile to nonmarital sex, but not to marital sex; marriage is obligatory for Islamic clergy. A patriarchal family can reinforce a totalitarian ethos. Hitler, Stalin, Franco, and Mussolini were all strongly pro-family, as is the Roman Catholic Church, despite its prohibiting clerical sex and marriage. The dictators wanted to increase the birthrate and thought that encouraging family formation was the most effective way of doing this. Pronatalism aside, the traditional patriarchal family might be thought to echo and reinforce an authoritarian political regime.

Sex is thus rather a side issue in the analysis of totalitarianism, but the idea that one is *always* under surveillance, no matter how alone one thinks one is, is central to Christianity. The Christian is under surveillance by God, and similarly the inhabitants of Oceania by Big Brother, who, like the Christian God, is "infallible and all-powerful. . . . Nobody has ever seen Big Brother. He is a face on the hoardings, a voice on the telescreen. We may be reasonably sure that he will never die, and there is already considerable uncertainty as to when he was born. Big Brother is the guise in which the Party chooses to exhibit itself to the world. His function is

---

[50] See Richard A. Posner, *Sex and Reason* (Cambridge: Harvard University Press, 1992), 239.

to act as a focusing point for love, fear, and reverence, emotions more easily felt toward an individual than toward an organization" (171).

The Inquisition was merely the pathological extreme of the Christian concern with what Orwell calls "crimethink." O'Brien, the Orwellian Grand Inquisitor, depicts the activities of the Ministry of Love as the perfection of the Inquisition. "We do not destroy the heretic because he resists us; so long as he resists us we never destroy him. We convert him, we capture his inner mind, we reshape him. We burn all evil and all illusion out of him; we bring him over to our side, not in appearance, but genuinely, heart and soul. We make him one of ourselves before we kill him. . . . By the time we had finished with them [three notorious traitors] they were only the shells of men. There was nothing left in them except sorrow for what they had done, and love for Big Brother. . . . They begged to be shot quickly, so that they could die while their minds were still clean" (210–11).[51]

My point in bringing out the parallels between the practice of totalitarianism in *Nineteen Eighty-Four* and the usages of the Catholic Church is not to be gratuitously offensive,[52] or to obscure the role of Catholicism post-Orwell, notably in Poland, in opposing totalitarianism. It is to bolster my earlier statement that brainwashing is not the story of today. Even the Catholic Church, which I am arguing is one of the models of the "Orwellian" state, has, though it remains immense and powerful, lost most of its control over people's minds, at least in the developed world. Gone are the Inquisition and the *index purgatorius*. Italy has a very high abortion rate and a very low birthrate, and even Ireland has now legalized divorce and abortion. Freethinking among even deeply religious people is the order of the day, not everywhere (in particular, not in all Muslim nations), but in most quarters of the wealthy nations and many of the nonwealthy ones as well. What remains a subject of genuine concern for our world, but one that neither novel casts much light on, is the juggernaut quality of technological progress, which for reasons that I stated at

---

[51] "Orwell plays brilliantly upon traditional religious language." Joseph Adelson, "The Self and Memory in *Nineteen Eighty-Four*," in *The Future of Nineteen Eighty-Four*, ed. Ejner J. Jensen (Ann Arbor: University of Michigan Press, 1984), 111, 116–17. To get the point, just substitute "God" for "Big Brother" and "burned at the stake" for "shot" in the passage quoted in the text.

[52] The parallels have been noted before, moreover. See, for example, William Steinhoff, *George Orwell and the Origins of 1984* (Ann Arbor: University of Michigan Press, 1975), 184–85; Jaroslav Krejci, "Religion and Anti-Religion: Experience of a Transition," *Sociological Analysis* 36 (1975): 108, 120–22. Steinhoff's book is an exhaustive study of the novel's sources. I want to make clear that the Catholicism with which I am comparing totalitarianism is traditional, not modern American, Catholicism. On the differences, see James D. Davidson and Andrea S. Williams, "Megatrends in Twentieth-Century American Catholicism," *Social Compass* 44 (1997): 507.

the outset—reasons that economics elucidates better than satire can, or either of our authors has—cannot be assumed to operate automatically to the net benefit of humankind.

## THE NOVELS AS LITERATURE

With 1984 receding into the past, and the memory of Stalinism and Mao-ism already dim in our rapidly changing world—with Orwell proved "wrong," and Huxley "right," or at least more right, by history—how is one to explain the fact that Orwell's novel is, I believe (without having been able to obtain statistics), more popular than Huxley's? The part of the answer that interests me is that Orwell's may be the "better" novel (my use of scare quotes acknowledging the inherently subjective character of such a judgment). As the political relevance of *Nineteen Eighty-Four* fades, its literary quality becomes more perspicuous. We can see it better today for what it is—a wonderfully vivid, suspenseful, atmospheric, and horrifying (in the sense, not meant pejoratively, that much of Henry James is horrifying, even gothic) romantic adventure story. In places it is even a melodrama, even a boy's adventure story, as when the villains, O'Brien and Charrington, recite nursery rhymes, or Charrington is seen without the disguise that had made him look old. The scenes in Charrington's shop bear the stamp of *The Secret Agent*, while the visit of Winston and Julia to O'Brien's apartment for induction into the rumored Brotherhood could be a scene in a John Buchan novel. The fairy-tale note is sounded in the very first sentence of Orwell's novel: "It was a bright cold day in April, and the clocks were striking thirteen" (5). We soon discover that there is nothing uncanny about a clock's striking thirteen in Oceania, because Oceania numbers the hours one to twenty-four, which is a clearer and simpler method for recording time than the a.m.-p.m. system, just as it uses the dollar rather than the nondecimal English currency of Orwell's day and just as it uses the metric system in place of English weights and measures. Yet these simple, "rationalizing" measures turn out to be sinis-ter in their own right. They illustrate the Party's effort to empty the culture of its historical residues, to make the present discontinuous with the past.

As for the telescreen, its *literary* significance has less to do with technol-ogy or privacy than with enhancing the perilousness of Winston's affair with Julia, the need for their elaborate rituals of concealment, and the inevitability of eventual detection and punishment. The suspense is so intense, right up to the dramatic arrest scene, that, inevitably, the third of the book that remains is anticlimactic. Indeed, except for the penultimate scene—the final meeting and parting of Winston and Julia—the last third has seemed to most readers, and seems to me, inferior to the first two-thirds of the novel from a literary standpoint. The problem is not that it is "didactic." The most didactic portion of the book is the long selection from *The Theory and Practice of Oligarchical Collectivism* that Winston reads (to us, as it were) just before he and Julia are arrested. The reading has enormous dramatic impact. The problem with the last third is that it is not well crafted. The first postarrest scene, with Winston in a holding cell with other political prisoners, is intended to be horrifying but succeeds only in being disgusting—and with the entry of Parsons, who expresses pride in his seven-year-old daughter for her having turned him in for thoughtcrime, even a bit ridiculous. That is also my reaction to the famous scene in which Winston is threatened with the rats and screams, "Do it to Julia! Do it to Julia!" (236).[53] The last sentence of the book— "He [Winston] loved Big Brother" (245)—also, it seems to me, verges on the bathetic.

Oddly, given Orwell's political aims, the last part of the book undermines the satire of communism by making the totalitarian dictators seem almost benign compared to O'Brien, who is, at least so far as the reader is given to understand him (for we see him only through Winston's eyes), a sadistic lunatic. Hitler and Stalin were cruel and paranoid, but they would hardly have said, or, probably, even thought, that "[p]rogress in our world will be progress toward more pain" or that "[w]e shall abolish the orgasm" (220).[54] This is overdone to the point of being ridiculous (though it echoes and parodies the ascetic strain in Christianity, and so is further evidence for the link that the novel forges between Catholicism and totalitarianism). So is O'Brien's insistence on getting Winston to accept that if the Party says that $2 + 2 = 5$, then it is so. That scene, a too deeply buried allusion to the Soviet Union's five-year plans,[55] and so again an error of literary craft, makes O'Brien seem more like a bullying schoolmaster trying to drum the rules of arithmetic into the head of a slow student than like a torturer. The basic problem is that no *political* purpose is served by the elaborate cat-and-mouse game that O'Brien plays with Winston and Julia. Neither of them has any valuable information about the "Brotherhood" (which probably does not exist) or is important enough to have to be brainwashed into making a public recantation of heresies. For remember that neither is a member of the Inner Party, let

[53] The scene in which Winston confronts in the mirror the damage that torture and starvation have done to his body is very effective, however.

[54] "The worst Nazi lived on something besides cruelty." George Kateb, "The Road to *1984*," in *Twentieth Century Interpretations of 1984*, ed. Samuel Hynes (Englewood Cliffs, N.J.: Prentice-Hall, 1971), 73, 75.

[55] The slogan "$2 + 2 = 5$" was popular in the Soviet Union during the first five-year plan; it expressed the aspiration of completing the plan in four years. Steinhoff, *George Orwell and the Origins of 1984*, 172.

alone an "old revolutionary" (like Jones, Aaronson, and Rutherford) whose taming is important to the Party's image of omnipotence and infallibility.

The basic flaw in the characterization of O'Brien—and, not incidentally, a departure from the realistic delineation of totalitarianism—is his being depicted as having no fear. It is because he is without fear that his treatment of Winston seems crazy. It is unrealistic to suppose the "Inner Party" of a totalitarian state dominated by lunatics or even sadists. A state so governed would be highly unstable. Inner Party members are cruel in order to maintain their positions. They fear their superiors, their rivals, and even a rising of the people; O'Brien has none of these fears.[56]

But these are details. All I want to argue is that we can begin to read Orwell's novel as we read Kafka, or *The Waste Land*, with which *Nineteen Eighty-Four* has some curious affinities, for the vividness of its nightmare vision relieved by the occasional poignant glimpse of redemptive possibilities. Reading it as literature (and cognizant of its literary imperfections), we resist, as Orwell sought to resist, the politicization of everything, the trend that has so damaged university English departments.[57] We also resist reducing the novel to a document of the author's biography, a common reduction in analyses of both our novels.[58]

In arguing for an aesthetic approach to literature and against treating works of literature as works of moral or political philosophy, I do not wish to be understood as advocating acontextual readings. A rich understanding of social context is often necessary to appreciate the wit and bite of a satire, a good—if somewhat obscure—example being O'Brien's effort to get Winston to believe that $2 + 2 = 5$. But it is one thing to require an understanding of political and other social issues as a precondition to fully appreciating a work of literature, and another to suppose that the significance of that work lies in its relation to those issues. The issues are not the point; they are rather the raw material on which the literary imagination operates to produce beauty.

[56] The only hint that he too is under surveillance is the statement in the novel that members of the Inner Party, though allowed to turn off the telescreens in their apartments, would be ill advised to do so for more than a half hour at a stretch.

[57] " 'On every campus . . . there is one department whose name need only be mentioned to make people laugh' . . . Everyone knows that if you want to locate the laughingstock on your local campus these days, your best bet is to stop by the English department." Andrew Delbanco, "The Decline and Fall of Literature," *New York Review of Books*, November 4, 1999, 32.

[58] I would go so far as to argue that literary interpretation is retarded, not advanced, by knowledge of the author's biography, as most readers, even when they are literary scholars or critics, have great trouble disregarding what they know about the writer's life and opinions when reading the works of literature that the writer produced. This is a conspicuous deformity of the literary scholarship and criticism of *Nineteen Eighty-Four*.

Surprisingly, when we do what I am suggesting—approach these novels as free from nonliterary preconceptions as is possible—we discover in both of them a deep, "Romantic" dissatisfaction with everyday modern life ("bovarism," after Madame Bovary). *Brave New World* has the more brilliant surface, and a sparkling wit that links it to the great British comic tradition,[59] but it is not a happy book; it has no characters who engage the reader's sympathy and no emotional depth. The conquest by science of the tragic realities of human life as we know it in our day is shown as destroying the possibility of romance. Conversely, the love affair that is the emotional core of *Nineteen Eighty-Four* is exalted by the proximity of terror and death. Julia is neither beautiful nor clever, is in fact rather shallow; and Winston, at thirty-nine, with his varicose veins, his five false teeth, his "pale and meager body" (118), is already middle-aged.[60] Their relationship—like that of Jordan and Maria in *For Whom the Bell Tolls* or Frederick and Catherine in *A Farewell to Arms*, like that of Andrei and Natasha in *War and Peace*, and like that of Julien Sorel and Madame de Rênal in *The Red and the Black*, which seem to me the appropriate precedents in the literary tradition[61]—would lack savor were it not for the background of terror and danger and the certainty of doom. His love for Julia is the last thing that Winston relinquishes under torture. The world of today, made so comfortable and safe by the technology foreseen by Huxley, has no place in it for Romanticism. The world has become disenchanted. That Julia is rather commonplace is not, as some feminists believe, a sign of Orwell's alleged misogyny; it is part of the point of the novel. (They also overlook her courage.)

From this perspective we see that the significance of the paperweight which Winston buys in Mr. Charrington's shop is not as a symbol of the charm of the ordinary. It is to show how even the most commonplace object can become luminous when it is bracketed with danger; one is put in mind of how some people get a greater kick out of sex when there is a risk of discovery.

A Weberian perspective can also help us see that people who think that *Nineteen Eighty-Four* is "about" technology in some deep sense are

---

[59] Its funniest scene is the madcap confrontation of the Director of Hatcheries and Conditioning by the Savage's mother, revealing that the Director had produced the Savage by "viviparous" reproduction, viewed as obscene in the society of *Brave New World*. Of course he resigns immediately.

[60] Julia is twenty-six years old, so thirteen years separate them—another sinister touch.

[61] Notice that in all these pairings, including Winston-Julia, the woman is quintessentially feminine and hence sharply differentiated from the man. (With reference to Julia, see Leslie Tentler, " 'I'm Not Literary, Dear': George Orwell on Women and the Family," in Jensen, *The Future of Nineteen Eighty-Four*, 47, 50–51.) This is a convention of Romantic literature.

confusing technology with technocracy. Technology is the application of rational methods to material production, and technocracy their application throughout the whole of life.[62] Weber's vision of human life become so completely rationalized that all enchantment would be squeezed out of the world[63] is profoundly anti-Romantic and therefore profoundly dismaying to persons of Romantic temperament.

To attribute to Orwell a Romantic fascination with the theme of love braided with cruelty and death will seem perverse to anyone who expects a work of imaginative literature to be continuous with the public persona and conscious self-understanding of the author. Orwell, as everyone knows, because he told us again and again (and because it was largely true), stood for honesty, simple decency, plain talking, common sense, abhorrence of cruelty, delight in the texture of ordinary life, and the other conventional English virtues. But to write imaginative literature one must have an imagination, and imagination draws on the unconscious depths of a person's mind. The author of *Nineteen Eighty-Four*, who objected to the publisher's blurb for the book because "it makes the book sound as though it were a thriller mixed up with a love story,"[64] was a more interesting person than we think, and perhaps than he knew.[65]

I noted earlier the distinction between the actual and the implied author of a novel. When as in the case of Orwell much is known about the intentions of the author in writing the novel, it is well-nigh irresistible to assume that the novel means what the author intended it to mean. Biography overwhelms the text. If one starts with the novel, setting aside, so far as possible, what one knows about the author, one may find that the novel means something quite different from what the author intended it to mean. One constructs by inference an implied author, the author whose

---

[62] " 'Technocracy' . . . signifies a social order organized on principles established by technical experts." W.H.G. Armytage, "The Rise of the Technocratic Class," in *Meaning and Control: Essays in Social Aspects of Science and Technology*, ed. D. O. Edge and J. N. Wolfe (London: Tavistock Publications, 1973), 65.

[63] The dehumanizing effects of a technocratic organization of society remains a popular theme. See, for example, Andrew Feenberg, *Alternative Modernity: The Technical Turn in Philosophy and Social Theory* (Berkeley and Los Angeles: University of California Press, 1995).

[64] George Orwell, letter to Roger Senhouse, December 26, 1948, in *Collected Letters, Essays and Journalism of George Orwell*, 4:460.

[65] I have found only one previous suggestion that *Nineteen Eighty-Four* can be understood as a Romantic work. W. Warren Wagar, "George Orwell as Political Secretary of the Zeitgeist," in Jensen, *The Future of Nineteen Eighty-Four*, 177. Orwell's "real allegiance was to the self, the romantic genius picturesquely estranged from everything and everybody, who must always be free to feel exactly what he feels and to say exactly what he pleases." Although Professor Wagar is on to something, he spoils it for me by denouncing Orwell as politically retrograde and expressing relief that Orwell died in 1950, thus sparing us "his first Holy Communion at the side of Malcolm Muggeridge" (196).

values and intentions are latent in the novel itself; and I am suggesting that the implied author of *Nineteen Eighty-Four* is a Romantic quite different from the "real" George Orwell.[66]

It would be absurd to deny political, even philosophical, significance, let alone purpose, to either novel; and that is not my aim. (But the economics in both novels is terrible!) Huxley's novel is a powerful satire of utilitarianism. Orwell's satire of communism has lost its urgency, but his reminder of the political importance of truth,[67] of the malleability of the historical record, and of the dependence of complex thought on a rich vocabulary (that is, that language is a medium of thought as well as of expression) remains both philosophically interesting,[68] and timely in an era in which history textbooks are being frantically rewritten to comply with the dictates of political correctness. That truth shall make us free, and that ignorance is weakness (to reverse one of the Party's slogans), have rarely been as powerfully shown as in *Nineteen Eighty-Four*. O'Brien is also an arresting spokesman for idealism in its zany philosophical as opposed to its political sense, denying that there is any reality apart from human consciousness; his program for rewriting history (and not just history textbooks) resonates with the long-standing philosophical debate over the epistemological robustness of testimony.[69] All these things are "in the book" in a perfectly valid sense. And while Orwell himself was not particularly interested in technology, it is easy to see how the recent advances in photographic simulation and computer data manipulation would facilitate a project of rewriting history. It is also easy to transform Winston's workstation into a computer terminal at which he edits "history" conveniently stored on-line. This is legitimate extrapolation as well.

But ultimately literature survives, if at all, as literature rather than as political or philosophical or even social commentary, for in the latter roles it is bound to be superseded sooner or later, and usually sooner. On that basis, and that basis alone, I predict a longer life for *Nineteen Eighty-Four* than for *Brave New World*. Literary judgments are matters of taste, not reason, so in suggesting that Orwell's novel is better than Huxley's I

---

[66] And, of course, the real George Orwell was really Eric Blair.

[67] In the sense of factuality—truth with a lowercase *t*, not the Truth of religious or political dogmatism.

[68] Young, *Totalitarian Language*, 11–18; cf. Peter Carruthers, *Language, Thought and Consciousness: An Essay in Philosophical Psychology* (New York: Cambridge University Press, 1996), 51–52.

[69] "The mutability of the past is the central tenet of Ingsoc. Past events, it is argued, have no objective existence, but survive only in written records and in human memories. The past is whatever the records and the memories agree upon. And since the Party is in full control . . . of the minds of its members [as well as of all records], it follows that the past is whatever the Party chooses to make it" (176). Compare C.A.J. Coady, *Testimony: A Philosophical Study* (New York: Oxford University Press, 1992).

am simply expressing my own preference for a literature of narrative tension and emotional depth to one of glittering caricature. The important point is that there is no contradiction in asserting that the novel which (though written earlier) predicted our current situation more accurately is the lesser work of literature.

# On the Internet and the Benign Invasions
## of *Nineteen Eighty-Four*

LAWRENCE LESSIG

I WENT TO Amazon.com and entered the search terms "Orwell" and "1984." A book popped onto my screen. I was in a hurry, and, not paying much attention to what was displayed, I hit the "One-Click" button to purchase the book. A book arrived a couple of days later. It wasn't Orwell's text. It was instead a book by Peter Huber—a polymath and lawyer—titled *Orwell's Revenge*.[1] It looked interesting enough, so I read it. And in Huber's book I found an illustration of the point I want to make about Orwell's book, *Nineteen Eighty-Four*.

There is a view of technology within *Nineteen Eighty-Four*—or so Huber argues. This view is consistent with what Orwell says elsewhere about the technologies his society was coming to know; the view is a pattern within Orwell's writing that has very few exceptions across the range of his texts. The view is loathing. Orwell hated technology. More particularly, he hated the then-emerging technologies of media—films, radio, and especially the gramophone. As Huber writes about Orwell's writings about the gramophone:

> He alludes to the instrument dozens and dozens of times in his writings, and always with revulsion. In 1934, Orwell even composes a horrible poem, "On a Ruined Farm Near his Master's Voice Gramophone Factory," blaming gramophones for the demise of farming.[2]

Or again:

> For Orwell . . . the electronic media are ugly, oppressive, mind-numbing—the enemies of quiet and the wreck of civilization. He ranks them right beside gambling as "cheap palliatives" for oppressed people.[3]

---

[1] Peter Huber, *Orwell's Revenge: The 1984 Palimpsest* (New York: Free Press, 1994). One extraordinary innovation in Huber's text is that he constructed it solely with Orwell's own words. Using *Nineteen Eighty-Four* as the source, Huber reconstructed *Nineteen Eighty-Four* to tell the story he tells in *Orwell's Revenge*.

[2] Ibid., 34.

[3] Ibid., 35.

Yet it is not just technology that inspires Orwell's hatred. His attacks on the market are just as strong. So too his attacks on the interaction between media and markets. His view is not that the technologies of media necessarily produce "tripe," or that the fidelity of a radio, for example, is impure. Rather, as Orwell writes in his 1945 essay "Poetry and the Microphone,"

> Nevertheless one ought not to confuse the capabilities of an instrument with the use it is actually put to. Broadcasting is what it is, not because there is something inherently vulgar, silly and dishonest about the whole apparatus of microphone and transmitter, but because all the broadcasting that now happens all over the world is under the control of governments or great monopoly companies.[4]

The fear is that markets inevitably produce monopolies, at least where markets are as tied to technology as was broadcasting in Orwell's day. As he continues,

> Something of the same kind [i.e., monopolization] has happened to the cinema, which, like the radio, made its appearance during the monopoly stage of capitalism and is fantastically expensive to operate. In all the arts the tendency is similar. More and more the channels of production are under control of bureaucrats. . . . [T]he totalitarianization which is now going on . . . must undoubtedly continue to go on, in every country in the world.[5]

Over and over, as Huber reports, Orwell inveighs against what he treats as a natural and unavoidable tendency in the modern technology of media: concentration.[6] And over and over again, he thus points to the conclusion of this process of concentration and control: the fantastic technology of control that in *Nineteen Eighty-Four* he calls the "telescreen."

In his understanding of markets, of course, Orwell was wrong. There was no necessity that these technologies, or the industries that they built, would move inevitably toward monopoly. Cartels can be broken; governments can break them. The then-dominant ideal of government support for monopoly could, and would, change. Indeed, in his time, as now, it wasn't inevitability that built monopolies. It was government. Once government rescinded support for these monopolies, these monopolies could go away. That may not have seemed possible at the time Orwell wrote. England then evinced ubiquitous monopoly; the rise of Fascism (when Fascism had a pretty face) may well have made monopoly seem

---

[4] George Orwell, "Poetry and the Microphone," in *The Penguin Essays of George Orwell* (London: Penguin, 1984), 245, reprinted in Huber, *Orwell's Revenge*, 73.

[5] Ibid., 250, reprinted in Huber, *Orwell's Revenge*, 74.

[6] Huber, *Orwell's Revenge*, 43–45.

inevitable everywhere. Yet we know enough now to recognize that the ubiquitous need not entail the inevitable.

But there is a deeper blindness in Orwell's text, and this is the focus of Huber's book. Orwell is mistaken not just about whether monopoly might be checked. More fundamentally, he is mistaken about the technology of communications in general,[7] and the central technological device of *Nineteen Eighty-Four*—the telescreen—in particular.

For as Huber notes, the remarkable fact about *Nineteen Eighty-Four* is that while the technology of the telescreen is central to the story, Orwell does practically nothing to introduce it, or to explain it, or to explain how it could work.[8] While Orwell spins forever to explain how Airstrip One comes into being (7, 13–14, 30–33, 45–47, 62–69, 74, 126–28), and tediously recounts, through Goldstein's writing, the history and logic of the present state (152–79), he tells us nothing about what makes the telescreen tick. We have no idea how it works. Or who runs it. Or how its capability is even possible. And thus, Huber argues, the Achilles' heel in Orwell's account. If you had to build a technology that could make possible the kind of monitoring and control that Orwell assigns to the telescreen, then you would understand something important about why Orwell's telescreen is impossible. If you imagine its architecture—if you think through what it would take to build it as Orwell describes—then you see, Huber argues, why the technology could not be the tool of totalitarians.[9]

Think, Huber argues, about what the telescreen does. First, it is a broadcast technology, perpetually streaming state-selected content to an audience that is paying only partial attention. Second, it is a monitoring technology, watching the bored viewers as some of them watch the telescreen. In the one scene where we see its monitoring working, Winston Smith is scolded for his failure to bend down deeply enough during calisthenics exercises (33–34).[10] As in a public school gym class, he is picked out of the crowd (of millions? thousands? just a few? we don't know) and told to touch his toes. Anyone his age, he is told, should be able to touch his toes.

---

[7] Ibid., 24–25, 55, 67–75.

[8] Ibid., 24–25 ("But how exactly does the telescreen work? What's connected to what? Where and how do all the people who are watching all the other people select whom they will watch? Orwell never explains. He is in fact remarkably unspecific about the single critical piece of technology on which his book so completely depends.").

[9] Ibid., 67 ("To put it in *1984* terms, tyrannies can't build telescreens. . . . [Neither can] [t]elescreens . . . abide tyranny").

[10] "And on that occasion—'Smith!' screamed the shrewish voice from the telescreen. '6079 Smith W! Yes, *you*! Bend lower, please! You can do better than that. You're not trying. Lower, please! *That's* better, comrade. Now stand at ease, the whole squad, and watch me.' "

The technological capacity to create such an interactive vehicle is very different from the technology of the TV. It requires, Huber argues, a very special design.[11] The telescreen is more than just a receiver. It is a broadcaster in reverse. It is not just "one to many." It is "many to one." And, as Huber argues, only a specific kind of architecture for communication could make this form of monitoring possible—especially if the technology also includes the ability to permit members of the Inner Party to switch the telescreen off.[12] So the design must enable not only the monitoring of the many by the few, but also the selective monitoring of some by the few.

It is here that Huber's text begins to displace Orwell's in its present-day significance. In an ingenious mixing of story and argument about the nature of architectures of communication, Huber quite successfully shows that an architecture that would enable the telescreen Orwell describes is an architecture that we are all now quite familiar with.[13] That architecture, Huber says, is the Internet. And if there is one thing we all know about the Internet, Huber argues, it is that it is not a technology of control. Rather, Huber maintains, the Internet is a technology of freedom.[14] If the wires were to be laid to make the telescreen possible, then inevitably, Huber suggests, they would also make possible Amazon.com or the pages of Matt Drudge. If intended to empower the government, they couldn't help but empower the citizen. If designed to permit control, they would also inevitably disable control. To build the telescreen is to

---

[11] Huber, *Orwell's Revenge*, 222–23 (explaining that the telescreen need not just broadcast but must additionally receive—must be addressable).

[12] Ibid., 24–25.

[13] Though when Huber wrote his book, the Internet was just beginning to become well known.

[14] Huber, *Orwell's Revenge*, 217–40 (explaining that the notion of the telescreen, today manifested as a variety of communications technologies, and further extrapolated toward its logical ends, makes the fears of Orwell appear nonsensical, e.g., "[i]n a telescreened society, records multiply far too fast to be systematically falsified. . . . [t]elescreens move pictures. If you move the pictures efficiently enough, you'll completely reverse the world's dreaded slide toward centralized monopoly. . . . [t]elescreens make possible collectivism by choice—a commonwealth society based on individual willingness to share and cooperate. . . . in the age of the ubiquitous telescreen, everyone will own a video-press. That should mean vastly more freedom of expression, not less. . . . [w]ith the telescreen, it is thus possible to have brotherhood, or at least as much brotherhood as free individuals can stand, without Big Brother. . . . [t]he telescreened world, which we see unfolding around us today, is thus the complete opposite of *1984*. . . . [i]f Orwell had doublethought his telescreen to its logical conclusion, he would have foreseen the day in which the proles do the watching, and the Party is whipped into submission. As Thiel de Sola Pool would record in 1983, telescreens are the technologies of freedom. . . . [i]f the Thought Police can use telescreens, so can others—that's just the way telescreens work, if they work at all. Networks as powerful as Orwell imagined cannot be built any other way. The world of Stalin filled with Apple computers belongs to Apple, not Stalin").

build the very architecture for the totalitarian state's demise. If the tele-screen works, then its architecture inevitably would enable freedom, not Orwell's control.

Huber believes he is offering an account of technology that is differ-ent from Orwell's, and of course, on one level, it certainly is. But what interests me about Huber's account is not its difference from Orwell's in *Nineteen Eighty-Four*, but its similarity. In one sense the books couldn't be more different. Yet in another sense, they both betray the same understanding of technology—an understanding that is wrong, however common.

Both books suffer from a kind of "is-ism"—that the way things are is the way things must be.[15] Orwell sees monopoly control over the media; he can imagine only its extension as media extends. Huber sees perfect freedom within the Internet; he can imagine only freedom expanding as the network expands. But in both cases "how something is" is not how it must be. And in particular for Huber, how the Internet is or, at the time he wrote the book, was—its embrace of freedom, its lack of control—is not how the Internet must be or is becoming. Huber sees the Internet producing the functionality the telescreen needs, and he concludes from this that the telescreen must embrace freedom. But there are obvious—and increasingly extant—ways that the Internet could be modified to elim-inate the freedom Huber celebrates. Hence there is no guarantee that the Internet will serve the end of freedom. Put differently, it isn't difficult to imagine architectures for the Internet that would allow it to become a technology of control—because changes in the Internet just now are pro-ducing just this kind of control.

To see how, contrast privacy on the Internet with privacy in the world Orwell describes. The telescreen effects a certain kind of monitoring. But though this will certainly seem counterintuitive, the monitoring of the telescreen is actually more protective of privacy than is the increasing monitoring on much of the Internet. And if we had to choose between the Internet and the telescreen—or, more specifically, if we had to choose between the two, given that a totalitarian regime were in control—the telescreen would be the far preferable technology. There is thus a re-deeming humanness to Orwell's monitor that is increasingly missing in the Internet's monitor.

To see this point, we need to abstract a bit from the other parts of Orwell's story—from the repressive political will, from the perpetual grimness of English life—and think about a feature of this telescreen that is quite important to the narrative Orwell recounts: the telescreen is trans-

---

[15] See Lawrence Lessig, *Code and Other Laws of Cyberspace* (New York: Basic Books, 1999), 24–29.

parent about whether, at any moment, you might be being watched. The telescreen doesn't hide that it is monitoring; and, more important, it shows you exactly the range of space that is being monitored. Winston can write a diary outside its view because he knows the scope of that view (9).[16] Indeed, this is the common feature of monitoring throughout the work: that the targets always know where they are capable of being monitored. Patrolling helicopters, children as spies, a language that betrays deviance, telescreens everywhere: everyone knows that (s)he is being watched. (Indeed, I can recall only once in the book where this rule is broken—in the room over the antique shop, where the telescreen was hidden behind a picture on the wall [182–85].)[17]

Not only is the monitoring of Orwell's telescreen transparent, it is also imperfect. We aren't told, but we can infer, that it must be humans on the other side of the telescreen. (If it takes an army of people to keep history up-to-date, then it must be an army of people who make the monitors function.) Thus it is humans who watch, and who must remember, or forget, just what they see. Yet humans can't easily gather and collate the data they collect. The data are trapped in human minds and no doubt quickly disappears from those minds.[18]

These two aspects of the telescreen produce an important kind of freedom. You can know where to go; you are reminded you are being watched; and the watching produces very little in the form of searchable

---

[16] "For some reason the telescreen in the living room was in an unusual position. Instead of being placed, as was normal, in the end wall, where it could command the whole room, it was in the longer wall, opposite the window. To one side of it there was a shallow alcove in which Winston was now sitting. . . . [b]y sitting in the alcove, and keeping well back, Winston was able to remain outside the range of the telescreen, so far as sight went. He could be heard, of course, but so long as he stayed in his present position he could not be seen. It was partly the unusual geography of the room that had suggested to him the thing that he was now about to do. . . . [t]he thing that he was about to do was to open a diary."

[17] " 'We are the dead,' he said. 'We are the dead,' echoed Julia dutifully. 'You are the dead,' said an iron voice behind them. They sprang apart. . . . 'You are the dead,' repeated the iron voice. 'It was behind the picture,' breathed Julia. 'It was behind the picture,' said the voice. . . . There was a snap as though a catch had been turned back, and a crash of breaking glass. The picture had fallen to the floor, uncovering the telescreen behind it."

[18] See Lessig, *Code and Other Laws of Cyberspace*, 150–51 ("The monitoring of modern life is indeed different in substance from the monitoring at the time of the founding [of the United States]. There is no doubt that life then was monitored . . . but that monitoring was different. It was done by people whose memories were imperfect. . . . These memories, moreover, could not be searched, or collected, or produced as records. . . . Gossipy neighbors might have watched [your activities, previous to modern technology], but their watching produced nothing as lasting or as reliable as videotape, a toll booth's records of when you entered and when you left, a credit card system's endless collection of data about your purchases, or the telephone system's records of who you called when and for how long. Today's monitoring is different because the technologies of monitoring—their efficiency and their power—are different").

records. The telescreen thus makes a very leaky system of control. It is costly and, even then, inefficient.

Compare the Internet: While the original architecture of the Internet made it very hard to know who someone was, or where they came from, this feature of the original architecture is changing.[19] Increasingly, the technology imbeds the ability to notice and track individual behavior. In this tracking, there is no equivalent to the freedom the telescreen affords. You can't easily know where you are subject to monitoring and where not; you can't easily know where you can hide. There is no "screen" on the Internet that distinguishes itself from a wall—the part where data are being collected as distinct from the part where it is not. Instead, every interaction on the Internet is potentially captured by a telescreen, and yet the network does nothing to tell you this. Where you go, where you came from, your address, your machine, the software you are using, whether you are able to use encrypted transactions—all these facts are perpetually monitored by the network as you use it. And when this monitoring is tied to technologies such as cookies, the monitoring makes it quite possible for other parties to know who the user is, and where the user is going. The system by default gathers these data always, and whether and where they are being used is hidden from the surfer.

For example, think again about Amazon.com. When I am in Amazon.com, the company watches where I surf.[20] It watches the books I'm interested in, and it collects data about what I buy. It uses those data, and all similar data from other users, to decide what I might like. It offers me recommendations if I request them. And for a while I could even get it to tell me stuff about other people as well. Amazon would report, for example, the top-selling books at various universities. On the morning of our 1999 Orwell conference, the top book at the University of Chicago was *Eurodollar Futures and Options*, while at Microsoft the top-seller was *How the Web was Won. Microsoft from Windows to the Web: The Inside Story of How Bill Gates and His Band of Internet Idealists Transformed a Software Empire.*

These data are gathered without your knowing or seeing. This watching is constant but invisible. There isn't a machine that you can see that is watching you; there isn't an agent following you around. The monitoring is invisible except to those who know how the Internet actually works— a small, naturally limited group. And the monitoring goes on perpetually in every part of the Net you might try to see.

---

[19] See ibid., 30–42.

[20] Amazon.com Privacy Notice ("By visiting Amazon.com, you are accepting the practices described in this Privacy Notice. . . . We receive and store any information you enter on our Web site or give us in any other way. . . . You provide most such information when

The Internet's lack of transparency is a first difference from the telescreen. Its lack of forgetfulness is a second. The telescreen had drones that
watched to make sure Smith bent low enough. But, no doubt, Smith was
just one Smith among many; who would remember the next time around?
But with the Net, the records that are collected are searchable any time
in the future. You can write an email to a friend; six months later, the
government can search through its collected records of email to that
friend's company and find this email. These records are out there and
remain permanent by default. To remove them requires effort. Keeping
them is cheaper.

The telescreen was thus transparent and forgetful; the Net is opaque
and perpetual. Most have no idea about the kinds of data that are collected; yet these collected data remain out there for others to search. The
system is not leaky; it is perfectly sealed. And it could produce, properly
architected, a perfect technology of control. As science fiction writer
Vernor Vinge describes it, the Net could produce "ubiquitous law enforcement," made possible by "fine-grained distributed systems" in the form
of computer chips linked by the Net to every part of social life—a portion
of which would be dedicated to the government's use.[21]

In the current debate about copyright protection, just such a system is
now being proposed. Copyright industries are keen to find a way to control the "sharing" of content on the Net. Unprotected music, for example,
is easily shared on the Net. Copyright holders view this sharing as a kind
of theft.[22] They thus push Congress to pass laws requiring computer manufacturers to build into their computers the capacity to control this "sharing."[23] This technology in turn would perpetually monitor who copied
what from whom. It would be a crime to build a computer that didn't
have this technology in it; it would be a crime to use a computer to exchange content that didn't have this technology in it. It would be criminal,
in other words, to use the network *except* in a way that perpetually and
accurately collected all the data it could about what music you listened
to, with what permissions, granted by whom. No such power was imagined for the telescreen.

Of course, copyright aside, for the most part (at least in liberal democracies) control on the Net is harmless (though again, the Soviets would
have chosen the Net over the telescreen in a flash). But my point is not

---

you search, buy, bid, post, participate in a contest or questionnaire, or communicate with
customer service . . .).

[21] See http://www.swiss.ai.mit.edu/projects/mac/cfp96/plenary-sf.html.

[22] See, e.g., "Valenti Warns of Devastating Economic Impact of Copyright Theft," at
http://www.mpaa.org/jack (February 28, 2002).

[23] See Consumer Broadband and Digital Television Promotion Act, S. 2048, 107th Cong.
(2002).

about danger. It is instead about the character of architectures. I'm not arguing that we should fear a new Stalinist state produced by the Internet (except for those who would share their CDs with their neighbors). My point is instead to call attention to the mistake that both Orwell and Huber make. Technologies of communications do not *naturally and inevitably* tend, as Orwell suggests, toward the telescreen; nor do they *naturally and inevitably* tend, as Huber argues, to the freedom of the original Net. In both cases, architectures *tend* as we choose. They develop as we design them, and we can design them to be more or less protective of freedom. There is no *nature* that determines either way; there are instead a million small decisions that in sum build a technology of freedom or of control.

More perversely, from the argument thus far we could well argue that the Internet would be more protective of freedom if it were more like the telescreen. If privacy on the Internet is to be protected, at a minimum the architecture must increase the transparency of the ways data about users are being collected. The Internet could facilitate that transparency: W3C has described, for example, a technology called P3P, which would enable users to select the kind of data they wanted to give away; and when sites tried to take more, they would be blocked.[24] Microsoft has now implemented this technology into its most recent browser.[25] This technology, if implemented generally, would thus enable the same transparency the telescreen gave. It would enable individuals to know where and when they were being watched. It would therefore also show them where they could write their diaries in peace.

Likewise would privacy and freedom on the Net be enhanced if the network were designed to be more forgetful, again, like the telescreen. Rather than perpetually producing searchable records that can be traced back to individuals, the system could be designed to break any obvious or simple links between data and individuals. Already there are sites on the Net that promise privacy by promising to throw away any data collected when the user is on the site. A site called Ziplip.com, for example, offers email that can't be linked back to any particular user. Sites like this thus make the system as a whole effectively more forgetful. Whatever they remember, it is nothing about me. Or again, they make the system as a whole more like the technology of the telescreen—whatever was noticed at one time is not directly accessible later.

Transparency and forgetfulness are thus two values that could be embedded within the Internet's architecture, making it more like the

[24] See W3C Platform for Privacy Preferences (P3P) Project, at http://www.w3.org/P3P/.
[25] See Microsoft Internet Explorer: Web Privacy, at http://www.microsoft.com/windows/ie/evaluation/overview/privacy.asp.

telescreen and more protective of privacy. They are, in other words, features that could be chosen for its design. And thus my point is not the obvious one—that technologies enable freedom or control—but one more easily missed: that this enabling depends upon how we build the technologies, and that building always involves choices.

❦

Huber himself gets this point, my story notwithstanding. For I lied about how I came across his book. I didn't get it on Amazon. He sent it to me as a gift. In it was a very kind inscription that spoke of the "happy ending" that his book describes as something "we have yet to write." For though his book sounds convinced that the Internet guarantees its own freedom, Huber himself is not. He understands that any freedom in the Internet comes from its design, and that its design can be changed. To defend the freedom in the Internet is thus to defend it against changes in its design. And he has personally been active in struggles to oppose those changes.

But whatever Huber himself sees, most see it as his book is written, and as Orwell writes it. Most take the values built into an architecture as given; few see the choices built into that architecture. More important for us, and especially in the context of the Internet, most don't even notice the regulatory effect of these architectural decisions. Most treat them as natural and, hence, not to be questioned. When the Internet protected freedom, this was the nature of its design. Now that the Internet increasingly enables control, most take this, too, to be a part of the nature of its design. The is-ism with which I charged Huber is actually an is-ism that is common to humanity generally. The regulations that get built into the technological environments we inhabit are more often invisible than noticed as constraints.

This fact about us will be increasingly important as more of our lives move onto the Internet. As the Internet is changed to enable a greater degree of control, we will display a fundamental aspect of humanity: the principle of bovinity. Large animals are controlled by very weak fences, and we are large animals. For most of us, most of the time, the regulations within the architectures of cyberspace are limits that we find. It will take a great deal of learning to see they are limits someone built, and that we can, and should, resist.

✤

# The Self-Preventing Prophecy; or, How a Dose of Nightmare Can Help Tame Tomorrow's Perils

DAVID BRIN

WHAT WILL the future be like?

The question is much on people's minds, and not only because we've entered a new century. One of our most deeply human qualities keeps us both fascinated with and worried about tomorrow's dangers. We all try to project our thoughts into the future, using special portions of our brains called the *prefrontal lobes* to mentally probe the murky realm ahead. These tiny neural organs let us envision, fantasize, and explore possible consequences of our actions, noticing some errors and avoiding some mistakes.

Humans have possessed these mysterious nubs of gray matter—sometimes called the "lamps on our brows"—since before the Neolithic. What has changed recently is our effectiveness in using them. Today, a substantial fraction of the modern economy is devoted to predicting, forecasting, planning, investing, making bets, or just preparing for times to come. Which variety of seer we listen to can often be a matter of style. Some prefer horoscopes, while others like to hear consultants in Armani suits present a convincing "business case."

Each of us hopes to prepare for what's coming and possibly improve our fate in the years ahead. Indeed, this trait may be one of the most profound distinctions between humanity and other denizens of the planet, helping to explain our mastery over the world.

Yet it is important to remember that a great many more things *might* happen than actually do. There are more plausibilities than likelihoods.

I

One of the most powerful novels of all time foresaw a dark future that never came to pass. That we escaped the destiny portrayed in George Orwell's *Nineteen Eighty-Four* may owe in part to the way his chilling

---

Parts of this paper were edited and revised from a series of articles about "the coming millennium" for Netscape's *iPlanet* magazine, copyright October 1999.

tale affected millions, who then girded themselves to fight "Big Brother" to their last breath. In other words, Orwell may have helped make his own scenario *not* come true.

Since then, many other "self-preventing prophecies" rocked the public's conscience or awareness, perhaps helping us deflect disaster. Rachel Carson foresaw a barren world if we ignored environmental abuse—a mistake we may have somewhat averted, partly thanks to warnings like *Silent Spring* and *Soylent Green*. Who can doubt that films such as *Dr. Strangelove*, *On the Beach*, and *Fail-Safe* helped caution us against dangers of inadvertent nuclear war? *The China Syndrome*, *The Hot Zone*—and even *Das Kapital*—arguably belong to this genre of works whose credibility and worrisome vividness may help prevent their own scenarios from coming true.

Whether these literary or cinematic works actually made a difference can never be proved. That each of them substantially motivated large numbers of people to pay increased attention to specific possible failure modes cannot be denied.

As for Big Brother—Orwell showed us the pit awaiting any civilization that combines panic with technology and the dark, cynical tradition of tyranny. In so doing, he armed us against that horrible fate. In contrast to the sheeplike compliance displayed by subject peoples in *Nineteen Eighty-Four*, it seems that a "rebel" image has taken charge of our shared imaginations. Every conceivable power center, from governments and corporations to criminal and techno-elites, has been repeatedly targeted by Hollywood's most relentless theme . . . suspicion of authority.

(Can you cite even a single popular film of the last forty years in which the protagonist does not bond with the audience by performing some act of defiance toward authority in the first ten minutes?)

These examples point to something bigger and more important than mere fiction. Our civilization's success depends at least as much on the mistakes we avoid as on the successes that we plan. Sadly, no one compiles lists of these narrow escapes, which seem less interesting than each week's fashionable crisis. People can point to a few species saved from extinction . . . and our good fortune at avoiding nuclear war. That's about it for famous near-misses. But once you start listing them, it turns out we have had quite an impressive roll call of dodged bullets and lucky breaks.

Learning *why* and *how* ought to be a high priority.

## II

History is a long and dreary litany of ruinous decisions made by rulers in all centuries and on all continents. No convoluted social theory is needed to explain this. A common thread weaves through most of these disasters; a flaw in human character—*self-deception*—eventually enticed even great leaders into taking fatal missteps, ignoring the warnings of others.

The problem is devastatingly simple, as the late physicist-author Richard Feynman put it. "The first principle is that you must not fool yourself—and you are the easiest person to fool."[1]

Many authors have railed against the cruelty and oppression of despots. But George Orwell focused also on the essential *stupidity* of tyranny, by portraying how the ferocious yet delusional oligarchs of Oceania were grinding their nation into a state of brutalized poverty. Their tools had been updated, but their rationalizations were essentially the same ones prescribed by oppressors for ages. By keeping the masses ill-educated, by whipping up hatred of scapegoats, and by quashing free speech, elites in nearly all cultures strove to eliminate criticism and preserve their short-term status . . . thus guaranteeing long-term disaster for the nations they led. This tragic and ubiquitous defect may have been the biggest factor chaining us far below our potential as a species. That is, till we stumbled onto a solution.

The solution of *many voices*. Each of us may be too stubbornly self-involved to catch our own mistakes. But in an open society, we can often count on *others* to notice them for us. Though we all hate irksome criticism and accountability, they are tools that work. The four great secular institutions that fostered our unprecedented wealth and freedom—science, justice, democracy, and markets—function best when all players get to see, hear, speak, know, argue, compete, and create without fear. One result is that the "pie" we are all dividing up keeps getting larger.

In other words, elites actually do better—in terms of *absolute* wealth—when they cannot conspire to keep the *relative* differences of wealth too great. And yet this ironic truth escaped notice by nearly all past aristocracies, obsessed as they were with staying as far above the riffraff as possible.

Orwell saw this pattern, perhaps more clearly than anyone, portraying it in the banal and witless justifications given by Oceania apparatchiki.[2]

---

[1] Richard Feynman, *What Do You Care What Other People Think?* (New York: Norton, 1988).

[2] Orwell's books are often cited as warnings against science and technology . . . a terrible misinterpretation. While Oceania's tyrants gladly use certain technological tools to reinforce their grip on power, their order stifles every human ingredient needed for science and free inquiry. Beyond tools of suppression and surveillance, technology is stagnant, productivity declining. Innovation is deemed subversive. It is a society that eats its seed corn and beats plowshares into useless statues. Yet many critics persuade themselves that the Oceania elite, while evil, is somehow clever at the same time.

A similar fixation can be seen in popular interpretations of Mary Shelley's masterwork, *Frankenstein*, which is widely perceived as a polemic against science and the arrogation of God's powers. Yet Shelley herself does not seem to hold that view. The "creature" begins in

How have we done with his warning? Today, in the modern neo-West, even elites cannot escape being pilloried by spotlights and scrutiny. They may not like it, but it does them (and especially us) worlds of good. Moreover, this openness has helped prevent the worst misuses of technology that Orwell feared. Though video cameras are now smaller, cheaper, and even more pervasive than he ever imagined, their arrival in numberless swarms has not had the totalitarian effect he prophesied, perhaps because—forewarned—we act to ensure that the lenses point both ways.

This knack of *holding the mighty accountable*, possibly our culture's most original achievement, owes largely to those who gazed at human history and saw the central paradox of power—what's good for the leader and what's good for the commonwealth only partly overlap and can often skew at right angles. In throwing out some of the rigid old command structures—the kings, priests, and demagogues who claimed to rule by inherent right—we seem to be gambling instead on an innovative combination: blending rambunctious individualism with mutual accountability.

Those two traits may at first sound incompatible. But any sensible person knows that one cannot thrive without the other.

## III

The Orwellian metaphor is pervasive. On disputative Web sites like Slashdot, every third posting seems to blare warnings about "Big Brother," as adversaries scream, "This is just like 1984!" whenever something vaguely bothersome turns up (e.g., wall-size TV screens, personality tests for high school students, the cat-brain camera).

Is government the chief enemy of freedom? That authority center does merit close scrutiny. Meanwhile other citizens worry about different power groups—aristocracies, corporations, criminal gangs, and technological elites. Can anyone justifiably claim exemption from accountability?

Orwell's metaphors have been expanded beyond his initial portrayal of a Stalinist nightmare-state to include all worrisome accumulations of influence, authority, or unreciprocal transparency. People tend to style

---

innocence and a state of tentative hopefulness. It is Victor Frankenstein's *subsequent* behavior that earns the reader's contempt. Frankenstein's vicious rejection and cruelty toward his own creation is the fault that brings pain to his world and unleashes his great punishment. Rather than rejecting science, the novel appears to support the moral "Don't be a lousy dad." (Which is interesting, given Mary Shelley's personal background.)

The central lesson of both tales is that technology can be abused when it is monopolized by a narrow, secretive, and self-deceiving elite, absent any accountability or outside criticism. Almost any modern scientist would call this obvious. And after growing up with such stories, many nonscientists find it apparent, as well. The warning is heard.

themselves, politically, according to which group they perceive threatening freedom. Elsewhere[3] I discuss the role that righteous indignation plays in helping to create what may be the first true social immune system against calamity. All four of those great social innovations mentioned above that fostered our unprecedented wealth and freedom (*science*, *justice*, *democracy*, and *regulated markets*) are based on harnessing this network of suspicion through vigorous and competitive application of mutual accountability. It may not be nice, but it works far better than hierarchical authority ever did.

These "accountability arenas" function well only when all players get fair access to information.

## IV

Technological advances like the Internet may help amplify this trend or may squelch it, depending on choices we make in the next few years. The implications of burgeoning information technology may be enormous. Soon the cognitive powers of human beings will expand immensely. Memory will be enhanced by vast, swift databases that you'll access almost at the speed of thought. Vision will explode in all directions as cameras grow ever smaller, cheaper, more mobile, and more densely interconnected.

*In such a world, it will be foolish ever to depend on the ignorance of others.*

If they don't know your secrets now, there is always a good chance that someone will pierce your veils tomorrow, perhaps without your ever becoming aware of it. The best firewalls and encryptions may be bypassed by a gnat-camera in your ceiling or a whistle-blower in your front office. How can you ever be sure it has not already happened?[4]

---

[3] *The Transparent Society: Will Technology Force Us to Choose between Freedom and Privacy?* (New York: Perseus, 1998).

[4] Criticism is the best antidote to error. Yet most humans, especially the mighty, try to avoid it. Leaders of past cultures crushed free speech and public access to information, a trend Orwell depicted as enhanced by technology in a future when elites control all the cameras. In part thanks to Orwell's warning, ours may be the first civilization systematically to avoid this cycle, whose roots lie in human nature. We have learned that few people are mature enough to hold themselves accountable, but in an open society adversaries eagerly pounce on each other's errors. To preserve our freedom, we must not try to limit the cameras—they are coming anyway, and no law will ever prevent the elites from seeing. Instead, we must make sure all citizens share the boon—and burden—of sight. This is already the world we live in. One where the people look hard at the mighty and look harder the mightier they are.

Orwell's dark future can't come true if confident citizens have a habit of protecting themselves by seeing and knowing.

Some businessfolk, like Jack Stack (author of *The Great Game of Business*), see the writing on the wall. By using open-book management, they reduce costs, enhance employee morale, foster error-detection, eliminate layers of management, speed their reaction time, and learn how to do business in ways that make it irrelevant how much their competitors know.

Companies that instead pay millions trying to conceal knowledge will strive endlessly to plug leaks yet will gain no long-term advantage or peace of mind. Because the number of *ways* to leak will expand geometrically as both software and the real world grow more complex. Because information is not like money or any other commodity. It will soon be like air.

## V

Let's take this a bit further. Say you are walking down the street. Your sunglasses are also cameras. Each face you encounter is scanned and fed into an Internet pattern-search.

Your glasses are also display screens. *Captions* seem to accompany pedestrians and passing drivers, giving their names and compact bios. You do an eye-flick, commanding a fresh view from an overhead satellite. A tap of your teeth retrieves in-depth data about the person in front of you, including family photos and commentary posted by friends, business associates . . . even enemies.

As you stroll along, you know that others see *you* similarly captioned, indexed, biographed.

Sound horrific? Well, then, here's the key question—how are you going to stop it? Outlawing the tools will only ensure that common folk can't use them. As Robert Heinlein said, the chief thing accomplished by a privacy law is to make the bugs smaller.

That, in turn, will only serve the interests of the mighty. As George Orwell would surely point out, elites (government, corporate, criminal, and so on) will get these new powers of sight, no matter what the rules say. So we might as well have them too.

The metaphor of Oceania's *telescreen* is central here. In Orwell's world, those at the top of a rigid pyramidal hierarchy controlled the flow of information with fierce totality. Only propaganda filtered downward, while every iota or datum about the lives of proles flowed upward. Accountability went in just one direction.

Despite repeated efforts by our own hierarchs to justify one-way information flows, the true record of the last generation has been an indisputable and overwhelming dispersal of knowledge and the power to see. People are becoming addicted to knowing. Take the events that surrounded the tragedies of September 11, 2001. Most of the video we saw was taken by private citizens, a potentially crucial element in future emergencies. Private cell phones spread word more rapidly than official media. So did email and instant messaging when the telephone system got swamped. Swarms of volunteers descended on the disaster sites, as local officials quickly dropped their everyday concerns about liability or professional status in order to use all willing hands. The sole effective action to thwart terrorist plans was taken by individuals aboard United Airlines Flight 93, armed with intelligence and communication tools—and a mandate—outside official channels.

Is this a true and unstoppable trend? Only time will tell. Has it been, in part, driven by the inoculative effects of cautionary fiction such as *Nineteen-Eighty Four*? I can't even begin to prove the hypothesis.

Is this a different way to look at the effects and importance of literature? You bet it is. Scholars aren't used to considering the pragmatic fruits of fictional gedankenexperimentation, but perhaps it's time they started.

## VI

Consider the issue of these dispersed information systems from another perspective. The best analogy I can come up with is the old *villages* that our ancestors lived in, till just a few decades ago. They, too, knew intimate details about almost everyone they met on a given day. Back then, you recognized maybe a thousand people. But *we* won't be limited by the capacity of organic vision and memory. Our enhanced eyes will scan ten billion fellow villagers. Our enhanced memories will know their reputations, and they will know ours.

This is obviously cause for mixed feelings and deep misgivings. Will it be the "good village" of Andy Hardy movies . . . safe, egalitarian and warmly tolerant of eccentricity? Or the bad village of Frank Capra's Potterstown, a place steeped in hierarchies, feuds, and petty bigotries, where the mighty and the narrow-minded suppress all deviance from dismal normality?

Or even the vast, stifling, all-knowing "village" of Orwell's Oceania?

We'd better start arguing about this now—how to make the scary parts less scary, and the good parts better—because the village is coming back, like it or not.

## VII

The key to our success—both personal and as a society—will be agility in dealing with whatever the future hurls our way. Moreover, there are reasons to think we already have what it takes. Consider the following hoary old cliché.

Too bad human decency and justice haven't kept pace with our technological progress.

Here is another.

No past era featured as much cruelty and misery as this one.

People seem to draw perverse pleasure from such statements, even though they are patently false.

In fact, more than half of those alive on Earth today never saw war, starvation, or major civil strife in their own backyard. Most never went more than a day without food. Only a small fraction have seen a city burn, heard the footsteps of a conquering army, or watched an overlord exercise capricious power of life and death over helpless peasants. Yet these events were routine for most of our ancestors.

Of course, when I speak of fractions, that still leaves hundreds of millions who *have* experienced such things. I won't minimize the terrors so many still endure. Our consciences should be prodded, by the relentless power of television, into compassion and vigorous action.

Still, it's worth noting that things have changed a bit since humanity wallowed in horror, back in the middle years of the twentieth century. The ratio of humans who now live modestly safe and comfortable lives—though in conditions modern North Americans might deem threadbare—has never been greater. It means the slope hasn't been all *downward*, since the despair of 1942. Some might even argue that progress has been made.

As for comparing technical and moral advances, there's just no contest. For example, while I truly love the Internet, its effects on real life have so far been rather exaggerated. Telephones and radio had far greater immediate effects on people's lives when they entered the home, opening the world to millions.

It is our *attitudes*—toward all sorts of injustices that used to be considered inherent—that have undergone a transformation unlike any in history.

Consider the famous Stanley Kubrick film *2001: A Space Odyssey*. Way back when it appeared, in 1967, two monumental projects transfixed the people of the United States—conquering outer space and tackling injustice to achieve a more honorable society.

Who would have imagined, back then, that *colonizing space* would prove such a grindingly slow job . . . yet by 1999 we would take for granted so many advances in tolerance, decency, and accountability? Or that we'd so ignore these achievements, focusing instead on the residual injustices that are left unsolved?

We still don't have the fancy space stations of *2001* . . . but there is another, more important difference. Our astronauts today come in all sexes and colors. Any kids who watch them on TV feel a bit less fettered by presumed limitations. Each of them may choose to hope, or not, without being told *you can't*.

At this rate, who will bet me that a woman or a person of color won't preside in the White House long before the first human being steps on Mars? Progress doesn't always go the way you expect it to.


## VIII

This is not the path prophesied in *Nineteen Eighty-Four*, which envisioned a bitter society—one that exploited every opportunity to stoke hatred and division among the ruled. One in which the common man is little better than a harried sheep, ignorant, disempowered, and unable to imagine another way. So far, we seem aimed at avoiding that particular failure mode. (At least those who read science fiction cannot be accused of lacking imagination.)

Do we owe this fact, in part, to anti-Cassandras like George Orwell whose warnings, once they were heeded, thus never came true?

Is fear of dystopian nightmare a greater motivator and effectuator of change than any utopian promise? Indeed, our tendency seems always to criticize whatever injustices continue to flourish, rather than ever to pause to rejoice in what's been accomplished. That alone shows how deeply the lesson has been learned. The worry that Orwell and others ignited in us still burns. It drives us on, far more effectively than any vague glowing promise of a better world.

We daren't let up. Not ever, because we've been shown the alternatives. The world that George Orwell presented was—and remains—just too scary.

# Part V

# SEX AND POLITICS

# Sexual Freedom and Political Freedom

## CASS R. SUNSTEIN

### ORWELL'S THESIS

One of the most vivid passages in *Nineteen Eighty-Four* appears in the middle of the novel, where Winston experiences what is meant to be a moment of revelation. The passage can be found immediately after Winston tells Julia about "his married life": as it happens Julia knew "the essential parts of it already." Thus she describes "to him, almost as though she had seen or felt it, the stiffening of Katharine's body as soon as he touched her." This was "the frigid little ceremony that Katharine had forced him to go through on the same night every week." Winston notes that she "hated it," but "nothing would make her stop doing it." What Katharine called it, Winston says, Julia will "never guess"; but of course Julia "promptly" guesses: "Our duty to the Party." Then Julia begins to "enlarge upon the subject":

> It was not merely that the sex instinct created a world of its own which was outside the Party's control and which therefore had to be destroyed if possible. What was more important was that sexual privation induced hysteria, which was desirable because it could be transformed into war fever and leader worship. The way she put it was:
>
> "When you make love you're using up energy; and afterwards you feel happy and don't give a damn for anything. They can't bear you to feel like that. They want you to be bursting with energy all the time. All this marching up and down and cheering and waving flags is simply sex gone sour. If you're happy inside yourself, why should you get excited about Big Brother and the Three-Year Plans and the Two Minutes Hate and all the rest of their bloody rot?"
>
> This was very true, he thought. There was a direct, intimate connection between chastity and political orthodoxy. (110–11)

This passage lies at the core of Orwell's stated account of sexuality, politics, and totalitarianism. We might discern from the passage a distinctive thesis: Totalitarian governments thrive on the repression of sexual drives; they repress sexuality in order to make room for mass "marching" and public "cheering," that is, "sex gone sour." Nor is it hard to think of governments, and political movements, that appear to provide at least indirect support for Orwell's claim. Consider, for example, highly eroticized political movements in America and elsewhere that thrive, at least in part, on the effort to combat sexual promiscuity, and that eroticize that very effort (sometimes by talking about sex so much).

My claim here, however, is that Orwell's claim is wrong—that there is no "direct, intimate connection between chastity and political orthodoxy." The links between "sexual privation" and "orthodoxy" are much less direct and intimate, and sometimes the two are antagonists, not allies. Orwell's treatment of the issue is diminished by the fact that Julia, most of all on this count, emerges as less a person than an adolescent male fantasy, a point that may also shed light on the weakness of the link that Orwell draws between sexual freedom and totalitarianism. Orwell has at most identified a mechanism, not a lawlike generalization.

The point has contemporary implications. Many people seem to share Orwell's belief that political totalitarian and sexual repression march hand in hand, both logically and empirically. On this view, it is no accident that authoritarian nations—Afghanistan under the Taliban, for example, or communist China—are concerned both to crush dissent and to suppress sexual liberty. In free and less free countries, those who insist on the protection of sexual liberty (in such domains as prostitution and pornography) often claim to be political dissidents, or close cousins of political dissidents, and urge that they deserve the same degree of respect accorded to those who attempt to topple a politically repressive regime. Nothing that I say here will challenge efforts to reduce government interference with sexual liberty, nor will I explore the question of what, concretely, sexual liberty should be understood to be. But I will offer reasons to challenge current manifestations of the tendency to find a link between sexual repression and political repression. I do believe that there is a close association between political repression and the repression of women, but Orwell is, unfortunately, quiet on that score.

## SEX, AND TWO LOVE STORIES, IN *NINETEEN EIGHTY-FOUR*

To deal with the relationship between sexual privation and political orthodoxy, it will be useful to begin more generally with Orwell's treatment of sex and love. This treatment superficially supports but actually outruns his own thesis about the purpose and effect of sexual frustration.

### Sex

Sex is portrayed in *Nineteen Eighty-Four* in several different ways. First, there is the dutiful, dead, frigid, antierotic, pro-Party sex of Winston's marriage, contrasted with the much freer relationship between Winston and Julia. But an alternative account of sex is offered early in the novel, during the Two Minutes Hate. Here Winston has "[v]ivid, beautiful hallucinations," involving "the dark-haired girl behind him." According to those hallucinations: "He would flog her to death with a rubber truncheon. He would tie her naked to a stake and shoot her full of arrows like Saint Sebastian. He would ravish her and cut her throat at the moment of climax. . . . He hated her because she was young and pretty and sexless, because he wanted to go to bed with her and would never do so, because round her sweet supple waist, which seemed to ask you to encircle it with your arm, there was only the odious scarlet sash, aggressive symbol of chastity" (16–17). (Chancing upon her some seventy pages later, he notices "that by running he could probably catch up with her. He could keep on her track till they were in some quiet place, and then smash her skull in with a cobblestone" [85–86].) This is the "girl" who turns out to be Julia. In their first real discussion, he tells her: "I wanted to rape you and then murder you afterwards. Two weeks ago I thought seriously of smashing your head in with a cobblestone" (101).

Of Orwell's three portrayals of sex, the most conventional involves the relationship between Winston and Julia. Their initial physical encounter is notably unerotic: "At the beginning he had no feeling except sheer incredulity. The youthful body was strained against his own, the mass of dark hair was against his face, and yes! Actually she had turned her face up and he was kissing the wide red mouth. . . . He had pulled her down on to the ground, she was utterly unresisting, he could do what he liked with her. But the truth was that he had no physical sensation except that of mere contact. All he felt was incredulity and pride. He was glad that this was happening, but he had no physical desire" (100). Later, after sexual intercourse: "Their embrace had been a battle, the climax a victory. It was a blow struck against the Party. It was a political act" (105). (Compare Julia's activity, feigned to be sure, for the Junior Anti-Sex League.)

### Love, and Love and Sex

While there are a number of portrayals of sex in *Nineteen Eighty-Four*, there are only two love stories, involving two couples: Julia and Winston is one, and Winston and O'Brien the other; the most erotically charged, even intense scenes involve the latter. In a way the whole book is structured around a love triangle, in which O'Brien extinguishes the erotic connection between Julia and Winston, marking the triumph of the Party against a "blow" that had threatened it, and reestablishing both chastity and political orthodoxy. (There is an obvious Oedipal dimension to the triangle, insofar as O'Brien is a kind of punitive father, splitting Winston from his beloved.)

The existence of a love triangle is signaled early on, where Orwell writes, of O'Brien, that Winston "felt deeply drawn to him, and not solely because he was intrigued by the contrast between O'Brien's urbane manner and his prize-fighter's physique. . . . [He] had the appearance of being a person that you could talk to, if somehow you could cheat the telescreen and get him alone" (13). Winston has had a dream, or it might be real, in which O'Brien whispers to him: "We shall meet in the place where there is no darkness." And this becomes the foundation for the long concluding section, which is portrayed as a series of sexually sadistic acts committed by O'Brien against Winston. In fact it is a sustained scene of rape and castration. (This is why *Nineteen Eighty-Four*, as opposed to, say, *Brave New World*, belongs as much to the genre of horror as to that of science fiction.)

Early on in the torture, when O'Brien momentarily takes away the pain, Orwell writes that as Winston "looked up gratefully at O'Brien," "his heart seemed to turn over. . . . He had never loved him so deeply as at this moment. . . . Perhaps one did not want to be loved so much as to be understood. O'Brien had tortured him to the edge of lunacy, and in a little while, it was certain, he would send him to his death. It made no difference. In some sense that went deeper than friendship, they were intimates" (208). When the more severe torture begins, O'Brien announces, lest there should be any question about what kind of scene this is, "You will be hollow. We shall squeeze you empty, and then we shall fill you with ourselves" (211). As this torture starts, "O'Brien laid a hand reassuringly, almost kindly, on his. 'This time it will not hurt,' he said. 'Keep your eyes fixed on mine.' " The equipment produces in him "a large patch of emptiness, as though a piece had been taken out of his brain" (212).

This is the rape scene; the castration scene follows. O'Brien forces Winston to take off his clothes, and while Winston is naked, O'Brien "seized one of Winston's remaining front teeth between his powerful thumb and forefinger. A twinge of pain shot through Winston's jaw. O'Brien had wrenched the loose tooth out by the roots. He tossed it across the cell." Then he commands: "Now put your clothes on again" (224). It is almost anticlimactic when, in the famous "rats" scene, O'Brien leads Winston to betray Julia.

The arc of the novel appears to fit well with Orwell's thesis. The erotic connection between Julia and Winston produces a threat to the Party. O'Brien has to sever the link in order to transfer Winston's erotic attention to Big Brother (thus Winston, in the final paragraphs, is portrayed as bride, grateful rape victim, repentant son, suckling infant: "He was back in the Ministry of Love . . . his soul white as snow. . . . The long-hoped-for bullet was entering his brain. . . . O stubborn, self-willed exile from the loving breast! . . . He loved Big Brother" [244–45]). There are pieces that do not quite fit; the relationship between Julia and Winston fuels, at least on Winston's part, political activity rather than not giving "a damn for anything" (110), and in the end Winston is perhaps less a sexually frustrated marcher (though he does cheer: "he was with the crowds outside, cheering himself deaf" [244]) than something hollowed-out and dead. But the basic picture seems to cohere.

## THE THESIS ELABORATED, AND SOME CONFLICTING THESES

Julia claims—and though this is not entirely clear, she seems to be speaking in Orwell's voice—that if people are sexually active, they "feel happy and don't give a damn for anything." Political orthodoxy is a consequence of sexual frustration, which governments can channel into marching and flag-waving and the Two Minutes Hate. Sexual satisfaction removes the taste for these forms of political participation; people will no longer "get excited" once they are happy "inside" themselves. (Compare: "Almost as swiftly as he had imagined it, she had torn her clothes off, and when she flung them aside it was with that same magnificent gesture by which a whole civilization seemed to be annihilated. Her body gleamed white in the sun" [104].) In short, political fevers are a product of sexual frustration, and this is one of the things that a totalitarian government knows best. (Compare Winston's approval of the fact that Julia had been with scores of men; his desire for her to have been with "hundreds—thousands"; his claim "I hate purity. I hate goodness. I don't want any virtue to exist anywhere"; his pleasure at her reaction to his question about her attitude toward the sex act itself, "I adore it": "Not merely the love of one person, but the animal instinct, the simple undifferentiated desire: that was the force that would tear the Party to pieces. He pressed her down upon the grass" [104–5].)

It is not easy to know how to test Orwell's thesis, which appears to be an empirical claim. But there are obvious problems. Many people who are sexually inactive, voluntarily or as a result of coercion, do not support the prevailing political orthodoxy. Why should we think that "hysteria," if that is what is induced by sexual deprivation, leads to approval of the political status quo? It is at least as plausible to think that sexual activity would lead to political rebelliousness as to believe that it is correlated with conformity. Some dissident groups take steps to repress sexual activity, sometimes with the thought that the repression will strengthen ties to the cause and hence further endanger the state. Or—to me more plausibly—it may be that the sort of people who are sexually active are often likely to be political rebels. In any case is it really true that sexual satisfaction makes people—in Julia's words—not "give a damn for anything"? This seems implausible. Perhaps some people who are immersed in an extremely passionate relationship do not like to think about anything else; but that is a different point.

Notice in this connection that before O'Brien's true nature is revealed, Winston and Julia, now sexual partners, do not abstain from politics but on the contrary enlist in what they think is a conspiracy against the Party. The conspiracy is one in which sacrifice for the cause—with one exception—is unlimited, in fact not so different, with that exception, from what the Party wants from its citizens:

> "You are prepared to give your lives?"
> "Yes."
> "You are prepared to commit murder?"
> "Yes."
> "To commit acts of sabotage which may cause the death of hundreds of innocent people?"
> "Yes."
> "To betray your country to foreign powers?"
> "Yes." . . .
> "You are prepared to commit suicide, if and when we order you to do so?"
> "Yes."
> "You are prepared, the two of you, to separate and never see one another again?"
> "No!" broke in Julia. (142–43)

The single exception embodied in Julia's "No!" shows that political loyalty can be undermined by an erotic relationship. But this is a quite different point from Orwell's thesis.

We might compare in this regard the very different presentation of the relation between sexual freedom and political freedom in Huxley's *Brave New World*. There sexual promiscuity is a kind of opiate of the masses, consistently encouraged partly in order to discourage political rebellion. Both novels portray the death of the individual soul, but with major differences: Where *Nineteen Eighty-Four* is a nightmare vision of Communism or Fascism, *Brave New World* is a nightmare vision of triumphant capitalism. We might even identify a Huxley hypothesis, one that appears to compete directly with Orwell's: Sexual activity diverts people from engaging in political causes, and it ought therefore to be encouraged by a government that seeks a quiescent population. On this view, sexual promiscuity is depoliticizing, soul-destroying, a twin to soma, antagonistic to rebellion. Some political movements have in fact accepted this view, and

|  | *Sexual repression* | *Sexual freedom* |
| --- | --- | --- |
| Political repression | Orwell's *Nineteen Eighty-Four* | Huxley's *Brave New World* |
| Political freedom | Many dissident groups | One understanding of contemporary America |

it is easy to see how it might be true. We can imagine the possibilities described in the accompanying matrix.

On this view, Huxley's hypothesis is the antonym to Orwell's. But along one dimension, it is only apparently competing. The key point is that Huxley, like Orwell, identifies sexual activity with political passivity. In Orwell, the state seeks marching, even a form of fanaticism; in Huxley, the state seeks a kind of pleased, vacant indifference. Sexual repression is, in *Nineteen Eighty-Four*, a necessary way of "bottling down some powerful instinct and using it as a driving force" (111); in *Brave New World*, the society is infantilized and pacified through catering to that same instinct. Thus it is that in Orwell's world, a form of sex that is not a "frigid little ceremony" (110) is a threat to the political order, whereas in Huxley's, the threat comes from a refusal of sex, or of soma, which will be and will produce rebellion. Compare Winston to Julia, who appears to have little interest in politics, and who says, "I'm not interested in the next generation, dear." When Winston says, "You're only a rebel from the waist downwards," she does not object but instead finds the statement "brilliantly witty" (129).

But there are other possibilities, very different from Orwell's and Huxley's shared view. It may be that sexual love can actually fuel political activity, by expanding the imagination and promoting empathic engagement with the lives of others. Probably we need to distinguish here, as Orwell does not, among different kinds of sexuality. It is not as if there is a choice only between "the Party's sexual puritanism" and "sexual privation" (Orwell's phrases) on the one hand and "making love" on the other. Promiscuous relationships are not all the same; nor are enduring, passionate relationships. Promiscuous relationships may have different effects from enduring, passionate relationships. The connection between any one of these and political activity depends on many independent variables.

All this may not be quite fair to Orwell. He also seems to have another point in mind. It has to do with how sexuality is connected with individuality and self-expression, with the rejection of conformity, with what he seems to see as the truest and most distinctive self, anarchic and not governable. It is this that presents the deepest danger to the Party. Orwell is not speaking here of love or of intimate relations with individual persons: "Not merely the love of one person, but the animal instinct, the simple undifferentiated desire: that was the force that would tear the Party to pieces" (105). Here, too, there is an interesting relationship with Huxley, who portrays promiscuity as soulless, as an erasure of individuality, as a form of conformity. Both Huxley and Orwell may have a particular conception of authentic sexuality in view, and they may not be so different. The contrast is that Orwell portrays "the animal instinct, the simple undifferentiated desire" as active and a threat to political orthodoxy, something that, once unleashed, will lead to rebellion. O'Brien appears to agree. Winston's torture and castration produce a kind of docility, even serenity, that paves the way for, or that is, acceptance of Big Brother and death.

Orwell's conception of sexuality as an "animal instinct," and as an expression of something ungovernable and personal, may be right; certainly there is truth in it. But sexuality can itself be a product of social practices; it should not be naturalized, and opposed, as "true self," to cultural constraint. We do not know the extent to which sexual drives are themselves a product of private and public authority. Orwell tends to naturalize the "sex instinct" (as the very term suggests). This is an underexplored point in the novel itself, where sexual drives seem to be something beyond the reach of politics or the Party, except through after-the-fact techniques of the kind used by O'Brien. Perhaps this is not Orwell's full position; Winston's early fantasies of sexual violence might be taken as a product of the particular social circumstances of Party domination. But this point is not much elaborated, nor is it brought into contact with Julia's claims about the nature and consequence of sexual activity.

## SOME IMPLICATIONS

Does a free society allow prostitution and pornography? Does a free society attempt to eliminate "sexual repression," understood as state interference with people's sexual choices? Much will depend on how we understand the idea of sexual liberty. Perhaps that form of liberty does not require mere freedom from governmental restraints. If preferences and values have social origins (at least in part), then the desire to go to a prostitute, or to be a prostitute, may reflect a lack of freedom. Notwithstanding this point, many contemporary critics do connect sexual freedom and political freedom. They seem to think that those who challenge sexual repression, or sexual orthodoxy, are in some sense striking a blow for political liberty as well.

If the discussion here is correct, the claimed link is illusory. Sexual freedom, at least in Orwell's sense, need not be connected with political freedom, and those who seek the one need have no interest in the other. There is no link logically or empirically. In some ways Orwell's conception of their relationship is a cousin of the conception of many dissident movements in the 1960s. Those movements combined an intense interest in sexual experimentation with an intense interest in political rebellion; they were a self-conscious challenge to conformity in various guises. But it is no coincidence that modern feminism outgrew those movements, in part because sexual liberty was understood, much of the time, as a matter of giving men greater sexual access to women. While I cannot support the claim here, I think that Orwell's conception of sexual freedom belongs in the same family, and indeed that sexual equality is a large neglected topic in a book that otherwise has so much to say about both freedom and sex.

## CONCLUSION

Orwell suggests that totalitarian governments favor "sexual puritanism," which induces "hysteria," something that such governments mobilize in their own favor. This is the image of patriotic frenzy as "sex gone sour." On this view, sexual freedom embodies freedom and individualism, and it is the deepest enemy of a totalitarian state. A state that allows sexual freedom will be unable to repress its citizens. This is why O'Brien must achieve victory over Julia.

But it is possible to imagine other, equally plausible views. "Sexual privation" might indeed induce hysteria, but of the sort that leads to rebellion and thus serves as an obstacle to a successful totalitarian government. I have suggested that in the face of existing social norms, many people who are sexually active are also likely to be political rebels, because of something in their character (itself perhaps a product of early childhood or genetic predispositions). And sexual freedom, even promiscuity, might be encouraged by totalitarian governments, in order to divert the citizenry and to induce apathy. (This is Huxley's thesis.) Or we might reject the idea that the only two options are "privation" and "freedom" (as understood by both Orwell and Huxley). The real question might be what sorts of intimate relationships people are allowed to make with one another.

In the end I believe that Orwell's thesis is a crude, vaguely Freudian cliché, implausible as an abstraction and in some ways undermined by the novel itself. It is true that some totalitarian states have attempted the approach he describes, and perhaps they have had some modest success. But Orwell was wrong to think that there is a "direct, intimate connection between chastity and political orthodoxy." The mechanisms that link sexual freedom and political freedom are extremely diverse. There are no lawlike generalizations here.

# Sex, Law, Power, and Community

ROBIN WEST

How SHOULD we think critically about—and then possibly reform—our laws regulating human sexuality? One possible way to do so is moralistic: by reference to a community's shared and long-standing moral or religious beliefs, we could determine what sexual practices are morally good and what practices are morally bad, and then we could attempt to pass laws that encourage the good and deter the bad. We could then criticize our laws, including our laws of sexual regulation, by reference to how well or how poorly they achieve this end. Another possible way to do so might be called liberal: in a liberal society, individuals are understood to be and encouraged to be autonomous—an autonomy that is in turn fostered by both the liberty entailed by the Rule of Law and the particular decisions individuals make regarding their own vision of the good, their own religious beliefs, their chosen family and marital structures, and, among much else, their chosen sexual practices. We should, then, critically evaluate law, sex, and our laws regulating sexuality by reference to this liberal ideal of autonomous individualism. These two positions—the social conservative's and the modern liberal's—are familiar: the first tilting in favor of a considerable amount of sexual regulation, the latter tilting against it. In this country, at this time, these two positions continue to dominate social as well as legal debate, amply evidenced by such public scandals as those of the Clinton era.

There are, however, at least two other, quite different, even nonstandard, ways of thinking about the relationship of law to sex, and of laws regulating sex, which also play some role in our current zeitgeist and perhaps an even greater role in our Western intellectual traditions. Neither fits easily on the conservative-to-liberal matrix quickly sketched above. The first very general way of thinking about these relations is political. We might ask, of sex and law, a series of essentially political questions, all aimed toward assessing the value of law, of sex, and of laws regulating sexual practices, laying bare their relation to various forms of pernicious *power*, rather than their relation to contested moral virtues or values. Then, we might assess the value of law, or the value of sex, or the value of regulation by reference to whether and how particular laws or legal regimes, or particular sexual practices or sexual regimes further politically desirable social organizations. The second very general and equally non-standard way of thinking about these questions might be called *humanistic*. We might assess the value of our sexual practices, and of the legal regulation of sex, by asking whether our laws and sexual practices express or generate desirable communities and a good quality of life for the individuals who inhabit them. We might think not so much of the distributions of power that sex, law, and the law of sex generate, but rather, about the harms caused, interests served, lives enhanced or lives diminished, and communities strengthened or weakened by our sexual practices, our legal institutions, and our sexual regulatory regime. From such questions—questions that go to the harms, interests, pains, pleasures, and individual and communal potentialities that our sexual and legal practices generate—we might then assess the value of various forms of sexual regulation.

Organized feminism has done much to highlight both of these nonstandard ways of thinking about the legal regulation of sexuality, but they by no means owe their origin to that political movement. Political theorists and communitarian moral philosophers, and some novelists, have long attended to the political and human costs—and promises—of regulating human sexuality. Orwell, notably, contributed to both. Thus in *Nineteen Eighty-Four*, the political novel for which he is best known, Orwell introduced—by negative, dystopian inference—an important political argument for sexual privacy that, although similar in outcome to liberal arguments for deregulation, is nevertheless different from them, and perhaps even idiosyncratic. In the first two sections of this paper, I will spell out briefly the political argument regarding sexual regulation that I believe is implicit in *Nineteen Eighty-Four* and will then criticize it.

If we turn away from Orwell's famous novel, however, and look instead at his biographical and literary essays—and in particular, his substantial essay on the life and fiction of Charles Dickens[1]—we find a quite different, and decidedly more humanistic, method of social criticism from anything suggested in *Nineteen Eighty-Four*. Although suggestive rather than explicit and never applied to laws regarding sexual practices, the Dickensian humanistic social criticism he there describes—the appeal to "honor and decency,"[2] the attempt to change society by improving upon the capacity for sympathy at the heart of our moral nature,[3] the fear that political change might be worse than the disease of injustice,[4] the conviction that the disease of injustice is nevertheless intolerable,[5] the faith that narrative

---

[1] George Orwell, "Charles Dickens," in *A Collection of Essays* (New York: Harcourt Brace & Co., 1981), 48.

[2] Ibid., 52, 101–3.

[3] Ibid., 51.

[4] Ibid., 53, 58–60.

[5] Ibid., 75.

is in some way at the heart of the task of social reform,[6] and even the "generous anger" that Orwell finds in Dickens's countenance[7]—all of this Orwell not only attributes to Dickens but also seemingly embraces himself. That Dickensian or Orwellian method of social reform and criticism, I want to suggest toward the end of this paper, is markedly different from the political vision put forward in *Nineteen Eighty-Four*. It provides a needed and timely corrective, I will suggest, not only to his own political analysis of sexual regulation suggested in *Nineteen Eighty-Four*, but to virtually all political analyses of law. The need for that corrective, today, is great, when our heightened and postmodern awareness of the realpolitik of social life and struggle threatens to overshadow all other forms of insight and resounds as an uncomfortable echo of Orwell's own day, when the British imperialism he so hated threatened to annihilate the lives and societies to whose betterment it was disingenuously dedicated. The final section of this paper will briefly spell out the assumptions of humanistic legal criticism, in the context of sexual regulation.

## SEX, LAW, AND POWER: AN ORWELLIAN ASSESSMENT

The Orwellian political argument for sexual privacy implied in *Nineteen Eighty-Four* rests primarily on a description of power, and only derivatively on a description of sex. Orwell held two assumptions regarding power, both of which contrast vividly with now conventional postmodern dogma. The first assumption—which runs not only through *Nineteen Eighty-Four*, but also through his memoirs—is that *power kills* (220).[8] Power is the willingness and ability to kill, control, manipulate, oppress, humiliate, and torture other human beings. Power is malignant. The second is that the form of power that is most dangerous is concentrated, unconstrained, unchecked *state* power. Of all possible distributions of power, the novel urges, the one in which the state holds an excessive amount is the most dangerous. Thus, in *Nineteen Eighty-Four*, virtually every misery suffered by the citizens of Oceania, from poor consumer goods, to literal bombardments from the sky, to the doublespeak imposed on them, the false consciousness that results, and the ever-present threat of imminent and arbitrary arrest and execution, is the result of the conjurings of unchecked, centralized state power, which is in turn motivated, not by a misguided paternalism, but by the sheer desire to kill, destroy,

---

[6] Ibid., 93–95.

[7] Ibid., 104.

[8] Peter Stansky and William Abrahams, *The Unknown Orwell and Orwell: The Transformation* (Stanford: Stanford University Press, 1994).

and control. *Nineteen Eighty-Four* quite clearly reflects the view, not un-common among socialist, left-leaning intellectuals at midcentury, that communism—socialism combined with a horrific degree of concentrated state power—was the great threat with which we all had to reckon, and unchecked state power was unquestionably the evil that lurked at its core.

These claims, obviously, are not idiosyncratic Orwellian beliefs, nor are they beliefs that were held exclusively by the great anticommunist novel-ists of midcentury: arguably, a distrust of power and a fear of the perni-cious consequences of unconstrained states are central, even defining com-mitments of a distinctively Western and liberal political orientation. The uniqueness of Orwell's political novel, I believe, and surely the distinc-tiveness of his idiosyncratic argument for sexual privacy that lies at its core, stem from the novel's embrace of two seemingly contradictory re-sponses to the potential threat posed to humanity by the specter of con-centrated state power. Both responses are common enough, but they are rarely held jointly. The first response, shared by countless liberal and not-so-liberal theorists of the state, is best stated as a foundational faith: a belief that the very *idea* of law, of lawfulness, of legal process, or in short of the Rule of Law, is an important antidote to the danger of unchecked state or public power. Although boosted, naturally, by the demonstrable contempt for legality and legal process evidenced by the mid-twentieth-century communist states that so impressed Orwell, anticommunism is not at the heart of this view. Rather, scores if not hundreds of Western liberal and not-so-liberal thinkers, from Aristotle,[9] to John Locke and the English social contract theorists,[10] to our own constitutional framers,[11] to Sigmund Freud,[12] Lon Fuller,[13] and innumerable nineteenth- and twenti-eth-century liberal-legal thinkers, have held out the hope that law is some-how different from power, and that because it is, the very idea of law—the Rule of Law itself—might effectively counter the potential or real evil of totalitarian, dictatorial states. The generality and abstractions required by the Rule of Law force a regard for a liberal and ecumenical universal-ism—a habit of mind—that in turn protects us against the whimsical dic-tates of overly particularistic, overly discriminating, overly personalized and overly personalizing, and hence tyrannical political sovereigns. Law,

---

[9] Aristotle, *The Politics*, trans. Benjamin Jowett (New York: Modern Library, 1943), 162–65.

[10] Thomas Hobbes, *Leviathan* (Cambridge: Cambridge University Press, 1991); John Locke, "An Essay Concerning the True Original Extent and End of Civil Government," in *Two Treatises of Government* (New York: Everyman Library, 1975), 183–205.

[11] *The Federalist*, Nos. 10, 51, 55, 57 (James Madison); *Marbury v. Madison*, 5 U.S. 137 (1803).

[12] Sigmund Freud, *Totem and Taboo*, trans. A. Brill (New York: New Republic, 1918).

[13] Lon Fuller, *The Morality of Law* (New Haven: Yale University Press, 1964), 33–94.

for many Western thinkers, is a potent counter to the threat of unchecked public power, and unchecked public power is the greatest political danger a political community can face.

The mature George Orwell of *Nineteen Eighty-Four* and *Animal Farm* obviously concurred. In his essay "England Your England," he neatly and crisply describes the belief, held by his British cocitizens, in law, and the Rule of Law, and the difference between law and power, as a childlike, irrational, and even contradictory faith; but rather than condescend to it, he makes clear in the essay that he both cherishes that faith and shares it.[14] *Nineteen Eighty-Four* is less ambiguous on the point. In *Nineteen Eighty-Four*, the citizens of Oceania, Orwell and his protagonist Winston Smith note repeatedly, lack a Rule of Law to protect them from power's malignancy: first they lack law itself—like the citizens under King Rex of Fuller's famous jurisprudential parable, they lack general, consistent rules promulgated beforehand in accordance with procedural criteria—but they also lack democracy, courts, and judicial process. They lack law no less than they lack privacy, security, love, intimacy, and a natural language. In his negative insight that law would be absent in a regime controlled by a central malignant power, Orwell gave voice to a fear and a hope that in many ways define our Western liberal tradition.

The oddity of *Nineteen Eighty-Four*, however, lies in its simultaneous embrace of another and very different sort of answer to the political question posed above. We turn to what is perhaps not as long a list of thinkers but is nevertheless an impressive one, including neo-Rousseaueans, Fourierians, Brook Farmers and other nineteenth-century utopians,[15] Emersonians and free-love enthusiasts of the early twentieth century, Marcusians and other Frankfurt School adherents of midcentury,[16] and various pro-sex feminists, Act Uppers, and sex radicals[17] of the century's late

---

[14] George Orwell, "England Your England," in *A Collection of Essays*, 252.

[15] John C. Spurlock, *Free Love: Marriage and Middle-Class Radicalism in America* (New York: New York University Press, 1988), 319–409. See also Hal D. Sears, *The Sex Radicals: Free Love in High Victorian America* (Lawrence: Regents Press of Kansas, 1977).

[16] Herbert Marcuse, *Eros and Civilization: A Philosophical Inquiry into Freud*, 2nd ed. (New York: Vintage Books, 1966); Herbert Marcuse, *An Essay on Liberation* (Boston: Beacon Press, 1969). For a general discussion of the relationship between a Marcusian view of sex and politics, on the one hand, and constitutional protections of privacy, on the other, see Thomas C. Grey, "Eros, Civilization, and the Burger Court," *Law and Contemporary Problems* 43 (Spring 1980): 83.

[17] Duncan Kennedy, "Sexual Abuse, Sexy Dressing, and the Eroticization of Domination," in *Sexy Dressing, etc.* (Cambridge: Harvard University Press, 1993); Mary Joe Frug, *Postmodern Legal Feminism* (New York: Routledge and Kegan Paul, 1992). For a general introduction to the positions of some of the so-called pro-sex feminists, see *Pleasure and Danger: Exploring Female Sexuality*, ed. Carole S. Vance (Boston: Routledge and Kegan Paul, 1984).

years. All of these have held out the hope that unregulated, naturalistic, animalistic, erotic, hedonistic, pleasure-for-pleasure's-sake sex can be a politically rebellious act and, particularly, a political act of defiance against states, state power, and state authority: its animalistic naturalism, its life force, its break with restraints, its defiant avoidance of authority, its chaotic passion, its anti-individualistic communion, its sheer devotion to pleasure, its uselessness, and its nonproductivity all make it a bulwark against the deadly, rationalistic regularity, the thanatos-driven thirst for order and predictability, the sterile instrumentalism, the dour attraction of the "principle of antipathy" (as Bentham provocatively called it), the alliance to the culture of pain, death, and sadism, that, so some think, lie at the heart of state power. For this group, erotic sexuality, we might say formulaically, is *itself* a bulwark against state power. If we put these two groups together, we find a curious yin-yang effect: an impressive array of Western political thinkers, from virtually all disciplines and walks of life, have argued, in various ways, that *either* general, abstract, rational law, *or* particular, concrete, impassioned, and irrational sex, can be potent as a political force against the evil of unconstrained state power.

These views, however, are almost never held jointly, and each is often held, at least by its most fervent proponents, to imply the negation of the other. Thus a commitment to the Rule of Law, for example, is rarely held to imply a commitment to sexual liberation and more often held to imply the reverse. Sigmund Freud famously regarded both the symbolic erection of the totemic Rule of Law and the suppression of erotic sexuality as necessary conditions of civilization—by which he clearly meant, among much else, life free from the tyrannical rule of personalized, paternal tyrants.[18] Sometimes echoing those Freudian sentiments, or presaging them, twentieth-century legal and political proponents of the Rule of Law have often regarded the preservation of the orderly, gently sentimental—but nevertheless generally hierarchic and patriarchal—procreative family as a component of private life that can not only serve the ends of order but also serve as further protection against an overly intrusive state; hence they have tended to regard nonfamilial, erotic, reckless sexuality as a threat to that familial order. This yields a strong case for the preservation of a realm of privacy around the traditional family but at the same time underwrites a mandate for regulating the erotic sexuality that exists outside of that sphere and that arguably threatens it. Likewise, on the other side, romantics, utopians, sex radicals, Marcusians, free-love proponents and their late twentieth-century counterparts typically collapse the "law" and the "state" and find in *both* the danger of concentrated power. For many, and quite explicitly for the mid- to late twentieth-century sex advo-

---

[18] Freud, *Totem and Taboo*, 182–87.

cates, law is itself nothing but the disingenuous articulations of power, and it is therefore against both that unbridled sexual passion and expression might constitute a legitimate and antiauthoritarian, rebellious, and even revolutionary political impulse.[19] For sex romantics, typically, the irrationality, concreteness, and particularity of sexual expression find as meaningful a target in the abstract generalities of law as its chaotic, spontaneous, and generative abandon finds in the deadening quest for control central to obsessive state power.

George Orwell, perhaps uniquely, seemingly embraced *both* of these convictions. The quiet and gentle pleasures of companionate, marital sex, Orwell makes clear, along with family intimacy and love quite generally, are destroyed by state control. But, oddly, for erotic, nonmarital, sex-for-its-own-sake sex, Orwell makes a stronger and quite different claim. Erotic sex, Winston Smith insists in *Nineteen Eighty-Four*, is a truly *political* and even revolutionary act (103–5). It is so, Winston Smith says, and Orwell apparently believed, *not* because it is itself an act of power—far from it. Rather, it is a revolutionary, political act because it is an *animalistic act of instinct*, and as such *it is power's antithesis*. Sex is what power isn't. Neither Orwell nor Winston elaborates, unfortunately, but it's not hard to fill in the argument: animalistic, instinctual, erotic sex is spontaneous rather than controlled or controlling; it is benign and life affirming rather than malign or deathly; it hedonistically seeks pleasure rather than sadistically seeking death; it is comforting and caressing rather than torturous and brutal; it is moved by the principle of sympathy rather than the principle of antipathy; it is passionate rather than calculating; it is a giving over of the self rather than an imposition of the self; it is a search for self-abandon rather than a manipulative search for control. Concentrated power might indeed destroy family love, marital sex, and companionate intimacy; familial intimacy is vulnerable to concentrated state power. But power stands in a different relation altogether to erotic sex: erotic sex is not just threatened by power; erotic sex is power's antithesis.

Law, too, Smith reminds us, is power's antithesis, but certainly not because it bears any resemblance to erotic sex. Rather, law is antithetical to power for almost the opposite reason: law is distinguished from power by its generality, rationality, regularity, abstraction, and regard for process. Thus Orwell seemingly found in *both* our capacity for erotic, hedonistic sexuality *and* our capacity for rational, general, universal legalism—in both our animalistic, instinctual pleasure in the bodies, touches, caresses, and comforts of others, and our ability to govern through rules—vehicles for our humanity and manifestations of our human freedom. Far from antithetical to each other, erotic sex and the Rule of Law both, Or-

---

[19] See Kennedy, "Sexual Abuse."

well suggests, are deep human impulses, each expressive of our freedom, each requiring the other, and both vulnerable to the deadening thirst for power—the ability and willingness to kill, torture, and humiliate—threatened by the rise of concentrated state power.

What, then, finally, of the legal regulation of sexuality? By embracing, so to speak, these two fundamental but also fundamentally different antiauthoritarian impulses, law and sex, we can derive a distinctively Orwellian argument for the constitutional protection of erotic sexuality—not sexuality as a part of family life, not sexuality as an aspect of reproductive life, not sexuality as part and parcel of larger "lifestyles," but, rather, for erotic sexuality itself—against moralistic or paternalistic state regulation. The Constitution, particularly according to Warren Court jurisprudence—which is the jurisprudence that came closest to embracing something like this, at least until its sexual privacy law was truncated by *Bowers v. Hardwick*—after all, is the voice of law And the raison d'être of law is precisely to speak to and constrain political power: enforced by a relatively powerless branch, interpreted by reference to general norms of reason rather than a mandate of political will, the Constitution constrains, limits, and breaks up the concentrations of state power that threaten freedom, respect, and dignity in even properly functioning (much less corrupt) working democracies. To this common enough understanding, we might then add the Orwellian claim that the physical, bodily, natural pleasures of erotic sexuality—no less than free speech, religion, or family life, and indeed perhaps more so—instill a regard and concern for one's own and others' natural, biological well-being, which is itself antithetical to the suppression of concern and regard characteristically induced by concentrated, malignant, or sadistic power. If both of these premises are granted, then the constitutional protection of sex—even and particularly the erotic, nonreproductive, nonfamilial, nonmarital, nonproductive, useless, unprofitable, and inefficient kind—would not be just an unfortunate by-product of other freedoms and ends, such as family autonomy and privilege, in turn protected for essentially statist reasons. Sex is, rather, itself a potent force that constrains the state by countering it. There is nothing anomalous, then, about using the former (law) to protect the latter (sex) against a common target—power. Constitutionalism in general, and a constitutional right of privacy aimed at protecting free sexual expression, would simply be one way of doing so.

## SEX, LAW, AND PRIVATE POWER: A CRITICAL ASSESSMENT

There is, however, as every post-1984 reader of *Nineteen Eighty-Four* will surely note, a major disconnect between Orwell's dystopian vision and our current political fears and hopes, not only for sex, but for law quite generally, and it is unsurprising that the Orwellian argument I constructed above from *Nineteen Eighty-Four*'s premises sounds a bit hollow as well. At the heart of the disconnect between Orwell's imaginings and our own modern fears and hopes lies his understanding of power and, derivatively, his understanding of sex. Readers today, even more than in the fifties, are likely to find his assumptions regarding both power and sex—that power kills, that state power is the greatest threat we face, and that sex is power's opposite—either naively romantic or baldly false, and if they are, or if some of them are, then obviously the Orwellian argument for constitutionally insulating sex from legislation is a bad one. In my own view, this global dismissal of Orwell's musings on sexuality and power oversimplifies: while there is obviously much to criticize, I think there is a grain of truth in all of his assumptions—regarding sex, law, and power—and more than a grain in his claim regarding the malignancy of power. What Orwell got wrong, I think, is relatively obvious, while what he got right is not at all obvious and might be more important. Our task is not to throw out the baby with the bathwater.

But first, to throw out the bathwater. Let me begin with the second of his assumptions regarding power—that state power is the greatest evil, or threat of evil, we face. Even if Orwell was right to distrust power, he might have been wrong to identify concentrated *state* power as our greatest political threat. On a global level, communism, after all, did not triumph— global markets did, and that fact more than any other makes reading *Nineteen Eighty-Four* an oddly disorienting experience. But even domestically, his insistence on the dangers of state power, to the neglect of the dangers of private power, seems psychologically as well as politically off the mark. What if, contra Orwell's predictive fantasy, the greatest danger we face presently is not the concentrated public power of the nation-state at all, but instead the concentrated private power of individuals, associations, religious, racial, or ethnic subcultures, and global corporations? What if, to put this in terms of young adult fiction, it is Golding's dystopian novel *Lord of the Flies*, rather than Orwell's parable *Nineteen Eighty-Four*, that presents the scariest, starkest, most recognizable depiction of our imminent demise? What if it is the very real bloodshed of Columbine or the rapes of Woodstock '99, rather than the fictional mind control of the malignant authority in Oceania or of the head nurse in *One Flew over the Cuckoo's Nest*, that leave us most shaken? What if the greatest danger to our natural language, our commitment to truth, and our conviction that language can and ought to convey it comes not from state control at all, but from the edgy, pushing-the-envelope, ironic, playful sarcasm of corporate advertisers? To put the point politically, what if Thomas Hobbes had it essentially right, and it is the neutered, weakened,

or nonexistent state—too little, rather than too much, state authority—
that most endangers us, and that we find most threatening? What if, in
Freudian terms, rather than parental intrusiveness, it is fratricide and parental abandonment that we most fear? What if, to combine the Freudian
and Hobbesian insights, we have more to fear from our violent, jealous,
envious, acquisitive brothers in the state of nature than we have from the
intrusive, omnipotent, tyrannical father?

Orwell was no stranger to the dangers of private power, particularly
private economic power. He was a committed and lifelong socialist. He
was spiritually, emotionally, intellectually, and even physically repulsed
by poverty. He detested the British class system and his own role within
it, and was well aware of the power of economic actors, no less than
political actors, to shape and distort both consciousness and human fellow feeling. He was also, however, convinced, or became convinced, that
economic injustice would disappear when and only when, from a sense
of decency, human beings willed it to do so, and he was openly fearful
that contrived political mechanisms for forcing that transformation might
be worse than the injustice it was meant to address. It may have seemed
quite natural for him to highlight in his fiction—particularly to his fellow
socialists—the dangers of concentrated state power simply because the
dangers in the solutions to which one is attracted are precisely the dangers
one is least likely to see or appreciate. The danger of the state-run-amok,
in other words, might have seemed, to Orwell, to be simply the most
hidden—and hence most worrisome—rather than the patently obvious
dangers of an unregulated market economy. He had no more reason than
anyone else did to be able to predict the global ascendancy of market
economies and the decline of command economies in the last quarter of
the twentieth century. That he warned the West against a danger that
never came to be does not undermine his prescience in describing the
consequences: England may never have succumbed to the dangers of state
control of language, thought, love, and truth, but Russia did, and the
convergence between Orwell's imaginings and Soviet life is by no means
rendered less remarkable by the fortunate fact that it did not happen here,
and to us.

But whatever the reason for Orwell's fixation in his fiction on the dangers and evils of state power, to the neglect of private power, the fixation
was real and affects the fecundity of his political insights. Briefly put, there
are obvious, and important, differences in the political value of law, and
less obvious although real differences in the way we might regard sex, if
we regard private, rather than public, power as our greatest political
threat. Those differences imply in turn a different picture of both the value
and the meaning of sexual regulation. Thus—even for those of us who
concur with Orwell's distrust of power—if it is private rather than public

power that carries the negative potentials he portrays, we might be led to different understandings of the political bases for regulating sexual behavior. Let me spell out some of those different understandings, and where they seem to lead regarding the legal regulation of sex.

First, the idea of law itself holds out a quite different set of promises, and thus takes on a quite different meaning, if we worry about the dangers of private rather than totalitarian or state power. If private power is the problem, then the idea and promise of the Rule of Law is that law might be a force with which to neuter effectively not the dangers of an omnipotent state but, rather, the dangers of the acquisitive, the violent, the envious, the antisocial, and the sociopath in our midst, by acquiring a monopoly on legitimate violence. Following Hobbes, we want a legal leviathan; however, we want it to deliver us not from the evils of state power but, rather, from the evils of a fear-driven, short, nasty, and brutish private competition, against which the danger of excessively concentrated state power simply pales. Law, then, either monarchical or democratic, exists to counter the evils of private power. This Hobbesian rather than Freudian understanding of law's value, and the Rule of Law's meaning, also finds an echo both in our constitutional traditions and in our constitutional heritage, from the anti-Federalists to the New Dealers to the civil rights movements. The danger of factions, the danger of concentrated economic power, the danger of private racism—all these might be countered, or at least contained, by a law that seeks to displace power from the physically threatening brother to either an embodied or a disembodied state.

Viewing private rather than public power as the threat against which law is aimed, however, doesn't necessarily lead to a different end point regarding the desirability of regulating sex. Rather, whether or not it does depends on the nature of sex. If sexual activity, whether erotic, reproductive, familial, sentimental, or nonfamilial—like economic activity or acquisitive violence—is a part of that Hobbesian private realm, not just polluted by but defined by power, then it is obviously a proper target of law. If it is something other, though—if it is part of the private realm but not an expression of power—then perhaps it is not. For Orwell, again, sex was power's antithesis, and there's no reason I can see for thinking he would have seen it as standing in a different relation to power held by private rather than public actors. It's fair to surmise, I think, that Orwell would likely have concurred—although for somewhat different reasons— with the now widely held liberal view that erotic sex, like family and marriage, although a part of the private realm, is distinctively not an expression of private *power*, and that it therefore represents a reprieve from, rather than extension of, the power relations that otherwise make the private realm such a violent, nasty, and brutish place.

Sex, marriage, and family, on this now quite standard liberal conception, are all parts of the safe haven in a heartless, even if not a brutally violent, world. Sexual intimacy is different from familial and marital intimacy—it is purely physical, hedonistic, and pleasure seeking rather than sentimental and affectionate; nevertheless, like the latter, sex is a part of the private but companionate and communitarian counter to the competitive world of Hobbesian individuals. It is a part of, even if only the decadent part of, the Shakespearean Belmont of home, hearth, and mercy, rather than the Venice of markets, chicanery, usurious interest rates, and competition. Sex, like intimacy generally, represents the feminine world of altruism, care, and compassion that takes the edge off—and thereby makes livable—the atomized world of competing centers of private and economic power. Erotic sex outside of marriage is different but not much different, on this view, from erotic or even reproductive sex within marriage: what they both share, and what distinguishes both from other private practices, is that they are *not* expressions of power. Again, sex is what power—private power this time—isn't. If between consenting companions, sex, in any combination or configuration, represents a reprieve from private struggle. There is no good reason to regulate it, and good reason not to. For the most part, sex is private, but it is not power, or at any rate, it is not the private power against which law is aimed. It is not part of the aggression, violence, and general nastiness, deliverance from which makes the leviathan a good bargain.

This liberal picture—law as a counter to private power, sex as a part of the private world but distinctively not an expression of power—provides a ready rationale (although different from the Orwellian argument I constructed above) to the constitutional right of privacy the Court has constructed around sex, marriage, and family. Particularly, it makes sense of the construction of such a right in the face of the post-*Lochner* revolution: it rationalizes, in other words, the otherwise anomalous tendency to permit and encourage legal regulation of the "private" world of commerce and work, but to insist on a realm of privacy around family, marriage, and sexuality. What the Constitution protects, on this view, among much else, is a distinction not so much between "public" and "private" as between the private, which can be and indeed *must be* legally regulated—that being, after all, the point of law—and the "intimate," which cannot be. The latter, along with our "private" thoughts, our closely held religious beliefs, speech, and associations, represents the sphere, in now familiar constitutional language, into which public demands, public responsibilities, and public authorities simply may not intrude, not because they are "private"—the private, after all, is what law regulates—but because they are "intimate." That is, they are part of the private sphere unpolluted by the Hobbesian power struggle and hence, by definition, part of the sphere of which public control is not required and is indeed unduly paternalist. On this view, it makes perfect sense, at least it is perfectly consistent, to hold that the Hobbesian private man requires the regulative arm of the state and enjoys no constitutional protection from it. Rather, it is the non-Hobbesian man within us, so to speak—the individual carving out, in a profoundly noncompetitive, intimate, and indeed socially harmless way, his own family life, his religious orientation, his own conception of life's meaning—it is this man, and this life, in an otherwise Hobbesian world, that need, deserve, and receive a constitutional right of privacy. Sexuality is a part of that intimate sphere. There is, then, no contradiction, and in fact there is very good reason, on this view—derived from an understanding of private power as the threat against which law is aimed—to constitutionalize a realm of sexual privacy, and to insulate it against the authority, even if relatively benign, of the state.

This picture changes quite radically, however, once we question Orwell's—and liberalism's—view of sex. Orwell might after all have been right to fear concentrated power but wrong to view sex as power's antithesis. Contemporary liberal Hobbesians might be right to view private power as competitive and potentially lethal—the very force against which law is properly directed—but wrong to regard sex, family, and marriage as the sentimental complement to, or reprieve from, that competitive, potentially lethal realm. These are the stark narrative dystopian assumptions, not of *Nineteen Eighty-Four*, or of *Lord of the Flies*, but rather of Andrea Dworkin's dystopian novel *Mercy*, and they are the stark political assumptions of a good deal of contemporary feminism. They are also assumptions that, although admittedly and even notoriously disturbing, do not seem wildly disjoined from reality. Power is, at least often, something it would behoove us to distrust. And private power is surely, at least sometimes, a greater threat to our well-being than is public power. And just as surely—contrary to Orwell's romantic, revolutionary conception of sex, and contrary to contemporary liberalism's sentimental portrait—while sex is indeed a part of the private and intimate realms of life, sex is also, at least sometimes, and maybe often, an expression of malignant, private power. It is sometimes, maybe often, an attempt to render the violated victim not just subdued but still—annihilated. Sex is, sometimes, not a reprieve from the harsh, overly individualistic boundaries of an alienated society, and even less an expression of animalistic, instinctual abandon, but instead an attempt to rend apart a victim's physical integrity; to tear her body apart. Sexual provocation, play, and suggestiveness are sometimes, maybe often, not a harmless flirtatious attempt to instill humor and humanity in a sterile, dry, and dehumanizing public or economic world, but an aggressive attempt to silence by humiliation; to terrorize by reduction; to still and quiet and drive out the will, or being, or subjectivity, of another. When sex is any of these things, it is not a revolutionary, spontaneous declaration of freedom against centralized state power. Nor is it a space for sentimental reprieve from the Hobbesian war of all against all. When sex is any of these things, it is an act of private violence. And when it is an act of private violence, protection against it is what the legal sovereign promises, and is obligated, to deliver. When sex is any of these things, legal regulation of it is not just called for— overall, a better idea than not. When sex is any of these things, regulation of it is at the heart of the sovereign's legitimacy, and concern for privacy, constitutional or otherwise, is wildly misplaced.

What these assumptions suggest, if we regard them with any seriousness at all, is that there is no viable justification for a constitutional right to sexual privacy, any more than there is a constitutional right to economic privacy. What they might suggest, more strongly, is that there may well be a constitutional right to sexual regulation. Sex is sometimes, and maybe often, an expression of private aggression, not an expression of sentiment or antiauthoritarian animalistic passion. If that's right, then sex, when it violates the security or autonomy of others, ought indeed to be regulated, and regulated by law, and for the most fundamental Hobbesian reason. It is, after all, the state's unconditional, even nondelegable, duty to protect us against the violence and aggression of others, and it is within the state's ability and power to do so by law. Indeed, it is our constitutional right, as well as the state's constitutional duty, that it do precisely that.

## SEX, POWER, AND COMMUNITY

Let me now turn to the baby we must be careful to hold on to when we throw out the bathwater: Orwell's constitutive, even defining, and surely bottomless, distrust of power, and his reasons for it. Surely, it is that distrust of power that most distinguishes his general philosophical and political orientation from that of contemporary postmodernists. It is illuminating, for example, to contrast his view on power with that of Michel Foucault.[20] Famously, Foucault, in the last twenty years of his life, urged us to shed the Orwellian habit of viewing power as something that emanates from sovereigns, and as necessarily destructive, censorial, and oppressive. Power, Foucault insisted, contrary to the fears of the moderns, is neither destructive nor controlling, but affirmative and creative, and

[20] Michel Foucault, *Discipline and Punish*, trans. A. Sheridan (New York: Pantheon, 1979); Michel Foucault, *History of Sexuality*, trans. R. Hurley, vol. 1 (New York: Vintage, 1980).

comes from all sorts of social pores, as well as from the whims of states or political sovereigns. This different orientation, even emotional orientation, toward power implies different attitudes toward both law and sex as well: Foucault himself held, and now scores of postmodern political theorists concur, that we should turn our attention not to the Orwellian or Hobbesian or generally "Enlightenment" project of uncovering the hidden workings of power (wherever it may be) so as to better recognize it, criticize it, and then speak truth to it, but, rather, to the Foucauldian project of participating in it, of constructing our social reality, of embracing its capacity to produce truth rather than decrying its ability to mask it. Power is not something to first vilify and then oppose to other sources or values, such as law or truth or sex; rather, law is one form of power, as is truth, and as is sex as well. Law, sex, and truth have all been constructed through various forms, disciplines, and mechanisms of social power. But this is not something to worry over; this is social reality to grasp and then participate in.

Read simply as a corrective to Orwell's denunciation of power, Foucault's account of power and even of sexual power at first sounds plausible: *Nineteen Eighty-Four*, obviously, was just a fantasy. Sex is not a natural force destroyed by a totalitarian dictator on high; it is a way of being, created by social forces manifesting power on all levels of social living and toward various conflicting social ends. Indeed, there is a way to read Foucault, and to read Orwell, that tempts the reader to simply strike a commonsense compromise between them: they occupy opposite ends of a spectrum. Orwell defines power as malignant, deadly, and always emanating from some sovereign on high, while Foucault defines power as constructive, life-affirming, and oozing from every social pore. Maybe both poles are just exaggerations and, as the cliché holds, the truth lies in the middle: sometimes power is destructive, sometimes constructive; sometimes affirming, sometimes negating; sometimes productive, sometimes censorious. Obviously, that is true of sexual power as well, and obviously that complicates the task of regulating sex: we need somehow to use law to prohibit or punish the malignant use of sexual power, while trying to preserve its potency as a sentimental reprieve from private competition and even perhaps as a political reprieve from other forms of abusive power. Orwell and Foucault can each be read as a check on the excessive philosophical tendencies of the other.

There is, though, a deeper incompatibility between Orwell and Foucault, and between Orwellians and Foucauldian postmodernists, than in their disparate understandings of the moral valence of power, an incompatibility that cannot be so readily compromised: their disparate moral judgments of it. In Orwell's unequivocal belief, the distortions that power effected upon our natural and biological and instinctual animalistic capacities—not just for sexual pleasure, but also for care, for maternal love, and for companionate intimacy—were something *to condemn*. Our capacity for love, maternalism, companionship, and sexual pleasure in the bodies of others, he thought, as well as our commitment to truth and our command of a natural language, was *natural* but by no means *inevitable*: the pleasure we take from loving others *can be* blunted and extinguished by malign power. Such repression, he believed, is deeply immoral; it is even the heart of evil. By contrast, it is the heart of the Foucauldian, postmodern, constructivist, and skeptical turn to deny even the sense of these Orwellian moral commitments—to insist, contra Orwell, that the "natural" is just some category mistake, and that moral condemnation of that which destroys it, rather than participation in the process of constructing it, rests on nothing but confusion. All that is, in effect, is a product of social power, and that surely includes our "nature"; it surely includes both the natural impulses we think we cherish and the natural truths about them we might think we rest on when we form moral judgments about that which destroys what we value.

This brings me, finally, to what I regard as the important truth—easily enough missed—in Orwell's fiction and essays. Orwell had a universally and globally pessimistic view of power that may well have been overstated; a perverse obsession, at least in his fiction, with public rather than private power that now seems oddly misplaced; and a view of sex as power's antithesis that seems today to be not just naive but downright odd. But however flawed his understanding of power, he also understood, and deeply believed, that power is not *all there is*. There is also *nature*—meaning, not just wilderness, but human nature and human naturalness: our natural compassion and sympathy, our natural capacity for care, our natural inclination toward intimacy, our natural instinctual protection and love of our young, our natural yearning for beauty, and even our natural attraction to truth. We experience more than the workings of power, and we are something other than its various intersections. Relatedly, then, power and its distribution do not, or should not, exhaust our moral criteria, and an understanding of power does not exhaust our moral capacity. We judge and should judge the value of human social constructs—sex or law—not only by reference to whether or not that construct contributes to a decent distribution of power, but also by reference to the quality of life experienced by individuals within communities. It was, finally, Orwell's willingness to exercise his moral judgment—firmly grounded in sympathy for others, a commitment to principle, and his beliefs about the natural world—that truly set him apart from the postmodernists even of his own time and, more starkly still, from the postmodernists of our own.

What, if anything, do these fundamental differences in the Orwellian and loosely postmodern understanding of power suggest as to the legal regulation of sex? And as to our critical understanding of it? Orwell's stance, I think, at least reminds us that there is much more to life, and to social life in particular, than power—there is honor and decency and community and suffering and joy—and there are accordingly ways to engage in social criticism and social reform that are both deeper and gentler than the eventually bland analyses of power and its vectors dictated by postmodernism's peculiar brand of philosophical minimalism. We can describe communities and individual lives and the sufferings and joys they contain as something other than intersections of power vectors, and we can urge a greater decency, a greater regard for others, a more encompassing concern, and a larger moral compass, when anyone acts in ways that might improve or diminish the happiness and sorrows of those lives. Moreover, we can do this, not toward the end of a redistribution of social or political power, but toward the end of bettering the individual and community lives affected. Clearly, we can urge changes on the basis of humanistic criticism in the creation and interpretation of our laws as well.

Finally, let me just suggest two additional reasons, within the context of the legal regulation of sex, for urging a humanistic rather than purely political, critical method. First, although sex is at times an expression of abusive power, much of the time it is not, and we need a way to describe, debate, and value the sex that is not, no less than a way to regulate the sex that is. The debate over the legalization of same-sex marriage amply demonstrates the point. If same-sex marriage is something we ought to honor, it can't simply be because doing so would redistribute social power between traditionalists and the gay community—to assert as much is baldly question-begging. If same-sex marriage is something we ought to recognize, it must be because we have come to understand the point of marriage itself in a way that encompasses the ideals of the same- as well as opposite-sex couples who desire it: to facilitate a generative, permanent love, partly expressed in monogamous sexual relations, that enriches and sustains the participants committed to it. And it must be because we have come to understand the monogamous sexual relations between same-sex couples as expressive of such affection, in a way not much different from that of opposite-sex couples. I believe that is the point of marriage, best understood, and that monogamous sexual relations within opposite-sex couples are of such a nature. To sustain such claims, however, requires us to use a humanistic language of description and evaluation, rather than a Foucauldian discourse of power. If same-sex marriage is something we ought legally to permit, and the Constitution is read so as to require that it be permitted, then it must be because such marriages would be good for the individuals participating in them, and good for the society that tolerates them. The case for the legalization of same-sex marriage, in other words, must be based on the quality of the various communities and individual lives such a reform would engender. As such, it cannot be made without reference to the full expanse of the subjective lived experience within those unions, and to a full moral description and understanding of the value or harm of the sex within them. The "discourse of power" urged by postmodern Foucauldians, no less than a sterile "rights discourse" urged by traditional liberals, is simply inadequate to that task. It does not give us a way to grasp the meaning of either the sex or the marriage, and it does not give us a way to affirm their value.

And a discourse of power, within the context of sexual regulation, is inadequate to the task even of criticizing: it cannot, for example, describe the damage sometimes occasioned by those sexual relationships between either same-sex or opposite-sex individuals of wildly disproportionate power, wealth, privilege, or status, but which are both consensual and welcome—and hence, are neither criminal rape nor sexual harassment. Again, the liberal language of rights is clearly and even notoriously insufficient to the task: it is not at all clear that such relationships—relationships between, say, a professor and a student, or the president of the United States and an intern, or the CEO of a corporation and a secretary—violate any rights of autonomy or any rights at all. But the Foucauldian discourse of power—that these relationships are exploitative, or subordinating, or flatly unequal—is also inadequate to the task. First, it is overinclusive and in many cases simply false to the facts: obviously all relationships involve inequalities, and sometimes those inequalities liberate and enrich the weaker member. The inequality of power *alone* says nothing about whether they are good or bad. Nevertheless, some of these relationships *are* extremely damaging to the weaker party and are so, in part, because of the power disparity: a student might, for example, learn to value only her sexuality if that is what her professor values, and thereby denigrate her intellectual competencies; she might as a consequence forgo what might otherwise be an important and rewarding life plan and wind up bored, tired, and full of self-contempt as a result. This might, furthermore, happen so frequently as a result of such unions that it might prompt us to want to urge strongly that such unions be avoided, or entered only with extreme caution. But again, just as the value of same-sex marriage cannot be conveyed within the discourse of power, so the harm occasioned by such unequal unions cannot be conveyed within such a discourse: we need to describe the *harms*—not just the inequality—in a way that makes them palpably clear. We cannot do so if we limit our moral understanding—and our moral vocabulary—to a discourse of power that expresses nothing but, at most, a vague and ultimately unsupported preference for egalitarianism.

*Nineteen Eighty-Four* is a book about power. It is, more specifically, about the terribly destructive capacity of the concentrated power of the state to flatten, indeed to kill, nature: our nature, our natural language, our natural animalism, our natural environment, and above all our instinctual desires—our desire to nurture our young, to honor our parents, to love each other, to enjoy and lust after the pleasures of each other's bodies, to enjoy together companionate, monogamous, lifelong marriages. It is not about everything, and even as fantasy it clearly falls short: its predictions regarding the state have proven to be wildly off the mark, and its view of sex is romantic but almost ridiculously naive.

Nevertheless, the book has a lot of heart, and it expresses it well, if simply. We should measure the worth of the political institutions we create, Orwell urged, in *Nineteen Eighty-Four* and elsewhere, by reference to their effect on the quality of our individual and communal lives. If our work is dishonest, our language in tatters, our enjoyments shabby, our relations with others fraught with fear and distrust, and above all if there is no love and sympathy and honest mutual regard for others in our lives, then we have reason to worry, and reason to change. We may need to change by challenging the market power of economic actors, or the patriarchal power of men, or the legal power of the state, and it may from time to time behoove us to use the power of the state, or the power of the market, or the power of the family, to challenge one of the other loci of power. We cannot even know whether that's the case, however, much less what to do about it, unless we acknowledge what Orwell urged throughout his life: that what and who we are can be damaged by, but never equated with, the workings of power. Neither we, our sex, our experiences, our truths, our loves, our laws, or our nature is exclusively a product of power. And because they are not, they can be destroyed by it. We, our nature, our sexual pleasures, our personal integrity, our subjectivity, our commitment to truth, our beauty, our love, and the justice of our laws, though, are every day and everywhere—always and already, as they say—at risk.

♥❧

# *Nineteen Eighty-Four*, Catholicism, and the Meaning of Human Sexuality

JOHN HALDANE

### I

I AIM, in this essay, to do three things. First, to say something about con-trasting readings of *Nineteen Eighty-Four* in respect of the themes of reli-gion and sexuality. Second, to relate these readings to Roman Catholic understandings of those themes. Third, to relate those understandings to contemporary concerns about sexual liberty and regulation.

### II

Let me begin, then, with a quotation taken from a fairly recent study of Orwell's text:

> *Nineteen Eighty-Four* is about love in our time, its present status and future prospects . . . like *Paradise Lost* it is at once a love story and an account of man's relationship to God.[1]

So writes Patrick Reilly in an interesting, if somewhat speculative study of the book's thematic structure and of its relationship to other mythic treatments of the human condition, such as those of Milton in *Paradise Lost* and of Swift in *Gulliver's Travels*. An initial reaction to Reilly's unor-thodox characterization is to say that given Orwell's avowed atheism, any exploration of a theological theme could only be as the dissection of an ideological and historical illusion or as a literary reductio ad absurdum of religious assumptions. Certainly there is plenty of evidence in Orwell's writings of antipathy to religion and of particular hostility toward Roman

---

A version of this essay was delivered as the first Royden Davis Memorial lecture at Georgetown University in May 2001. I am grateful to Georgetown for appointing me to the Royden Davis chair of Humanities during the 2001–2 academic year.
[1] Patrick Reilly, *Nineteen Eighty-Four: Past, Present and Future* (Boston: Twayne, 1989), 57.

Catholicism. *A Clergyman's Daughter* (1935) charts the inadequacy of the Christian faith (in its Anglican form) to deal with intimations of mortality and contemplates the impossibility of recovering religious belief once it is lost. More directly to the point, throughout Orwell's writings, but particularly in his earlier ones, Roman Catholicism is disparaged as arrogant, illiberal, and morally immature.

In the early 1930s at a time of Catholic revival, when conversion was, if not a fashion, then at least a distinctive trend, Orwell wrote an unsigned review for the *New English Weekly* of a work by a German priest, Father Karl Adam, entitled *The Spirit of Catholicism*. After a characteristic complaint about overly long and convoluted sentences, Orwell pays Adam the compliment of not producing a work of apologetics but of attempting instead to show something of what Orwell terms "the Catholic soul." He writes:

> It is interesting to compare his book with some English book of similar tendency, for instance with Father Martindale's recent book *The Roman Faith*. [Martindale was a convert to Catholicism, a prominent Jesuit then serving at Farm Street in the smart and exclusive Mayfair area of central London.] The contrast between the Catholic who simply believes, and the convert who must for ever be justifying his conversion, is like the contrast between a Buddha and a performing fakir. . . . Father Martindale, being committed to the statement that faith is essentially reasonable, can neither stand up to his difficulties nor ignore them. Consequently he evades them with considerable nimbleness . . . Father Adam, who has started by saying that faith is not to be approached in the same spirit as "the profane sciences", has no need of these tricks. With a creed that is safe from "profane" criticism, he is in a very strong position; it gives him the chance to develop his own ideas, and to say something constructive and interesting.
>
> . . . [I]n an objective way, something can be learned, or rather re-learned, namely the Hebrew-like pride and exclusiveness of the genuine Catholic mind. When Father Adam writes of the Communion of Saints, one gets an impression of the Church not so much as a body of thought as of a kind of glorified family bank—a limited company paying enormous dividends, with non-members rigidly excluded from benefits. . . .

The smallest shareholder draws his bonus on the profits made by Augustine or Aquinas. The point is missed if one forgets that the "family" means the Church and the Church alone; the rest of humanity, stray saints apart, being so much negligible matter, for whom there can be nothing save a slightly rigid pity, for *extra ecclesiam nulla salus*, and "dogmatic intolerance", as Father Adam puts it, "is a duty to the infinite truth".

[And later Orwell writes] Very few people, apart from the Catholics themselves, seem to have grasped that the Church is to be taken seriously.[2]

This review is interesting in a variety of ways for what it reveals about Orwell's attitudes to religion and his degree of understanding of the Catholic view about the relationship of faith and reason. First, there is the apparent preference for fideism, represented by the one "who simply believes," over religious rationalism as represented by the convert's desire for intellectual justification. I say "apparent" to acknowledge that this may be read as ironic: if religious belief is necessarily irrational as well as false, then at least a fideistic approach does not add pretense to error. Second, there is the questionable application of the simple-belief vs. rational-justification opposition in the context of Catholicism, an attribution made all the more curious by the recognition of the importance to the Catholic view of the intellectual contribution of Aquinas. After all, the author of the *Summa Theologiae* and of the *Summa Contra Gentiles* was both a devout and assured believer and a byword of religious rationalism. Whatever else, Thomas Aquinas cannot be read as craving intellectual reassurance in response to personal doubt. Furthermore, it had long been a standard objection posed by the more scripturally or fideistically disposed versions of Christianity with which Orwell was familiar that Catholicism in general is markedly intellectualist and accords special significance to natural theology.

In addition, and in the present circumstance of greater importance, is the fact that while this passage unquestionably expresses hostility to the Catholic religion, it also suggests a degree of resentful exclusion and indicates that matters may not, after all, be so simple as the standard interpretations maintain. Among people of Orwell's generation, class, and literary and social interests, it was not uncommon, first, to feel disillusion with the existing political structures; second, to seek an ennobling conception of the human condition; and third, to judge that this might be found, if at all, in only one of two places: in a comprehensive political-cum-cultural ideology or in religion. For those whose experience and disposition inclined them to the political Left, the options often came down to nihilism, communism, or Catholicism. It is interesting, therefore, to find Orwell identifying this range of possibilities in 1942 in his review of T. S. Eliot's *Burnt Norton, East Coker, The Dry Salvages*. He writes:

Sooner or later one is obliged to adopt a positive stance towards life and society. It would be putting it too crudely to say that every poet in our time

[2] Review of *The Spirit of Catholicism* by Karl Adam (1932), in *Collected Essays, Journalism and Letters of George Orwell*, ed. Sonia Orwell and Ian Angus, vol. 1, *An Age Like This* (London: Secker & Warburg, 1968), 79–80.

must either die young, enter the Catholic Church, or join the Communist Party, but in fact the escape from the consciousness of futility is along these general lines.[3]

It is worth comparing this assessment with that of Dimitry Mirsky in his book *The Intelligentsia of Great Britain*, published in 1935:

> Catholicism more and more becomes the magnetic guide of the live bourgeoisie and intelligentsia pointing the road to the anti-Communist citadel. The intelligentsia . . . is steadily beginning to see that only two possibilities lie before it—catholicism and communism. To which he should turn is the dilemma of many an intellectual.[4]

In fact, for intellectuals of Orwell's generation and those proximate to it the situation was more complex, for there was a fair degree of movement to and fro between these possibilities, with remains of previously held positions and anticipations of prospective ones giving their work a degree of ambiguity that reflected their own search and uncertainty. In this connection one need only think of Graham Greene in England and of Walker Percy in the United States, and once one lifts the political criterion many more figures come into view including Elizabeth Bowen, G. K. Chesterton, Christopher Dawson, Alfred Douglas, Christopher Hollis, Flannery O'Connor, Muriel Spark, Evelyn Waugh, and plenty of lesser figures besides.

Of itself this hardly establishes the warrant of a positive religious interpretation of *Nineteen Eighty-Four*, let alone one congenial to Catholic ideas, but it does suggest the need for caution in dismissing the very possibility of such. One obvious and widely shared reading, of course, is that the narrative parodies the relentless oppression of the individual in a tyrannical theocracy. Certainly Orwell expressed the view that Catholicism, like Communism and Fascism, was a threat to the autonomous individual—though significantly he distinguished between the religious orthodoxy of medieval Europe and modern totalitarianism in respect of the extent to which they control thought, writing at one point in *Nineteen Eighty-Four* that "[e]ven the Catholic Church of the Middle Ages was tolerant by modern standards" (169). In a BBC radio talk broadcast in 1941 he had explored another aspect of the difference between old and new forms of thought control:

---

[3] Review of *Burnt Norton, East Coker, The Dry Salvages* by T. S. Eliot (originally in *Poetry London*, October–November 1942), in *Collected Essays, Journalism and Letters of George Orwell*, ed. Sonia Orwell and Ian Angus, vol. 2, *My Country Right or Left* (London: Secker & Warburg, 1968), 240.

[4] This is drawn from a longer passage quoted by Richard Johnstone in *The Will to Believe* (Oxford: Oxford University Press, 1982), a highly relevant study of attitudes among writers of the 1930s.

. . . In medieval Europe the Church dictated what you should believe, but at least it allowed you to retain the same beliefs from birth to death. . . .

Now with totalitarianism, exactly the opposite is true. The peculiarity of the totalitarian state is that though it controls thought, it does not fix it. It sets up unquestionable dogmas, and it alters them from day to day.[5]

Notwithstanding this purported difference, the fact remains that for Orwell both old and new ideologies are tyrannies, and on that basis one might be encouraged to suppose that Ingsoc is the "religion" of Oceania (a word the sung praise of which sounds rather like "Hosanna"); that Big Brother is its ubiquitously depicted but actually unseen deity; and that O'Brien is an (Irish?) duplicitous and bullying chief priest-cum-inquisitor hearing confession and securing the restoration to grace effected by the trials leading finally to Room 101. In this interpretation we will also find consecrated virgins, saints, heretics, and the rest. Even mystical passion, of a Latin sort, finds its expression at the end of the Hate devotion:

> The little sandy-haired woman had flung herself forward over the back of the chair in front of her. With a tremulous murmur that sounded like "My Saviour!" she extended her arms toward the screen [from which Big Brother's image had faded away]. Then she buried her face in her hands. It was apparent that she was uttering a prayer. (17)

There is, however, a different reading of what is, I think, a more ambiguous text than is generally allowed. According to this alternative interpretation, true religion is to be found not in the institutions of Oceania but in the counterculture associated with the Brotherhood followers of a dissident, troublemaking Jew, *Emmanuel* Goldstein, and in the salvific text, *the book*. Here we might detect a parallel to the position of early Christianity in Roman Palestine. A new culture hostile to religion suppresses it in the name of the emperor, but an indigenous preacher arises and acquires followers, and a new testament begins to be formed and circulated. Whatever the points of disanalogy, the prospect pursued by Winston is of liberation from tyranny through the word of an (as it turns out) imagined prophet of Israel. That suggests, I think, at least a note of appreciation of the meaning of the Christian gospel.

Moreover, if this line is pursued, it leads toward an acknowledgment of the possible appeal for Orwell of aspects of Catholic Christianity, signaled, for example, through the acknowledgment of the powerful Madonna-and-child motif. The first occurrence of this appears in Winston's opening diary entry, in the unsettling account of a film showing an attack on a ship full of refugees in which a woman desperately tries to protect a

---

[5] "Literature and Totalitarianism," in *Collected Essays*, 2:136.

child from attack. Writing largely without punctuation, Winston records the scene:

> . . . *you saw a lifeboat full of children with a helicopter hovering over it. there was a middleaged woman might have been a jewess sitting up in the bow with a little boy about three years old in her arms. little boy screaming with fright and hiding his head between her breasts as if he was trying to burrow right into her and the woman putting her arms around him and comforting him although she was blue with fright herself. all the time covering him up as much as possible as if she thought her arms could keep the bullets off him.*
> (11)

Later, through the scenic framework of a dream and his connected memories, the link is made between this unknown victim and Winston's own mother:

> The dream had also been comprehended by—indeed, in some sense it had consisted in—a gesture of the arm made by his mother, and made again thirty years later by the Jewish woman he had seen on the news film, trying to shelter the small boy from the bullets, before the helicopters blew them both to pieces.
>
> . . . Her large shapely body seemed to relapse naturally into stillness. For hours at a time she would sit almost immobile on the bed, nursing his young sister, a tiny, ailing, very silent child of two or three, with a face made simian by thinness.
>
> . . . His mother drew her arm round the child and pressed its face against her breast. Something in the gesture told him that his sister was dying. (132–33, 135)

Finally, there is the moment of reflection prior to their arrest as Winston and Julia look down into a yard in which a matronly prole is hanging family washing:

> The solid, contourless body, like a block of granite, and the rasping red skin, bore the same relation to the body of a girl as the rose-hip to the rose. Why should the fruit be held inferior to the flower?
>
> "She's beautiful," he murmured.
>
> "She's a meter across the hips, easily," said Julia.
>
> "That's the style of her beauty," said Winston.
>
> He held Julia's supple waist easily encircled by his arm. From the hip to the knee her flank was against his. Out of their bodies no child ever would come. That was the one thing they could never do. (181)

There is also the striking choice of Catholic-sounding names for Winston's fellow citizens (real and constructed) of the Oceanic state: the poet "Ampleforth" (the name of a famous Benedictine boarding school), the heroic comrade "Ogilvy" (John Ogilvie was the first Scottish Jesuit martyr and was beatified by Pius XI in 1929),[6] and "Parsons," "Syme," and "Charrington" (names akin to those of old recusant Catholic families such as Paston, Smythe, and Charlton).

More pervasive even than the mother-and-child theme, though encompassing the latter, is the fact that Winston's search for freedom proceeds in parallel with his experience of love. Here, as before, the obvious liberal interpretation has a conservative and ultimately Christian competitor. Undoubtedly the most common reading of the treatment of sexuality in the novel sees it as a welcome escape from the oppressive puritanism of the state. To quote:

[S]he had grasped the inner meaning of the Party's sexual puritanism. . . . "When you make love you're using up energy; and afterwards you feel happy and don't give a damn for anything." (110)

On this interpretation Winston's only shared expressions of liberty are illicit sex, first with a stranger, and then with a vibrant lover in the woods or in a secret apartment. By contrast, his state-approved marriage was a passionless union with a woman apparently rendered frigid by her subscription to the restrictedly reproductive norms of Ingsoc: "As soon as he touched her she seemed to wince and stiffen. . . . She would lie there with shut eyes, neither resisting nor co-operating, but *submitting*" (58). And even these reproductive norms are treated as permissives rather than as enduring obligations, temporary necessities to be replaced by "artsem," which will render even passionless sex an avoidable vice.

In this account Orwell emerges as an advocate of sexual liberty against puritanical constraint such as might well be associated with the Catholic emphasis on chastity. But again I would suggest that a more reflective reading reveals other possibilities. To begin with, the separation of sex, love, and reproduction is hardly to be associated with Catholic Christianity. Even in Orwell's time Roman teaching against contraception was a matter of controversy, and the Catholic case involving the normative integration of these three aspects was regularly rehearsed and challenged in books, pamphlets, and articles.

Not only did Orwell know how things stood in the Catholic view, but his narrative bears a Catholic reading—that is to say, one congenial to Catholic analysis. Consider first that the encounter with the stranger was a loveless purchase with a prole prostitute hag, and that the initial mutual satisfaction with Julia quickly gives way to a more familial embodiment of sexual love. From animal turf we move to human domesticity as Winston establishes a home for his underground "bride." A room or nest

[6] Later canonized by Paul VI in 1970.

is established, and an item of settled Victorian domesticity—the coral paperweight—is installed as a mysterious token of an order lost but hankered after. Winston dreams of "talking of trivialities and buying odds and ends for the household" (116). Even the lust-driven Julia enters into the nest-making ritual, bringing precious provisions into the newly established home.

Not only does the setting of their lovemaking change, but so too does its style. Recall that Winston's first thoughts about Julia are ones of sexual sadism: "Vivid, beautiful hallucinations flashed through his mind. He would flog her to death with a rubber truncheon. . . . He would ravish her and cut her throat at the moment of climax" (16). Vicious fantasy is transformed through personal contact into more wholesome passion. To begin with, the sex is as raw as the literary and publishing conventions allowed, but soon there is more talk than action, and it is not long before Winston has become Julia's "darling" and is sitting up in bed reading to his sleeping love. It is not long either before he is admiring and commending the motherly prole seen hanging family washing in the courtyard below. In short, what began in lust has soon been transformed into a quasi-traditional domestic setting—recall that the room is a presumed relic of a past pre-Ingsoc wedded order.

We saw Winston reflecting that "no child would ever come" but that was an acknowledgment of external constraint, not a matter of choice. It is hard to believe that had the relationship been able to continue, Winston would not have been pressing the question of starting a family—not for reasons of obeying the state, as had been the case in his marriage to Katharine, but for ones having to do with expressing mutual love and lifelong commitment in the having and raising of children. Consider the text: "He wished above all that they had some place where they could be alone together without feeling the obligation to make love every time they met" (116). Then later as he and Julia look down upon the diaper-hanging washer-mother, his admiring reflections on her continue:

> He wondered how many children she had given birth to. It might easily be fifteen . . . her life had been laundering, scrubbing, darning, cooking, sweeping, polishing, mending, scrubbing, laundering, first for children, then for grandchildren, over thirty unbroken years. At the end of it she was still singing. . . . [he felt a] mystical reverence . . . for her. . . . If there was hope, it lay in the proles! (181)

This passage is of great importance, coming at a moment of transition from happiness to pain as the state breaks in to reassert its control on life by announcing its declaration of death:

> [E]verywhere [throughout the world] stood the same solid unconquerable figure [the prole woman], made monstrous by work and childbearing, toiling

from birth to death and still singing. Out of those mighty loins a race of conscious beings must one day come. You were the dead; theirs was the future. . . .

"We are the dead," he said.

"We are the dead," echoed Julia dutifully.

"You are the dead," said an iron voice behind them. (182)

All of this prompts the question of which is better in Orwell's eyes: sex, love, and reproduction *conjoined?* or *disjoined?* Its focus on fertility and protofamilial domesticity also raises questions of sexual ethics and politics—past, present, and future—which we have to consider and answer for ourselves independent of Orwell's book.

## III

The evolved Roman Catholic view on these matters is not always understood or even well expressed by its advocates. First, it is not, in contrast to what it has often been in the Reformed Christian tradition, a product of theological doubt about the legitimacy of sexual desire. Famously, in his First Letter to the Corinthians, Saint Paul warns his correspondents against sexual appetite:

> Now concerning the matters about which you wrote. It is well for a man not to touch a woman. But because of the temptation to immorality each man should have his own wife and each woman her own husband . . . do not refuse one another except perhaps by agreement for a season, that you may devote yourselves to prayer; but then come together again, lest Satan tempt you through lack of self-control. I say this by way of concession, not of command. I wish that all were as I myself am [i.e., celibate].[7]

Following on from this, and influenced also by Plotinian neo-Platonism, Augustine sees sexual activity as something generally to be avoided and permitted only in the narrowest contexts of reproduction. He writes:

> A man turns to good use the evil of concupiscence . . . when he bridles and restrains its rage . . . and never relaxes its hold upon it except when intent on offspring, and then controls and applies it to the carnal generation of children.[8]

---

[7] 1 Corinthians 7:1–7. *The Holy Bible*, Revised Standard Version, Catholic Edition (London: Catholic Truth Society, 1966).

[8] Augustine, *De nuptis et concupiscentia, On Marriage and Concupiscence*, bk. 1., chap. 9, in *The Works of Aurelius Augustine, Bishop of Hippo*, ed. Marcus Dods (Edinburgh: T. & T. Clark, 1874), vol. 12.

Aquinas, by contrast, takes a rather different view, in no small part as a result of integrating Aristotle's philosophical naturalism with Christian sacred and moral theologies. In his account, which was certainly deemed authoritative in the pre-Vatican Church of Orwell's day, both the fact of sexual reproduction and its sensual pleasure are aspects of God's original and continuing design and not a consequence of the Fall. In the Prima Pars of the *Summa Theologiae* Aquinas addresses these issues directly and in opposition to the opinions of earlier church fathers such as Saints Gregory of Nyssa, John Chrysostom, and John Damascene and of the medievals Bonaventure and Alexander of Hales:

> [E]ven if man had not sinned, there would have been such intercourse to which the distinction of the sexes is ordained . . . what is natural to man was neither acquired nor forfeited by sin. Now it is clear that generation by co-ition is natural to man by reason of his animal life. . . .
>
> . . . In the [prelapsarian] state of innocence [concupiscence] would have been regulated by reason not because there would have been less pleasure as some say—for the sensual delight would have been the greater in proportion to the greater purity of nature and the greater sensibility of the body—but because the force of desire . . . would have been moderated by reason which does not lessen sensual pleasure but prevents desire from being attached to the pleasure in an inordinate way.[9]

Elsewhere Aquinas explains that sexual sin occurs not through inter-course as such but only when the orders of nature and reason are violated. This happens in two ways. First, through intentional sexual activity that, though potentially generative, violates the integrity and status of others, such as rape, incest, and adultery; and, second, when sexual acts are inten-tionally nongenerative, either because solitary, or with the wrong kind of partner, or of the wrong sort.[10] This last undergirds the teaching expressed by Paul VI in *Humanae Vitae* when he wrote that "conjugal acts made intentionally infecund are wrong . . . [for] . . . each and every marriage act . . . must remain open to the transmission of life."[11]

Since it may be presumed that Aquinas's strictures against potentially generative sex outside of marriage could derive only from Christian teach-ing, it is worth pointing out, first, that he himself characterizes matrimony in nonreligious terms as "commitment to one woman" and takes it to be part of the natural law; and, second, perhaps more strikingly, that Aris-totle, in whose *Nicomachean Ethics* no religious considerations feature,

[9] *Summa Theologiae*, Ia, q. 98, a 2, adapted from the translation by the English Domini-can Fathers (London: R & T Washbourne, 1914).

[10] Ibid., IIa, IIae, q. 154.

[11] *Humanae Vitae* (London: Catholic Truth Society, 1970), §11.

nonetheless includes adultery among those kinds of action that reason shows to be always and everywhere wrong.[12]

In the Catholic view, active sexuality is legitimate when it respects norms constituted by its three nonaccidentally related aspects: love, procreation, and marriage. It is relevant to this that Catholic doctrine regards the couple as the agents of the sacrament of marriage, and not civil or political society or even the Church. A sacramentally valid marriage is something only the partners themselves, with God's grace, can effect, and it is consummated in sexual union. It is not a state or condition imposed by a human authority, and in extremis it may be entered into without the presence of a priest. In moral theology the usual scenarios for this are ones of a stranded couple, or else of people enduringly remote from the services of the Church—such, in fact, as are the circumstances of Julia and Winston.

All of this indicates an outlook far removed from body-hating Christian puritanism, and from Ingsoc's Anti-Sex League, which seeks the triumph of the will over the orgasm and looks forward eagerly to neurophysiological technologies that would neutralize such ecstasy, and to artsem that will sever reproduction from sex. That very hatred of sexuality has ironic consequences, such as Julia's employment in Pornosec, the porn section of Oceanic publishing. Here Orwell may have been prophetic of the decline of public culture effected in part by its brutish sexualization; as he was, I think, in seeing that the severing of sex from love and marriage will lead to, and be further effected by, reproductive technologies.

IV

Let me conclude with a couple of points: one about liberal and more radical responses to the Catholic view of the meaning of human sexuality; and one about the ways in which that view has been expressed both by advocates and by opponents of it.

A significant strand within philosophical and political liberalism seeks to remove sexual morality from the public sphere and to locate it in the area of private relations. But there is reason to doubt the desirability or indeed the possibility of this, even given liberal political aspirations. Admittedly the liberalism of John Stuart Mill officially permits restrictive legislation only on grounds of limiting harm, and that would quite severely limit the state's role in matters of sexual practice. But it is not hard to show that Mill himself seemed disposed to entertain the possibility that gross offense might provide adequate grounds to consider legislative

---

[12] *Nicomachean Ethics*, bk. 2, chap. 6.

prohibition. For having written the famous words "the only purpose for which power can rightfully be exercised over any member of a civilized community against his will, is to prevent harm to others," he then went on to observe that "coming thus within the category of offenses against others, [a violation of good manners] may rightly be prohibited. Of this kind are offenses against decency, on which it is unnecessary to dwell."[13] Beyond the question of Mill's self-contradiction lies the fact that the threat of harm is neither a necessary nor a sufficient ground for restrictive legislation. Contact sports and market competition each produce harms but are not on that account deemed suitable cases for prohibition. By the same token rights violations such as are committed by voyeurs may reasonably be prohibited by law, though they do not necessarily cause harm.

Less obvious but no less telling, I think, is the consideration that quite apart from the need of the state to constrain activity that constitutes harm, offense, or rights violations with regard to others, it has an interest in protecting and even promoting certain nonpolitical values. If citizens are to recognize the authority of and give allegiance to the liberal polity, they have to see it not only as arbitrating between current contests over freedom, but as embracing needs and entitlements of other sorts, including ones arising from the past and extending into the future. They must also have confidence in its willingness to deal with new and so far unseen requirements. Accordingly, the state has to respond to intergenerational concerns and to protect and promote forms of social arrangement such as the family that serve to establish and cultivate subpolitical dispositions. Without them, ordinary citizens (as contrasted with those for whom politics is an end in itself) would have little reason to be concerned about political liberties, or about the maintenance of a state organized so as to protect them now and in the future. For that reason, and on grounds of respecting reasonable sensibilities, sexual and familial norms are of legitimate, if limited, concern to the liberal polity.

More radical critics may, of course, argue that this style of philosophical reasoning, like Catholic philosophy and moral theology, assumes norms of objective rationality and of value commensurability that may now be set aside as among the deeper errors of premodern and modernist projects. Apart from the dubious coherence of such criticism the point then needs to be noted that it ill-behooves the relativist to launch a principled campaign against the Catholic or indeed the liberal view. He or she must rest content with the incommensurable pluralism they would have us celebrate.

[13] The two passages come from J. S. Mill, *On Liberty* (London: Dent, 1957), respectively from the "Introductory" (72–73) and chap. 5 (153).

Finally, I remarked that the Catholic account of the meaning of human sexuality has not always been adequately rendered. The main issue here, I think, is the tendency for arguments about the function of sex to be construed along lines of reductive physiological functionalism—as if the matter were wholly determinable by reference to the shape and operation of the sexual organs. But just as Aquinas argues, again following Aristotle, that in human beings vegetative and sentient functions are subsumed under the governance of the rational soul that is the form of the body, so the teleology of sex has to be understood in terms of reflective consciousness and of shared social values.

To see what is at issue, consider the attempt to teach a child how it ought to eat—that is to say, how it ought to arrange itself at the table, use the implements provided, and engage in sociable conversation. One account of the matter might attempt to reduce all of this to the mechanics of lifting food from the plate into the mouth, of chewing it, and then of letting the digestive system do its work. Certainly we sit at table in order to feed ourselves. As Aquinas might put it, "It is clear that nutrition by digestion is natural to man by reason of his animal life." However, that provides only the material substratum of the human practice of eating, which in itself is a complex of psychological, aesthetic, dietary, social, and cultural elements. Dogs eat and so do human beings, but in the case of the latter, sentient animality is subordinated to rational purposes and values. Such is the difference between the two activities that one might say they are distinct operations. In truth they are neither one and the same, nor are they altogether different; rather, they are analogous: alike in some respects (food is consumed) and not in others (dogs do not observe ritual fasts, go on diets, or take one another out to dinner).

Likewise in the case of sexual activity. The anatomical similarity between dogs and men is not sufficient to allow the claim that intercourse between male and female of each species is one and the same activity. This fact subverts Hume's well-known argument designed to show that since parent-offspring coupling among animals is not objected to as immoral, there can be no rational ground (as opposed to emotive cause) for objecting to incest among humans. Hume writes:

> I would fain ask anyone, why incest in the human species is criminal, and why the very same action, and the same relations in animals, have not the smallest moral turpitude and deformity? . . . Animals are susceptible of the same relations, with respect to each other as the human species, and therefore would also be susceptible of the same morality, if the essence of morality consisted in these same relations.[14]

[14] David Hume, *A Treatise of Human Nature*, ed. L. A. Selby-Bigge (Oxford: Oxford University Press, 1958), bk. 3, pt. 1, sec. 1, 468.

The argument commits a fallacy of equivocation or failed analogy. The relations between animals and between human beings are not evidently one and the same ("begetter" and "parent" differ in meaning); and what dogs do and what humans do sexually are not in all respects the same activity. At the level of physiology there may be broad isomorphism (though note that in the human case thought and emotion have a bearing upon even these matters); but physiology stands to intentional, phenomenologically informed human sex rather as pigment stands to a painting or as sound stands to a musical composition. In each case the first element is a material component of a formally structured whole that transcends it. Put in terms of the metaphysics that Aquinas adopted from Aristotle, the human being and his or her activities are hylomorphically constituted. Failure to appreciate both the truth of this and its role in Catholic sexual ethics is liable to undermine both presentation and criticism of the latter.

Thus the interest of John Paul II's Thomistic-cum-phenomenological style, and thus the interest also of such literary exploration of the effects of the separation of sex, love, and marriage as is pursued, I think, in *Nineteen Eighty-Four.*

According to Karol Wojtyla (John Paul II):

> [Personal love] is by its very nature not unilateral but bilateral. . . . Love is not just something in one person and something in another—for in that case there would properly speaking be two loves—but is something common to both . . . not their separate loves for each other but something *between* two persons, something shared;

and later he writes:

> When the idea that 'I may become a father'/'I may become a mother' is totally rejected in the mind and will nothing is left of the relationship, objectively speaking, except mere sexual enjoyment. One person becomes an object of use for another person.[15]

That is what Ingsoc had achieved in forming the sexualities of Winston and Julia, but it is also what they were moving away from until their protomarital setting was so cruelly violated. In bringing these facts to mind, Orwell's radical critique of political tyranny may also be something of a morally conservative tract on behalf of the inseparability of sex, love, and marriage—a radical conservatism in the tradition of such other complex figures as Burke, Johnson, and Chesterton.

[15] Karol Wojtyla, *Love and Responsibility* (New York: Farrar, Straus & Giroux, 1981), 85 and 239.

V

I began by quoting from a study that views *Nineteen Eighty-Four* as "an account of man's relationship to God" and remarked that this is a somewhat speculative interpretation. Yet by this point I have argued that it may even be worth reading the text in terms of certain Roman Catholic themes and interests. A reader may therefore feel that if the first is "somewhat speculative," then the second must simply be an absurd attempt to grab Orwell for the Catholic cause. Alternatively, it might be pointed out that God is one thing and Catholicism quite another.

The first complaint is reminiscent of a point Orwell himself makes in his essay on Charles Dickens:

> Dickens is one of those authors who are well worth stealing. . . . When Chesterton wrote his introductions to the Everyman Edition of Dickens's works, it seemed quite natural to him to credit Dickens with his own highly individual brand of medievalism, and more recently a Marxist writer, Mr. T. A. Jackson, has made spirited efforts to turn Dickens into a bloodthirsty revolutionary. The Marxist claims him as "almost" a Marxist, the Catholic claims him as "almost" a Catholic.[16]

Lest there be any doubt, therefore, let me make it clear that I am not seeking to appropriate Orwell or *Nineteen Eighty-Four* for Catholicism, or to claim that Orwell was "almost" a Catholic, but only suggesting that it can be read in a way that renders it congenial to Catholic views of which Orwell was aware. So far as the second complaint is concerned—that God is one thing and Catholicism quite another—however that remark is intended, it would not necessarily disturb my reading. For the fact of the matter is that in the period of Orwell's lifetime, as in periods before and after it, an appreciative interest in things Catholic has not always been combined with an unambiguous belief in God. It would be the work of a quite different essay to determine why that might be so and how, if it should be, it might be rectified.

---

[16] *Collected Essays*, 1:413–14.

# CONCLUSION

# The Death of Pity: Orwell and American Political Life

MARTHA C. NUSSBAUM

It was a vast, luminous dream in which his whole life seemed to stretch out before him like a landscape on a summer evening after rain. It had all occurred inside the glass paperweight, but the surface of the glass was the dome of the sky, and inside the dome everything was flooded with clear soft light in which one could see into interminable distances. The dream had also been comprehended by—indeed, in some sense it had consisted in— a gesture of the arm made by his mother, and made again thirty years later by the Jewish woman he had seen on the news film, trying to shelter the small boy from the bullets, before the helicopters blew them both to pieces.
—*Nineteen Eighty-Four* (132)

"The old civilizations claimed that they were founded on love and justice. Ours is founded upon hatred. In our world there will be no emotions except fear, rage, triumph, and self-abasement. . . . There will be no love, except the love of Big Brother. There will be no laughter, except the laugh of triumph over a defeated enemy."
—*Nineteen Eighty-Four*, O'Brien to Winston (220)

The patient felt very moved by the idea that the real-life nightingale came back at last, to sing by the dying Emperor's window, and thus saved his life. . . . The survival of the real, good nightingale in the story reaffirmed the patient's faith in the existence of a good being who was still available and had not been killed, in spite of all the Emperor's—and the patient's—greed and destructiveness. The Emperor was saved because he had kept inside of himself such a good and forgiving object.
—Otto Kernberg, *Borderline Conditions and Pathological Narcissism*

I am very grateful to Felicia Ackerman, John Deigh, Abbott Gleason, Jack Goldsmith, Ian Malcolm, Richard Posner, and Cass Sunstein for their valuable comments on an earlier draft of this paper.

## A SHELTERING ARM, A DOME OF LIGHT

A gesture haunts this novel, as it haunts the mind of Winston Smith. Routine, daily, undeliberated, the gesture is also hopelessly distant, its radiance the stuff of dreams. No one can make this gesture any longer. Politics has destroyed it.

It is a gesture of the arm: a mother encircles her children, protecting them from harm. This gesture is the first thing Winston writes about in his diary: in the middle of cheerful war films about the bombing in the Mediterranean, he sees a lifeboat full of children about to be bombed by a helicopter overhead—and in it a Jewish woman, who puts her arms around her frightened little boy and covers him "as if she thought her arms could keep the bullets off him" (11). Although the journal entry quickly shifts to more approved sentiments of hatred and triumph, as Winston cheers the "wonderful shot of a childs arm going up up up right up into the air" (11), the gesture haunts his mind, prompting his later dream of the luminous place.

The later dream is a dream of "his whole life" (132)—imagined as occurring inside the glass paperweight that he bought from the old man in the shop. This paperweight, a "round, smooth thing" that he loves for its beauty and its uselessness (80–81), encloses at its heart a curved piece of coral, "a strange, pink, convoluted object that recalled a rose or a sea anemone" (80). In the dream, his whole life is inside that magical object. Within its dome, "everything was flooded with clear soft light" (132). For Winston the dream of the dome is comprehended by, indeed consists in, the gesture of the arm that his mother made, sheltering him and his sister, the same gesture that the Jewish woman made so many years later. It is apparently his "last glimpse of his mother" (133), and hours later the dream is "still vivid in his mind, especially the enveloping, protecting gesture of the arm in which its whole meaning seemed to be contained" (135).

But the paperweight is eventually broken. The tiny lump of coral, "a tiny crinkle of pink like a sugar rosebud from a cake" (183–84), rolls across the floor. "How small, thought Winston, how small it always was!" (184). His fascination with its beauty was a trap, the old man who sold it a member of the Thought Police. The paperweight and the gesture of the arm in which it consists are annihilated, not only by the state, but, at a deeper level, by Winston's own capacity for betrayal and destruction. And the only "loving breast" he finds, in the end, is the love of Big Brother.

## AN ORWELLIAN NATION?

In the aftermath of the tragic events of September 11, 2001, Orwell's novel keeps surfacing, as people try to make sense of the current political climate in our nation. Many have connected the novel's theme of perpetual war to aspects of current political rhetoric, which suggests that we are engaged in a "war" that has no clear terminus and that may be nothing less than a war against "evil" itself. With such a perpetual enemy, the suggestion is, how could one not suppose that war must be perpetual, as it is in Oceania, and, indeed, that only War is Peace?

Other writers about recent events in the United States have drawn attention to Orwellian issues of history, memory, and truth. In "The Memory Hole,"[1] economist Paul Krugman, focusing on the Bush administration's claims about the budget deficit, uses the novel to charge the administration with retrospective rewriting of history. A month later, Krugman again focused on *Nineteen Eighty-Four*, citing the administration's slippery use of language about Social Security as a classic instance of "doublethink" and "newspeak, the redefinition of words to rule out disloyal thoughts."[2]

Such connections are well worth investigating and debating. But there is something else Orwellian in the air, something more insidious, more troubling, I think, than the fact that politicians tell lies (in a climate of free speech in which lies can be publicly unmasked). Embedded in some major examples of public rhetoric responding to 9/11, but rooted in a longer series of changes going back to the Reagan Revolution of the 1980s, is a political approach to the emotions in general and compassion in particular. This approach is all too reminiscent of the novel and the political project depicted there: the project of extinguishing compassion and the complex forms of personal love and mourning that are its sources, and of replacing them with simple depersonalized forms of hatred, aggression, triumph, and fear. Phrases like "Axis of Evil" and "America's New War,' our president's "They started it, we'll finish it"—these summon up attitudes of unilateralism and confrontation that remind us ominously of O'Brien's cherished goal. We are implicitly urged not to see complexities within a nation or its history, not to have emotions acknowledging the presence of poverty, misery, and injustice in distant nations, or our own possible complicity in the genesis of those problems. Nothing will do but an us-them view of the world, in which the goal is to assail anyone who threatens our "preeminence." The emotions proper to that view of the world are indeed, as O'Brien says, fear, hatred, and triumph. These emo-

[1] *New York Times*, op-ed page, August 6, 2002.
[2] "The Bully Pulpit," *New York Times*, op-ed page, September 6, 2002.

tions may at times be accompanied, and in the aftermath of 9/11 they certainly were, by a strong compassion for America and its people; but even this compassion has its limits, as we shall later see. And this limited compassion can itself stand in the way of recognizing the reality of distant people.[3] To these present-day issues I shall later return; they lie at the heart of Orwell's novel.

*Nineteen Eighty-Four* is not just about lies and totalitarian projects of domination. It is about the end of human beings as we know them, the political overthrow of the human heart. Winston Smith is the last human being. The gesture of compassionate protection is the dream to which his humanity is anchored. O'Brien's boast is not simply that the regime is successful; it is that it has remade human nature. Now I believe that some of what Orwell has to say about this remaking is off-target—relying, for example, on a simplistic distinction between the public and the private realms, and (as other contributors to the present volume have mentioned) a naive view of sexuality as instinctual and resistant to social shaping. I also believe, and will argue, that his conclusion is far too bleak and, even in the novel's own terms, unearned: Winston's collapse is not the collapse of the human as such, dooming us all, but the sad shattering of an already haunted and guilt-ridden soul that never managed to find forgiveness for its own aggressive wishes. We can hope for more from ourselves and our future. But we had better watch out.

## "TRAGEDY . . . BELONGED TO THE ANCIENT TIME"

I have called the maternal gesture a gesture of compassion; but we could also call it a gesture of pity, the emotion central to Greek tragedy. (Although the English term "pity" has acquired nuances of condescension to suffering in recent times, the Greek term it translated did not have such connotations; indeed, Aristotle says that it requires fellow feeling, a belief that one's own possibilities and vulnerabilities are similar to those of the suffering person. Rousseau, using the French word *pitié*, makes a similar claim. So let us be clear from now on that we are discussing the death of that emotion, Aristotle's *eleos*, Rousseau's *pitié*, however these are most appropriately rendered into English.)[4]

Why does Winston think that this emotion, and the gesture that expresses it, belong to "the ancient time" (29), along with deep sorrow, along with the tragedies that represent sorrow and evoke pity? His moth-

---

[3] On this, see my "Compassion and Terror," in *Daedalus*, Winter 2003.

[4] All this is discussed in detail in my *Upheavals of Thought: The Intelligence of Emotions* (New York and Cambridge: Cambridge University Press, 2001), chap. 6.

er's death, he reflects, "had been tragic and sorrowful in a way that was no longer possible. Tragedy, he perceived, belonged to the ancient time. . . . Such things, he saw, could not happen today. Today there were fear, hatred, and pain, but no dignity of emotion, or deep or complex sorrows" (28–29). Winston associates his hunger for the ancient gestures with the name "Shakespeare," awakening with this name on his lips (29). Why these connections?

Why, in a similar manner, does O'Brien claim to have eliminated art and literature, as well as science? And why does he, like Winston, connect the death of art with the death of a particular type of love, the kind that is not encompassed in the love of Big Brother? (220).

*Nineteen Eighty-Four* is a novel, not a philosophical argument; but one may speculatively construct an argument to make sense of these connections. Tragedy requires and rests upon a sense of the enormous importance of particular human attachments. Even though ultimately tragic pity may take many objects—*Julius Caesar*, after all, is a tragedy about the death of the Roman Republic—the emotions that sustain it rest, genetically at least, on a sense of profound love and loyalty toward a small number of people, loyalty that cannot be shifted as the whims of political circumstance shift. What produces tragedy is just that sense of the enormous intrinsic value of someone or something that can be hurt and changed. Pity, the tragic emotion, requires the thought that someone or something that matters greatly to one's whole sense of life and its significance is suffering greatly. The tragic emotion internally records the magnitude and significance of the suffering, not only for the person who suffers, but also for the person who pities. The sheltering gesture is pity's natural outgrowth: seeing disaster striking someone whom one has already endowed with profound value in one's own scheme of ends, one's whole being rushes forward to protect and shelter.

That is my own analysis, but I think it does explain what Winston feels and thinks. For he believes that tragedy is possible only in a time that contains a sense of the irreducible intrinsic value of the people whom one loves, and thus "a conception of loyalty that was private and unalterable" (28). And that conception of loyalty belongs to a time when there were still "privacy, love, and friendship, and when the members of a family stood by one another without needing to know the reason" (28). Deep uncompromising attachment to a small number of people, seen as lying at the very root of one's existence: that is what the "ancient time" contained, and what current times have uprooted. Formerly, people "were governed by private loyalties which they did not question. What mattered were individual relationships, and a completely helpless gesture, an embrace, a tear, a word spoken to a dying man, could have value in itself" (136).

Although Orwell repeatedly links these emotions with a simple distinction between the "private" and the "public" realms, nothing in my own argument requires such a general distinction: what is required is intense attachments toward a small number of people, typically imagined as beginning in childhood, in the setting of the family. It is not required that the family be imagined as altogether off-limits to law, although some degree of protection of personal space and personal choice is clearly part of the picture of love that we are investigating.

Why do Winston and Orwell connect, in this way, the intense loyalties of the family with the very possibility of pity? One might think that they don't necessarily go together; indeed, one might even think that the emotions of the family subvert a valuable type of pity, the sort in which we link our imaginations to the sufferings of people at a distance. The type of pity a good modern politics needs might not be the sort that binds mothers unquestioningly to their own particular children: what about a larger and more general attitude of pity/compassion for sufferings of all suffering people?

Interestingly enough, on this point Orwell is in agreement with the ancient Stoics: however it may be extended, pity has particularistic roots. It cannot be born without intense particularistic attachments, and these attachments live on even in its mature and extended form. When the Stoics set out to make morality evenhanded, and to extend moral concern to all human beings on a basis of equality, they consequently saw the enterprise as requiring not the reform of pity and tragedy but their complete removal. Stoics have several reasons for objecting to tragedy, but one, at least, is the thought that its emotions teach us to care too much for this or that person, this or that mother or father or even city. That is so, they believe, because tragedy rests on a notion of the irreplaceability and the great intrinsic worth of that to which harm can come—and, in their view, such attachments are typically, even necessarily, mediated by a moral imagination that is erotic, particularistic, connected to the sharp sense of shared life and possibility that does indeed bind together members of a family. Even if eventually such intense emotions, as a child develops, can be extended to a city, or even to larger groupings of human beings, they always begin at home, remain to some extent deeply rooted there, and are in consequence liable to become destabilized, in their extension, by those early roots in family attachment. The result, as the Stoics see it, is that pity is uneven and unreliable, a bad guide for the person seeking evenhanded justice.

The Stoic project is not O'Brien's. Their deliberate removal of pity stems from morally high-minded motives. Far from wanting to remove pity in order to build society upon hatred and fear, they want to remove it in order to remove some very destructive sources of hatred and fear, the local particularism that all too often produces factionalism, rivalry, civil strife, and so on. Their goal is a society that extends concern equally to all human beings. And yet, when we see what becomes of human connection when one does systematically uproot these local attachments, we have some reason to question even such high-minded programs of emotional reform, and to sympathize with Orwell's claim that the emotions of the family lie at the heart of our moral humanity. Plato did away with the family, in his ideal city, in order to make love more evenhanded, anticipating the Stoic idea. Aristotle protests: "There are two things above all that make people love and care for something: the thought that it is all yours, and the thought that it is the only one you have. Neither of these will be present in that city" (*Politics* 1262b21–24, my translation). A study of Stoic antitragic texts gives strong support to Aristotle's critique: for one does see in Marcus Aurelius, for example, a yawning loneliness, a sense of the meaninglessness of all human endeavor, evenhandedness without any sense of why evenhandedness should matter. When local and familial passions are uprooted, perhaps we do lose touch with humanity, and with the springs of morality within it. Even if pity is a threat to impartiality, it is premature to cast it away if moral impotence is the likely result.[5]

In Stoicism, the death of pity may leave a lack of motivational energy for good, but it does not lead to evil. Indeed, there is much to admire in the commitment to respect all human beings as equals, whatever motivational and psychological difficulties it entails. In the society depicted in *Nineteen Eighty-Four*, by contrast, the removal of pity is accompanied by the removal of all moral concern and the deliberate construction of antimoral emotions. O'Brien denies that a civilization that uproots tragedy and its particular loves need be motivationally impotent. It can care intensely, indeed have a rich emotional life. Other sources of political motivation survive the death of tragedy: "Fear, rage, triumph, and self-abasement." But why do O'Brien—and ultimately Orwell and Winston—think that these emotions can survive the removal of family love, while pity and grief cannot?

What the people of Oceania have come to lack is any sense of any human being as an end. No individual human being is endowed with intrinsic value, and no group of human beings. Lacking the intense emotions of the family, so imbued with tension and erotic wonder, lacking the vision of the small coral object inside the luminous dome, they never learn

---

[5] I discuss this in more detail in "The Worth of Human Dignity: Two Tensions in Stoic Cosmopolitanism," in *Philosophy and Power in the Graeco-Roman World: Essays in Honour of Miriam Griffin*, ed. G. Clark and T. Rajak (Oxford: Oxford University Press, 2002), 31–49.

to regard anything in the world with wonder or profound love. They are brought up to think that everything can be sacrificed, and that one must be prepared to sacrifice anything and anyone at any moment. Betrayal is not betrayal, disloyalty not disloyalty; in their place we have the useful execution of public requirements. In place of the love of parents, children spying on and denouncing parents; in place of erotic love, the betrayal of lovers and love. By requiring that all attachments be held provisionally and instrumentally, held only insofar as useful to the state, Oceania uproots deep love and the possibility of grief.

But it does not uproot fear. Fear for one's own safety, a narrow selfish instrumentalizing fear, is the engine that makes the whole thing work. You can indeed have fear without love and grief—if you are wrapped in a narcissism so terrified and so all-enclosing that it does not acknowledge the full reality of any other entity but the self. You can also have rage and triumph, in a certain form.

To be sure, you cannot have the sort of anger that is closely bound up with love—the anger that responds to an assault on one's parent or child or country, the anger that reacts to a betrayal of love. These forms of anger require a sense of intrinsic value. But there is a type of anger that is next door to selfish fear: rage at that which threatens one's own safety and the safety of the political entity with which one's sense of personal safety is identified. This is the sort of rage that psychoanalysts have called narcissistic rage, rage against any threat to the domination and full control of the self. And of course there is a corresponding narcissistic kind of triumph—not the joy that endows another person or city or nation with reality and value, but the joy of removing an obstacle to one's total control.

In short, the sense of the intrinsic value of a human being is not innate. It is a developmental achievement, and it can be blocked. What Oceania does, with fiendish sagacity, is to obstruct childhood development at a critical point, blocking this achievement. As infants we are all narcissists. Infants do not comprehend the reality of people outside themselves; nor do they clearly distinguish between self and nonself. Wrapped up totally in their own experiences, they conceive of the world entirely from the point of view of those experiences—now blissful symbiosis, now excruciating lack. Oscillating between the sense of omnipotence well captured by Freud's famous phrase "His Majesty the Baby" and a terrified sense of helplessness, they do not yet grasp the reality of any other whole person. Others are there just to satisfy their needs. Indeed, others are not really either fully whole or fully other. Not whole, because they are just instruments of satisfaction or nonsatisfaction, comfort or noncomfort. As Melanie Klein aptly puts it, the mother is not a whole mother, but just the "good breast" that feeds and the "bad breast" that withholds. Not fully other, because to recognize a person as other requires recognizing that she has a life apart, a life not utterly dedicated to the needs of the infant.

This infantile life still contains fear, when nourishment and comfort do not arrive at the right moment. It contains rage at all withholding, rage at the very existence of any obstacle that would thwart the supremacy and completeness of the self. It contains triumph, when the child has managed to dragoon reality into the service of its wants. And it also contains a primitive type of shame or self-abasement, when helplessness is all too apparent.

Human development might in fact stop at this point. Recognizing another person's reality comes hard: for it means surrendering omnipotence, and recognizing that one's own demands for attention and constant love, one's wish to be the center of the universe, are inappropriate demands. Seeing a parent as both whole and other means that she has rights and is entitled to a separate existence. But if she has those rightful claims to a life of her own, then sadness ensues: for the golden age of omnipotence has come to an end. And, worse than sadness, guilt ensues: for the child must now recognize that its aggressive desires for mastery and control have been inappropriate demands. Here morality begins, in the struggle to atone, and to make reparation, for having directed aggression at the same whole object that one also loves.

This stage of emotional development is absolutely pivotal to the very possibility of a liberal political culture. For such a political culture is based on the acknowledgment of the separateness and worth of each and every person, and the rights of each and every person to exist, to go his or her own way, to limit the rapacious claims of others, or of the collectivity, in the name of personal dignity. An adult patient of Donald Winnicott's, who was only just beginning to be able to enter this developmental stage, memorably remarks to the therapist—whom he has for the first time been able to see as a separate person—"The alarming thing is that we are both then children, and the question is, Where is father? We know where we are, if one of us is the father."[6] In other words, recognizing another person as an end turns one into a vulnerable childlike self, rather than an omnipotent self. And that is alarming, in a way that the child's narcissistic fear is not alarming. Liberalism entails that profound fear, and, with it, grief and sorrow.

What Oceania does is to cut development off before that stage arrives. Primary narcissism is all there is. Each person, out of a combination of

[6] D. W. Winnicott, *Holding and Interpretation: Fragment of an Analysis* (New York: Grove Press, 1986).

terror, need, and omnipotence, thinks of others as mere instruments. Thus others are neither whole nor fully separate.

What about the collectivity? you will ask. Surely the people of Oceania identify strongly with the state and see its triumphs as their own. Precisely. Lacking a clear sense of the boundaries between self and other, lacking, indeed, any robust sense of *other*, they gain narcissistic triumph through absorption in the state. They are fed at the omnipotent breast of Big Brother. Helplessness makes itself felt every day in the fabric of daily life: no razor blades, no coffee, miserable cold and damp. But with the state continually feeding the message of victory and satisfaction, there is no need to suffer deeply or to experience the real vulnerability of the separate and incomplete human being. For the ego achieves a sense of invulnerability through its subjection to and total alliance with the state. Loving Big Brother really means attaching oneself to a "loving breast": one becomes complete, omnipotent, invulnerable. The collectivity is a vehicle of narcissistic triumph, not a real political entity toward which people hold complex emotions of love, anger, and grief. We know where we are, indeed, when one of us is Big Brother.

We have spoken of fear, rage, and triumph, less of self-abasement, the fourth emotion in O'Brien's catalog. But paradoxically, narcissistic triumph requires continual self-abasement. The fragile self (which has never achieved even a clear sense of its differentiation from others) can achieve triumph only by complete submission to the will of the collectivity, thus a continual abnegation of its own distinctness, its own rightful claims. Individual self-assertion means being, first, a separate individual, and that entails a terrifying kind of vulnerability. The only safety is in symbiotic merging with the loving breast.

Narcissism is a part of human development. Most human beings, however, in our still-ancient time (which, let us hope, will remain so), eventually transcend narcissism—to some degree at any rate, since adulthood is a difficult and unstable achievement—in the direction of an acknowledgment of the reality of other human beings. Typically, this recognition does take place in the family; but wherever it takes place, it always requires close attachment to a small number of people. Only when narcissistic goals have been to some degree renounced does one see the emergence of love, grief, and the understanding of narratives of deep sadness.

Psychologists who treat narcissistic personality disorders draw attention to the close connection between narcissistic grandiosity and a pathological type of rage—not the anger that responds to a sense of wrongdoing or injustice, but a blind rage that strikes out at all obstacles to the self's fragile projects. That rage is the emotion that supports war in Oceania. Its backdrop is the continual fear bred of the knowledge that one is always in key respects helpless. Terrified, with no sense of personal value or richness of life to sustain them, narcissists strike out.[7]

A recurrent observation in the literature on narcissism is that such patients lack a response to poetry, and to imaginative literature more generally. We can by now see why this might be so: such works invite the mind to enter the world of another, and thus to people the world with distinct bearers of identity and value. To one for whom nothing outside the self is real, this makes no sense at all.

So tragedy belongs to the ancient time, the time when human beings saw themselves as partial, vulnerable, limited by both chance and the rightful needs and demands of others. To the time of tragedy and morality, coming into the child's world together with real unequivocal love of the other.

### "SUCKED DOWN TO DEATH"

Winston Smith is not a narcissist. Indeed, he is set before us by Orwell as the last human being, the last relic of the ancient time. He understands the tragic emotions; he values the tragic works of literature that express and fortify them. And yet Winston Smith can be broken. He ends up surrendering to the love of Big Brother. Orwell suggests, I believe, that Winston is a good case of human aspiration, and thus that his doom spells doom for humanity, at least under duress of the type depicted here. Is this correct? In Winston's defeat do we really see the defeat of humanity as a whole, or do we see only the sad collapse of a very incomplete and unfortunate man?

To answer this question, we must investigate the role of guilt in Winston's life. We will see, I think, that although Winston's development did progress beyond primitive narcissistic emotions, it was nonetheless cut short at a critical juncture, leaving him all too prone to narcissistic retreat and collapse.

Winston's whole life is dominated by guilt over the role he played in the death of his mother and sister. His first dream, in the novel, is a dream of their death:

> At that moment his mother was sitting in some place deep down beneath him, with his young sister in her arms. . . . They were in the saloon of a sinking ship, looking up at him through the darkening water. . . . He was out in the light and air while they were being sucked down to death, and they were

[7] See, for example, Otto Kernberg, *Borderline Conditions and Pathological Narcissism* (Northvale, N.J.: Jason Aronson, 1985); Andrew Morrison, *Shame, the Underside of Narcissism* (Hillsdale, N.J.: The Analytic Press, 1989).

down there *because* he was up here. He knew it and they knew it, and he could see the knowledge in their faces. . . . the knowledge that they must die in order that he might remain alive. (28)

This dream expresses guilt of a particular sort: guilt connected to the fact of his own freedom, agency, and boyish aggression. Again and again, Winston chastises himself for inadequate love of his mother: "she had died loving him, when he was too young and selfish to love her in return" (28). His selfish act, snatching the chocolate from his little sister, is eminently forgivable, in a starving small boy. But he himself has never forgiven himself, in part because of the sheer bad luck that his mother and sister were taken away (presumably to death) right after that event (134–35). He connects the two incidents causally in his mind, albeit irrationally; never seeing them again, he never found any way to atone or achieve restoration to the loving group. He is indeed in "exile from the loving breast" (245). He can't get back to it, so it is not so surprising that he turns, in the end, to a deformed substitute.

Orwell draws attention to Winston's intense and eroticized love of his mother, and his inability to atone for her death, as a ubiquitous theme in all Winston's vulnerability. The paperweight, the physical object that he loves, and which, in the good dream, represents his whole life, is emblematic, in its crinkly pinkness surrounded by radiant light, of maternal flesh. The water in which mother and daughter are sinking is itself, perhaps, an image of female sexuality and passivity, by contrast to his male free aggression. The rats that seem on the verge of eating his face, the fear that ultimately breaks him, have a power that is closely connected to a horror of his own capacity for betrayal and destructiveness. And the Chestnut Street Café, where Winston lives out the remnants of his miserable life— that place where "*[u]nder the spreading chestnut tree / I sold you and you sold me*" (66)—alludes, it would seem, to the image of a boy sheltered within his mother's hair or even pubic hair, and to a deep guilt connected with that very love. At the same time, we should remember that the original poem to which the verse makes reference is Longfellow's "The Village Blacksmith," which follows the first line Orwell quotes with "the village smithy stands; / The smith a mighty man is he / with large and sinewy hands." So the reference is at the same time a reference to male force, connecting that force to destruction and betrayal—a connection confirmed by the way Winston remembers his own selfish act—as the act of a strong obstreperous boy taking something from two weak women.

In developmental terms, as I said, Winston is no narcissist. But he has been abandoned by sources of love and comfort at a critical juncture: just the time at which he has recognized his own aggressiveness and guilt, but before he has found any way to achieve reconciliation and forgiveness.

All children who progress beyond narcissism recognize at some point that the very person they love is the person against whom they have also directed rage and aggression. Not "the good breast" and "the bad breast," but one whole person whom they both love and hate. This recognition of ambivalence is typically very frightening, and children often respond to it with a period of profound sadness and mourning, in which they experience themselves as unable to find any way back to the golden world they once lived in, or, indeed, any way forward to a new world that is not golden but in a sense better than golden, in which morality exists and guilt may find forgiveness.[8]

This, I think, is Winston's situation, so vividly expressed by his recurrent fantasies of a "golden place," a place of light and freedom, and, at the same time, by his sense that he is in the light only because others are drowning. He can find no way forward into a world where people accept one another's flaws and learn to apologize and seek forgiveness for aggressive deeds and words. (We might not implausibly call this the world of liberalism.) He is thus left highly vulnerable to the forces of destruction inside himself, and to the destruction of his personality through the idea of himself as the one who has betrayed and doomed others. Instead of understanding himself as a flawed person capable of both bad and good deeds, and capable of making reparation for the bad with the good, he is left with the terrifying and engulfing sense of limitless badness in himself—because the forgiving object has simply disappeared from his life. Unlike the Kernberg patient depicted in my epigraph,[9] Winston has no good and forgiving objects inside him. His good objects are dead, dead on account of his selfishness.

He lives always, then, on the borderline of narcissistic collapse. It is not so surprising that O'Brien can engineer that collapse.

Why is Winston left in this state? In one way, he just had bad luck: his mother disappeared right at a pivotal moment, before she could become the agent of forgiveness and mercy, and show him how to have mercy on himself. But we should also mention the political duress under which his whole childhood has been lived. The day before she disappears, he takes great joy in playing the children's game of Snakes and Ladders: that is his most robust happy memory. And it is indeed through imaginative play that children often find an exit from the prison of guilt to a more constructive sense of reciprocity and interplay. Winston never had a real chance to learn to play. And then the culture of Oceania takes over, sending con-

---

[8] See my discussion, with many references to the clinical literature, in *Upheavals of Thought*, chap. 4.

[9] See Kernberg, *Borderline Conditions*, 259–60. I discuss the case further in *Hiding from Humanity: Disgust, Shame, and the Law* (Princeton: Princeton University Press, 2004).

tinually the messages of narcissism, rather than any messages connected with responsible moral citizenship, atonement, and decent regard for the rights of others. So he has no prop for his weak and besieged sense of self.

Even Winston's sense of the tragic is actually quite incomplete. It contains deep sorrow, and a kind of pity for his mother and sister. And yet the pity is so mingled with guilt and self-disgust that it does not fully emerge as pity for another separate being. We might say that there can be pity in its full-fledged form only where there is also mercy for self: for the self engulfed by a sense of its own utter blackness can never win through to a sufficient recognition of the sorrows of the other as other.

I suggest, then, that Winston's escape at the novel's end into utter selfishness, and complete antitragic narcissism, is not a sharp reversal. It is a breakdown to which his personality was prone all along. Good support from family and society might have changed the ending; but he is a fragile reed on which to rest our hopes for humanity.

Does Orwell think this too? I have my doubts. There is so much in Winston that is suggestive of the sadness of George Orwell himself, too much, perhaps, for us to take the portrait of Winston as that of an individual whom we are intended to see as flawed and a weak case of human aspiration. Moreover, if we were intended to see Winston in that way, the entire novel would have to be seen as deeply odd in its construction: for what could we, or should we, conclude from the failure of an individual whom we are intended all along to see as peculiar, sad, and deeply incomplete? So I suggest that Orwell did intend Winston to be a good case of the human spirit and of the possibilities of creativity and resistance of which that spirit is capable.

In this I believe him to be quite wrong. If Winston is, as I suggest, a sad little boy who never had a real chance to develop into a successful mature personality, then we can conclude little from his breakdown. And while no civilization has been as completely successful in its totalitarian projects as the novel's Oceania, that is in large part because the human spirit is not so easy to break, because again and again artists, thinkers, and people from every walk of life resist being broken, creating subcultures of resistance that display complex forms of reciprocity and tragic pity.

## A "FACILITATING ENVIRONMENT"?

Nonetheless, there is much to worry about. If the novel does not show convincingly that any human being can be broken, it is more convincing in its suggestion that many can be. Our personalities are always fragile, delicately poised between narcissistic demands that keep on reasserting themselves and the recognition of the worth and dignity of others. Morality and liberal citizenship are achievements that have to be made and remade; they require what Donald Winnicott called a "facilitating environment,"[10] both in the family and in the wider social world. It makes sense to ask, then, to what extent our culture in the United States today is that sort of facilitating environment.

There are aspects of U.S. public culture that pose standing dangers, reinforcing narcissism: an unusual degree of emphasis on manly pride and control; a persistent tendency to think of all threats to preeminence as obstacles to be removed; the suggestion of gratification without limit or price; the denial of mortality and limit, in favor of the idea that you can do and be anything; the suggestion that age and perhaps even death need not defeat us.[11]

These traits are frequently coupled, as in Oceania, albeit less extremely, by a distaste for, or even lack of comprehension of, the tragic. Every obstacle can be overcome—so there is no real tragedy.[12] The form of the cliché Western, in which the good hero simply wipes out the bad guys, is an antitragic form, containing no real pity, no mourning, no ambivalence even. It encourages the thought that evil is simple and utterly external, and can be defeated by simple aggression. By contrast, antinarcissistic art would be art that encourages the development of the ability to imagine the suffering of others, to see ambivalence in oneself and in others, and to look critically, and yet not unmercifully, at the forces of aggression in oneself, and at the harm they have purposed or done. Greek tragedy was an antinarcissistic art form. It peopled the mind with whole beings who exert distinct claims, asking us to imagine the suffering of distinct beings at circumstances both fate and human malice bring their way. We do not have enough tragic art in our lives.

---

[10] Donald Winnicott, *The Maturational Processes and the Facilitating Environment* (Madison, Conn.: International Universities Press, 1965).

[11] Morrison describes a common fantasy of American parents this way:

> The child shall have a better time than his parents; he shall not be subject to the necessities which they have recognized as paramount in life. Illness, death, renunciation of enjoyment, restrictions on his own will, shall not touch him; the laws of nature and of society shall be abrogated in his favour; he shall once more really be the centre and core of creation—'His Majesty the Baby', as we once fancied ourselves. . . . At the most touchy point in the narcissistic system, the immortality of the ego, which is so hard pressed by reality, security is achieved by taking refuge in the child.

> Morrison, in *Essential Papers on Narcissism*, ed. Morrison (New York and London: New York University Press, 1986), 33–34.

[12] Jonathan Lear, "A Counterblast in the War on Freud: The Shrink Is In," *New Republic*, December 25, 1995; a slightly different version was published as "On Killing Freud (Again)," in Lear, *Open Minded: Working Out the Logic of the Soul* (Cambridge: Harvard University Press, 1998), 16–32.

Recent studies of young people, especially young males, in the United States reinforce the idea that narcissism is a danger to watch out for. In their impressive book on troubled teenage boys, *Raising Cain*,[13] psychologists Dan Kindlon and Michael Thompson describe the way in which all too many boys grow up illiterate emotionally, utterly unable to imagine the suffering of other people, and, in consequence, unable to comprehend fully those people's distinct otherness. By the same token, such boys are also obtuse investigators of their own inner world. The fear and lack of control that, being human, they continually experience remains unacknowledged and is typically channeled into aggression. Subduing the other is a way of not confronting one's own helplessness. Kindlon and Thompson see this emotional narcissism at work in the humiliation of other children. They observe that it leads to crude and exploitative relations with women, modeled on masturbatory fantasies of domination and control.

Kindlon's more recent book, *Too Much of a Good Thing*,[14] focuses on the connection between the narcissistic personality and a culture of material accumulation. Teenagers at elite schools compete with one another in flaunting designer clothing, expensive ski vacations, luxury cars. They humiliate kids who do not have these possessions. Rarely do they seem to comprehend that life might contain more other-regarding values; never do they appear to take pride in performing outstanding deeds of public service or commitment to justice.

Such pictures tell only one part of the story. It is obvious that American culture also contains religious and secular values that emphasize service, sacrifice, and philanthropy, and that U.S. citizens have a strong sense of fair play and the importance of civil liberties, liberal values that require a sense of the worth and dignity of each person. Our constitutional and legal culture embodies such norms.

And yet during the past two decades there has been a marked shift in the direction of narcissism. The Reagan era was the beginning of a sea change in U.S. political culture. Appeals to justice and equity became unfashionable; appeals to self-interest and competitive values began to carry the day. Today the rhetoric of the Great Society (and of the New Deal before it) sounds distant, quaint, unlike language that would move Americans to action. That is not because human beings cannot be moved to action by Roosevelt's ideal of economic and social entitlements for all, and freedom from want and fear. It is because citizens of the United States

---

[13] Dan Kindlon and Michael Thompson, *Raising Cain: Protecting the Emotional Lives of Boys* (New York: Ballantine Books, 1999).

[14] Dan Kindlon, *Too Much of a Good Thing: Raising Children of Character in an Indulgent Age* (New York: Miramax, 2001).

have become, to some extent, different from the human beings they once were, different in the values they care about and in what will move them. "Ask yourself whether you are better off this year than you were last year," said Reagan at the conclusion of one of his debates with Walter Mondale. And Mondale's reply—that well-being has many components, of which fairness to others is one—fell on deaf ears. Today no speechwriter who wanted to keep his job would write such a line in the first place.[15]

The drift toward narcissism is prominent in international as well as domestic policy. Both political parties are culpable. Much in our recent political rhetoric suggests a cowboy picture of international relations: we charge into a place, we shoot up the evil folks, then we gallop off into the sunset—with no long-term commitment to the complex task of helping a devastated society advance toward economic stability and democratic self-governance. The phrase "Axis of Evil" suggests a unitary power of darkness, rather than what we find in reality, three distinct nations with utterly different problems and histories. And even if the term "Evil" is applied to governments only, and not to people, the implicit polarization between the evil "Them" and the good "Us" is positively Orwellian in its flattening of complex conflict into moral crusade. "The enemy of the moment always represented absolute evil, and it followed that any past or future agreement with him was impossible" (32). It discourages the thought that the goal of our interaction ought to be a long-term commit-ment to build strong institutions in Afghanistan, or in Iraq. Instead, the thought becomes, knock out the bad guy and get out, and all will be well. And of course it also obscures the realization that much of the human suffering in today's world is caused not by bad individuals, but by hunger, illness, and lack of education—problems for some of which, at least, the wealthy nations, and their narcissism, bear at least some of the responsi-bility. (Thus the number of deaths from AIDS in Africa is directly related to the greed of some U.S. and European pharmaceutical companies.)

What U.S. citizens deeply need at this time is to develop a larger capac-ity to imagine the experiences of people of many kinds in other countries, whose lives are affected daily by the actions of U.S. citizens—as consum-ers and businesspeople in an era of globalization, as members of a polity that engages with other nations. Our leadership, and our media, have on the whole done far too little to promote such a constructive, imaginative, and multifaceted engagement with the world. As a result, our own person-alities remain shallow, untouched by a sense of what our own acquisitive-ness means for others at a distance, untouched even by a sense of what daily life is like for many poor people in our own nation. As inequalities between rich and poor grow greater, the rich seem increasingly to live in

---

[15] Mondale's chief speechwriter at the time was political philosopher William Galston.

another world, insulated from the reality of suffering or struggle.[16] Like the kings and nobles depicted by Rousseau in his discussion of pity in *Emile*, it has never fully dawned on them that they are actually human, subject to the same problems that all human beings share. (And of course that failure of imagination is born of denial, not mere ignorance. We can therefore expect the boundaries of this narcissistic refusal to be aggressively policed.)

What Kindlon reports about the limits of imagination in the teenage children of the rich is true more generally of many aspects of U.S. society, where the ultrarich are increasingly insulated from the rest of the society, and where competitive and acquisitive values go increasingly unchallenged. One might contemplate, for example, the culture that has emerged in the typical large law firm: ethics courses are required by the Bar Association, but the guiding values of most firms are those of competition and accumulation.[17]

Such a culture could be challenged by the political culture, but that now happens rarely. Values of equal human dignity that are vital to the health of a democracy are surely threatened by the political culture (of both parties, for the most part), which cozies up to the superrich, talks about their excesses when it is politically necessary to do so, but then goes right back to business as usual (for example, cutting the additional funds that were appropriated for oversight of the SEC). Orwell's Oceania did not come about because of the disproportionate political influence of a clique of ultrarich people; but something like Oceania might come about in some such way, as democratic processes become increasingly unimportant and the real wielders of influence increasingly distance themselves from the lives that average people live.

And of course, even if we put aside issues about inequality in the United States, there are inequalities between the United States and poorer nations that command our imaginative engagement, since our actions daily affect these nations through the global market. To ignore these inequalities is a kind of group narcissism, and this group narcissism is daily reinforced by

[16] See Paul Krugman, "For Richer: How the Permissive Capitalism of the Boom Destroyed American Equality," *New York Times Magazine*, October 20, 2002, 62–67, 76–77, 141.

[17] Elmer Johnson, the insightful and highly ethical lawyer who for several years was CEO of the Aspen Institute, resigned both from that institute and from his original law firm for related reasons, having to do with the difficulty of pursuing an ethical mission in an environment dedicated to competitive values. In his letter of resignation of August 23, 2002, he speaks of "fundamental philosophical differences" that made for "considerable friction" in the implementation of programs based on ethical ideals. (I am grateful to Johnson for permission to quote from this letter.) He moved to a firm (Jenner and Block) that in his view has different values; he is currently forming an ethics group to think about why the lawyers who should have been gatekeepers permitted criminal greedy acts to occur.

our media, which are much more interested in the lifestyles of the rich than in the reality of daily life in some nation Americans know little about. Our leadership is, to say the least, not directing our attention to these matters. Our relationship to the world is depicted, almost always, in narcissistic terms, as one of control and preeminence—not one of responsibility even, and surely not one of guilt.

Oceania is not on our doorstep. But there are some worrying signs. Orwell was a great genius precisely because he knew how to give worrying signs an indelible and a terrifying form. If we are not too far gone to feel pity and terror for Winston Smith, we might be prompted to a critical scrutiny of the Oceanian elements in our own society. That, I think, would be a very good thing.

## EXILE FROM THE LOVING BREAST

What would we do, if we wanted to respond constructively to these worries? To work at all, the response would have to begin in each child's development in its family and larger social world. What development would need to produce is nothing less than an adult human being.

And what is that, you ask? By "an adult human being," I mean a human being who accepts the reality of exile from the loving breast, and who therefore does not seek, in politics or in relationships with others, a surrogate experience of fullness, control, and perfection. A human being who has accepted humanity. Well, that is a hard trick to pull off, especially when it means accepting the fact that one is going to die. But by "accepting" I do not mean "being happy about." I just mean "confronting the reality of," or even "grappling continually with the reality of." This human being would have noticed, early on, that the loving breast is not just a breast, but a part of a whole person who is separate from the self. A return to symbiosis with that breast is thus not only impossible but actually wrong: for that separate person has rights and a life of her own, and one should not even seek to turn another human being into a source and agent of one's own completeness. This recognition of separateness would be accompanied—it always is—by mourning, sorrow for the "golden country" of bliss and symbiosis that is no longer, and also by guilt for the persistent wish that no human being ever loses, to make that bliss return and to *make* that obstinate separate person the mere agent of one's will.

Let us hope, however, that this child we are imagining will have resources in her environment that take her further than poor Winston Smith was able to go—helping her to find within herself a merciful and forgiving object that can heal the ambivalence and pain of the discovery of one's own guilty aggression. These resources prominently include play and storytelling, and, as the child grows older, works of art that develop a rich inner world, the ability to imagine the separate experiences of another, and the ability to transmute mourning into pity and constructive action aimed at justice. Education should continually focus on this goal, developing children's ability to imagine the reality of other lives in increasingly complex forms. This means learning a lot more than Americans typically do about lives in places outside America, and seeing those lives as complex, rich, fully human. America is so isolated and so powerful that Americans are able to go through life without learning much about other nations; in this they face an obstacle to understanding that is less common for non-Americans. This obstacle must be addressed as Orwell sought to address it: through a continual confrontation with history and with facts about the situation in distant parts of the world. Both media and educational institutions must focus on this task.

In education at all stages, the defeat of Oceania in ourselves also requires a commitment to the arts, especially the tragic arts, and to the development of complex emotions suited to confront the ambivalences of human life. Comic art is also of the greatest importance, because it fosters a recognition of our rather powerless situation in this world—but a recognition that contains joy rather than disgust. People who can laugh at themselves are marginally less likely to need to lord it over others.

The defeat of Oceania will also require fostering a critical culture of argument and counterargument, in which people model the liberal value of respect for others by showing respect for the argument of an opponent, at the same time showing respect for their own independent thought and inner life.

The leadership of our nation, and its general approach to the world, will support Oceania if it presents the United States as a completely good engulfing breast that eclipses and suffocates any challenge from the world of separate nations and their people. By contrast, an anti-Oceanian politics would focus on the needs and limitations that all human beings share, depicting the United States' relation to the world as one of responsibility and interdependence. It would construct foreign policy in terms of the acknowledgment of the right of all human beings to live and enjoy decent lives. U.S. engagement would focus on supporting those lives, as well as on national security. The idea of preeminence, and the removal of all obstacles to self-sufficiency, would be replaced by an idea (already in the dominant tradition of natural-law internationalism, at least since Grotius) of the world as a society of human beings, in which nations play a very important role, protecting people's rights and expressing their values, but in which the larger world community also plays a role. Leaders would educate the U.S. public to see itself as part of such an interlocking world.

In the context of such a vision of humanity, extreme wealth would be seen as a source of public shame, rather than as a source of narcissistic triumph.[18]

Internally, an anti-Oceanian politics would support a critical culture aimed at expressing respect for those who are different from the majority, both for their ideas and for their legitimate rights. It would also support the arts, even and especially when the arts challenge complacent views of American complacency and supremacy. How nice it would be to have leaders, maybe even a president, of whom it could be believed that one day he or she might wake up with the word "Shakespeare" on his or her lips, after a sorrowful or hopeful dream of glass and clear soft light.

There are rich resources in the United States for the defeat of Oceania. But the defeat of Oceania requires not just a commitment to truth, a vigilance about history, and a zealous defense of civil liberties. It demands, deep beneath these matters, a commitment to the formation of a personality that sees itself as incomplete and needy, and yet not without resource, capable of both pity and mercy. That, history and Orwell show us, is a commitment very difficult indeed to make, and yet more difficult to fulfill.

---

[18] That this is no mere fantasy is clear if one lives for a time in Finland or one of the other Nordic countries. People really do feel shame at having much more than others, and sometimes at having a car at all. At least it is an indulgence that requires continual guilty explanation.

# Contributors

HOMI K. BHABHA is Anne F. Rothenberg Professor of English and American Literature and Chair of the Program in History and Literature at Harvard University, and Visiting Professor in the Humanities at University College, London. The author of *The Location of Culture* (Routledge, 1994) and editor of the essay collection *Nation and Narration* (Routledge, 1990), Bhabha is currently at work on *A Measure of Dwelling*, a theory of vernacular cosmopolitanism forthcoming from Harvard University Press, and *The Right to Narrate*, forthcoming from Columbia University Press.

DAVID BRIN is a scientist and author whose novels include *Earth*, *The Postman*, and *Startide Rising*. Brin's nonfiction book—*The Transparent Society: Will Technology Make Us Choose between Freedom and Privacy?*—won the 2000 Freedom of Speech Award of the American Library Association.

JAMES CONANT is Professor of Philosophy at the University of Chicago and the author of numerous articles on topics in aesthetics, philosophy of language, and the philosophy of mind, and on figures such as Kant, Nietzsche, Kierkegaard, William James, Frege, Carnap, and Wittgenstein, among others.

MARGARET DRABBLE was born in Sheffield, England, in 1939, and educated at Newnham College, Cambridge, where she studied English literature. Her first novel, *A Summer Bird-cage*, was published in 1963, and recent novels include *The Peppered Moth* (2000), *The Seven Sisters* (2002), and *The Red Queen* (2004). She edited the fifth and sixth editions of *The Oxford Companion to English Literature* (1985, 2000) and has written biographies of British novelists Arnold Bennett (1974) and Angus Wilson (1995).

RICHARD A. EPSTEIN is the James Parker Hall Distinguished Service Professor of Law at the University of Chicago, where he has taught since 1972, and is a director of the John M. Olin Program in Law and Economics. His books include *Skepticism and Freedom: A Modern Case for Classical Liberalism* (University of Chicago Press, 2003) and *Cases and Materials on Torts*, 8th ed. (Aspen Law & Business, 2004). He has also written numerous articles on a wide range of legal and interdisciplinary subjects.

ABBOTT GLEASON is Barnaby Conrad and Mary Critchfield Keeney Professor of History at Brown University. He received his B.A. and Ph.D.

from Harvard University and has served as the Director of the Kennan Institute for Advanced Russian Studies at the Woodrow Wilson Center.

JACK GOLDSMITH is Professor of Law at Harvard University. In January 2005 he will be publishing his first book, *The Limits of International Law*, with Oxford University Press (coauthored with Eric Posner).

JOHN HALDANE is Professor of Philosophy and Director of the Centre for Ethics, Philosophy and Public Affairs at the University of St. Andrews, Scotland. He writes in several areas of philosophy as well as on art and religion. His recent books include, with J.J.C. Smart, *Atheism and Theism*, 2nd ed. (Blackwell, 2003); *An Intelligent Person's Guide to Religion* (Duckworth, 2003); and *Faithful Reason: Essays Catholic and Philosophical* (Routledge, 2004).

EDWARD S. HERMAN is an economist and media analyst, Professor Emeritus of Finance, Wharton School, University of Pennsylvania, and an author of numerous books and articles on economics, foreign affairs, and the workings of the mainstream media. Among his books are *Corporate Control, Corporate Power*; *The Political Economy of Human Rights* (2 vols.) and *Manufacturing Consent* (both coauthored with Noam Chomsky); *The Real Terror Network*; *Triumph of the Market*; *The Myth of the Liberal Media*; and *Beyond Hypocrisy: Decoding the News in an Age of Propaganda*.

BARBARA S. KIRSHNER is Professor of Pediatrics and Medicine at the University of Chicago, with subspecialty training in pediatric gastroenterology and nutrition. In addition to having written more than one hundred articles and book chapters relating to chronic inflammatory bowel disease in children, she has an active role in teaching medical students and house staff.

LAWRENCE LESSIG is the John A. Wilson Distinguished Scholar and Professor of Law at Stanford Law School. His writings include *Free Culture* (Penguin, 2004), *The Future of Ideas* (Random House, 2001), and *Code and Other Laws of Cyberspace* (Basic Books, 1999).

MARTHA C. NUSSBAUM is the Ernst Freund Distinguished Service Professor of Law and Ethics in the Philosophy Department, Law School, and Divinity School at the University of Chicago. She is an Associate in the Departments of Classics and Political Science, an Affiliate of the Committee on Southern Asian Studies, a Board Member of the Human Rights Program, and the Coordinator of the Center for Comparative Constitutionalism. Her most recent book is *Hiding from Humanity: Disgust, Shame, and the Law* (Princeton University Press, 2004).

RICHARD A. POSNER is Judge, U.S. Court of Appeals for the Seventh Circuit, and Senior Lecturer at the University of Chicago Law School. He is also the author of many books, including *Law and Literature*, rev. and enl. ed. (Harvard University Press, 1998), and *Public Intellectuals: A Study of Decline* (Harvard University Press, 2001).

DARIUS REJALI, Professor of Political Science at Reed College, is an internationally recognized expert on violence, focusing on government torture and interrogation. He is the author of *Torture and Modernity: Self, Society and State in Modern Iran* (Westview, 1994), the forthcoming *Torture and Democracy* (Princeton University Press, 2005), and *Approaches to Violence* (Princeton University Press, forthcoming).

ELAINE SCARRY teaches in the English department at Harvard University, where she is Walter M. Cabot Professor of Aesthetics and the General Theory of Value. She is the author of *On Beauty and Being Just*, *The Body in Pain*, *Resisting Representation*, *Dreaming by the Book*, and many articles on war and social contract.

CASS R. SUNSTEIN is the Karl N. Llewellyn Professor of Jurisprudence at the University of Chicago Law School and Department of Political Science. He is the author of numerous books, including *Democracy and the Problem of Free Speech*, *The Partial Constitution*, *After the Rights Revolution*, *Free Markets and Social Justice*, *One Case at a Time: Judicial Minimalism on the Supreme Court*, *Republic.com*, *Designing Democracy*, *Risk and Reason*, *Why Societies Need Dissent*, and *The Second Bill of Rights: FDR's Constitutional Vision and Why We Need It More Than Ever*. He has also written extensively on constitutional law, the First Amendment, and jurisprudence.

ROBIN WEST is Professor of Law at Georgetown University Law Center, the author most recently of *Re-Imagining Justice* (Ashgate Press, 2003), and editor of the volume entitled *Rights*, of the *Encyclopedia of International Legal Theory*.

PHILIP G. ZIMBARDO is Professor of Psychology at Stanford University (since 1968). His current research interests are in the domain of experimental social psychology, with emphasis on the psychology of social influence, mind control, cults, violence, terrorism, evil, hypnosis, time perspective, the normal bases of madness, and shyness. His research, theorizing, and teaching interests have resulted in more than three hundred professional and technical articles, along with fifty books, text and trade, workbooks, and teaching manuals.

# Index